The Gospel of Luke

A new English translation from the
Robinson-Pierpont Greek text
by David Robert Palmer

with notes and commentary
by David Robert Palmer

August 2023 Edition
(first Amazon ed. June 2022)

ISBN: 978-1-958612-01-9

CONTENTS

NOTES TO THE READER

Footnotes are provided indicating many of the variant readings in the Greek text, and which list the manuscript support for each variant. This is called a "critical apparatus." Here is an example footnote on variant readings found in this volume:

24:42 txt μερος 𝔓^{75} ℵ A B D L W it^{d,e} syr^{s} cop^{sa,bopt} Clem Or^{vid} Cyr½ Ps-Ath Aug¼ Diatess-Arab½ SBL TH NA28 {B} ‖ μερος και κηριον it^{a} Jerome Diatess-Arab½ ‖ μερος και απο μελισσιου κηριου E^{c} N 𝔐 it^{b,q} syr$^{c,p,pal,h\ with*}$ cop^{bopt} Justin^{dub} Amphil Tert Cyr½ Epiph Jer TR RP ‖ μερος και απο μελισσιου κηριον E* it$^{aur,t,ff^2,l,r^1}$ vg arm geo Cyril-Jerusalem Proclus; Aug¾ Varimadum ‖ *lac* 𝔓^{45} C P Q T

The bold 24:42 is the chapter and verse number, "txt" means this first variant is the Greek text which the translation in English is translated from; the Greek words following "txt" are the words of the txt reading, and the variant readings are separated by the ‖ slanted double lines. Next are the symbols for the manuscripts and other witnesses which support that reading. Papyri are listed first, then majuscule or "uncial" Greek manuscripts, then minuscule Greek manuscripts, then "versions," which means early translations into other languages: Old Latin first (it$^{a,b,c,ff^2,l}$), then Vulgate editions, Syriac, Coptic, Armenian, Georgian, Ethiopic, Gothic. If the reading is the majority reading by simple Greek manuscript count, the symbol 𝔐 is gvien. Next, the witness of early church fathers is given. After that, two-letter abbreviations for Greek New Testament editions which adopt that variant reading are given. Consistently cited editions are five: TR RP SBL TH NA28. But when the Byzantine majority is split, or the whole body of witnesses is especially variously divided, sometimes other editions are cited as well, such as AT BG HF TG VS WH. Following is a list of abbreviations thereof and their meaning:

TR - Textus Receptus, specifically, "The New Testament in the Original Greek according to the text followed in the Authorised Version; F. H. A. Scrivener; Cambridge, 1894; but also Stephens 1550, Erasmus, Elzivir, Beza may be cited where different)
RP – Robinson-Pierpont GNT, "The Byzantine Textform," 2018 edition
SBL – Society for Biblical Literature, 2010, Edited by Michael W. Holmes
TH – Tyndale House Greek New Testament, © 2017 by Tyndale House, Cambridge; Edited by Dirk Jongkind
NA28 – Nestle-Aland 28th Edition GNT, © Deutche Bibelgesellschaft, Stuttgart (The same Greek text as the UBS5)
AT – Antoniades GNT, 1904 (the Greek Orthodox Patriarchal text)
BG - Byzantine Greek New Testament, © 2014 CSPMT (The Center for the Study and Preservation of the Majority Text, Rockville, Maryland): the Kr/Family 35 Textform (originally promoted mainly by Wilbur Pickering)
HF – Hodges/Farstad "majority text"
TG – Tregelles, Samuel P., Greek New Testament
VS – Hermann von Soden GNT, 1913
WH – Westcott & Hort GNT, 1881

Following the two-letter Edition abbreviations, are two "braces," { } enclosing either a capital letter or a slash: {C} or {\}. Those containing letters are found in the United Bible Societies' Greek editions, and in this volume represent those found in the UBS 5th edition. The United Bible Societies' Editorial Committee uses these to indicate their evaluation of evidence for the text, as follows.

"By means of the letters A, B, C, and D, enclosed within "braces" { } at the beginning of each set of textual variants, the Committee has sought to indicate the relative degree of certainty, arrived at on the basis of internal considerations as well as of external evidence; for the reading adopted as the text.
{A} signifies that the text is virtually certain,
{B} indicates that there is some degree of doubt.
{C} means that there is considerable degree of doubt whether the text or the apparatus contains the superior reading,
{D} shows that there is a very high degree of doubt concerning the reading selected for the text."

The braces containg a slash {\} are provided by this author to indicate that the UBS5 contains no textual apparatus footnote about that variant.

The final variant given is *// lac* which lists witnesses which have a "lacuna" there; that is, where the manuscript is defective or damaged or that section is gone, and/or the manuscript otherwise is unable to provide witness.

For a table listing the primary ancient manuscripts and witnesses to the Gospel of Luke, see the table at the end of this document entitled "Table of Witnesses."

For a list of the abbreviations and dates of early Versions and Fathers, see https://www.katapi.org.uk/UBSGrNT/Intro2.htm.

.

Chapter 1

Introduction

Lk 1:1 Ἐπειδήπερ πολλοὶ ἐπεχείρησαν ἀνατάξασθαι διήγησιν περὶ τῶν πεπληροφορημένων ἐν ἡμῖν πραγμάτων,

1Since many have undertaken to draw up an account of the things fully attested among us,

Lk 1:2 καθὼς παρέδοσαν ἡμῖν οἱ ἀπ' ἀρχῆς αὐτόπται καὶ ὑπηρέται γενόμενοι τοῦ λόγου,

2as delivered to us by the original eyewitnesses who became stewards of the word,[1]

Lk 1:3 ἔδοξεν κἀμοί, παρηκολουθηκότι ἄνωθεν πᾶσιν ἀκριβῶς, καθεξῆς σοι γράψαι, κράτιστε Θεόφιλε,

3it seemed good to me also, having meticulously traced everything again from the top, to write it down in sequence for you, O most excellent Theophilus,

Lk 1:4 ἵνα ἐπιγνῷς περὶ ὧν κατηχήθης λόγων τὴν ἀσφάλειαν.

4so that you may know the reliability of things you have been told.

The Birth of John the Baptizer Foretold

Lk 1:5 Ἐγένετο ἐν ταῖς ἡμέραις Ἡρῴδου βασιλέως[2] τῆς Ἰουδαίας ἱερεύς τις ὀνόματι Ζαχαρίας, ἐξ ἐφημερίας Ἀβιά• καὶ γυνὴ αὐτῷ[3] ἐκ τῶν θυγατέρων Ἀαρών, καὶ τὸ ὄνομα αὐτῆς Ἐλισάβετ.

5It came about in the days of Herod, king of Judea, that there was a priest, Zechariah by name, of the rotation of Abijah.[4] And his wife was from the daughters of Aaron, and her name was Elizabeth.

---

[1] **1:2** Or, "as delivered to us by those who from the beginning were eyewitnesses and servants of the word." The word I translated "became" is the Greek word γίνομαι - gínomai, which usually means became, or came about, or happen. But Luke often uses γίνομαι in place of the simple word in Greek for "to be." That is why most translations translate it here as simply "were." But the reason I did not translate it that way, is that it would result in a non-Lukan use of the title "the Word" for Jesus. For you see, if we say, they were eyewitnesses and servants of the word from the beginning, that would be the only possible explanation of the idea of "being eyewitness of the word." That means they beheld Jesus as the word, in the Johannine concept of I John 1:1 and John 1. Otherwise, what would it mean? That they saw Jesus write the word down? But I do not believe that is what Luke is saying. I believe he is saying that the men who were the first eyewitness of Jesus, were given the trust of being stewards of the word, of the message. See Acts 1:21-22, which Luke also wrote. There we read how it was decided that the original eyewitnesses became official stewards of the word.

[2] **1:5a** txt βασιλέως TH NA28 ‖ τοῦ βασιλέως TR RP

[3] **1:5b** txt γυνὴ αὐτῷ TH NA28 ‖ ἡ γυνὴ αὐτοῦ TR RP

[4] **1:5c** The priests were divided up into divisions that took turns in rotation, doing the priestly duties.

Lk 1:6 Ἦσαν δὲ δίκαιοι ἀμφότεροι ἐναντίον[5] τοῦ θεοῦ, πορευόμενοι ἐν πάσαις ταῖς ἐντολαῖς καὶ δικαιώμασιν τοῦ κυρίου ἄμεμπτοι.

6Both were upright in the sight of God, walking blamelessly in all the commandments and requirements of the Lord.

Lk 1:7 Καὶ οὐκ ἦν αὐτοῖς τέκνον, καθότι ἦν ἡ Ἐλισάβετ στεῖρα,[6] καὶ ἀμφότεροι προβεβηκότες ἐν ταῖς ἡμέραις αὐτῶν ἦσαν.

7But a child they did not have, because Elizabeth was barren. And they were both advanced in age.

Lk 1:8 ¶ Ἐγένετο δὲ ἐν τῷ ἱερατεύειν αὐτὸν ἐν τῇ τάξει τῆς ἐφημερίας αὐτοῦ ἔναντι τοῦ θεοῦ,

8And it came about, that once when his rotation was on duty and he was serving as priest before God, his lot fell

Lk 1:9 κατὰ τὸ ἔθος τῆς ἱερατείας, ἔλαχε τοῦ θυμιᾶσαι εἰσελθὼν εἰς τὸν ναὸν τοῦ κυρίου.

9(normal custom for the priesthood) to go into the temple of the Lord, and to burn incense.[7]

Lk 1:10 Καὶ πᾶν τὸ πλῆθος ἦν τοῦ λαοῦ προσευχόμενον ἔξω τῇ ὥρᾳ τοῦ θυμιάματος.

10The hour of incense came, and all the people in the assembly were praying outside.

Lk 1:11 Ὤφθη δὲ αὐτῷ ἄγγελος κυρίου, ἑστὼς ἐκ δεξιῶν τοῦ θυσιαστηρίου τοῦ θυμιάματος.

11Then an angel of the Lord appeared to him, standing at the right side of the altar of incense.

Lk 1:12 Καὶ ἐταράχθη Ζαχαρίας ἰδών, καὶ φόβος ἐπέπεσεν ἐπ' αὐτόν.

12Seeing it disturbed Zechariah, and fear fell over[8] him.

Lk 1:13 Εἶπεν δὲ πρὸς αὐτὸν ὁ ἄγγελος, Μὴ φοβοῦ, Ζαχαρία· διότι εἰσηκούσθη ἡ δέησίς σου, καὶ ἡ γυνή σου Ἐλισάβετ γεννήσει υἱόν σοι, καὶ καλέσεις τὸ ὄνομα αὐτοῦ Ἰωάννην.

13But the angel said to him: "Fear not, Zechariah, for your request was heard. Your wife Elizabeth will bear you a son, and you shall call his name John.

Lk 1:14 Καὶ ἔσται χαρά σοι καὶ ἀγαλλίασις, καὶ πολλοὶ ἐπὶ τῇ γενέσει[9] αὐτοῦ χαρήσονται.

14Joy and gladness will be with you, and many will rejoice over his birth.

---

5 **1:6** txt ἐναντίον TH NA28 ‖ ἐνώπιον TR RP

6 **1:7** txt ἦν ἡ Ἐλισάβετ TH NA28 ‖ ἡ Ἐλισάβετ ἦν TR RP

7 **1:9** It is said that a priest received only once in his lifetime, if at all, the privilege to enter inside the shrine to burn incense. The Levites were divided into 48 semi-annual rotations. So a particular priest's rotation was on duty only about twice a year. Then as to the individual who would go inside to burn incense, it was the custom of the priesthood to decide whose turn it was by casting lots. Zechariah's lot fell.

8 **1:12** See the Septuagint, Psalm 54:5.

9 **1:14** txt γενέσει ℵ A B C D E K L M P S U W Y Δ Θ Λ Π Ω *pm* TH NA28 ‖ γεννήσει G Γ Ψ f^1 f^{13} 33 *pm* TR RP ‖ *lac* 𝔓^{75} F H N Q T Ξ

Lk 1:15 Ἔσται γὰρ μέγας ἐνώπιον τοῦ κυρίου,[10] καὶ οἶνον καὶ σίκερα οὐ μὴ πίῃ, καὶ πνεύματος ἁγίου πλησθήσεται ἔτι ἐκ κοιλίας μητρὸς αὐτοῦ.

15For he will be great in the eyes of the Lord. Wine and intoxicating beverages by no means shall he drink, and he will be filled with the Holy Spirit, beginning yet in his mother's womb.[11]

Lk 1:16 Καὶ πολλοὺς τῶν υἱῶν Ἰσραὴλ ἐπιστρέψει ἐπὶ κύριον τὸν θεὸν αὐτῶν•

16He will turn many of the children of Israel toward the Lord their God.

Lk 1:17 καὶ αὐτὸς προελεύσεται ἐνώπιον αὐτοῦ ἐν πνεύματι καὶ δυνάμει Ἠλίου, ἐπιστρέψαι καρδίας πατέρων ἐπὶ τέκνα, καὶ ἀπειθεῖς ἐν φρονήσει δικαίων, ἑτοιμάσαι κυρίῳ λαὸν κατεσκευασμένον.

17And he will proceed in front of Him, in the spirit and power of Elijah, such that the hearts of fathers will turn[12] toward their children,[13] and the disobedient toward the outlook of the righteous: a prepared people will be arranged for the Lord."

---

[10] **1:15a** txt τοῦ κυρίου B D K Lc M U W Γ Δ Λ Π 28 565 892 *pm* Ir-lat TR RP NA28-[τοῦ] // κυρίου ℵ A C L* Ω f^1 2 33 579 1241 2542 *pm* Cyr WH // τοῦ θεοῦ Θ Ψ f^{13} 157 700 1071 1424 // *lac* 𝔓[75] F H N Q T Ξ

[11] **1:15b** John will be a nazirite, like Samson was, so it would be natural to compare the Greek phrase here, ἔτι ἐκ κοιλίας μητρὸς αὐτοῦ with that in Judges 13:5: Ναζὶρ θεοῦ ἔσται τὸ παιδάριον ἀπὸ τῆς κοιλίας (and v. 7, where his mother changes Nazirite to holy, and κοιλίας to γαστήρ) and 16:17: ἅγιος Θεοῦ ἐγό εἰμι ἀπὸ κοιλίας μητρός μου. The big difference is that in Luke here about John, the word ἔτι is used, meaning something "while still." And we know from Luke 1:44 that he was in fact filled with the Holy Spirit while still in his mother's womb. In Isaiah 44:2, 24, God said, "I am the one who formed you from the womb," ὁ πλάσας σε ἐκ κοιλίας, where even though it says "from" the womb, we know the forming began while still in the womb. The addition of the word ἔτι in the Luke passage here just makes it all the more clear that God meant John would be filled with the Spirit while still in his mother's womb, and forward from then on.

[12] **1:17a** The Greek says John will proceed in the power of Elijah "to turn." The verb for turn, ἐπιστρέφω - epistrephw, is in the infinitive form, ἐπιστρέψαι - epistrepsai. This is an "infinitive of result," a Hebraism.

[13] **1:17b** The wording "the Fathers," in English tends to mean "all the fathers." But in this context, the number of fathers is set by verse 16, "He will turn many." Thus, there would be many fathers whose hearts will turn ἐπὶ τέκνα - epi tekna (toward children.) There is no possessive pronoun "their" here in the Greek. But if we leave it out here, in English, if someone's heart "turns toward children," that might be understood to mean, he decides he now wants to have children. This verse must be an allusion to Malachi 4:6 in the Hebrew, and not the Septuagint. In the Hebrew it is fathers, plural, and children, generic. The Septuagint says ὃς ἀποκαταστήσει καρδίαν πατρός πρὸς υἱὸν, "who will turn the heart of the father to the son." Several translations make the word πατήρ (pateer) generic here, and so translate it as "parents to their children." I can understand that. But so many people already have an understanding of this verse, based on what seems to be a reality in this world that there are more children and fathers estranged, than children from their mothers. For example, the Bible says "Who ever heard of such a thing as a mother killing her child and eating him?" Apparently, it is harder to believe that a mother would do that to her child, than a father. Note that Malachi in the Hebrew also says that He will turn the hearts of the sons to the fathers. The question is, what is broken? Is it more fathers estranged from their children, and children angry at their fathers? Or mothers to the same extent? I think it is the former. That is why I am leaving it fathers and children, because that is more what is broken in the absence of the power of the Spirit.

Lk 1:18 Καὶ εἶπεν Ζαχαρίας πρὸς τὸν ἄγγελον, Κατὰ τί γνώσομαι τοῦτο; Ἐγὼ γάρ εἰμι πρεσβύτης, καὶ ἡ γυνή μου προβεβηκυῖα ἐν ταῖς ἡμέραις αὐτῆς.

18And Zechariah said to the angel, "By what will I know this?[14] For I am old, and my wife is well advanced in age."

Lk 1:19 Καὶ ἀποκριθεὶς ὁ ἄγγελος εἶπεν αὐτῷ, Ἐγώ εἰμι Γαβριὴλ ὁ παρεστηκὼς ἐνώπιον τοῦ θεοῦ• καὶ ἀπεστάλην λαλῆσαι πρός σε, καὶ εὐαγγελίσασθαί σοι ταῦτα.

19And in answer the angel said to him, "I am Gabriel, one who stands in the presence of God, and I have been sent to speak to you and to tell you these glad announcements.

Lk 1:20 Καὶ ἰδού, ἔσῃ σιωπῶν καὶ μὴ δυνάμενος λαλῆσαι, ἄχρι ἧς ἡμέρας γένηται ταῦτα, ἀνθ' ὧν οὐκ ἐπίστευσας τοῖς λόγοις μου, οἵτινες πληρωθήσονται εἰς τὸν καιρὸν αὐτῶν.

20And behold, you will be silent and unable to speak, until the day these things take place, because you did not believe my words, which will be fulfilled in their time."

Lk 1:21 Καὶ ἦν ὁ λαὸς προσδοκῶν τὸν Ζαχαρίαν, καὶ ἐθαύμαζον ἐν τῷ χρονίζειν ἐν τῷ ναῷ αὐτόν.[15]

21And the people were waiting for Zechariah, and wondering about his delay in the temple.

Lk 1:22 Ἐξελθὼν δὲ οὐκ ἐδύνατο[16] λαλῆσαι αὐτοῖς• καὶ ἐπέγνωσαν ὅτι ὀπτασίαν ἑώρακεν ἐν τῷ ναῷ• καὶ αὐτὸς ἦν διανεύων αὐτοῖς, καὶ διέμενεν κωφός.

22And when he came out, he was not able to speak to them, and they knew: a vision he had seen in the temple. He kept motioning to them, and remained mute.

Lk 1:23 Καὶ ἐγένετο, ὡς ἐπλήσθησαν αἱ ἡμέραι τῆς λειτουργίας αὐτοῦ, ἀπῆλθεν εἰς τὸν οἶκον αὐτοῦ.

23And when his days of service were completed, he went home.

Lk 1:24 Μετὰ δὲ ταύτας τὰς ἡμέρας συνέλαβεν Ἐλισάβετ ἡ γυνὴ αὐτοῦ, καὶ περιέκρυβεν ἑαυτὴν μῆνας πέντε, λέγουσα

24After those days, his wife Elizabeth conceived, and she hid herself for five months.

Lk 1:25 ὅτι Οὕτως μοι πεποίηκεν κύριος[17] ἐν ἡμέραις αἷς ἐπεῖδεν ἀφελεῖν ὄνειδός[18] μου ἐν ἀνθρώποις.

25"The way the Lord has done this for me," she said, "these are days he has looked with concern upon me, to take away my disgrace among the people."

---

[14] **1:18** Zechariah may have felt his question justified because of the fact that Abraham asked the same thing- for a sign. See Genesis 15:8. But this shows a lack of belief in God's statements. Jesus said later, "A wicked and adulterous generation asks for a miraculous sign, but none will be given it except the sign of Jonah." (Diatess. 11:17-18; Mt 12:38-39; Lk 11:16, 20) The apostle Paul said, "For Jews require a sign, and Greeks seek after wisdom..." (I Cor. 1:22)

[15] **1:21** txt ἐν τῷ ναῷ αὐτόν TH NA28 ‖ αὐτὸν ἐν τῷ ναῷ TR RP

[16] **1:22** txt ἐδύνατο TH NA28 ‖ ἠδύνατο TR RP

[17] **1:25a** txt κύριος TH NA28 ‖ ὁ κύριος TR RP

[18] **1:25b** txt ὄνειδός TH NA28 ‖ τὸ ὄνειδός TR RP

The Birth of Jesus Foretold

Lk 1:26 ¶ Ἐν δὲ τῷ μηνὶ τῷ ἕκτῳ ἀπεστάλη ὁ ἄγγελος Γαβριὴλ ὑπὸ ἀπὸ τοῦ θεοῦ
εἰς πόλιν τῆς Γαλιλαίας, ᾗ ὄνομα Ναζαρέθ,[19]
26And in the sixth month, the angel Gabriel was sent out from[20] God, to a town
in Galilee named Nazareth,
Lk 1:27 πρὸς παρθένον μεμνηστευμένην ἐμνηστευμένην[21] ἀνδρί ᾧ ὄνομα
Ἰωσήφ, ἐξ οἴκου Δαυίδ• καὶ τὸ ὄνομα τῆς παρθένου Μαριάμ.
27to a virgin pledged to be married to a man named Joseph, of the house of
David. And the virgin's name was Mary.
Lk 1:28 Καὶ εἰσελθὼν ὁ ἄγγελος[22] πρὸς αὐτὴν εἶπεν, Χαῖρε, κεχαριτωμένη• ὁ
κύριος μετὰ σοῦ.
28And the angel went in to her, and said, "Hail, O favored one! The Lord is
with you."[23]
Lk 1:29 Ἡ δὲ ἐπὶ τῷ λόγῳ διεταράχθη καὶ διελογίζετο ποταπὸς εἴη ὁ ἀσπασμὸς
οὗτος.
29But[24] she was very troubled by the utterance,[25] and wondered what sort of
greeting this might be.
Lk 1:30 Καὶ εἶπεν ὁ ἄγγελος αὐτῇ, Μὴ φοβοῦ, Μαριάμ• εὗρες γὰρ χάριν παρὰ τῷ
θεῷ.
30And the angel said to her, "Fear not, Mary, for you have found favor with
God.
Lk 1:31 Καὶ ἰδού, συλλήμψῃ[26] ἐν γαστρί, καὶ τέξῃ υἱόν, καὶ καλέσεις τὸ ὄνομα
αὐτοῦ Ἰησοῦν.
31And behold, you shall conceive in your womb, and shall bear a son, and you
are to call his name Jesus.
Lk 1:32 Οὗτος ἔσται μέγας, καὶ υἱὸς ὑψίστου κληθήσεται• καὶ δώσει αὐτῷ κύριος
ὁ θεὸς τὸν θρόνον Δαυὶδ τοῦ πατρὸς αὐτοῦ,
32This man will be great, and will be called the Son of the Most High. And the
Lord God will give him the throne of his father David,

---

19 **1:26a** Ναζαρέθ NA28 ‖ Ναζαρέτ TR RP TH

20 **1:26b** txt ἀπὸ TH NA28 ‖ ὑπὸ TR RP

21 **1:27** txt ἐμνηστευμένην TH NA28 ‖ μεμνηστευμένην RP

22 **1:28a** txt ὁ ἄγγελος TR RP ‖ *omit* TH NA28

23 **1:28b** txt σοῦ א B L W Ψ f[1] 565 579 700 1241 syr[pal] cop[sa,bo] arm geo Origenlem Ps-Gregory-Thaumaturgus Peter-Alexandria[acc. to Cyril] Serapion Gregory-Nyssa[*vid*] Epiphanius Hesychius John-Damascus; Jerome Quadvultdeus TH NA28 {A} ‖ σοῦ. εὐλογημένη σὺ ἐν γυναιξίν. "...you. Blessed are you among women." A C D E G H K M U Γ Δ Θ Λ Π 0233 f[13] 2 28 33 118 157 180 205 597 892 1006 1010 1071 1243 1292 1342 1424 1505 2542 *Lect* it[a,aur,b,c,d,e,f,ff2,l,q,r1] vg syr[p,h] cop[bomss] eth slav Diatessaron Eusebius Ps-Athanasius Theodotus-Ancryra[*vid*]; Tertullian Ambrose Augustine TR RP ‖ *lac* 𝔓[45] 𝔓[75] F Y N P Q T Ξ Ω.

24 **1:29a** txt *omit* TH NA28 ‖ ἰδοῦσα TR RP

25 **1:29b** txt ἐπὶ τῷ λόγῳ διεταράχθη NA28 ‖ διεταράχθη ἐπὶ τῷ λόγῳ αὐτοῦ TR RP

26 **1:31** txt συλλήμψῃ NA28 ‖ συλλήψῃ TR RP

Lk 1:33 καὶ βασιλεύσει ἐπὶ τὸν οἶκον Ἰακὼβ εἰς τοὺς αἰῶνας, καὶ τῆς βασιλείας αὐτοῦ οὐκ ἔσται τέλος.

33and he will reign over the house of Jacob for ever; and of his kingdom there will be no end."

Lk 1:34 Εἶπεν δὲ Μαριὰμ πρὸς τὸν ἄγγελον, Πῶς ἔσται τοῦτο, ἐπεὶ ἄνδρα οὐ γινώσκω;

34And Mary said to the angel, "How will this happen, since I am not knowing a man?"[27]

Lk 1:35 Καὶ ἀποκριθεὶς ὁ ἄγγελος εἶπεν αὐτῇ, Πνεῦμα ἅγιον ἐπελεύσεται ἐπὶ σέ, καὶ δύναμις ὑψίστου ἐπισκιάσει σοι• διὸ καὶ τὸ γεννώμενον ἅγιον κληθήσεται υἱὸς θεοῦ.

35And in answer the angel said to her, "The Holy Spirit will come upon you, and the power of the Most High will overshadow you. For this reason also, the one to be born will be called holy,[28] the Son of God.

Lk 1:36 Καὶ ἰδού, Ἐλισάβετ ἡ συγγενίς[29] σου, καὶ αὐτὴ συνείληφεν[30] υἱὸν ἐν γήρει αὐτῆς• καὶ οὗτος μὴν ἕκτος ἐστὶν αὐτῇ τῇ καλουμένῃ στείρᾳ.

36And behold, Elizabeth your relative, even she in her old age, has conceived a son, and this is the sixth month with her, she who was called barren.

Lk 1:37 Ὅτι οὐκ ἀδυνατήσει παρὰ τοῦ θεοῦ πᾶν ῥῆμα.

37Therefore with God,[31] nothing[32] will be impossible."

Lk 1:38 Εἶπεν δὲ Μαριάμ, Ἰδού, ἡ δούλη κυρίου• γένοιτό μοι κατὰ τὸ ῥῆμά σου. Καὶ ἀπῆλθεν ἀπ' αὐτῆς ὁ ἄγγελος.

38"Here am I, the slave girl of the Lord," Mary said. "May it be to me according to your statement." And the angel left her.

---

[27] **1:34** "I am not knowing a man," with the verb for know in the continuous aspect, is a euphemism meaning, "I am not being intimate- having sex with a man, now or in the near future."

[28] **1:35** The one to be born would already have been called holy, in that it would be a firstborn male; see Exodus 13:2, 14-16.

[29] **1:36a** txt συγγενίς TH NA28 ‖ συγγενής RP

[30] **1:36b** txt συνείληφεν NA28 ‖ συνειληφυῖα RP

[31] **1:37a** txt τοῦ θεοῦ TH NA28 ‖ τῷ θεῷ RP. A more correct rendering of τοῦ θεοῦ would be, "Therefore for God..." But I did not write that because I did not want 2 "for"s in a row, auditorally.

[32] **1:37b** Literally, "Because with God every saying will not be impossible," ὅτι οὐκ ἀδυνατησει παρὰ τοῦ θεοῦ πᾶν ῥῆμα. The BDF grammar states that ῥῆμα - hrēma here is Hebraistic in use: "thing, matter, event," and that οὐκ...πᾶν is also a Semitism, resulting in the whole to mean, "nothing will be impossible with God." But I can't help but feel that Mary's response, "Let it be to me according to your ῥῆμα," harks back to the use of ῥῆμα by the angel, and that the angel told of Elizabeth's case as assurance that "therefore, in view of this, as for my statements to you also, not one statement will be impossible." Still, this is reminiscent of Genesis 18:14 in the Septuagint: Μὴ ἀδυνατήσει παρὰ τῷ Θεῷ ῥῆμα? "Is anything too hard for the LORD?" That was when the angel of the LORD had announced to the aged Sarah that she would bear a son. There, the word ῥῆμα - hrēma is used as meaning "anything."

Mary Stays With Elizabeth

Lk 1:39 Ἀναστᾶσα δὲ Μαριὰμ ἐν ταῖς ἡμέραις ταύταις ἐπορεύθη εἰς τὴν ὀρεινὴν μετὰ σπουδῆς, εἰς πόλιν Ἰούδα,

39At that time Mary got up and went with speed to the hill country, to a town of Judah,

Lk 1:40 καὶ εἰσῆλθεν εἰς τὸν οἶκον Ζαχαρίου, καὶ ἠσπάσατο τὴν Ἐλισάβετ.

40where she entered the house of Zechariah, and greeted Elizabeth.

Lk 1:41 Καὶ ἐγένετο ὡς ἤκουσεν τὸν ἀσπασμὸν τῆς Μαρίας ἡ Ἐλισάβετ,[33] ἐσκίρτησεν τὸ βρέφος ἐν τῇ κοιλίᾳ αὐτῆς· καὶ ἐπλήσθη πνεύματος ἁγίου ἡ Ἐλισάβετ,

41And it came about that when Elizabeth heard Mary's greeting, the baby in her womb did leap, and Elizabeth was filled with the Holy Spirit.

Lk 1:42 καὶ ἀνεφώνησεν φωνῇ μεγάλῃ, καὶ εἶπεν, Εὐλογημένη σὺ ἐν γυναιξίν, καὶ εὐλογημένος ὁ καρπὸς τῆς κοιλίας σου.

42And she shouted out in a loud voice,[34] saying, "Blessed are you among women, and blessed is the fruit of your womb!

Lk 1:43 Καὶ πόθεν μοι τοῦτο, ἵνα ἔλθῃ ἡ μήτηρ τοῦ κυρίου μου πρός ἐμέ;[35]

43And why does it come to me, that to me the mother of my Lord should come?

Lk 1:44 Ἰδοὺ γάρ, ὡς ἐγένετο ἡ φωνὴ τοῦ ἀσπασμοῦ σου εἰς τὰ ὦτά μου, ἐσκίρτησεν ἐν ἀγαλλιάσει τὸ βρέφος[36] ἐν τῇ κοιλίᾳ μου.

44For when the sound of your greeting came into my ears, the baby in my womb did leap in exultation.[37]

Lk 1:45 Καὶ μακαρία ἡ πιστεύσασα, ὅτι ἔσται τελείωσις τοῖς λελαλημένοις αὐτῇ παρὰ κυρίου.

45Blessed is she who has believed that there will be a completion of the things announced to her from the Lord!"

Mary's Song

Lk 1:46 Καὶ εἶπεν Μαριάμ, Μεγαλύνει ἡ ψυχή μου τὸν κύριον,

46And Mary said: "My soul does magnify the Lord,[38]

---

33 **1:41** txt τὸν ἀσπασμὸν τῆς Μαρίας ἡ Ἐλισάβετ TH NA28 ‖ ἡ Ἐλισάβετ τὸν ἀσπασμὸν τῆς Μαρίας RP

34 **1:42** txt ἀνεφώνησεν φωνῇ A TR RP ‖ ἀνεφώνησεν κραυγῇ B TH NA28 ‖ ἀνεβόησεν φωνῇ א

35 **1:43** txt ἐμέ NA28 ‖ με TR RP

36 **1:44a** txt ἐν ἀγαλλιάσει τὸ βρέφος TR TH NA28 ‖ τὸ βρέφος ἐν ἀγαλλιάσει RP

37 **1:44b** Leapt in ἀγαλλιάσις. This word is found only in Biblical and ecclesiastical literature. It refers primarily to messianic exultation. Some of the other occurrences are: later in this chapter, v. 46, where Mary rejoiced in "God my Savior," i.e., God + a form of the word Yeshua; in Psalm 44:8, exulting in God; Hebrews 1:9, the Messiah is anointed with the oil of gladness more than his peers; Acts 2:46, the church fellowshiped in Messianic exultation; and Jude 24, it is an exceeding joy found in the presence of God himself.

38 **1:46** Mary probably had in mind Psalm 34:3, "O magnify the Lord with me, and let us exalt his name together," and "My soul shall make its boast in the Lord," Psalm 34:2. And so she says, "My soul **does** magnify the Lord." It is reminiscent also of the "Bless the Lord, O my

Lk 1:47 καὶ ἠγαλλίασεν τὸ πνεῦμά μου ἐπὶ τῷ θεῷ τῷ σωτῆρί μου.

47and my spirit did rejoice in God my Savior,

Lk 1:48 Ὅτι ἐπέβλεψεν ἐπὶ τὴν ταπείνωσιν τῆς δούλης αὐτοῦ. Ἰδοὺ γάρ, ἀπὸ τοῦ νῦν μακαριοῦσίν με πᾶσαι αἱ γενεαί.

48because he looked toward the lowly station of his servant. So behold: all the generations after now will consider me blessed,

Lk 1:49 Ὅτι ἐποίησέν μοι μεγάλα[39] ὁ δυνατός, καὶ ἅγιον τὸ ὄνομα αὐτοῦ.

49because the Mighty One did great things for me. And holy will be his name,[40]

Lk 1:50 Καὶ τὸ ἔλεος αὐτοῦ εἰς γενεὰς καὶ γενεὰς[41] τοῖς φοβουμένοις αὐτόν.

50and his mercy to those who fear him, into age after age.[42]

---

soul...bless his holy name" of Psalm 103:1; and also of 104:1, 35, and 146:1, where in the Septuagint the Greek sentence is startlingly identical to Mary's, only that the imperative mood of the verb 'magnify' is changed to the indicative. Note: It was Semitic to use the nominative case for vocative, so Mary could still have been addressing her soul, as in the Psalms, i.e., "Magnify the Lord, O my soul." The songs of Mary and Zechariah are the most Semitic parts of Luke.

39 **1:49a** txt μεγάλα TH NA28 // μεγαλεῖα TR RP

40 **1:49b** ...ὁ δυνατός, καὶ ἅγιον τὸ ὄνομα αὐτοῦ, καὶ τὸ ἔλεος αὐτοῦ εἰς γενεὰς καὶ γενεὰς τοῖς φοβουμένοις αὐτόν. Traditionally, this ὁ δυνατός, καὶ ἅγιον τὸ ὄνομα is considered an example of the Hebraistic use of καί to co-ordinate words with independent clauses; so Friedrich Blass, and thus read: "The Mighty One did great things for me, wherefore his name is holy." But ἅγιον is ambiguously both masculine and neuter, and the flow seemed to group together "his name and his mercy" as that which is holy. In the Greek, ἅγιον τὸ ὄνομα αὐτοῦ, καὶ τὸ ἔλεος αὐτοῦ...τοῖς φοβουμένοις, "holy his name and his mercy," the words 'holy,' 'name,' and 'mercy' are all three neuter singular; 'name' and 'mercy' are subjects; and 'holy' is the predicate adjective, and there is no verb, except the implied copula verb ἐστίν, 'is'. The O-V-S syntax is more common when a single verb has a double subject. Ἐστίν is by far the copula most frequently omitted but implied in Greek, and a preference for omission is observed in (1) proverbs, (2) impersonal constructions, especially those expressing possibility or necessity, (3) questions, and (4) exclamations. And the τοῖς φοβουμένοις, "to those who fear him," is something like an "ethical dative," (also a Semitism), thus meaning, "his name and his mercy will be holy in the eyes of those who fear him." For is not the kindness and forbearance of God meant to lead you to repentance and holiness? (Romans 2:4) For other examples of the ethical dative, see Jonah 3:3, Acts 7:20, II Peter 3:14, and possibly the ἔρχομαί σοι of Rev. 2:5. We have examples of the ethical dative in English literature also. See Milton's Paradise Lost, Book I, Lines 25-26: "I may assert Eternal Providence, And justify the ways of God to men." In other words, justify the ways of God in the eyes of men, in the sight of men.

41 **1:50a** txt γενεὰς καὶ γενεὰς TH NA28 // γενεὰς γενεῶν TR RP

42 **1:50b** Mary through the anointing of the Holy Spirit looks both backward and forward: backward to the "from everlasting to everlasting, to generation of generations" of Psalm 103:17, and forward, as in Psalm 146:10, "into age after age," in harmony with Paul in Ephesians 2:7, that God sent Yeshua "so that in the ages to come he might show the exceeding riches of his grace in his kindness toward us through Christ Jesus." In Psalm 89:1, the "From everlasting until everlasting" covers both past, present and future. But the "time" tense here is still relative to and set by verse 48 as the future, where she speaks of "all the ages from now on." Her phrase in the Greek, "into age after age," εις γενεὰς καὶ γενεὰς, is almost identical to the Greek phrase of Psalm 146:10. This same phrase is also used in Lamentations 5:19, and Psalm 49:11 (and many others) as a parallelism to "for ever." Psalm 146 is clearly a Psalm she loved. Psalm 45:17 says, "I will cause your name to be celebrated in

Lk 1:51 Ἐποίησεν κράτος ἐν βραχίονι αὐτοῦ• διεσκόρπισεν ὑπερηφάνους διανοίᾳ καρδίας αὐτῶν.

51Power he wrought with his arm. He scattered those who were proud in the thoughts of their heart.

Lk 1:52 Καθεῖλεν δυνάστας ἀπὸ θρόνων, καὶ ὕψωσεν ταπεινούς.

52He pulled down rulers from their thrones and lifted high the humble.

Lk 1:53 Πεινῶντας ἐνέπλησεν ἀγαθῶν, καὶ πλουτοῦντας ἐξαπέστειλεν κενούς.

53Hungry ones he filled up with good things and rich ones he sent away empty.

Lk 1:54 Ἀντελάβετο Ἰσραὴλ παιδὸς αὐτοῦ, μνησθῆναι ἐλέους,

54He helped his servant Israel, and remembered[43] about mercy

Lk 1:55 καθὼς ἐλάλησεν πρὸς τοὺς πατέρας ἡμῶν, τῷ Ἀβραὰμ καὶ τῷ σπέρματι αὐτοῦ εἰς τὸν αἰῶνα.

55"to Abraham and his seed for ever,' as he said to our fathers."

Lk 1:56 Ἔμεινεν δὲ Μαριὰμ σὺν αὐτῇ ὡς[44] μῆνας τρεῖς, καὶ ὑπέστρεψεν εἰς τὸν οἶκον αὐτῆς.

56And Mary remained with her about three months, and then returned to her home.

The Birth of John the Baptizer

Lk 1:57 Τῇ δὲ Ἐλισάβετ ἐπλήσθη ὁ χρόνος τοῦ τεκεῖν αὐτήν, καὶ ἐγέννησεν υἱόν.

57And the time was fulfilled for Elizabeth to give birth, and she produced a son.

Lk 1:58 Καὶ ἤκουσαν οἱ περίοικοι καὶ οἱ συγγενεῖς αὐτῆς ὅτι ἐμεγάλυνεν κύριος τὸ ἔλεος αὐτοῦ μετ' αὐτῆς, καὶ συνέχαιρον αὐτῇ.

58And her neighbors and relatives heard that the Lord had magnified his mercy to her, and they rejoiced with her.

Lk 1:59 Καὶ ἐγένετο ἐν τῇ ἡμέρᾳ τῇ ὀγδόῃ,[45] ἦλθον περιτεμεῖν τὸ παιδίον• καὶ ἐκάλουν αὐτὸ ἐπὶ τῷ ὀνόματι τοῦ πατρὸς αὐτοῦ Ζαχαρίαν.

59And it came about that on the eighth day, they came to circumcise the child, and they were about to call him by the name of his father, Zechariah,

Lk 1:60 Καὶ ἀποκριθεῖσα ἡ μήτηρ αὐτοῦ εἶπεν, Οὐχί, ἀλλὰ κληθήσεται Ἰωάννης.

60and his mother responded and said, "No! He shall be called John."

---

all generations; therefore the peoples will praise you for ever and ever." This shows that "all generations" is a parallelism to "for ever and ever." See the preceding footnote about the verb "is" being omitted when expressing possibility. "And holy may be his name, and his mercy to those who fear him."

43 **1:54** The Greek verb is an infinitive, an infinitive of illustration or result, a Hebraism; so also several instances in Zechariah's song.

44 **1:56** txt ὡς TH NA28 ‖ ὡσεὶ TR RP

45 **1:59** txt ἡμέρᾳ τῇ ὀγδόῃ TH NA28 ‖ ὀγδόῃ ἡμέρᾳ TR RP

Lk 1:61 Καὶ εἶπαν πρὸς αὐτὴν ὅτι Οὐδείς ἐστιν ἐν τῇ συγγενείᾳ[46] σου ὃς καλεῖται τῷ ὀνόματι τούτῳ.

61And they said to her, "There is no one among your relatives called by that name."

Lk 1:62 Ἐνένευον δὲ τῷ πατρὶ αὐτοῦ, τὸ τί ἂν θέλοι καλεῖσθαι αὐτό.[47]

62Then they signaled to his father, to find out what he wanted him to be called.

Lk 1:63 Καὶ αἰτήσας πινακίδιον ἔγραψεν, λέγων, Ἰωάννης ἐστὶν ὄνομα[48] αὐτοῦ• καὶ ἐθαύμασαν πάντες.

63And he asked for a tablet, and wrote as follows,[49] "His name is John." Everyone was surprised.

Lk 1:64 Ἀνεῴχθη δὲ τὸ στόμα αὐτοῦ παραχρῆμα καὶ ἡ γλῶσσα αὐτοῦ, καὶ ἐλάλει εὐλογῶν τὸν θεόν.

64And immediately his mouth was opened, and also his tongue, and he spoke, blessing God.

Lk 1:65 Καὶ ἐγένετο ἐπὶ πάντας φόβος τοὺς περιοικοῦντας αὐτούς• καὶ ἐν ὅλῃ τῇ ὀρεινῇ τῆς Ἰουδαίας διελαλεῖτο πάντα τὰ ῥήματα ταῦτα.

65And an awe came over everyone who lived around them. And all through the hill country of Judea, these things were being discussed.

Lk 1:66 Καὶ ἔθεντο πάντες οἱ ἀκούσαντες ἐν τῇ καρδίᾳ αὐτῶν, λέγοντες, Τί ἄρα τὸ παιδίον τοῦτο ἔσται; Καὶ γὰρ χεὶρ κυρίου ἦν μετ' αὐτοῦ.

66And everyone who heard, kept thinking about it, saying, "What then will this child be?" For the hand of the Lord was certainly[50] with him.

Zechariah's Song

Lk 1:67 Καὶ Ζαχαρίας ὁ πατὴρ αὐτοῦ ἐπλήσθη πνεύματος ἁγίου, καὶ ἐπροφήτευσεν,[51] λέγων,

67And his father Zechariah was filled with the Holy Spirit, and he prophesied, saying:

Lk 1:68 Εὐλογητὸς κύριος ὁ θεὸς τοῦ Ἰσραήλ, ὅτι ἐπεσκέψατο καὶ ἐποίησεν λύτρωσιν τῷ λαῷ αὐτοῦ,

68"Blessed be the Lord, the God of Israel, because he has turned to concern himself and has accomplished redemption for his people.

Lk 1:69 καὶ ἤγειρεν κέρας σωτηρίας ἡμῖν ἐν οἴκῳ Δαυὶδ[52] παιδὸς αὐτοῦ—

69He has raised up a horn[53] of salvation for us in the house of David his servant

---

[46] **1:61** txt ἐν τῇ συγγενείᾳ TR RP ‖ ἐκ τῆς συγγενείας TH NA28

[47] **1:62** txt αὐτο TH NA28 ‖ αὐτόν TR RP

[48] **1:63a** txt ὄνομα NA28 ‖ τὸ ὄνομα TR RP TH

[49] **1:63b** Literally, "he wrote, saying..," ἔγραψεν λέγων, a Semitism for "he wrote as follows:..."

[50] **1:66** txt γαρ 𝔓4 א B TH NA28 ‖ *omit* A TR RP

[51] **1:67** txt ἐπροφήτευσεν TH NA28 ‖ προεφήτευσεν TR RP

[52] **1:69a** txt οἴκῳ Δαυὶδ NA28 ‖ τῷ οἴκῳ Δαυὶδ τοῦ TR RP

Lk 1:70 καθὼς ἐλάλησεν διὰ στόματος τῶν ἁγίων ἀπ' αἰῶνος προφητῶν αὐτοῦ—
70as he has said through the mouths of his holy prophets since[54] eons ago,
Lk 1:71 σωτηρίαν ἐξ ἐχθρῶν ἡμῶν, καὶ ἐκ χειρὸς πάντων τῶν μισούντων ἡμᾶς•
71salvation from our enemies and from the hand of all who hate us—
Lk 1:72 ποιῆσαι ἔλεος μετὰ τῶν πατέρων ἡμῶν, καὶ μνησθῆναι διαθήκης ἁγίας
αὐτοῦ,
72to demonstrate mercy to our fathers to remember his holy covenant,
Lk 1:73 ὅρκον ὃν ὤμοσεν πρὸς Ἀβραὰμ τὸν πατέρα ἡμῶν, τοῦ δοῦναι ἡμῖν
73the oath he swore to our father Abraham, to give us
Lk 1:74 ἀφόβως ἐκ χειρὸς ἐχθρῶν[55] ἡμῶν ῥυσθέντας, λατρεύειν αὐτῷ
74rescue from the hand of our enemies, that we may serve him without fear
Lk 1:75 ἐν ὁσιότητι καὶ δικαιοσύνῃ ἐνώπιον αὐτοῦ πάσαις ταῖς ἡμέραις ἡμῶν.
75in holiness and righteousness before him all our days.[56]
Lk 1:76 Καὶ σὺ δέ, παιδίον, προφήτης ὑψίστου κληθήσῃ• προπορεύσῃ γὰρ
ἐνώπιον κυρίου ἑτοιμάσαι ὁδοὺς αὐτοῦ•
76Yes and you,[57] child, will be called a prophet of the Most High; for you will
go on before[58] the Lord to prepare his paths,
Lk 1:77 τοῦ δοῦναι γνῶσιν σωτηρίας τῷ λαῷ αὐτοῦ ἐν ἀφέσει ἁμαρτιῶν αὐτῶν,
77to give his people the knowledge of salvation through the forgiveness of
their sins,
Lk 1:78 διὰ σπλάγχνα ἐλέους θεοῦ ἡμῶν, ἐν οἷς ἡμᾶς ἀνατολὴ ἐξ ὕψους,
78because of the tender feelings of our God with which the Sunrise from on
high will[59] look over us
Lk 1:79 ἐπιφᾶναι τοῖς ἐν σκότει καὶ σκιᾷ θανάτου καθημένοις, τοῦ κατευθῦναι
τοὺς πόδας ἡμῶν εἰς ὁδὸν εἰρήνης.
79to appear to those sitting in darkness and in the shadow of death, to guide
our feet along the path of peace."
Lk 1:80 ¶ Τὸ δὲ παιδίον ηὔξανεν καὶ ἐκραταιοῦτο πνεύματι, καὶ ἦν ἐν ταῖς
ἐρήμοις ἕως ἡμέρας ἀναδείξεως αὐτοῦ πρὸς τὸν Ἰσραήλ.
80And the child grew and became strong in spirit; and he was in the deserts,
until the days of his being presented to Israel.

---

53 **1:69b** *Horn* in the Old Testament symbolizes *strength.*

54 **1:70** txt ἀπ' TH NA28 ‖ τῶν ἀπ' TR RP

55 **1:74** txt ἐχθρῶν TH NA28 ‖ τῶν ἐχθρῶν ἡμῶν TR RP

56 **1:75** txt πάσαις ταῖς ἡμέραις ἡμῶν TH NA28 ‖ πάσας τὰς ἡμέρας τῆς ζωῆς ἡμῶν TR RP

57 **1:76a** txt καὶ σὺ δέ TH NA28 ‖ καὶ σύ TR RP

58 **1:76b** txt ἐνώπιον TH NA28 ‖ πρὸ προσώπου TR RP

59 **1:78** txt ἐπισκέψεται TH NA28 ‖ ἐπεσκέψατο TR RP

Chapter 2

The Birth of Jesus

Lk 2:1 Ἐγένετο δὲ ἐν ταῖς ἡμέραις ἐκείναις, ἐξῆλθεν δόγμα παρὰ Καίσαρος Αὐγούστου, ἀπογράφεσθαι πᾶσαν τὴν οἰκουμένην.

1And it came about in those days, that a decree went out from Caesar Augustus, that all the inhabited earth should be registered.[60]

Lk 2:2 Αὕτη ἀπογραφὴ[61] πρώτη ἐγένετο ἡγεμονεύοντος τῆς Συρίας Κυρηνίου.

2This was the first registration that took place while Quirinius was governor of Syria.

Lk 2:3 Καὶ ἐπορεύοντο πάντες ἀπογράφεσθαι, ἕκαστος εἰς τὴν ἰδίαν ἑαυτοῦ[62] πόλιν.

3And all were making their way to be registered, each to his own town.

Lk 2:4 Ἀνέβη δὲ καὶ Ἰωσὴφ ἀπὸ τῆς Γαλιλαίας, ἐκ πόλεως Ναζαρέθ,[63] εἰς τὴν Ἰουδαίαν, εἰς πόλιν Δαυίδ, ἥτις καλεῖται Βηθλέεμ, διὰ τὸ εἶναι αὐτὸν ἐξ οἴκου καὶ πατριᾶς Δαυίδ,

4Thus Joseph also went up, from the town of Nazareth in Galilee, to Judea, to the town of David, which is called Bethlehem, because he was from the house and line of David;

Lk 2:5 ἀπογράψασθαι σὺν Μαριὰμ τῇ ἐμνηστευμένῃ αὐτῷ, οὔσῃ ἐγκύῳ.

5to be registered along with Mary, the one pledged to him,[64] who was pregnant.

Lk 2:6 Ἐγένετο δὲ ἐν τῷ εἶναι αὐτοὺς ἐκεῖ, ἐπλήσθησαν αἱ ἡμέραι τοῦ τεκεῖν αὐτήν.

6And it came about that while they were there, the days for her to give birth were completed,

Lk 2:7 Καὶ ἔτεκεν τὸν υἱὸν αὐτῆς τὸν πρωτότοκον, καὶ ἐσπαργάνωσεν αὐτόν, καὶ ἀνέκλινεν αὐτὸν ἐν φάτνῃ,[65] διότι οὐκ ἦν αὐτοῖς τόπος ἐν τῷ καταλύματι.

7and she bore her firstborn son. And she swaddled him[66] and placed him in a feeding trough, because there was no room for them in the inn.

---

60 **2:1** *The whole inhabited earth...* This is hype on the part of Rome, commonly used in order to magnify the emperors. The meaning is *the whole empire.* The registration here is the recording of the names for the purpose of adding everyone to the tax rolls. The phrase could also be translated *that a census should be taken of all the inhabited earth.* The tax is a poll tax, or head tax, or a capitation, as forbidden in the constitution for the U.S.A. This was a form of tribute forced upon the conquered by the conqueror.

61 **2:2** txt ἀπογραφὴ TH NA28 ‖ ἡ ἀπογραφὴ TR RP

62 **2:3** txt ἑαυτοῦ TH NA28 ‖ ἰδίαν TR RP

63 **2:4** txt ναζαρεθ ℵ D F G H M S U Y Γ Θ Λ Ψ f^1 f^{13} 2 28 565 Eras-1516, 1522, 1527; Elz-1624 Scriv-1894 SBL NA28 ‖ ναζαραθ A C Δ ‖ ναζαρετ B E^{sup} K L W Ξ Ω 33 118 157 579 700^c 1071 1424 Compl Steph-1550 Beza-1588, 1598 Walton-1657 Mill-1710 Scriv-1887 VS TG AT BG RP TH ‖ ναζετ 700* ‖ *lac* $\mathfrak{P}^{45}$ $\mathfrak{P}^{75}$ E N P Q T Π

64 **2:5** txt ἐμνηστευμένῃ αὐτῷ TH NA28 ‖ μεμνηστευμένῃ αὐτῷ γυναικί TR RP

65 **2:7a** txt φάτνῃ TH NA28 ‖ τῇ φάτνῃ TR RP

The Shepherds and the Angels

Lk 2:8 ¶ Καὶ ποιμένες ἦσαν ἐν τῇ χώρᾳ τῇ αὐτῇ ἀγραυλοῦντες καὶ φυλάσσοντες φυλακὰς τῆς νυκτὸς ἐπὶ τὴν ποίμνην αὐτῶν.

8And there were shepherds in that same region, camping out in the fields, keeping watch over their flocks by night.

Lk 2:9 Καὶ ἄγγελος κυρίου ἐπέστη αὐτοῖς, καὶ δόξα κυρίου περιέλαμψεν αὐτούς• καὶ ἐφοβήθησαν φόβον μέγαν.

9And[67] an angel of the Lord came upon them, and the glory of the Lord shone all around them, and they were terrified.

Lk 2:10 Καὶ εἶπεν αὐτοῖς ὁ ἄγγελος, Μὴ φοβεῖσθε• ἰδοὺ γάρ, εὐαγγελίζομαι ὑμῖν χαρὰν μεγάλην, ἥτις ἔσται παντὶ τῷ λαῷ•

10And the angel said to them, "Fear not. For behold, I am announcing to you a great joy that will be with all the people.

Lk 2:11 ὅτι ἐτέχθη ὑμῖν σήμερον σωτήρ, ὅς ἐστιν χριστὸς κύριος, ἐν πόλει Δαυίδ.

11Because for you is born this day, in the town of David, a Savior, who is Messiah the Lord.

Lk 2:12 Καὶ τοῦτο ὑμῖν τὸ σημεῖον• εὑρήσετε βρέφος ἐσπαργανωμένον, καὶ κείμενον ἐν φάτνῃ.

12And this will be a sign to you: you will find a baby swaddled, and[68] lying in a feeding trough."

Lk 2:13 Καὶ ἐξαίφνης ἐγένετο σὺν τῷ ἀγγέλῳ πλῆθος στρατιᾶς οὐρανίου, αἰνούντων τὸν θεόν, καὶ λεγόντων,

13And suddenly, there was with the angel a great company of the army of heaven, praising God and saying,

Lk 2:14 Δόξα ἐν ὑψίστοις θεῷ, καὶ ἐπὶ γῆς εἰρήνη• ἐν ἀνθρώποις εὐδοκία.

14"Glory to God in the highest realms! And on earth peace, good will toward men!" [69]

---

66 **2:7b** Or swathed, or podded. In this practice, the baby was bound up tight with bands of cloth =*band*-ages, for reasons which may be reasonably guessed. The cloth would absorb any blood, amniotic fluid and wax still present after cleaning; this would have both practical and ceremonial cleanness ramifications, since the mother's blood was ceremonially unclean. The dead were wrapped somewhat similarly. Furthermore, the infant wrapped in such a way would be prevented from rolling. This last reason could have been especially applicable in Jesus' case, since he was placed in a stone feeding trough. The stone surface was not necessarily level or even. In addition, swaddling could have prevented the infant from rolling or flopping its limbs during travel on an animal. Native Americans swaddled a papoose to a sled of sorts to facilitate traveling. Traveling or not, a woman of that circumstance had a heavy burden of chores, and the swaddling could have kept the infant out of trouble while mother's eye was not upon it. Many Mediterranean lands practiced swaddling well over a thousand years later. See also Job 38:8,9; Ezekiel 16:4-6. Note that the Ezekiel passage implies that a baby not swaddled, is unclean, and undignified. (The passage refers to Jerusalem.) It is important that a translation of this Luke text use the same word as used in Job and Ezekiel, so that the reader catches the connection.

67 **2:9** txt και TH NA28 ‖ καὶ ἰδού TR RP

68 **2:12** txt καὶ κείμενον TH NA28 ‖ κείμενον TR RP

Lk 2:15 Καὶ ἐγένετο, ὡς ἀπῆλθον ἀπ' αὐτῶν εἰς τὸν οὐρανὸν οἱ ἄγγελοι, οἱ ποιμένες ἐλάλουν πρὸς ἀλλήλους, Διέλθωμεν δὴ ἕως Βηθλέεμ, καὶ ἴδωμεν τὸ ῥῆμα τοῦτο τὸ γεγονός, ὃ ὁ κύριος ἐγνώρισεν ἡμῖν.

15And it came about that when the angels had departed from them into heaven, the shepherds[70] were saying[71] to one another, "Let's go over to Bethlehem, and see this thing that has happened, which the Lord has made known to us."

Lk 2:16 Καὶ ἦλθαν σπεύσαντες, καὶ ἀνεῦραν τήν τε Μαριὰμ καὶ τὸν Ἰωσήφ, καὶ τὸ βρέφος κείμενον ἐν τῇ φάτνῃ.

16And they went speeding, and found both Mary and Joseph, and the baby lying in the feeding trough.

Lk 2:17 Ἰδόντες δὲ διεγνώρισαν περὶ τοῦ ῥήματος τοῦ λαληθέντος αὐτοῖς περὶ τοῦ παιδίου τούτου.

---

69 **2:14** {D} txt ἐν ἀνθρώποις εὐδοκία ℵ^{2} B^{2} E G H K L M P U Γ Δ Θ Λ Ξ Ψ 053 0233^{vid} *f*^{1} *f*^{13} 2 28 157 180 205 565 579 597 700 892 1006 1009 1010 1071 1079 1195 1216 1241 1242 1243 1253 1292 1342 1344 1365 1424 1505 1546 1646 2148 2174 2882 *Byz Lect* (syr$^{pal mss}$ εὐδοκία σου) cop^{bo} arm eth geo slav Origen$^{2/5}$ Ps-Gregory-Thaumaturgus Eusebius Ps-Athanasius Apostolic Consitutions Didymus-Philo-Carpasia Epiphanius Severian Chrysostom Marcus-Eremita Paul-Emesa Cyril Proclus Theodotus-Ancyra Hesychius Theodoret TR RP ‖ ἐν ἀνθρώποις εὐδοκίας "to mortals of his good pleasure" ℵ* A B* D W 23 it^{d} vg^{ww,st} cop^{sa} goth Irenaeus^{lat} Origen$^{gr2/5,lat}$ Cyril-Jerusalem Gaudentius Jerome$^{4/15}$ Augustine$^{2/41}$ SBL TH NA28 {A} ‖ *hominibus bonae voluntatis* (=ἀνθρώποις εὐδοκίας 372) it$^{a,aur,b,β,c,e,f,(ff2),l,q,r1}$ vg^{cl} Irenaeus^{lat} Origen^{lat} Athanasius^{lat}; Hilary Ambrosiaster Ambrose Chromatius Jerome$^{11/15}$ Augustine$^{39/41}$ ms$^{acc. to Erasmus}$ ‖ καὶ ἐν ἀνθρώποις εὐδοκία syr$^{(s),(p),h}$ Origen$^{1/5}$ ‖ *lac* C N Π? 33. The UBS textual commentary says that the majority text reading is probably a scribal oversight, because, "at the end of a line εὐδοκίας would differ from εὐδοκία only by the presence of the smallest lunar sigma, little more than a point, for which it might have been taken— thus ευδοκιαc." Also according to the UBS textual commentary, the earlier reading is a Semitizing construction characteristic of Luke chapters 1 and 2. This Semitic expression is found in Hebrew in the Dead Sea Scrolls in several Qumran Hymns: "the sons of his (God's) good pleasure," 1 QH iv.32 f.; xi.9; and "the elect of his (God's) good pleasure," viii.6; and also in Aramaic, in a fragment from Qumran, "among men of his good pleasure," see J. A. Fitzmeyer, S.J. (Theological studies, XIX [1958], pp. 225-227. The Sahidic translation of this phrase of the angels' song reads, "And peace upon earth among men of his desire." Similarly, later in this gospel, a voice from heaven says about Jesus, "You are my beloved son; in you I had good pleasure." See Galatians 6:16. Interesting that the same people who object to the NA28 text in Luke 2:14 where instead of "peace, goodwill toward men," it limits the blessing to "men of his good pleasure," yet in Revelation 22:21 where the NA28 text says "the grace of the Lord Jesus be with all," they object, and prefer that that blessing be only to the saints.

70 **2:15a** txt οἱ ποιμένες ℵ B L W Θ Ξ 1 565 700 1071 1582* it^{a,aur,b,β,e,f,ff2,l,r1} vg syr^{s,p,pal} cop^{sa,bo} arm geo Or-lat Eus TH NA28 ‖ καὶ οἱ ἄνθρωποι οἱ ποιμένες A D E F G H K M P S U Y Γ Δ Λ Ψ Ω 053 *f*^{13} 2 28 33 118 157 892 1009 1010 1079 1195 1216 1230 1241 1242 1344 1424 1546 1582^{c} 2148 2174 𝔐 *Lect*^{m} it$^{(e),d,q}$ syr^{h} Diatess^{a,n,t} TR RP ‖ καὶ οἱ ποιμένες 579 1365 ‖ *lac* 𝔓^{45} 𝔓^{75} C N Q T Π. The expression οἱ ἄνθρωποι οἱ ποιμένες is considered a "pleonasm," and thus most translations of the majority text say simply "shepherds." See also expressions such as Ἄνδρες ἀδελφοὶ in Acts 7:2, which is also considered a pleonasm, and rendered simply "brothers."

71 **2:15b** txt ἐλάλουν TH NA28 ‖ εἶπον TR RP

17And once they had seen, they gave an exact report[72] of the message spoken to them concerning this child.
Lk 2:18 Καὶ πάντες οἱ ἀκούσαντες ἐθαύμασαν περὶ τῶν λαληθέντων ὑπὸ τῶν ποιμένων πρὸς αὐτούς.
18And all who heard it were amazed at what the shepherds said to them.
Lk 2:19 Ἡ δὲ Μαριὰμ πάντα συνετήρει τὰ ῥήματα ταῦτα, συμβάλλουσα ἐν τῇ καρδίᾳ αὐτῆς.
19As for Mary, she memorized these words, and pondered them in her heart.
Lk 2:20 Καὶ ὑπέστρεψαν οἱ ποιμένες, δοξάζοντες καὶ αἰνοῦντες τὸν θεὸν ἐπὶ πᾶσιν οἷς ἤκουσαν καὶ εἶδον, καθὼς ἐλαλήθη πρὸς αὐτούς.
20And the shepherds returned, glorifying and praising God, because of the fact that all the things which they had heard and seen, were just as it had been told to them.

Jesus Presented in the Temple

Lk 2:21 Καὶ ὅτε ἐπλήσθησαν ἡμέραι ὀκτὼ τοῦ περιτεμεῖν αὐτόν, καὶ ἐκλήθη τὸ ὄνομα αὐτοῦ Ἰησοῦς, τὸ κληθὲν ὑπὸ τοῦ ἀγγέλου πρὸ τοῦ συλλημφθῆναι αὐτὸν ἐν τῇ κοιλίᾳ.
21And when the eighth day had arrived, the time to circumcise him, he was called the name Jesus, the name called by the angel before he was conceived in the womb.
Lk 2:22 ¶ Καὶ ὅτε ἐπλήσθησαν αἱ ἡμέραι τοῦ καθαρισμοῦ αὐτῶν κατὰ τὸν νόμον Μωϋσέως, ἀνήγαγον αὐτὸν εἰς Ἱεροσόλυμα, παραστῆσαι τῷ κυρίῳ -
22And when the days of their[73] cleansing according to the Law of Moses[74] had been completed, they took him up to Jerusalem to present him to the Lord,
Lk 2:23 καθὼς γέγραπται ἐν νόμῳ κυρίου ὅτι Πᾶν ἄρσεν διανοῖγον μήτραν ἅγιον τῷ κυρίῳ κληθήσεται -
23as it is written in the Law of the Lord, "Every male to open a womb[75] shall be called holy to the Lord,"[76]
Lk 2:24 καὶ τοῦ δοῦναι θυσίαν κατὰ τὸ εἰρημένον ἐν τῷ νόμῳ κυρίου, Ζεῦγος τρυγόνων ἢ δύο νοσσοὺς περιστερῶν.
24and to offer a sacrifice, in keeping with what is said in the Law of the Lord: "a pair of doves or two young pigeons."[77]

---

72 **2:17** txt διεγνώρισαν TR RP ‖ ἐγνώρισαν TH NA28

73 **2:22a** txt αυτων 76 *rell. Gk.* it^{q} syr^{p,h} cop^{sa,bopt} AT RP TH NA28 ‖ αυτου D 118 205 209 it^{a,aur,b,c,d,e,f,ff2,g1,l,r1} vg syr^{s} cop^{sams} arm Ir-lat (*Adv. Haer* 3.10.5.157-9) ‖ αυτον Θ* ‖ *omit* cop^{bopt} Chrys Diatess-Pers. ‖ αυτης TR ‖ *lac* 𝔓^{45} 𝔓^{75} C F N P Q T. The TR reading is found only in the Catenae. Manuscript 76 is listed for the majority reading since some had claimed it reads as the TR, but this has been confirmed as not true.

74 **2:22b** Leviticus 12:1-8

75 **2:23a** Or, "every male to inaugurate a womb," or "every offspring first to open a womb, if it is male."

76 **2:23b** Exodus 13:2,12-16

77 **2:24** Leviticus 12:8

Lk 2:25 Καὶ ἰδού, ἄνθρωπος ἦν ἐν Ἱερουσαλήμ, ᾧ ὄνομα Συμεών, καὶ ὁ ἄνθρωπος οὗτος δίκαιος καὶ εὐλαβής, προσδεχόμενος παράκλησιν τοῦ Ἰσραήλ, καὶ πνεῦμα ἦν ἅγιον ἐπ' αὐτόν.

25And behold, a man was in Jerusalem whose name was Simeon. This man was righteous and devout, waiting for the consolation of Israel, and the Holy Spirit was upon him.

Lk 2:26 Καὶ ἦν αὐτῷ κεχρηματισμένον ὑπὸ τοῦ πνεύματος τοῦ ἁγίου, μὴ ἰδεῖν θάνατον πρὶν ἂν ἴδῃ[78] τὸν χριστὸν κυρίου.

26It had been communicated to him by the Holy Spirit, that he would not see death before he had seen the Lord's Anointed.

Lk 2:27 Καὶ ἦλθεν ἐν τῷ πνεύματι εἰς τὸ ἱερόν• καὶ ἐν τῷ εἰσαγαγεῖν τοὺς γονεῖς τὸ παιδίον Ἰησοῦν, τοῦ ποιῆσαι αὐτοὺς κατὰ τὸ εἰθισμένον τοῦ νόμου περὶ αὐτοῦ,

27And he came by the Spirit into the temple, at the same time that the parents of the child Jesus brought him to do for him what the custom of the Law required.

Lk 2:28 καὶ αὐτὸς ἐδέξατο αὐτὸ εἰς τὰς ἀγκάλας,[79] καὶ εὐλόγησεν τὸν θεόν, καὶ εἶπεν,

28And he took him into his arms, and blessed God, and said:

Lk 2:29 Νῦν ἀπολύεις τὸν δοῦλόν σου, δέσποτα, κατὰ τὸ ῥῆμά σου, ἐν εἰρήνῃ•

29"Now, Master, keeping your word, you are dismissing your slave in peace.

Lk 2:30 ὅτι εἶδον οἱ ὀφθαλμοί μου τὸ σωτήριόν σου,

30For my eyes have seen your salvation,

Lk 2:31 ὃ ἡτοίμασας κατὰ πρόσωπον πάντων τῶν λαῶν•

31which you have prepared in the sight of all the peoples;

Lk 2:32 φῶς εἰς ἀποκάλυψιν ἐθνῶν, καὶ δόξαν λαοῦ σου Ἰσραήλ.

32a light to be a revelation for the Gentiles,[80] and the glory of your people Israel."

Lk 2:33 Καὶ ἦν ὁ πατὴρ αὐτοῦ καὶ ἡ μήτηρ αὐτοῦ θαυμάζοντες ἐπὶ τοῖς λαλουμένοις περὶ αὐτοῦ.

33And the child's father[81] and mother were marveling at the things being said about him.

---

78 **2:26** txt πρὶν ἢ ἴδῃ TR RP TH ‖ πρὶν ἢ ἂν ἴδῃ SBL ‖ πρὶν [ἢ] ἂν ἴδῃ NA28

79 **2:28** txt τὰς ἀγκάλας TH NA28 ‖ τὰς ἀγκάλας αὐτοῦ TR RP

80 **2:32** In a physical sense, as is intended here, a *Gentile* is any person or nation that is not Israelite; that is, not a blood descendant of Jacob. (God had changed Jacob's name to *Israel.*).

81 **2:33** txt ὁ πατηρ αὐτοῦ 𝔓[141*vid*] ℵ B D L W 131 700 1241 *f*[1] vg it[d] syr[s] cop[sa,bopt] Cyril-Jerusalem Jerome Aug TH NA28 {B} ‖ Ἰωσηφ ὁ πατηρ αὐτοῦ 157 165 176 eth[PP] ‖ ὁ Ἰωσηφ A N Ψ 579 ‖ Ἰωσηφ E G K M U Γ Δ Θ Λ Π *f*[13] 2 28 33 180 205 565 597 892 1006 1010 1071 1243 1292 1342 1424 1505 1582[C] it[a,aur,b,β,c,e,f,ff²2,l,q,r¹] vg[mss] syr[p,h,pal] cop[bopt] (eth[TH]) Hesychius[*vid*] Hilary TR RP ‖ *lac* 𝔓[45] 𝔓[75] C F P Q T Ξ. Erasmus has πατηρ "father" in all 5 of his editions. Said he, "In some Greek manuscript I read 'Joseph' instead of 'father'; in my opinion it has been changed by someone who feared that Joseph be called Jesus' father" ("*In Graecis aliquot codicibus lego pro pater, Ioseph; quod arbitror immutatum a quopiam, qui vereretur Ioseph vocare patrem Iesu...*"; '*aliquot*' added in 1519—ASD VI-5, p. 484 ll. 42–44; similarly in *Resp. ad annot. Ed. Lei*, ASD IX-4, p. 126 ll. 506–509). So we see that Erasmus figured that copyists changed the original "father"

Lk 2:34 Καὶ εὐλόγησεν αὐτοὺς Συμεών, καὶ εἶπεν πρὸς Μαριὰμ τὴν μητέρα αὐτοῦ, Ἰδού, οὗτος κεῖται εἰς πτῶσιν καὶ ἀνάστασιν πολλῶν ἐν τῷ Ἰσραήλ, καὶ εἰς σημεῖον ἀντιλεγόμενον•

34And Simeon blessed them, and said to Mary, his mother: "Behold, this one is being laid down to cause the stumbling or rising of many in Israel,[82] and to be a sign that will be continually denounced—

Lk 2:35 καὶ σοῦ δὲ αὐτῆς τὴν ψυχὴν διελεύσεται ῥομφαία• ὅπως ἂν ἀποκαλυφθῶσιν ἐκ πολλῶν καρδιῶν διαλογισμοί.

35yes a sword will be run through your own soul too–[83] so that the thoughts of many hearts will be revealed."

Lk 2:36 Καὶ ἦν Ἅννα προφῆτις, θυγάτηρ Φανουήλ, ἐκ φυλῆς Ἀσήρ - αὕτη προβεβηκυῖα ἐν ἡμέραις πολλαῖς, ζήσασα μετὰ ἀνδρὸς ἔτη ἑπτὰ ἀπὸ τῆς παρθενίας αὐτῆς,

36And there was also a prophetess, Hannah, daughter of Penuel, of the tribe of Asher. This woman had grown to be very old, having lived with a husband for seven years after her virginity,

Lk 2:37 καὶ αὕτη χήρα ἕως ἐτῶν ὀγδοήκοντα τεσσάρων - ἣ οὐκ ἀφίστατο τοῦ ἱεροῦ, νηστείαις καὶ δεήσεσιν λατρεύουσα νύκτα καὶ ἡμέραν.

37and then being a widow to[84] eighty-four years of age, one who hardly left the temple,[85] but served night and day, in fasting and praying.

Lk 2:38 Καὶ αὕτη αὐτῇ[86] τῇ ὥρᾳ ἐπιστᾶσα ἀνθωμολογεῖτο τῷ θεῷ καὶ ἐλάλει περὶ αὐτοῦ πᾶσιν τοῖς προσδεχομένοις λύτρωσιν ἐν Ἱερουσαλήμ.

38And coming up at that very time, she gave thanks to God,[87] and spoke about the child to all those expecting redemption in Jerusalem.[88]

---

to Joseph, for the very same reasons that KJV Onlyists prefer the reading "Joseph." But they forget that the KJV calls Joseph Jesus' father in several other passages. Erasmus was correct, but the KJV does not follow him here. The newly transcribed Papyrus 141 from the 3rd century reads _ πηρ αυτου "his father", with a lacuna just before it, so not showing the definite article ὁ, but it more than likely had it, and so reads the same as ℵ B D L W TH NA28.

82 **2:34** "I lay in Zion for a foundation a stone."..."A stone of stumbling, a rock of offense..." "The person who trips over that stone, will be turned to powder..." On the other hand, many new Israelites will rise or stand up, as a result of Gentiles being grafted into the Olive Tree. This is the same word as used for resurrection, and also for some brand new thing or person coming into existence. See Isaiah 56:6-8

83 **2:35** txt καὶ σοῦ δὲ TR RP TH // καὶ σοῦ [δὲ] NA28

84 **2:37a** txt ἕως ℵ* A B L N Ξ Ψ 0130 33 579 ℓ844 it[f] vg TH NA28 {/} // ὡς ℵ[2] E K M W Γ Δ Θ Λ Π f[1] f[13] 2 28 157 565 700 892 1071 1241 1424 2542 𝔐 TR RP // *omit* D ℓ2211 it // *lac* 𝔓[45] 𝔓[75] C F P Q T

85 **2:37b** txt τοῦ ἱεροῦ ℵ[2a] B D L W TH NA28 {/} // ἀπὸ τοῦ ἱεροῦ A N 𝔐 TR RP // ἐκ τοῦ ἱεροῦ ℵ[*,2b] // *lac* C P Q T

86 **2:38a** txt αὕτη αὐτῇ τῇ ὥρᾳ TR RP // αὐτῇ τῇ ὥρᾳ TH NA28

87 **2:38b** txt θεῷ ℵ B D L N W Ξ 579 it[a,d] syr[h] cop[bo] TH NA28 // κυρίῳ A E G H K M S U Y Γ Δ Θ Λ Π Ψ Ω f[1] f[13] 2 28 33 157 565 700 1424 𝔐 syr[p] cop[sa] TR RP // *lac* 𝔓[45] 𝔓[75] C F P Q T

88 **2:38c** txt ἐν Ἱερουσαλήμ TR RP // Ἱερουσαλήμ TH NA28 {A}

Lk 2:39 Καὶ ὡς ἐτέλεσαν ἅπαντα πάντα τὰ κατὰ τὸν νόμον κυρίου, ἐπέστρεψαν εἰς τὴν Γαλιλαίαν, εἰς πόλιν ἑαυτῶν Ναζαρέθ.

39And when they had completed everything required by the Law of the Lord, they returned to their own town of Nazareth.

Lk 2:40 Τὸ δὲ παιδίον ηὔξανεν, καὶ ἐκραταιοῦτο, πληρούμενον σοφίᾳ• καὶ χάρις θεοῦ ἦν ἐπ' αὐτό.

40And the child grew and became strong;[89] he was filled with wisdom, and the grace of God was upon him.

The Boy Jesus at the Temple

Lk 2:41 Καὶ ἐπορεύοντο οἱ γονεῖς αὐτοῦ κατ' ἔτος εἰς Ἰερουσαλὴμ τῇ ἑορτῇ τοῦ Πάσχα.

41Now his parents would go every year to Jerusalem for the festival of Passover.

Lk 2:42 Καὶ ὅτε ἐγένετο ἐτῶν δώδεκα, ἀναβαινόντων αὐτῶν κατὰ τὸ ἔθος τῆς ἑορτῆς,

42And when he turned twelve years old,[90] they went up,[91] according to the custom of the Festival.

Lk 2:43 καὶ τελειωσάντων τὰς ἡμέρας, ἐν τῷ ὑποστρέφειν αὐτούς, ὑπέμεινεν Ἰησοῦς ὁ παῖς ἐν Ἰερουσαλήμ• καὶ οὐκ ἔγνωσαν οἱ γονεῖς αὐτοῦ•

43And when the days were completed and they were returning home, the boy Jesus remained in Jerusalem, and his parents[92] were not aware of it.

Lk 2:44 νομίσαντες δὲ αὐτὸν εἶναι ἐν τῇ συνοδίᾳ, ἦλθον ἡμέρας ὁδόν, καὶ ἀνεζήτουν αὐτὸν ἐν τοῖς συγγενέσιν καὶ[93] τοῖς γνωστοῖς•

---

89 **2:40** txt ἐκραταιοῦτο ℵ B D L W lat syr^{s} cop Or^{lat} TH NA28 {/} ‖ ἐκραταιοῦτο πνεύματι (from 1:80) A E G H K M N S U Y Γ Δ Θ Λ Π Ψ Ω *f*^{1} *f*^{13} 2 28 33 157 565 579 700 892 1071 1241 1424 2542 ℓ844 ℓ2211 𝔐 it$^{aur,f,q,(r^1)}$ syr^{p,h} cop$^{bo^{mss}}$ (Epiph) TR RP ‖ *lac* 𝔓45 𝔓75 C F P Q T Ξ

90 **2:42a** Greek, καὶ ὅτε ἐγένετο, "and when he became" twelve... Luke does not use καὶ ὅτε ἐγένετο as a transitional phrase. Never once in his gospel or in Acts did Luke use even just the word "hote" in a transitional phrase, but rather, he always used it to indicate precisely the timing of something. Here Jesus, the Lamb of God, is just turning twelve shortly before the Passover festival. This may mean that Jesus' birthday was in our late March or early April.

91 **2:42b** txt ἀναβαινόντων αὐτῶν TH NA28 {\} ‖ ἀναβάντων αὐτῶν εἰς Ἱεροσόλυμα TR RP

92 **2:43** txt εγνωσαν οι γονεις ℵ B D L W Θ 33 157 579 1241 lat syr$^{(s),h^{mg}}$ cop$^{sa,bo^{pt}}$ SBL TH NA28 {/} ‖ εγινωσκων οι γονεις 700 ‖ εγνωσανιωσηφ και η μητηρ 892 1071 2542 ‖ εγνωσαν ο ιωσηφ και η μητηρ Δ 1424 ‖ εγνω ιωσηφ και η μητηρ A C K M N U Γ Λ Π Ψ 0130 2 28 69 565 it (syr^{p,h}) cop$^{bo^{pt}}$ 𝔐 TR RP
Interesting that most translations of the Byzantine text, or of the Textus Receptus, do not show that the verb εγνω is singular. For example, the KJV says "Joseph and his mother knew not of it." In contrast, the Geneva Bible shows that the verb is singular, by rendering it as follows: "Ioseph knew not, nor his mother." What is really potentially informative here is the word coming before the more famous variant. Which form of the verb γινωσκω came first and led to the other, and why?

93 **2:44** txt και τοις γνωστοις ℵ B C* L N W TH NA28 {\} ‖ και εν τοις γνωστοις A C^{c} D 𝔐 TR RP

44Thinking he was in their company, they went a day's journey, and then began looking for him among their relatives and acquaintances.

Lk 2:45 καὶ μὴ εὑρόντες αὐτόν,[94] ὑπέστρεψαν εἰς Ἰερουσαλὴμ ἀναζητοῦντες[95] αὐτόν.

45And when they did not find him, they went back to Jerusalem to look for him.

Lk 2:46 Καὶ ἐγένετο, μετὰ[96] ἡμέρας τρεῖς εὗρον αὐτὸν ἐν τῷ ἱερῷ, καθεζόμενον ἐν μέσῳ τῶν διδασκάλων, καὶ ἀκούοντα αὐτῶν, καὶ ἐπερωτῶντα αὐτούς.

46And it came about that after three days they found him, sitting in the temple, in the midst of the teachers, both listening to them and questioning them.

Lk 2:47 Ἐξίσταντο δὲ πάντες οἱ ἀκούοντες αὐτοῦ ἐπὶ τῇ συνέσει καὶ ταῖς ἀποκρίσεσιν αὐτοῦ.

47And all those who heard him were amazed at the understanding of his responses.[97]

Lk 2:48 Καὶ ἰδόντες αὐτὸν ἐξεπλάγησαν• καὶ εἶπεν πρὸς αὐτὸν ἡ μήτηρ αὐτοῦ, Τέκνον, τί ἐποίησας ἡμῖν οὕτως; Ἰδού, ὁ πατήρ σου κἀγὼ ὀδυνώμενοι ἐζητοῦμέν σε.

48And when *his parents* saw him, they were stunned. His mother said to him, "Son, why have you treated us this way? Look at how distressed your father and I are, searching for you."

Lk 2:49 Καὶ εἶπεν πρὸς αὐτούς, Τί ὅτι ἐζητεῖτέ με; Οὐκ ᾔδειτε ὅτι ἐν τοῖς τοῦ πατρός μου δεῖ εἶναί με;

49And he said to them, "Why would you be searching for me? Shouldn't you have known that I would have to be among my Father's things?"[98]

Lk 2:50 Καὶ αὐτοὶ οὐ συνῆκαν τὸ ῥῆμα ὃ ἐλάλησεν αὐτοῖς.

50But they did not understand what he said to them.

Lk 2:51 Καὶ κατέβη μετ' αὐτῶν, καὶ ἦλθεν εἰς Ναζαρέθ καὶ ἦν ὑποτασσόμενος αὐτοῖς. Καὶ ἡ μήτηρ αὐτοῦ διετήρει πάντα τὰ ῥήματα[99] ἐν τῇ καρδίᾳ αὐτῆς.

51Then he went down with them, and arrived in Nazareth, and continued to subordinate himself to them. But his mother was recording all these words in her heart.[100]

---

94 **2:45a** txt ευροντες TH NA28 {\} // ευροντες αυτον TR RP

95 **2:45b** txt αναζητουντες TH NA28 {\} ζητουντες TR RP

96 **2:46** txt μετα TH NA28 {\} // μεθ' TR RP

97 **2:47** Literally, "were amazed at his understanding and his responses." This is probably an example of hendiadys, which according to BDF §442(16), when used with the conjunction καί, accomplishes the coordination of two ideas, one of which is dependent on the other, and serves in the NT to avoid a series of dependent genitives. Blass gives this verse, Lk 2:47, as an example of hendiadys.

98 **2:49** Jesus is not remarking against the fact that his parents came to find him, but that it took them a 3-day search to find him. But Jesus is saying that no searching around was necessary because they should have figured he would be in the temple, and look there first. For the temple is "his Father's things."

99 **2:51a** txt τα ρηματα TH NA28 {\} // τα ρηματα ταυτα TR RP SBL

100 **2:51b** Compare Genesis 37:11.

Lk 2:52 ¶ Καὶ Ἰησοῦς προέκοπτεν σοφίᾳ[101] καὶ ἡλικίᾳ, καὶ χάριτι παρὰ θεῷ καὶ ἀνθρώποις.

52And Jesus kept growing in wisdom and stature, and in favor with God and with people.

Chapter 3

John the Baptizer Prepares the Way

Lk 3:1 Ἐν ἔτει δὲ πεντεκαιδεκάτῳ τῆς ἡγεμονίας Τιβερίου Καίσαρος, ἡγεμονεύοντος Ποντίου Πιλάτου τῆς Ἰουδαίας, καὶ τετρααρχοῦντος[102] τῆς Γαλιλαίας Ἡρῴδου, Φιλίππου δὲ τοῦ ἀδελφοῦ αὐτοῦ τετρααρχοῦντος τῆς Ἰτουραίας καὶ Τραχωνίτιδος χώρας, καὶ Λυσανίου τῆς Ἀβιληνῆς τετρααρχοῦντος,

1In the fifteenth year of the reign of Tiberius Caesar, with Pontius Pilate governor of Judea, and Herod as tetrarch[103] of Galilee, his brother Philip tetrarch of Iturea and Trachonitis, and Lysanias as tetrarch of Abilene,

Lk 3:2 ἐπὶ ἀρχιερέως Ἅννα καὶ Καϊάφα, ἐγένετο ῥῆμα θεοῦ ἐπὶ Ἰωάννην τὸν Ζαχαρίου υἱὸν ἐν τῇ ἐρήμῳ.

2during the high priesthood of Hananiah[104] and Kayafas, the word of God came upon John the son of Zechariah in the desert.

Lk 3:3 Καὶ ἦλθεν εἰς πᾶσαν τὴν περίχωρον τοῦ Ἰορδάνου, κηρύσσων βάπτισμα μετανοίας εἰς ἄφεσιν ἁμαρτιῶν•

3And he appeared, in all the areas around the Jordan, proclaiming a baptism of repentance for forgiveness of sins,

Lk 3:4 ὡς γέγραπται ἐν βίβλῳ λόγων Ἠσαΐου τοῦ προφήτου,[105] Φωνὴ βοῶντος ἐν τῇ ἐρήμῳ, Ἑτοιμάσατε τὴν ὁδὸν κυρίου• εὐθείας ποιεῖτε τὰς τρίβους αὐτοῦ.

4as it is written in the scroll of the words of Isaiah the prophet: "The voice of one calling in the desert, 'Prepare the way for the Lord, make the paths straight for him.

---

101 **2:52** txt σοφίᾳ TR RP SBL TH // [ἐν τῇ] σοφίᾳ NA28 {\}

102 **3:1a** txt τετρααρχουντος ℵ* A C SBL NA28 {\} // τετραρχουντος ℵc B E L N W 𝔐 TR RP TH // *omit* D // *lac* 𝔓45 𝔓75 F P Q T Ξ. This variant occurs 3 times in this verse Luke 3:1. Codex A reads with NA28 in the first instance, and with 𝔐 in the others. Though Codex D omits the first one, it reads with 𝔐 in the others. The purpose for omitting one of the two adjacent vowels, in this case an alpha, is sometimes called "euphony." That is, it sounds better. But I don't think it needs any purpose; it is just a phonological phenomenon of the flow of the speech organs taking the path of least resistance, which happens in most all languages. The BDF grammar in §124 states: "Koine often neglects euphony for the sake of etymological clarity (§§17 and 19). So, in an effort to achieve clear isolation of the elements, hiatus is not avoided in composition (contrary to Attic), especially in numerals." The word τετρα-άρχης - αρχεῖν is given as the second example.

103 **3:1b** From the Greek *tetra,* four, and *arche,* to rule. As a *monarch* is a one and only ruler of a realm, in the same way a *tetrarch* is a ruler of one fourth of a realm. (Which implies that there must exist three other one-fourth divisions of the realm.)

104 **3:2** The Greek says *Hannas,* which is short for the Greek, *Hananos,* which in turn is the Greek form of the Hebrew name *Hananiah.*

105 **3:4** txt προφητου TH NA28 {\} // προφητου λεγοντος TR RP

Lk 3:5 Πᾶσα φάραγξ πληρωθήσεται, καὶ πᾶν ὄρος καὶ βουνὸς ταπεινωθήσεται• καὶ ἔσται τὰ σκολιὰ εἰς εὐθεῖαν, καὶ αἱ τραχεῖαι εἰς ὁδοὺς λείας•

5Every valley shall be filled up, every mountain and hill laid low. The crooked places shall be made straight, the rough ways smooth.

Lk 3:6 καὶ ὄψεται πᾶσα σὰρξ τὸ σωτήριον τοῦ θεοῦ.

6And all flesh shall see the salvation of God.'[106]"

Lk 3:7 Ἔλεγεν οὖν τοῖς ἐκπορευομένοις ὄχλοις βαπτισθῆναι ὑπ' αὐτοῦ, Γεννήματα ἐχιδνῶν, τίς ὑπέδειξεν ὑμῖν φυγεῖν ἀπὸ τῆς μελλούσης ὀργῆς;

7So John would say to the crowds coming out to be baptized by him, "You spawn of snakes! Who warned you to flee from the coming wrath?

Lk 3:8 Ποιήσατε οὖν καρποὺς ἀξίους τῆς μετανοίας• καὶ μὴ ἄρξησθε λέγειν ἐν ἑαυτοῖς, Πατέρα ἔχομεν τὸν Ἀβραάμ• λέγω γὰρ ὑμῖν ὅτι δύναται ὁ θεὸς ἐκ τῶν λίθων τούτων ἐγεῖραι τέκνα τῷ Ἀβραάμ.

8Then produce fruit characteristic of repentance. And do not begin to say to yourselves, 'We have Abraham as our father.' For I tell you that God can raise up children for Abraham from these stones.

Lk 3:9 Ἤδη δὲ καὶ ἡ ἀξίνη πρὸς τὴν ῥίζαν τῶν δένδρων κεῖται• πᾶν οὖν δένδρον μὴ ποιοῦν καρπὸν καλὸν ἐκκόπτεται καὶ εἰς πῦρ βάλλεται.

9Even now the axe is poised at the root of the trees, and every tree that does not produce good fruit will be cut down and thrown into the fire."

Lk 3:10 Καὶ ἐπηρώτων αὐτὸν οἱ ὄχλοι λέγοντες, Τί οὖν ποιήσωμεν;[107]

10And the crowds would ask him, "What should we do then?"

Lk 3:11 Ἀποκριθεὶς δὲ ἔλεγεν[108] αὐτοῖς, Ὁ ἔχων δύο χιτῶνας μεταδότω τῷ μὴ ἔχοντι• καὶ ὁ ἔχων βρώματα ὁμοίως ποιείτω.

11And in answer he would say to them, "The person who has two tunics should give away to the one who has none, and the person who has foodstuffs should do the same."

Lk 3:12 Ἦλθον δὲ καὶ τελῶναι βαπτισθῆναι, καὶ εἶπαν[109] πρὸς αὐτόν, Διδάσκαλε, τί ποιήσωμεν;[110]

12Revenue agents also came to be baptized, and they asked him, "Teacher, what should we do?"

---

106 **3:6** Isaiah 40:3-5a

107 **3:10** txt ποιησωμεν 𝔓4 ℵ A B C D L N W TH NA28 {\} ‖ ποιησομεν 𝔐 TR RP ‖ *lac* 𝔓45 𝔓75 E P T Ξ

108 **3:11** txt ελεγεν 𝔓4 ℵ B C* L N TH NA28 {\} ‖ ειπεν W ‖ λεγει A C2 D 𝔐 TR RP ‖ *lac* 𝔓45 𝔓75 E P Q T Ξ. I suspect that none of these 3 are authorial text. None of them are necessary for the sense, and in fact, in the book of Acts, written by Luke the same author as this gospel, Luke often omits such words of saying. The Byzantine reading λεγει is not Luke's style, but is Mark's and John's. The NA28 reading ελεγεν would be more Luke's style, and continues the imperfect of the verb in the previous verse, επηρωτων.

109 **3:12a** txt ειπαν C D W NA28 {\} ‖ ειπον 𝔓4 ℵ A B L N Ξ 𝔐 TR RP TH ‖ *lac* 𝔓45 𝔓75 E P Q T

110 **3:12b** txt ποιησωμεν 𝔓4 ℵ A B C D F H K L M N S W Y Γ Δ Θ Λ Ξ Π Ψ Ω f13 2* 28 33 565 579 700 1071 1582* 1424 TH NA28 {\} ‖ ποιησομεν G U 1 2c 118 157 1582c TR RP ‖ *lac* 𝔓45 𝔓75 E P Q T. Don't quote me on this, but it appears to me that the Syriac Peshitta and the Sahidic and Bohairic Coptic versions support ποιησομεν, and the Latin Vulgate supports ποιησωμεν. This is the weakest Majority Text reading I have seen so far in the gospel of Luke.

Lk 3:13 Ὁ δὲ εἶπεν πρὸς αὐτούς, Μηδὲν πλέον παρὰ τὸ διατεταγμένον ὑμῖν πράσσετε.

13He said to them, "Collect nothing in excess, beyond what is prescribed for you."

Lk 3:14 Ἐπηρώτων δὲ αὐτὸν καὶ στρατευόμενοι, λέγοντες, Τί ποιήσωμεν καὶ ἡμεῖς; Καὶ εἶπεν αὐτοῖς,[111] Μηδένα διασείσητε, μηδὲ συκοφαντήσητε• καὶ ἀρκεῖσθε τοῖς ὀψωνίοις ὑμῶν.

14Some soldiers were also questioning him, saying, "And us, what should we do?" And he told them, "You should no longer shake down anyone, nor frame anyone, always staying content with your pay."

Lk 3:15 Προσδοκῶντος δὲ τοῦ λαοῦ, καὶ διαλογιζομένων πάντων ἐν ταῖς καρδίαις αὐτῶν περὶ τοῦ Ἰωάννου, μήποτε αὐτὸς εἴη ὁ χριστός,

15And all the people were waiting expectantly, wondering in their hearts if John might possibly be the Anointed One.

Lk 3:16 ἀπεκρίνατο λέγων πᾶσιν ὁ Ἰωάννης, Ἐγὼ μὲν ὕδατι βαπτίζω ὑμᾶς• ἔρχεται δὲ ὁ ἰσχυρότερός μου, οὗ οὐκ εἰμὶ ἱκανὸς λῦσαι τὸν ἱμάντα τῶν ὑποδημάτων αὐτοῦ• αὐτὸς ὑμᾶς βαπτίσει ἐν πνεύματι ἁγίῳ καὶ πυρί•

16John responded speaking to everyone, "I baptize you in water, but one who is more powerful than I is coming, the thongs of whose sandals I am not worthy to untie. He will baptize you in the Holy Spirit and in fire:

Lk 3:17 οὗ τὸ πτύον ἐν τῇ χειρὶ αὐτοῦ, διακαθᾶραι[112] τὴν ἅλωνα αὐτοῦ, καὶ συναγαγεῖν[113] τὸν σῖτον εἰς τὴν ἀποθήκην αὐτοῦ, τὸ δὲ ἄχυρον κατακαύσει πυρὶ ἀσβέστῳ.

17his winnowing fork is in his hand to clear out his threshing floor, gathering the wheat into the barn. But the chaff he will burn up in unquenchable fire."

Lk 3:18 Πολλὰ μὲν οὖν καὶ ἕτερα παρακαλῶν εὐηγγελίζετο τὸν λαόν•

18And with many and varied other exhortations John was preaching the good news to the people.

Lk 3:19 ὁ δὲ Ἡρῴδης ὁ τετραάρχης, ἐλεγχόμενος ὑπ' αὐτοῦ περὶ Ἡρῳδιάδος τῆς γυναικὸς τοῦ ἀδελφοῦ αὐτοῦ, καὶ περὶ πάντων ὧν ἐποίησεν πονηρῶν ὁ Ἡρῴδης,

19But when Herod the Tetrarch was rebuked by him, regarding Herodias his brother's wife, and all the other evil things he had done,

Lk 3:20 προσέθηκεν καὶ τοῦτο ἐπὶ πᾶσιν,[114] κατέκλεισεν τὸν Ἰωάννην ἐν φυλακῇ.

20Herod piled this on top of them all: he shut John up in prison.

---

111 **3:14** txt αυτοις 𝔓^{4} B C* D L Ξ TH NA28 {\} ‖ προς αυτους ℵ A C^{3} N W 𝔐 syr^{h} TR RP ‖ *lac* 𝔓^{75} E P Q T

112 **3:17a** txt διακαθαραι 𝔓^{4} ℵ* B it$^{(a),e}$ cop^{samss,bopt} Ir-lat TH NA28 {\} ‖ και διακαθαριει ℵ^{1} A C D E L N W Ξ 𝔐 lat cop^{sams,bopt} TR RP ‖ *lac* 𝔓^{45} 𝔓^{75} P Q T. (Cf. Matt 3:12)

113 **3:17b** txt συναγαγειν 𝔓^{4} ℵ* it^{e} cop^{samss,bopt} B TH NA28 {\} ‖ συναξαι ℵ^{1} ‖ συναξει ℵ^{2} A C (D) E L N W Ξ 𝔐 lat cop^{sams,bopt} Ir-lat TR RP ‖ *lac* 𝔓^{45} 𝔓^{75} P Q T (Cf. Matt 3:12)

114 **3:20** txt πασιν 𝔓^{75} ℵ* B D Ξ it^{b,d,e} cop TD TG SBL TH ‖ πασιν [και] NA28 {\} ‖ πασιν και ℵ^{2} A C E L N W 070 𝔐 lat syr TR RP ‖ *lac* 𝔓^{4} 𝔓^{45} P Q T. One theory for the cause of addition of και is that it was to avoid asyndeton.

The Baptism of Jesus

Lk 3:21 Ἐγένετο δὲ ἐν τῷ βαπτισθῆναι ἅπαντα τὸν λαόν, καὶ Ἰησοῦ βαπτισθέντος καὶ προσευχομένου, ἀνεῳχθῆναι τὸν οὐρανόν,

21When all the people were being baptized, Jesus was baptized too. And as he was praying, the heavens were torn open,

Lk 3:22 καὶ καταβῆναι τὸ πνεῦμα τὸ ἅγιον σωματικῷ εἴδει ὡς περιστερὰν ἐπ' αὐτόν, καὶ φωνὴν ἐξ οὐρανοῦ γενέσθαι,[115] Σὺ εἶ ὁ υἱός μου ὁ ἀγαπητός, ἐν σοὶ εὐδόκησα.

22and the Holy Spirit descended on him in the bodily form of a dove. And a voice from said, "You are my Son, whom I love; with you I am well pleased."

The Genealogy of Jesus

Lk 3:23 Καὶ αὐτὸς ἦν Ἰησοῦς ἀρχόμενος ὡσεὶ ἐτῶν τριάκοντα, ὢν υἱός, ὡς ἐνομίζετο, Ἰωσήφ, τοῦ Ἡλί,

23And this Jesus, being about thirty years old,[116] was the son, so it was thought, of Joseph,[117] the son[118] of Eili,

---

115 **3:22** txt γενεσθαι 𝔓⁴ ℵ B D L W TH NA28 {\} ‖ γενεσθαι λεγουσαν A E N 𝔐 TR RP ‖ *lac* 𝔓⁴⁵ 𝔓⁷⁵ C P Q T Ξ

116 **3:23a** καὶ αὐτὸς ἦν Ἰησοῦς ἀρχόμενος ὡσει ἐτῶν τριάκοντα. Most translations render this something like, "And Jesus himself was about thirty years old when he began his ministry." The trouble with that is that the words "his ministry" are not in the Greek. The usual reasoning for this rendering is that the word "began," αρχω is reminiscent of Luke's use of the same word, and in the same middle voice, in Acts 1:1, where he says he wrote about all that Jesus "began both to do and to teach." I find this an unacceptable leap. The KJV says, "And Jesus himself began to be about thirty years of age..." The trouble with that is, how can you *begin* to be *about* thirty? The thirtieth year has a beginning, but "about thirty" does not. So what was it that was beginning? The lexical authorities on koine Greek tell us that the word αρχω in the middle voice is often *pleonastic* or superfluous, in accordance with late Jewish usage; so Josephus, Dalman, Worte; and JWHunkin on the Pleonastic αρχομαι in the New Testament. Acts 1:1 is specifically given as an example of this; thus Acts 1:1 would be "everything he did and taught." Here in Luke 3:23, both ειμι and αρχω are in the continuous aspect. The word αυτος could be its demonstrative use. Thus I translated this passage, "And *this* Jesus, being about thirty years old, was the son, so it was thought, of Joseph..."

117 **3:23b** See the endnote at the end of this document, comparing this genealogy to Matthew's genealogy.

118 **3:23c** Probably, son-in-law of Eili. (In Hebrew this name Eili starts with the consonant Ayin, a gutteral stop. The NA28/UBS Greek text and the 1550 Textus Receptus have it spelled Eili, but the Hodges & Farstad "Majority Text" has a Greek rough breathing mark in front, so spelled "Heli.") In that culture, the word "son" was used more broadly. Ben Crick of England has a good commentary on this, as follows: "The genealogies in Matthew 1 and Luke 3 are both ostensibly of Joseph, not of Mary. But whereas Matt. 1:16 gives Jacob as the father of Joseph, Luke 3:23 states that Joseph was the son of Heli. How do we explain this? We know that Mary had a sister (John 19:25), but nowhere is a brother mentioned. So if Heli had no son, his inheritance would pass to his nearest male relative, in this case his son-in-law (Numbers 27:1-11), provided he was of the same tribe (Numbers 36:1-9). Therefore we should read in Luke 3:23 that Joseph was son-in-law of Heli. So Heli was Mary's father, and Mary was

Lk 3:24 τοῦ Μαθθάτ, τοῦ Λευΐ, τοῦ Μελχί, τοῦ Ἰανναί, τοῦ Ἰωσήφ,

24 the son of Matthat, the son of Levi, the son of Melki, the son of Yannai,[119] the son of Joseph,

Lk 3:25 τοῦ Ματταθίου, τοῦ Ἀμώς, τοῦ Ναούμ, τοῦ Ἑσλί, τοῦ Ναγγαί,

25 the son of Mattathias, the son of Amos, the son of Nahum, the son of Esli, the son of Naggai,

Lk 3:26 τοῦ Μαάθ, τοῦ Ματταθίου, τοῦ Σεμεΐν, τοῦ Ἰωσήχ, τοῦ Ἰωδά,

26 the son of Maath, the son of Mattathias, the son of Semein, the son of Josech,[120] the son of Joda,

Lk 3:27 τοῦ Ἰωανάν, τοῦ Ῥησά, τοῦ Ζοροβάβελ, τοῦ Σαλαθιήλ, τοῦ Νηρί,

27 the son of Yoanan,[121] the son of Rhesa, the son of Zerubbabel, the son of Shealtiel, the son of Neri,

Lk 3:28 τοῦ Μελχί, τοῦ Ἀδδί, τοῦ Κωσάμ, τοῦ Ἐλμαδάμ, τοῦ Ἤρ,

28 the son of Melki, the son of Addi, the son of Cosam, the son of Elmadam,[122] the son of Er,

Lk 3:29 τοῦ Ἰησοῦ, τοῦ Ἐλιέζερ, τοῦ Ἰωρίμ, τοῦ Μαθθάτ, τοῦ Λευΐ,

29 the son of Joshua,[123] the son of Eliezer, the son of Jorim, the son of Matthat, the son of Levi,

Lk 3:30 τοῦ Συμεών, τοῦ Ἰούδα, τοῦ Ἰωσήφ, τοῦ Ἰωνάμ, τοῦ Ἐλιακίμ,

30 the son of Simeon, the son of Judah, the son of Joseph, the son of Jonam,[124] the son of Eliakim,

Lk 3:31 τοῦ Μελεᾶ, τοῦ Μεννά, τοῦ Ματταθά, τοῦ Ναθάμ, τοῦ Δαυίδ,

31 the son of Melea, the son of Menna,[125] the son of Mattatha, the son of Nathan, the son of David,

Lk 3:32 τοῦ Ἰεσσαί, τοῦ Ὠβήδ, τοῦ Βοόζ, τοῦ Σαλμών, τοῦ Ναασσών,

32 the son of Jesse, the son of Obed, the son of Boaz, the son of Salmon,[126] the son of Nahshon,

---

descended from David. Gabriel's words to Mary, "the Lord God shall give unto Him the throne of His father David," (Luke 1:32) confirm this.

119 **3:24** txt ιανναι 𝔓^{4} ℵ B L syr^{p} cop^{sa} TH NA28 {\} || *Iannae* vg || ιαννα A E^{c} TR RP || ιωαννα E* N || *alt genealogy* D || *omit entire genealogy* W || *lac* 𝔓^{45} 𝔓^{75} C P Q T Ξ

120 **3:26** txt ιωσηχ 𝔓^{4} ℵ B L TH NA28 {\} || ιωσηφ A E N 𝔐 TR RP || *alt genealogy* D || *omit entire genealogy* W || *lac* 𝔓^{45} 𝔓^{75} C P Q T Ξ

121 **3:27** txt ιωαναν 𝔓^{4} ℵ^{1} A B 𝔐 cop^{sa,bo} RP TH NA28 {\} || ιωανναν L || ιωναν ℵ* || ιωαννα syr^{p} TR || *Iohanna* vg || *omit* του ιωαναν του ρησα N || *alt genealogy* D || *omit entire genealogy* W || *lac* 𝔓^{45} 𝔓^{75} C P Q T Ξ

122 **3:28** txt ελμαδαμ ℵ B L N^{vid} (070) lat TH NA28 {\} || ελμασαμ 𝔓^{4} || ελμωδαμ A 0102 𝔐 it^{aur,f,q} TR RP || *alt genealogy* D || *omit entire genealogy:* W || *lac* 𝔓^{45} 𝔓^{75} C P Q T Ξ

123 **3:29** txt ιησου 𝔓^{4} ℵ B L TH NA28 {\} || ιωση A E N TR RP || *alt genealogy* D || *omit entire genealogy* W || *lac* 𝔓^{45} 𝔓^{75} C P Q T Ξ

124 **3:30** txt ιωναμ ℵ B TH NA28 {\} || ιωαναν A E L 𝔐 TR RP || ιωανα N || *alt genealogy* D || *omit entire genealogy* W || *lac* 𝔓^{4} 𝔓^{45} 𝔓^{75} C P Q T Ξ

125 **3:31** txt μεννα ℵ B L vg cop^{sa,bo} TH NA28 {\} || μαιναν E N RP || μεναμ TR || *omit* του μεννα A || *alt genealogy* D || *omit entire genealogy* W || *lac* 𝔓^{4} 𝔓^{45} 𝔓^{75} C P Q T Ξ

Lk 3:33 τοῦ Ἀμιναδάβ, τοῦ Ἀράμ, τοῦ Ἑσρώμ, τοῦ Φαρές, τοῦ Ἰούδα,
33 the son of Amminadab, the son of Aram,[127] the son of Hezron, the son of Perez, the son of Judah,
Lk 3:34 τοῦ Ἰακώβ, τοῦ Ἰσαάκ, τοῦ Ἀβραάμ, τοῦ Θάρρα, τοῦ Ναχώρ,
34 the son of Jacob, the son of Isaac, the son of Abraham, the son of Terah, the son of Nahor,
Lk 3:35 τοῦ Σερούχ, τοῦ Ῥαγαῦ, τοῦ Φαλέκ,[128] τοῦ Ἑβέρ, τοῦ Σαλά,
35 the son of Serug, the son of Reu, the son of Peleg, the son of Eber, the son of Shelah,
Lk 3:36 τοῦ Καϊνάμ, τοῦ Ἀρφαξάδ, τοῦ Σήμ, τοῦ Νῶε, τοῦ Λάμεχ,
36 the son of Cainan,[129] the son of Arphaxad, the son of Shem, the son of Noah, the son of Lamech,

---

126 **3:32** txt ωβηδ του βοοζ του σαλμων N^{c} 𝔐 latt syr^{p,h} TR RP // ωβηδ του σαλμων N* // ωβηδ του βοος του σαλμων D^{2} ℓ2211 // ιωβηδ του βοος του σαλμων ℵ^{2} A // ιωβηδ του βοος του σαλμων L // ιωβηλ του βοοζ του σαλμων cop^{bo} // ωβηλ του βοος του σαλμων D* // ιωβηδ του βοος του σαλα cop^{sa} TH NA28 {\} // ιωβητ του βοος του σαλα 𝔓^{4vid} // ιωβηλ του βαλλς του σαλα ℵ* // ιωβηλ του βοος του σαλα B syr^{s} // *lac* 𝔓^{45} 𝔓^{75} C P Q T Ξ 070 (0102 except σαλμων)

127 **3:33** txt τοῦ Ἀμιναδὰβ τοῦ Ἀράμ (Matt 1:3,4) A (D Ἀμειναδαβ) E G H N^{C} U 565 1079 1230 1253 *Byz*^{pt} ℓ184 ℓ292 ℓ2211 ℓ^{AD} it^{a,aur,c,d,f,ff2,l,q,r1} vg syr^{p} goth geo^{2} TR RP // τοῦ Ἀμιναδὰμ τοῦ Ἀράμ Π Ω 2 33 118 1424 // τοῦ Ἀδὰμ τοῦ Ἀδμὶν τοῦ Ἀρνει 𝔓^{4vid} ℵ* 1241 cop^{sa} and other versions // τοῦ Ἀμιναδὰβ τοῦ Ἀδμὶν τοῦ Ἀρὰμ 0102 // τοῦ Ἀμιναδὰμ τοῦ Ἀδμὶν τοῦ Ἀρὰμ 1216 // τοῦ Ἀδὰμ τοῦ Ἀρνει (syr^{S} added "between the lines: Burkitt) WH^{mg} // τοῦ Ἀμιναδὰβ τοῦ Ἀδμὶν τοῦ Ἀρνὶ (ℵ^{1} TH Ἀρνει) (L TH Ἀδμεὶν) X (*f*^{13} Ἀρηΐ for Ἀρνὶ) 69 124 346 788 cop^{bo} NA28 {C} // Ἀμιναδὰμ τοῦ Ἀμὴν τοῦ Ἀρνὶ 157 // Ἀμιναδὰβ τοῦ Ἀλμεὶν τοῦ Ἀρνὶ Γ // τοῦ Ἀμιναδὰβ τοῦ Ἀράμ τοῦ Ἀλμεὶ τοῦ Ἀρνεὶ 1582 // τοῦ Ἀμιναδὰμ τοῦ Ἀράμ τοῦ Ἀλμεὶ τοῦ Ἀρνεὶ 1 // τοῦ Ἀδμειν τοῦ Ἀρνει B WH // τοῦ Ἀμιναδὰβ τοῦ Ἀράμ τοῦ Ἰωραμ K M^{C} Y Δ Λ Ψ (180 1010 Ἰωαρὰμ) 700 (892) 2542 2882 it^{b,e} (syr^{h}) // τοῦ Ἀμιναδὰμ τοῦ Ἀράμ τοῦ Ἰωραμ M* S // τοῦ Ἀμιναδὰβ τοῦ Ἀράμ τοῦ Ἀρνὶ N // τοῦ Ἀμιναδὰβ τοῦ Ἀράμ τοῦ Ἀδμὶ τοῦ Ἀρνὶ Θ *pc* arm geo // Ἀμιναδὰμ τοῦ Ἰαρὰμ τοῦ Ἀρὰμ 28* // Ἀμιναδὰμ τοῦ Ἀρὰμ τοῦ Ἰωράμ 1242 1344 // Ἀμιναδὰμ τοῦ Ἰωρὰμ τοῦ Ἀρὰμ 28^{C} 205 (1292 Ἰωαρὰμ) // τοῦ Ἀμιναδὰμ τοῦ Ἀρὰμ τοῦ Ἀλμεὶ του Ἀρνί τοῦ Ἰωράμ 1365 // του Ἀμιναδὰβ τοῦ Ἀδμὶν τοῦ Ἀράμ τοῦ Ἰωράμ 1646 2174 // τοῦ Ἀρὰμ τοῦ Ἀμιναδὰβ του Ἀρμὶν του Ἀρνίν syr$^{pal ms,(ms)}$ // τοῦ Ἀμιναδὰμ τοῦ Ἰωρὰμ τοῦ Ἀράμ 1009 // τοῦ Νηρὶ τοῦ Ἀμιναδὰμ τοῦ Μελχὶ τοῦ Ἀρὰμ τοῦ Ἀδδί 1546 // *lac* 𝔓^{45} 𝔓^{75} C F P Q T Ξ 070 syr^{C}. There is, in the words of the Editorial Committee of the UBS' Greek New Testament, a "bewildering array of readings" for the first half of this verse. They go on: "the Committee adopted what seems to be the least unsatisfactory form of text, a reading that was current in the Alexandrian church at an early period. Although the reading τοῦ Ἀμιναδὰβ τοῦ Ἀράμ is supported by an impressive range of witnesses (A D 33 565 1079 many versions), with a reading that involves three names (such as that adopted by the Committee) Luke's entire genealogy of Jesus falls into an artistically planned pattern, even more elaborate than Matthew's (cf. Mt 1:17); thus, from Adam to Abraham, 3 x 7 generations; from Isaac to David, 2 x 7 generations; from Nathan to Salathiel (pre-exilic), 3 x 7 generations; from Zerubbabel (post-exilic) to Jesus, 3 x 7 generations, making a total of 11 x 7, or 77 generations from Adam to Jesus."

128 **3:35** txt φαλεκ ℵ B D L N *pm* cop^{sa} TR NA28 {\} // φαλεχ cop^{bopt} // φαλεγ A E 0102 ℓ2211 *pm* RP // *omit genealogy* W // *lac* 𝔓^{4} 𝔓^{75} C P Q T Ξ 070

129 **3:36** txt τοῦ Καϊναμ 𝔓^{4vid} ℵ B L *f*^{1} 33 pc SBL TH NA28 {\} // τοῦ Καϊναν A K M N U Γ Δ Θ Λ Π Ψ 0102 *f*^{13} 2 (28) 69 118 124 157 700 (1071) 1424 𝔐 syr^{p,h} cop$^{sa mss,bopt}$ TR RP // τοῦ Καϊνα 565 //

Lk 3:37 τοῦ Μαθουσάλα, τοῦ Ἐνώχ, τοῦ Ἰάρετ, τοῦ Μαλελεήλ, τοῦ Καϊνάμ,
37the son of Methuselah, the son of Enoch, the son of Jared, the son of
Mahalaleel, the son of Cainan,
Lk 3:38 τοῦ Ἐνώς, τοῦ Σήθ, τοῦ Ἀδάμ, τοῦ θεοῦ.
38the son of Enos, the son of Seth, the son of Adam, the son of God.

Chapter 4

The Temptation of Jesus

Lk 4:1 Ἰησοῦς δὲ πλήρης πνεύματος ἁγίου ὑπέστρεψεν ἀπὸ τοῦ Ἰορδάνου, καὶ
ἤγετο ἐν τῷ πνεύματι ἐν τῇ ἐρήμῳ,
1Jesus, full of the Holy Spirit, returned from the Jordan, and was led by the
Spirit into the desert,
Lk 4:2 ἡμέρας τεσσεράκοντα πειραζόμενος ὑπὸ τοῦ διαβόλου. Καὶ οὐκ ἔφαγεν
οὐδὲν ἐν ταῖς ἡμέραις ἐκείναις• καὶ συντελεσθεισῶν αὐτῶν, ἐπείνασεν.
2being tempted forty days by the devil. And he ate nothing during those days,
and at the end of them he was hungry.[130]
Lk 4:3 Εἶπεν δὲ αὐτῷ ὁ διάβολος, Εἰ υἱὸς εἶ τοῦ θεοῦ, εἰπὲ τῷ λίθῳ τούτῳ ἵνα
γένηται ἄρτος.
3And the devil said to him, "If you are the Son of God, speak to this stone, that
it become a loaf of bread."
Lk 4:4 Καὶ ἀπεκρίθη πρὸς αὐτὸν ὁ Ἰησοῦς, Γέγραπται ὅτι Οὐκ ἐπ' ἄρτῳ μόνῳ
ζήσεται ὁ ἄνθρωπος.
4And Jesus responded to him, "It is written, 'A human being shall not live on
bread alone.'[131]"
Lk 4:5 Καὶ ἀναγαγὼν αὐτὸν ἔδειξεν αὐτῷ πάσας τὰς βασιλείας τῆς οἰκουμένης ἐν
στιγμῇ χρόνου.
5Then leading him upward,[132] the devil showed him all the kingdoms of the
inhabited earth, in a moment of time.

Elam syr^{s} ‖ *omit* 𝔓^{75vid} D it^{d} ‖ *lac* 𝔓^{45} C F P Q T Ξ syr^{c}. The man Kainan does not appear in this spot in the Hebrew text, but does in the Septuagint. The genealogy in the Sepuagint differs very greatly from that in the Hebrew. Which also changes the number of years in human history.

[130] **4:2** txt ἐπείνασεν NA28 {\} ‖ ὕστερον ἐπείνασεν TR RP

[131] **4:4** txt ἄνθρωπος א B L W syr^{s} cop^{sa,bo} Or^{Gr½,lat} NA28 {B} ‖ ἄνθρωπος, ἀλλ' ἐπὶ παντὶ ῥήματι θεοῦ A E 0233 𝔐 syr^{p,h} arm geo Or^{½} Titus-Bostra Asterius-Amasea TR RP ‖ ἄνθρωπος, ἀλλ' ἐν παντὶ ῥήματι θεοῦ D 0102 latt ‖ ἄνθρωπος, ἀλλ' ἐν παντὶ ῥήματι ἐκπορευομένῳ διὰ στόματος θεοῦ cop^{bopt} eth Diatess. Deuteronomy 8:3 The Editorial Committee for the United Bible Societies' Greek text says, "The shortest reading, which has good and early support, must be original; the longer forms of text have been assimilated by copyists to the Matthaean parallel (Mt 4:4) or to the Septuagint of Dt 8:3, either verbatim or according to the general sense. If any of the longer forms of text had been original, its omission from א B L W 1241 syr^{s} cop^{sa,bo} would be unaccountable."

[132] **4:5** txt αὐτὸν NA28 {\} ‖ αὐτὸν ὁ διάβολος εἰς ὄρος ὑψηλὸν TR RP

Lk 4:6 Καὶ εἶπεν αὐτῷ ὁ διάβολος, Σοὶ δώσω τὴν ἐξουσίαν ταύτην ἅπασαν καὶ τὴν δόξαν αὐτῶν• ὅτι ἐμοὶ παραδέδοται, καὶ ᾧ ἐὰν θέλω δίδωμι αὐτήν.

6 And the devil said to him, "All this authority and their glory I will give to you, for it has been handed over to me, and I give it to whomever I wish.

Lk 4:7 Σὺ οὖν ἐὰν προσκυνήσῃς ἐνώπιον ἐμοῦ, ἔσται σοῦ πᾶσα.

7 Now then, if you worship in front of me, it will all be yours."

Lk 4:8 Καὶ ἀποκριθεὶς ὁ Ἰησοῦς εἶπεν αὐτῷ, γέγραπται, Κύριον τὸν θεόν σου προσκυνήσεις, καὶ αὐτῷ μόνῳ λατρεύσεις.

8 In answer Jesus said to him,[133] "It is written: 'You shall worship Yahweh your God, and him only shall you serve.'[134]"

Lk 4:9 Ἤγαγεν δὲ αὐτὸν εἰς Ἱερουσαλήμ, καὶ ἔστησεν ἐπὶ τὸ πτερύγιον τοῦ ἱεροῦ, καὶ εἶπεν αὐτῷ, Εἰ υἱὸς εἶ τοῦ θεοῦ, βάλε σεαυτὸν ἐντεῦθεν κάτω•

9 Then the devil led him into Jerusalem, and had him stand on the gable of the temple. And he said to him, "If you are the Son of God, throw yourself down from here.

Lk 4:10 γέγραπται γὰρ ὅτι Τοῖς ἀγγέλοις αὐτοῦ ἐντελεῖται περὶ σοῦ, τοῦ διαφυλάξαι σε•

10 For it is written: 'He will command his angels concerning you to guard you carefully,

Lk 4:11 καὶ ὅτι[135] ἐπὶ χειρῶν ἀροῦσίν σε, μήποτε προσκόψῃς πρὸς λίθον τὸν πόδα σου.

11 and they will bear you up in their hands, so you will not strike your foot against a stone.'[136]"

Lk 4:12 Καὶ ἀποκριθεὶς εἶπεν αὐτῷ ὁ Ἰησοῦς ὅτι Εἴρηται, Οὐκ ἐκπειράσεις κύριον τὸν θεόν σου.

12 Jesus answered and said to him, "It says: 'You shall not test Yahweh your God.'[137]"

Lk 4:13 Καὶ συντελέσας πάντα πειρασμὸν ὁ διάβολος ἀπέστη ἀπ' αὐτοῦ ἄχρι καιροῦ.

13 And having carried out every sort of temptation, the devil left him until an opportune time.

Jesus Begins to Preach

Lk 4:14 Καὶ ὑπέστρεψεν ὁ Ἰησοῦς ἐν τῇ δυνάμει τοῦ πνεύματος εἰς τὴν Γαλιλαίαν• καὶ φήμη ἐξῆλθεν καθ' ὅλης τῆς περιχώρου περὶ αὐτοῦ.

14 And Jesus returned to Galilee in the power of the Spirit, and a rumor about him spread throughout the whole region.

---

133 **4:8a** txt *omit* ℵ B D L W Ξ ℓ2211 lat syr^{s,p} cop^{sa,bopt} arm geo NA28 {\} ‖ Ὕπαγε ὀπίσω μου Σατανᾶ A E 0102 𝔐 it syr^{h} (cop^{bopt}) TR RP

134 **4:8b** Deuteronomy 6:13

135 **4:11** txt ὅτι ℵ A B L W Ξ TR NA28 {\} ‖ *omit* D E 0102 𝔐 it cop^{sa,bopt} RP

136 **4:10-11** Psalm 91:11,12

137 **4:12** Deuteronomy 6:16

Lk 4:15 Καὶ αὐτὸς ἐδίδασκεν ἐν ταῖς συναγωγαῖς αὐτῶν, δοξαζόμενος ὑπὸ πάντων.

15 And he taught in their synagogues, being praised by everyone.

Jesus Rejected at Nazareth

Lk 4:16 ¶ Καὶ ἦλθεν εἰς Ναζαρά,[138] οὗ ἦν τεθραμμένος· καὶ εἰσῆλθεν, κατὰ τὸ εἰωθὸς αὐτῷ, ἐν τῇ ἡμέρᾳ τῶν σαββάτων εἰς τὴν συναγωγήν, καὶ ἀνέστη ἀναγνῶναι.

16 And he came to Nazareth, where he had been brought up, and went into the synagogue on the Sabbath day, as was his custom. And he stood up to read.

Lk 4:17 Καὶ ἐπεδόθη αὐτῷ βιβλίον τοῦ προφήτου Ἠσαΐου. Καὶ ἀναπτύξας τὸ βιβλίον, εὗρεν τὸν τόπον οὗ ἦν γεγραμμένον,

17 And the scroll of the prophet Isaiah was handed to him. Unrolling the scroll, he found the place where it is written:

Lk 4:18 Πνεῦμα κυρίου ἐπ' ἐμέ, οὗ εἵνεκεν ἔχρισέν με εὐαγγελίσασθαι πτωχοῖς· ἀπέσταλκέν με κηρύξαι αἰχμαλώτοις ἄφεσιν, καὶ τυφλοῖς ἀνάβλεψιν, ἀποστεῖλαι τεθραυσμένους ἐν ἀφέσει,

18 "The Spirit of Yahweh is upon me, because he has anointed me; He has sent me[139] to preach good news to the poor, to announce release for the prisoners and sight for the blind, to send off the crushed into liberty,

Lk 4:19 κηρύξαι ἐνιαυτὸν κυρίου δεκτόν.

19 to proclaim the year of Yahweh's favor..."[140]

---

138 **4:16** txt ναζαρα ℵ B* Ξ it^{e} cop^{samss} Or NA28 {\} ‖ την ναζαρα 33 ‖ την ναζαρατ A 0102 ‖ ναζαρεδ D ‖ ναζαρετ B^{2} L 579 700 892 1241 1582 2542 ‖ την ναζαρετ F K Π 118 157 565 1071 1424 *pm* RP ‖ την ναζαρεθ G M U Y Γ Ψ *f*^{13} 2 28 *pm* TR ‖ ναζαρεθ W Λ 1 788 ‖ ναζαρατ Θ ‖ ναζαραθ Δ ‖ *lac* 𝔓^{45} 𝔓^{75} C N P Q T

139 **4:18** txt *omit* ℵ B D L W Ξ *f*^{13} 33 579* 700 892* lat syr^{s} cop^{sa,bo} Or Eus Did NA28 {\} ‖ *include* ἰάσασθαι τοὺς συντετριμμένους τὴν καρδίαν "to heal the broken-hearted" A F K M U Γ Δ Θ Λ Π Ψ 0102 *f*^{1} 2 28 69 124 157 346 565 788 1071 1241 1424 2882 𝔐 it^{f} vg^{cl} syr^{p,h,pal} cop^{bomss} Ir^{lat} TR RP ‖ *lac* 𝔓^{45} 𝔓^{75} C N P Q T. The standard textual criticism arguments are: (1), *lectio brevior lectio potior* ("the shorter reading is the better reading" - unless homoioteleuton or otherwise explains omission), and (2), that the first reading best explains the other reading; that is, there is no good explanation why scribes might have omitted the phrase, but an explanation why scribes might have added the phrase is that the additional phrase completes the gap compared to the Isaiah passage- it harmonizes Luke to Isaiah. But there would be nothing remarkable about Jesus selecting and reading only the phrases that were pertinent to what he wanted to say. Indeed, all Greeek editions agree that Jesus did not finish the sentence from Isaiah; and that is why some translations, including mine, end the quotation with an ellipsis..." Moreover, Jesus also adds a phrase from a totally different passage in Isaiah, 58:6, "to set at liberty those who are oppressed." To me, the fact that Jesus selected another phrase from a completely different passage as well, just proves how selective he was being for phrases, and that lends more credibility to the idea that he skipped one phrase from the Isaiah 61 passage. Another interesting fact is that the phrase sight to the blind here in Luke 4:18 is not found in the Hebrew of Isaiah 61, but only in the Septuagint, the ancient translation of the Old Testament into Greek.

140 **4:19** Isaiah 61:1,2 When Jesus read this passage, he did not read to the end of the sentence. The next phrase was about the Lord's vengeance.

Lk 4:20 Καὶ πτύξας τὸ βιβλίον, ἀποδοὺς τῷ ὑπηρέτῃ, ἐκάθισεν• καὶ πάντων οἱ ὀφθαλμοὶ ἐν τῇ συναγωγῇ ἦσαν ἀτενίζοντες αὐτῷ.

20And having closed the scroll, he gave it back to the attendant and sat down. The eyes of everyone in the synagogue were fastened on him.

Lk 4:21 Ἤρξατο δὲ λέγειν πρὸς αὐτοὺς ὅτι Σήμερον πεπλήρωται ἡ γραφὴ αὕτη ἐν τοῖς ὠσὶν ὑμῶν.

21And he began to speak to them: "Today this scripture is fulfilled in your hearing."

Lk 4:22 Καὶ πάντες ἐμαρτύρουν αὐτῷ, καὶ ἐθαύμαζον ἐπὶ τοῖς λόγοις τῆς χάριτος τοῖς ἐκπορευομένοις ἐκ τοῦ στόματος αὐτοῦ, καὶ ἔλεγον, Οὐχὶ υἱός ἐστιν Ἰωσὴφ οὗτος;

22All were speaking well of him and amazed at the gracious words coming from his mouth. And they were saying, "Isn't this Joseph's son?"

Lk 4:23 Καὶ εἶπεν πρὸς αὐτούς, Πάντως ἐρεῖτέ μοι τὴν παραβολὴν ταύτην, Ἰατρέ, θεράπευσον σεαυτόν• ὅσα ἠκούσαμεν γενόμενα εἰς τὴν Καφαρναούμ, ποίησον καὶ ὧδε ἐν τῇ πατρίδι σου.

23And he said to them, "No doubt you will quote to me this proverb: 'Physician, heal yourself! The things we heard were happening in Capernaum, do here in your home town.'"

Lk 4:24 Εἶπεν δέ, Ἀμὴν λέγω ὑμῖν ὅτι οὐδεὶς προφήτης δεκτός ἐστιν ἐν τῇ πατρίδι αὐτοῦ.

24And he said, "Truly I tell you, no prophet is accepted in his home town.

Lk 4:25 Ἐπ' ἀληθείας δὲ λέγω ὑμῖν, πολλαὶ χῆραι ἦσαν ἐν ταῖς ἡμέραις Ἠλίου ἐν τῷ Ἰσραήλ, ὅτε ἐκλείσθη ὁ οὐρανὸς ἐπὶ ἔτη τρία καὶ μῆνας ἕξ, ὡς ἐγένετο λιμὸς μέγας ἐπὶ πᾶσαν τὴν γῆν•

25I tell you, in Elijah's days, during the three years and six months that the sky was shut and there was a great famine covering the whole land, it is a fact that there were plenty of widows in Israel.

Lk 4:26 καὶ πρὸς οὐδεμίαν αὐτῶν ἐπέμφθη Ἠλίας, εἰ μὴ εἰς Σάρεπτα τῆς Σιδωνίας πρὸς γυναῖκα χήραν.

26Yet it was not to any of them that Elijah was sent, but to Zarephath *in the country* of Sidon, to a widow woman *there.*

Lk 4:27 Καὶ πολλοὶ λεπροὶ ἦσαν ἐν τῷ Ἰσραὴλ ἐπὶ Ἐλισαίου τοῦ προφήτου• καὶ οὐδεὶς αὐτῶν ἐκαθαρίσθη, εἰ μὴ Ναιμὰν ὁ Σύρος.

27Again, in the case of Elisha the prophet, there were plenty of lepers in Israel, and not one of them was cleansed; only Naaman the Syrian."

Lk 4:28 Καὶ ἐπλήσθησαν πάντες θυμοῦ ἐν τῇ συναγωγῇ, ἀκούοντες ταῦτα,

28And all the people in the synagogue were furious when they heard these things.

Lk 4:29 καὶ ἀναστάντες ἐξέβαλον αὐτὸν ἔξω τῆς πόλεως, καὶ ἤγαγον αὐτὸν ἕως ὀφρύος τοῦ ὄρους ἐφ' οὗ ἡ πόλις ᾠκοδόμητο αὐτῶν ὥστε[141] κατακρημνίσαι αὐτόν.

29They got up and drove him outside the town, intending to throw him down the cliff.

141 **4:29** ᾠκοδόμητο αὐτῶν ὥστε NA28 {/} ‖ αὐτῶν ᾠκοδόμητο εἰς τὸ TR RP

Lk 4:30 Αὐτὸς δὲ διελθὼν διὰ μέσου αὐτῶν ἐπορεύετο.
30But he walked right through them, and went on his way.

Jesus' Teaching Has Authority

Lk 4:31 Καὶ κατῆλθεν εἰς Καφαρναοὺμ πόλιν τῆς Γαλιλαίας• καὶ ἦν διδάσκων αὐτοὺς ἐν τοῖς σάββασιν.
31And he went down to Capernaum, a town in Galilee, and on the Sabbath began to teach them.
Lk 4:32 Καὶ ἐξεπλήσσοντο ἐπὶ τῇ διδαχῇ αὐτοῦ, ὅτι ἐν ἐξουσίᾳ ἦν ὁ λόγος αὐτοῦ.
32And they were amazed at his teaching, because his word was authoritative.
Lk 4:33 Καὶ ἐν τῇ συναγωγῇ ἦν ἄνθρωπος ἔχων πνεῦμα δαιμονίου ἀκαθάρτου, καὶ ἀνέκραξεν φωνῇ μεγάλῃ,
33And in the synagogue there was a man who had a demon, an unclean spirit. He shouted out with a very loud voice,
Lk 4:34 Ἔα, τί ἡμῖν καὶ σοί, Ἰησοῦ Ναζαρηνέ; Ἦλθες ἀπολέσαι ἡμᾶς; Οἶδά σε τίς εἶ, ὁ ἅγιος τοῦ θεοῦ.
34"Ha! What business do you have with us, Jesus, you Nazarene? Have you come to destroy us? I know who you are— the Holy One of God!"
Lk 4:35 Καὶ ἐπετίμησεν αὐτῷ ὁ Ἰησοῦς, λέγων, Φιμώθητι, καὶ ἔξελθε ἀπ' αὐτοῦ. Καὶ ῥίψαν αὐτὸν τὸ δαιμόνιον εἰς τὸ μέσον ἐξῆλθεν ἀπ' αὐτοῦ, μηδὲν βλάψαν αὐτόν.
35And Jesus rebuked him, saying, "Be quiet and come out of him!" And the demon threw him down before them all and came out of him, doing him no damage.
Lk 4:36 Καὶ ἐγένετο θάμβος ἐπὶ πάντας, καὶ συνελάλουν πρὸς ἀλλήλους, λέγοντες, Τίς ὁ λόγος οὗτος, ὅτι ἐν ἐξουσίᾳ καὶ δυνάμει ἐπιτάσσει τοῖς ἀκαθάρτοις πνεύμασιν, καὶ ἐξέρχονται;
36And astonishment overwhelmed them all, and they spoke to each other, saying, "What is this message, that with authority and power he commands unclean spirits, and they come out?"
Lk 4:37 Καὶ ἐξεπορεύετο ἦχος περὶ αὐτοῦ εἰς πάντα τόπον τῆς περιχώρου.
37And a rumor went out about him into every place in that region.

Jesus Heals All in Capernaum

Lk 4:38 ¶ Ἀναστὰς δὲ ἀπὸ τῆς συναγωγῆς, εἰσῆλθεν εἰς τὴν οἰκίαν Σίμωνος• πενθερὰ δὲ τοῦ Σίμωνος ἦν συνεχομένη πυρετῷ μεγάλῳ• καὶ ἠρώτησαν αὐτὸν περὶ αὐτῆς.
38And rising up out of the synagogue, he went into the home of Simon. And Simon's mother-in-law was suffering a high fever, and they asked him about her.
Lk 4:39 Καὶ ἐπιστὰς ἐπάνω αὐτῆς, ἐπετίμησεν τῷ πυρετῷ, καὶ ἀφῆκεν αὐτήν• παραχρῆμα δὲ ἀναστᾶσα διηκόνει αὐτοῖς.
39So he stood over her and rebuked the fever, and it left her. And she got up at once and proceeded to wait on them.

Lk 4:40 ¶ Δύνοντος δὲ τοῦ ἡλίου, ἅπαντες ὅσοι εἶχον ἀσθενοῦντας νόσοις ποικίλαις ἤγαγον αὐτοὺς πρὸς αὐτόν• ὁ δὲ ἑνὶ ἑκάστῳ αὐτῶν τὰς χεῖρας ἐπιτιθεὶς ἐθεράπευεν αὐτούς.

40And as the sun was setting, everyone who had anyone ill with various kinds of sickness brought them to him, and laying his hands on each one of them, he was healing[142] them.

Lk 4:41 Ἐξήρχετο δὲ καὶ δαιμόνια ἀπὸ πολλῶν, κράζοντα καὶ λέγοντα ὅτι Σὺ εἶ ὁ υἱὸς τοῦ θεοῦ. Καὶ ἐπιτιμῶν οὐκ εἴα αὐτὰ λαλεῖν, ὅτι ᾔδεισαν τὸν χριστὸν αὐτὸν εἶναι.

41Moreover, demons were coming out from many, shouting and saying, "You are the Son of God!"[143] And he would rebuke *them*, not allowing them to speak, because they knew him to be the Messiah.

Jesus Keeps Moving

Lk 4:42 Γενομένης δὲ ἡμέρας, ἐξελθὼν ἐπορεύθη εἰς ἔρημον τόπον, καὶ οἱ ὄχλοι ἐπεζήτουν αὐτόν, καὶ ἦλθον ἕως αὐτοῦ, καὶ κατεῖχον αὐτὸν τοῦ μὴ πορεύεσθαι ἀπ' αὐτῶν.

42And when day came, he left and went off to a solitary place. And the crowds were searching for him, and they came up to him and detained him from leaving them.

Lk 4:43 Ὁ δὲ εἶπεν πρὸς αὐτοὺς ὅτι Καὶ ταῖς ἑτέραις πόλεσιν εὐαγγελίσασθαί με δεῖ τὴν βασιλείαν τοῦ θεοῦ• ὅτι ἐπὶ τοῦτο ἀπεστάλην.

43But he said to them, "I must preach the kingdom of God to the other towns also, because on that basis I was sent."[144]

Lk 4:44 Καὶ ἦν κηρύσσων εἰς τὰς συναγωγὰς τῆς Ἰουδαίας.

44And he kept on preaching in the synagogues of Jewdom.[145]

---

142 **4:40** txt ἐπιτιθεὶς ἐθεράπευεν NA28 {/} ‖ ἐπιθεὶς ἐθεράπευσεν TR RP

143 **4:41** txt ὁ υἱὸς 𝔓^{75} א B C D L W Ξ lat syr^{s} cop^{sa,bopt} Marcion^{T} Or NA28 {/} ‖ ὁ χριστὸς ὁ υἱὸς A Q 0102 𝔐 it^{f,q} syr^{p,h} cop^{bopt} TR RP

144 **4:43** txt ὅτι ἐπὶ τοῦτο ἀπεστάλην 𝔓^{75} א B L W NA28 {/} ‖ ὅτι εἰς τοῦτο ἀπεστάλην C ‖ εἰς τοῦτο γὰρ ἀπεστάλην D ‖ ὅτι εἰς τοῦτο ἀπέσταλμαι A ℓ2211 𝔐 TR RP ‖ *lac* Ξ

145 **4:44** txt εἰς τὰς συναγωγὰς τῆς Ἰουδαίας 𝔓^{75} א B Q^{vid} syr^{s,h} cop^{sa,bopt} NA28 {B} ‖ ἐν ταῖς συναγωγαῖς τῆς Ἰουδαίας C L ‖ εἰς τὰς συναγωγὰς τῶν Ἰουδαίων W ‖ εἰς τὰς συναγωγὰς τῆς Γαλιλαίας D arm? ‖ ἐν ταῖς συναγωγαῖς τῆς Γαλιλαίας A E 𝔐 it$^{a,aur,b,d,e,f,ff^2,l,q,r^1}$ vg syr^{p,hmg} cop^{bopt} eth arm? geo TR RP ‖ *lac* N P T Ξ. Where the earliest say he was preaching in the synagogues "of Judea," some manuscripts say, "of the Jews," others say, "to the Jews," others (most) say, "of Galilee," and others "their synagogues." It is apparent that the copyists responsible for the reading "of Galilee" were trying to correct the seeming difficulty of the words "of Judea," when the context before and after indicates that Jesus was traveling in Galilee; and other copyists were motivated by the desire to harmonize Luke with the accounts of Matthew and Mark. The reading "of Judea," however, can be translated as "the land of the Jews," or something to that effect, which in meaning would be inclusive of Galilee.

Chapter 5

The Calling of Simon, Andrew, James, and John

Lk 5:1 Ἐγένετο δὲ ἐν τῷ τὸν ὄχλον ἐπικεῖσθαι αὐτῷ καὶ ἀκούειν τὸν λόγον τοῦ θεοῦ, καὶ αὐτὸς ἦν ἑστὼς παρὰ τὴν λίμνην Γεννησαρέτ•

1And it came about that as he was standing by the Lake of Gennesaret, with the crowd pressing urgently around him and listening to the word of God,

Lk 5:2 καὶ εἶδεν δύο πλοῖα ἑστῶτα παρὰ τὴν λίμνην• οἱ δὲ ἁλιεῖς ἀπ' αὐτῶν ἀποβάντες ἔπλυνον τὰ δίκτυα.

2he saw two boats standing idle by the lake; the fishers had gotten out of them, washing the nets.[146]

Lk 5:3 Ἐμβὰς δὲ εἰς ἓν τῶν πλοίων, ὃ ἦν Σίμωνος, ἠρώτησεν αὐτὸν ἀπὸ τῆς γῆς ἐπαναγαγεῖν ὀλίγον. Καθίσας δὲ ἐκ τοῦ πλοίου ἐδίδασκεν τοὺς ὄχλους.

3And getting on board one of the boats, which was Simon's, he asked him to put out a little from shore. And sitting down, he taught the people from the boat.

Lk 5:4 Ὡς δὲ ἐπαύσατο λαλῶν, εἶπεν πρὸς τὸν Σίμωνα, Ἐπανάγαγε εἰς τὸ βάθος, καὶ χαλάσατε τὰ δίκτυα ὑμῶν εἰς ἄγραν.

4And when he had finished speaking, he said to Simon, "Put out into the deep, and let down your nets for a catch."

Lk 5:5 Καὶ ἀποκριθεὶς Σίμων εἶπεν, Ἐπιστάτα, δι' ὅλης νυκτὸς κοπιάσαντες οὐδὲν ἐλάβομεν• ἐπὶ δὲ τῷ ῥήματί σου χαλάσω τὰ δίκτυα.

5And in response Simon said, "Master, working hard through the whole night we took nothing. But on the basis of your word, I will let down the nets."[147]

Lk 5:6 Καὶ τοῦτο ποιήσαντες, συνέκλεισαν πλῆθος ἰχθύων πολύ• διερρήσσετο δὲ τὰ δίκτυα αὐτῶν•

6And when they had done so, they had enclosed a great number of fish, and their nets[148] were beginning to tear.

Lk 5:7 καὶ κατένευσαν τοῖς μετόχοις ἐν τῷ ἑτέρῳ πλοίῳ, τοῦ ἐλθόντας συλλαβέσθαι αὐτοῖς• καὶ ἦλθον καὶ ἔπλησαν ἀμφότερα τὰ πλοῖα, ὥστε βυθίζεσθαι αὐτά.

7So they signaled to their partners in[149] the other boat to come and help them, and they came, and they filled both the boats, such that they began to sink.

Lk 5:8 Ἰδὼν δὲ Σίμων Πέτρος προσέπεσεν τοῖς γόνασιν Ἰησοῦ, λέγων, Ἔξελθε ἀπ' ἐμοῦ, ὅτι ἀνὴρ ἁμαρτωλός εἰμι, κύριε.

8And when Simon Peter saw *this*, he fell at Jesus' knees and said, "Go away from me Lord; I am a sinful man!"

---

146 **5:2** txt ἔπλυνον 𝔓^{75} B D Q W NA28 {/} ‖ ἔπλυναν ℵ C* L ‖ ἀπέπλυναν A E 𝔐 TR RP

147 **5:5** txt τὰ δίκτυα 𝔓^{75vid} ℵ B D L W it$^{aur,(e),q}$ cop$^{sa^{mss},bo^{pt}}$ NA28 {/} ‖ τὸ δίκτυον A C E 𝔐 lat syr^{p,h} (cop$^{sa^{ms},bo^{pt}}$) TR RP ‖ *lac* 𝔓^{4}

148 **5:6** txt τὰ δίκτυα 𝔓^{4} 𝔓^{75} ℵ B D L W it syr^{s} NA28 {/} ‖ τὸ δίκτυον A C E 𝔐 it^{b} vg syr^{p,h} TR RP

149 **5:7** txt ἐν 𝔓^{4} 𝔓^{75} ℵ B D L W it^{a} NA28 {/} ‖ τοῖς ἐν A C E 𝔐 lat cop^{sa} TR RP

Lk 5:9 Θάμβος γὰρ περιέσχεν αὐτὸν καὶ πάντας τοὺς σὺν αὐτῷ, ἐπὶ τῇ ἄγρᾳ τῶν
ἰχθύων ὧν[150] συνέλαβον•
9For astonishment had seized him and all those with him, at the catch of fish
that they had taken, and likewise also James and John the sons of Zebedee, who
were partners with Simon.
Lk 5:10 ὁμοίως δὲ καὶ Ἰάκωβον καὶ Ἰωάννην, υἱοὺς Ζεβεδαίου, οἳ ἦσαν κοινωνοὶ
τῷ Σίμωνι. Καὶ εἶπεν πρὸς τὸν Σίμωνα ὁ Ἰησοῦς, Μὴ φοβοῦ• ἀπὸ τοῦ νῦν
ἀνθρώπους ἔσῃ ζωγρῶν.
10But Jesus said to Simon, "Don't be afraid. From now on you will be catching
human beings."
Lk 5:11 Καὶ καταγαγόντες τὰ πλοῖα ἐπὶ τὴν γῆν, ἀφέντες πάντα, ἠκολούθησαν
αὐτῷ. 11And when they had pulled the boats to shore, they gave it all up and
followed him.

A Leper Healed Spreads the Word

Lk 5:12 Καὶ ἐγένετο, ἐν τῷ εἶναι αὐτὸν ἐν μιᾷ τῶν πόλεων, καὶ ἰδού, ἀνὴρ
πλήρης λέπρας• ἰδὼν δὲ τὸν Ἰησοῦν, πεσὼν ἐπὶ πρόσωπον, ἐδεήθη αὐτοῦ,
λέγων, Κύριε, ἐὰν θέλῃς, δύνασαί με καθαρίσαι.
12And it came about that he was in one of the towns, and behold, a man
covered with leprosy.[151] And when he saw Jesus, he fell on his face and begged
him, saying, "Lord, if you are willing, you can cleanse me."
Lk 5:13 Καὶ ἐκτείνας τὴν χεῖρα ἥψατο αὐτοῦ, λέγων, Θέλω, καθαρίσθητι. Καὶ
εὐθέως ἡ λέπρα ἀπῆλθεν ἀπ' αὐτοῦ.
13And reaching out his hand, he touched him, saying, "I am willing. Be
cleansed." And immediately the leprosy left him.
Lk 5:14 Καὶ αὐτὸς παρήγγειλεν αὐτῷ μηδενὶ εἰπεῖν• ἀλλὰ ἀπελθὼν δεῖξον
σεαυτὸν τῷ ἱερεῖ, καὶ προσένεγκε περὶ τοῦ καθαρισμοῦ σου, καθὼς προσέταξεν
Μωϋσῆς, εἰς μαρτύριον αὐτοῖς.
14And he ordered him to tell no one, but "Go, show yourself to the priest, and
offer for your cleansing what Moses commanded, as a testimony to them."[152]
Lk 5:15 Διήρχετο δὲ μᾶλλον ὁ λόγος περὶ αὐτοῦ• καὶ συνήρχοντο ὄχλοι πολλοὶ
ἀκούειν, καὶ θεραπεύεσθαι ἀπὸ τῶν ἀσθενειῶν αὐτῶν.
15But word about him was spreading all the more, and many crowds would
walk alongside to listen, and to be healed[153] of their sicknesses.
Lk 5:16 Αὐτὸς δὲ ἦν ὑποχωρῶν ἐν ταῖς ἐρήμοις καὶ προσευχόμενος.
16And he would take retreat in deserted places, and pray.

---

150 **5:9** txt ὧν 𝔓75 B D it^{aur} cop^{bo} NA28 {/} ‖ ᾗ ℵ A C E L W ℓ2211 𝔐 lat syr^{h} cop^{sa} TR RP

151 **5:12** The Greek word was used for various diseases of the skin— not necessarily leprosy.

152 **5:13** Jesus is following the Law, Leviticus 14, as to what to do regarding healing of leprosy. In all the history of Israel subsequent to the giving of the Law and Leviticus 14, no Jew had ever been verified as healed of leprosy.

153 **5:15** txt *omit* ℵ B C* D L W latt syr^{s,p} cop^{sa,bopt} NA28 {/} ‖ ἀπ' αὐτοῦ A ‖ ὑπ' αὐτοῦ E N ℓ2211 𝔐 syr^{h} TR RP

The Paralytic Lowered Through the Roof

Lk 5:17 Καὶ ἐγένετο ἐν μιᾷ τῶν ἡμερῶν, καὶ αὐτὸς ἦν διδάσκων· καὶ ἦσαν καθήμενοι Φαρισαῖοι καὶ νομοδιδάσκαλοι, οἳ ἦσαν ἐληλυθότες ἐκ πάσης κώμης τῆς Γαλιλαίας καὶ Ἰουδαίας καὶ Ἱερουσαλήμ· καὶ δύναμις κυρίου ἦν εἰς τὸ ἰᾶσθαι αὐτόν.

17And it came about during one of the days that, as he was teaching, Pharisees and teachers of the Torah also were sitting there, who had come from every village of Galilee and from Judea and Jerusalem. And the power of the Lord was present for him to heal.[154]

Lk 5:18 Καὶ ἰδού, ἄνδρες φέροντες ἐπὶ κλίνης ἄνθρωπον ὃς ἦν παραλελυμένος, καὶ ἐζήτουν αὐτὸν εἰσενεγκεῖν καὶ θεῖναι[155] ἐνώπιον αὐτοῦ·

18And behold, men carrying on a pallet a man who was paralyzed. And they were trying to carry him in, to lay him before him.

Lk 5:19 καὶ μὴ εὑρόντες ποίας εἰσενέγκωσιν αὐτὸν διὰ τὸν ὄχλον, ἀναβάντες ἐπὶ τὸ δῶμα, διὰ τῶν κεράμων καθῆκαν αὐτὸν σὺν τῷ κλινιδίῳ εἰς τὸ μέσον ἔμπροσθεν τοῦ Ἰησοῦ.

19And not finding a way to carry in because of the crowd, they went up onto the roof, and lowered him with his bed down through the tiles, into the middle, in front of Jesus.

Lk 5:20 Καὶ ἰδὼν τὴν πίστιν αὐτῶν, εἶπεν, Ἄνθρωπε, ἀφέωνταί σοι αἱ ἁμαρτίαι σου.

20And when Jesus saw their faith, he said,[156] "Friend, your sins are forgiven you."

Lk 5:21 Καὶ ἤρξαντο διαλογίζεσθαι οἱ γραμματεῖς καὶ οἱ Φαρισαῖοι, λέγοντες, Τίς ἐστιν οὗτος ὃς λαλεῖ βλασφημίας; Τίς δύναται ἁμαρτίας ἀφεῖναι, εἰ μὴ μόνος ὁ θεός;

21And the Torah scholars and Pharisees began to reason as follows: "Who is this fellow who speaks blasphemy![157] Who can forgive sins but God alone?"

Lk 5:22 Ἐπιγνοὺς δὲ ὁ Ἰησοῦς τοὺς διαλογισμοὺς αὐτῶν ἀποκριθεὶς εἶπεν πρὸς αὐτούς, Τί διαλογίζεσθε ἐν ταῖς καρδίαις ὑμῶν;

22But knowing their reasonings, Jesus in response said to them, "Why are you debating *this* in your hearts?

Lk 5:23 Τί ἐστιν εὐκοπώτερον, εἰπεῖν, Ἀφέωνταί σοι αἱ ἁμαρτίαι σου, ἢ εἰπεῖν, Ἔγειρε καὶ περιπάτει;

23Which is easier: to say 'Your sins are forgiven you,' or to say, 'Get up and walk'?

---

154 **5:17** txt αὐτόν ℵ B L W Ξ syr^{s} Did NA28 {/} ‖ αὐτούς A C D E N 𝔐 latt syr^{p,h} cop^{bo} TR RP.

155 **5:18** txt θειναι ℵ A C D E N 𝔐 TR RP SBL TH ‖ θειναι [αυτον] B L Ξ NA28 {/}

156 **5:20** txt *omit* ℵ B L Ξ it^{ff2} vg cop^{sa} NA28 {/} ‖ τῷ παραλυτικῷ C D 124 syr^{p} cop^{bo} Cyr ‖ τῷ ἀνθρώπω f^{1} it^{a,b,e,l,q} eth ‖ αὐτῷ A E N W 𝔐 it^{d} syr^{h} arm TR RP

157 **5:21** The Greek for blasphemy is in the plural, an idiomatic pluralization of abstract topics that frequently serves as a designation of concrete phenomena. Here it would mean something more like "words of blasphemy," referring to the one incident of blasphemy in verse 20. Other examples of this kind of plural are Matthew 14:9, 15:19.

Lk 5:24 Ἵνα δὲ εἰδῆτε ὅτι ὁ υἱὸς τοῦ ἀνθρώπου ἐξουσίαν ἔχει ἐπὶ τῆς γῆς ἀφιέναι ἁμαρτίας - εἶπεν τῷ παραλελυμένῳ - Σοὶ λέγω, ἔγειρε, καὶ ἄρας τὸ κλινίδιόν σου, πορεύου εἰς τὸν οἶκόν σου.

24But so that you may know that the Son of Man has authority on earth to forgive sins..." He said to the paralyzed man, "I tell you, get up, pick up your mat and be on your way home."

Lk 5:25 Καὶ παραχρῆμα ἀναστὰς ἐνώπιον αὐτῶν, ἄρας ἐφ' ὃ κατέκειτο, ἀπῆλθεν εἰς τὸν οἶκον αὐτοῦ, δοξάζων τὸν θεόν.

25And immediately he stood up, in full view of them, and taking up that upon which he had been lying, he went away toward home, praising God.

Lk 5:26 Καὶ ἔκστασις ἔλαβεν ἅπαντας, καὶ ἐδόξαζον τὸν θεόν, καὶ ἐπλήσθησαν φόβου, λέγοντες ὅτι Εἴδομεν παράδοξα σήμερον.

26Everyone was stunned with amazement. And they glorified God, and were filled with awe, saying, "We have seen remarkable things today."

A Revenue Agent Joins Jesus

Lk 5:27 Καὶ μετὰ ταῦτα ἐξῆλθεν, καὶ ἐθεάσατο τελώνην, ὀνόματι Λευΐν, καθήμενον ἐπὶ τὸ τελώνιον, καὶ εἶπεν αὐτῷ, Ἀκολούθει μοι.

27And after these things he went out, and he saw a revenue agent[158] by the name of Levi, sitting at the taxes post, and he said to him, "Follow me."

Lk 5:28 Καὶ καταλιπὼν πάντα, ἀναστὰς ἠκολούθει αὐτῷ.

28And he rose up and followed him, giving it all up.

Lk 5:29 Καὶ ἐποίησεν δοχὴν μεγάλην Λευῒς αὐτῷ ἐν τῇ οἰκίᾳ αὐτοῦ• καὶ ἦν ὄχλος πολὺς τελωνῶν, καὶ ἄλλων οἳ ἦσαν μετ' αὐτῶν κατακείμενοι.

29Then Levi held a great banquet for him at his house. And there was also a large crowd of revenue agents and others who were reclining with him.

Lk 5:30 Καὶ ἐγόγγυζον οἱ Φαρισαῖοι καὶ οἱ γραμματεῖς αὐτῶν πρὸς τοὺς μαθητὰς αὐτοῦ λέγοντες, Διὰ τί μετὰ τῶν τελωνῶν καὶ ἁμαρτωλῶν ἐσθίετε καὶ πίνετε;

30And the Pharisees and their Torah scholars[159] grumbled to his disciples, saying, "Why do you eat and drink with revenue agents and sinners?"[160]

---

158 **5:27** The Greek word here translated "revenue agent" is τελώνης, a combination of the words τέλος for excise off the end tally, and the word ὠνέομαι which means to "buy." Hence, tax-buyers, or tax owners. The accounts receivable which the due taxes represented were purchased by something like collection agencies. According to Bauer, the τελῶναι were not the holders of the 'tax farming' contracts themselves, (the actual holders were called publicani), but were subordinates (Latin, portitores) hired by the publicani. The higher officials, the publicans, were usually foreigners, but their underlings were taken, as a rule, from the native population, from the subjugated people. The prevailing system of tax collection afforded the collector many opportunities to exercise his greed and unfairness. Moreover, since the tax was forced upon the conquered by the conqueror, the collectors of the tax were personal reminders to the populace that they, the payers of the tax, were conquered. Hence the collectors of the tax were particularly hated and despised as a class. They were pre-judged to be both embezzlers, and traitors or collaborators with the occupying foreign power.

159 **5:30a** txt φαρισαιοι και οι γραμματεις αυτων B C L W Ξ $\mathbf{f}^1$ 33 157 579 700 892 1241 2542 lat SBL NA28 {/} ‖ φαρισαιοι και οι γραμματεις ℵ (D) it cop$^{sa^{mss},bo}$ ‖ γραμματεις και οι φαρισαιοι F

Lk 5:31 Καὶ ἀποκριθεὶς ὁ Ἰησοῦς εἶπεν πρὸς αὐτούς, Οὐ χρείαν ἔχουσιν οἱ ὑγιαίνοντες ἰατροῦ, ἀλλὰ οἱ κακῶς ἔχοντες.

31 And Jesus responded and said to them, "It is not the healthy who need a doctor, but those who are sick.

Lk 5:32 Οὐκ ἐλήλυθα καλέσαι δικαίους, ἀλλὰ ἁμαρτωλοὺς εἰς μετάνοιαν.

32 I have not come to call the righteous, but sinners to repentance."

Jesus Questioned About Fasting

Lk 5:33 Οἱ δὲ εἶπαν πρὸς αὐτόν, Οἱ μαθηταὶ Ἰωάννου νηστεύουσιν πυκνά, καὶ δεήσεις ποιοῦνται, ὁμοίως καὶ οἱ τῶν Φαρισαίων• οἱ δὲ σοὶ ἐσθίουσιν καὶ πίνουσιν.

33 They then said to him, "The[161] disciples of John are often fasting and making prayers, and likewise those of the Pharisees, but yours go on eating and drinking."

Lk 5:34 Ὁ δὲ Ἰησοῦς εἶπεν πρὸς αὐτούς, Μὴ δύνασθε τοὺς υἱοὺς τοῦ νυμφῶνος, ἐν ᾧ ὁ νυμφίος μετ' αὐτῶν ἐστιν, ποιῆσαι νηστεῦσαι;

34 And Jesus said to them, "Can you make the members of the bridegroom's party fast during *days* in which the bridegroom is with them?

Lk 5:35 Ἐλεύσονται δὲ ἡμέραι, καὶ ὅταν ἀπαρθῇ ἀπ' αὐτῶν ὁ νυμφίος, τότε νηστεύσουσιν ἐν ἐκείναις ταῖς ἡμέραις.

35 But the days will come. Yes, when the bridegroom is taken away from them, then in those days they will fast."

Lk 5:36 Ἔλεγεν δὲ καὶ παραβολὴν πρὸς αὐτοὺς ὅτι Οὐδεὶς ἐπίβλημα ἀπὸ ἱματίου καινοῦ σχίσας ἐπιβάλλει ἐπὶ ἱμάτιον παλαιόν• εἰ δὲ μή γε, καὶ τὸ καινὸν σχίσει καὶ τῷ παλαιῷ οὐ συμφωνήσει τὸ ἐπίβλημα τὸ ἀπὸ τοῦ καινοῦ.

36 And he also spoke a parable to them: "No one tears[162] a patch from a new garment *and* places it onto an old garment. For then, he will both tear[163] the new, and the patch[164] from the new will not match[165] the old.

---

118 788 1071 ‖ γραμματεις αυτων και οι φαρισαιοι A K M N U Γ Δ Θ Λ Ψ *f*^{13} (except 788) 565 1424 𝔐 it^{r1} (cop$^{sa^{ms},bo^{ms}}$) TR RP ‖ *lac* 𝔓^{4} 𝔓^{45} 𝔓^{75} G H P Q T. These are meaningfully different, since having the possessive pronoun first, as in "their Torah scholars and Pharisees" makes it sound like "their" refers to the Jews as possessors, and both Torah scholars and Pharisees as the subject, whereas "the Pharisees and their Torah scholars" makes it sound like only a subset of the Torah scholars, those belonging to the sect of the Pharisees, is being talked about. Compare Mark 2:16.

160 **5:30b** The Mishnah associated tax collectors with murderers and highway robbers. (*Nedarim* 3:4 and *Bava Qamma* 10:2)

161 **5:33** txt Οἱ 𝔓^{4} א^{1} B L W Ξ cop^{sa,bopt} NA28 {B} ‖ Διὰ τί οἱ א^{*,2} A C D E N 0233 𝔐 it$^{a,aur,b,d,ef,ff^2,l,q,r^1}$ vg syr^{p,h,pal} cop^{bopt} arm eth geo Aug TR RP

162 **5:36a** txt σχίσας 𝔓^{4} א B D L W Ξ it^{d} (syr^{p}) cop^{sa,bo} NA28 {/} ‖ *omit* A C E 𝔐 lat syr^{h} TR RP

163 **5:36b** txt σχίσει 𝔓^{4} א B C D L W NA28 {/} ‖ σχίζει A E 𝔐 TR RP. τὸ καινὸν is the subject doing the "tearing," but I have paraphrased a little to make it clear.

164 **5:36c** txt τὸ ἐπίβλημα 𝔓^{4} א B C (D) L W lat syr cop NA28 {/} ‖ ἐπίβλημα TR ‖ *omit* A E 𝔐 RP. I think the NA reading is a clarification, and the RP reading is original.

165 **5:36d** txt συμφωνήσει 𝔓^{4} א A B C D L W NA28 {/} ‖ συμφωνεῖ E 𝔐 RP

Lk 5:37 Καὶ οὐδεὶς βάλλει οἶνον νέον εἰς ἀσκοὺς παλαιούς• εἰ δὲ μή γε, ῥήξει ὁ οἶνος ὁ νέος τοὺς ἀσκούς, καὶ αὐτὸς ἐκχυθήσεται, καὶ οἱ ἀσκοὶ ἀπολοῦνται.

37 And no one puts new wine into old wineskins. For then, the new wine will burst the wineskins, and it will be spilled, and the wineskins will be ruined.

Lk 5:38 Ἀλλὰ οἶνον νέον εἰς ἀσκοὺς καινοὺς βλητέον.

38 On the contrary, new wine must be put in new wineskins.[166]

Lk 5:39 Καὶ οὐδεὶς πιὼν παλαιὸν θέλει νέον• λέγει γάρ, Ὁ παλαιὸς χρηστός ἐστιν.

39 And no one after drinking old wine wants[167] the new, for he says, 'The old is better.' "[168]

Chapter 6

Man Over the Sabbath

Lk 6:1 Ἐγένετο δὲ ἐν σαββάτῳ διαπορεύεσθαι αὐτὸν διὰ σπορίμων• καὶ ἔτιλλον οἱ μαθηταὶ αὐτοῦ καὶ ἤσθιον τοὺς στάχυας, καὶ ἤσθιον, ψώχοντες ταῖς χερσίν.

1 And he happened during a Sabbath[169] to be passing through grainfields, and his disciples were plucking and eating the heads, rubbing them in their hands.[170]

---

166 **5:38** txt *omit* 𝔓^{4} 𝔓^{75} א B L W cop NA28 {/} ‖ καὶ ἀμφότεροι συντηροῦνται (Matt 9:17) A C D E latt syr cop^{bomss} TR RP

167 **5:39a** txt θέλει 𝔓^{4} 𝔓^{75} א B C* L W cop^{sa,bo} arm NA28 {/} ‖ εὐθέως θέλει A E 𝔐 latt syr^{p,h} TR RP ‖ *omit v. 39* D it$^{a,b,d,e,ff^2,l,r^1}$

168 **5:39b** txt χρηστός 𝔓^{4} 𝔓^{75vid} א B L W syr^{p} cop^{sa,bo} NA28 {A} ‖ χρηστότερός A C E 𝔐 it^{aur,f,q} vg syr^{h,pal} arm eth geo TR RP ‖ *omit v. 39* D it$^{a,b,d,e,ff^2,l,r^1}$

169 **6:1a** txt σαββάτῳ 𝔓^{4} א B L W 1 22 33 69 118 157 205 588 579 697 788 791 1005 1210 1241 1365 1582* 2372 2542 2670 it$^{b,c,l,q,r^1}$ syr^{p,hmg,pal} cop^{sa,bopt} eth NA28 {C} ‖ τοῖς σάββασιν *Lect* cop^{bopt} (Mt 12:1; Mk 2:23 ‖ σαββάτῳ δευτεροπρώτῳ A C D E H K M U Y Γ Δ Θ Λ Π Ψ 0233 2^{c} 124^{c} 180 565 597 700 892 1006 1010 1292 1342 1424 1505 1582^{c} it$^{a,aur,d,f,ff^2}$ vg syr^{h} arm slav goth Epiph Chrys Isid Ambr TR RP ‖ σαββάτῳ δευτέρω πρώτω 2* 13 28 124* 346 543 826 828 983 1071 1243 1709 ‖ σαββάτῳ δευτεροπρῲ Ω ‖ σαββάτῳ δευτέρῳ geo ‖ *sabbato mane* it^{e} ‖ *lac* 𝔓^{45} F G N P Q T. The UBS textual commentary: "In the opinion of a majority of the Committee, although σαββάτῳ δευτεροπρώτῳ is certainly the more difficult reading, it must not for that reason be adopted. The word δευτεροπρῶτος occurs nowhere else, and appears to be a *vox nulla* that arose accidentally through a transcriptional blunder. (Perhaps some copyist introduced πρώτῳ as a correlative of ἐν ἑτέρῳ σαββάτῳ in ver. 6, and a second copyist, in view of 4:31, wrote δευτέρῳ, deleting πρώτῳ by using dots over the letters—which was the customary way of cancelling a word. A subsequent transcriber, not noticing the dots, mistakenly combined the two words into one, which he introduced into the text.)"

170 **6:1b** This was the allowable practice of "plucking the heads," see Deuteronomy 23:24, 25, "If you enter your neighbor's vineyard, you may eat grapes until you are fully satisfied, but do not put any in a container. If you enter your neighbor's grainfield, you may pluck the heads with your hands, but you must not put a sickle to your neighbor's standing grain." But, the Mishnah and Traditions of the Elders forbade: MISHNA II.: The principal acts of labor (prohibited on the Sabbath) are forty less one--viz.: Sowing, ploughing, reaping, binding into sheaves, threshing, winnowing, fruit-cleaning, grinding, sifting, kneading, baking, wool-shearing, bleaching, combing, dyeing, spinning, warping, making two spindle-trees, weaving

Lk 6:2 Τινὲς δὲ τῶν Φαρισαίων εἶπαν, Τί ποιεῖτε ὃ οὐκ ἔξεστιν ἐν τοῖς σάββασιν;

[2]But some of the Pharisees said, "Why are you doing what on a Sabbath is not permissible?"[171]

Lk 6:3 Καὶ ἀποκριθεὶς πρὸς αὐτοὺς εἶπεν ὁ Ἰησοῦς, Οὐδὲ τοῦτο ἀνέγνωτε, ὃ ἐποίησεν Δαυίδ, ὅτε ἐπείνασεν αὐτὸς καὶ οἱ μετ' αὐτοῦ ὄντες;

[3]And in answer to them Jesus said, "Have you never read what David did when he and those with him were hungry?

Lk 6:4 Ὡς εἰσῆλθεν εἰς τὸν οἶκον τοῦ θεοῦ, καὶ τοὺς ἄρτους τῆς προθέσεως λαβὼν ἔφαγεν καὶ ἔδωκεν τοῖς μετ' αὐτοῦ, οὓς οὐκ ἔξεστιν φαγεῖν εἰ μὴ μόνους τοὺς ἱερεῖς;

[4]How he went into the house of God, and taking the loaves of offering, he ate, and gave to the ones with him, which was not permissible to eat, except for the priests only?"

Lk 6:5 Καὶ ἔλεγεν αὐτοῖς, Κύριός ἐστιν τοῦ σαββάτου ὁ υἱὸς τοῦ ἀνθρώπου.

[5]Then he said to them, "The Son of Man is lord of the Sabbath."[172]

Lk 6:6 Ἐγένετο δὲ ἐν ἑτέρῳ σαββάτῳ εἰσελθεῖν αὐτὸν εἰς τὴν συναγωγὴν καὶ διδάσκειν• καὶ ἦν ἄνθρωπος ἐκεῖ, καὶ ἡ χεὶρ αὐτοῦ ἡ δεξιὰ ἦν ξηρά.

[6]And it came about that on another Sabbath, he went into the synagogue and was teaching, and a man was there whose right hand was shriveled.

Lk 6:7 Παρετηροῦντο δὲ αὐτὸν οἱ γραμματεῖς καὶ οἱ Φαρισαῖοι, εἰ ἐν τῷ σαββάτῳ θεραπεύει• ἵνα εὕρωσιν κατηγορεῖν αὐτοῦ.

[7]And the Torah scholars and the Pharisees were carefully watching him, whether he would heal on the Sabbath, in order to obtain cause to prosecute him.

Lk 6:8 Αὐτὸς δὲ ᾔδει τοὺς διαλογισμοὺς αὐτῶν, εἶπεν δὲ τῷ ἀνδρὶ[173] τῷ ξηρὰν ἔχοντι τὴν χεῖρα, Ἔγειρε καὶ στῆθι εἰς τὸ μέσον. Καὶ ἀναστὰς ἔστη.

[8]But he knew their reasoning, and said to the man with the shriveled hand, "Get up and stand in view." And he got up and stood.

---

two threads, separating two threads (in the warp), tying a knot, untying a knot, sewing on with two stitches, tearing in order to sew together with two stitches, hunting deer, slaughtering the same, skinning them, salting them, preparing the hide, scraping the hair off, cutting it, writing two (single) letters (characters), erasing in order to write two letters, building, demolishing (in order to rebuild), kindling, extinguishing (fire), hammering, transferring from one place into another. These are the principal acts of labor--forty less one. http://www.jewishvirtuallibrary.org/jsource/Talmud/shabbat7.html

[171] **6:2** The Greek word translated "permissible" is the impersonal participle ἔξεστιν, which is derived from the same root as ἐξουσία, the word for authority. If an activity was ἔξεστιν, that means it was "loosed," or ruled by the rabbis to be something "allowed" by the Torah. If something was not ἔξεστιν, as is the case here, that means it was "bound," that is, the rabbis had adjudged that it was forbidden by the Torah.

[172] **6:5** txt του σαββατου ο υιος του ανθρωπου ℵ B W syr$^{p,(pal)}$ cop$^{(sa),bopt}$ eth diatess NA28 {B} ‖ και του σαββατου ο υιος του ανθρωπου 𝔓^{4vid} ‖ ο υιος του ανθρωπου και του σαββατου A (D it^{d}, but v. 5 placed after v. 10) E L 𝔐 it$^{a,aur,b,e,f,ff^2,l,q,r^1}$ vg syr^{h} cop^{bopt} arm geo Marcion$^{AccToEpiphan.}$ Ambrosiaster TR RP ‖ *lac* C Ξ syr^{s}

[173] **6:8** txt εἶπεν δὲ τῷ ἀνδρὶ 𝔓^{4} ℵ B L NA28 {/} ‖ λέγε D ‖ εἶπεν δὲ τῷ ἀνθρώπῳ W ‖ καὶ εἶπεν τῷ ἀνθρώπῳ A E 𝔐 TR RP ‖ *lac* 𝔓^{45} C N P Q T Ξ

Lk 6:9 Εἶπεν δὲ ὁ Ἰησοῦς πρὸς αὐτούς, Ἐπερωτῶ ὑμᾶς, Εἰ ἔξεστιν τῷ σαββάτῳ ἀγαθοποιῆσαι ἢ κακοποιῆσαι; Ψυχὴν σῶσαι ἢ ἀπολέσαι;

9Then Jesus said to them, "I ask you, is it permissible on the Sabbath to do good or to do evil, to save life or to destroy it?"

Lk 6:10 Καὶ περιβλεψάμενος πάντας αὐτούς, εἶπεν αὐτῷ, Ἔκτεινον τὴν χεῖρά σου. Ὁ δὲ ἐποίησεν καὶ ἀπεκατεστάθη ἡ χεὶρ αὐτοῦ.

10And looking around at them all, he said to him, "Stretch out your hand." He did so, and his hand was restored.

Lk 6:11 Αὐτοὶ δὲ ἐπλήσθησαν ἀνοίας• καὶ διελάλουν πρὸς ἀλλήλους, τί ἂν ποιήσαιεν τῷ Ἰησοῦ.

11And they were filled with rage,[174] and discussed with each other what they should do to Jesus.

The Twelve Apostles

Lk 6:12 Ἐγένετο δὲ ἐν ταῖς ἡμέραις ταύταις ἐξελθεῖν αὐτὸν εἰς τὸ ὄρος προσεύξασθαι• καὶ ἦν διανυκτερεύων ἐν τῇ προσευχῇ τοῦ θεοῦ.

12And it came about in those days that he went out into the hills to pray, and spent the whole night praying to God.

Lk 6:13 Καὶ ὅτε ἐγένετο ἡμέρα, προσεφώνησεν τοὺς μαθητὰς αὐτοῦ• καὶ ἐκλεξάμενος ἀπ' αὐτῶν δώδεκα, οὓς καὶ ἀποστόλους ὠνόμασεν,

13And when it was day, he called his disciples to him, and from them he selected twelve, whom he then designated apostles:

Lk 6:14 Σίμωνα ὃν καὶ ὠνόμασεν Πέτρον, καὶ Ἀνδρέαν τὸν ἀδελφὸν αὐτοῦ, καὶ Ἰάκωβον καὶ Ἰωάννην, καὶ Φίλιππον καὶ Βαρθολομαῖον,

14Simon, whom he also named Peter, and his brother Andrew; James and John; Philip and Bartholomew;

Lk 6:15 καὶ Μαθθαῖον καὶ Θωμᾶν, καὶ Ἰάκωβον Ἁλφαίου, καὶ Σίμωνα τὸν καλούμενον Ζηλωτήν,

15Matthew and Thomas; James son of Halphaeus and Simon the Zealot; and Judas son[175] of James;

Lk 6:16 καὶ Ἰούδαν Ἰακώβου, καὶ Ἰούδαν Ἰσκαριώτην'Ισκαριώθ, ὃς ἐγένετο προδότης.

16and Judas of Kerioth,[176] who became a betrayer.

---

174 **6:11** Greek ἀνοία - anoia, a word much like our English word 'mad,' in that it can mean both anger and insanity. You could say Jesus' opponents went out of their minds with rage. Anger often overcomes better judgment. Thus anoia is often translated as 'folly.'

175 **6:16a** Or *brother*

176 **6:16b** This man's name is usually written Judas Iscariot. "Iscariot" is probably from the Hebrew words אִישׁ קְרִיּוֹת, ish Qerioth, which mean *a man from Kerioth.* Kerioth was a town in southern Judea, which would make this Judas the only one in the circle of thirteen (Jesus and the twelve disciples) that was not from Galilee.

Blessings and Woes

Lk 6:17 Καὶ καταβὰς μετ' αὐτῶν, ἔστη ἐπὶ τόπου πεδινοῦ, καὶ ὄχλος πολὺς μαθητῶν αὐτοῦ, καὶ πλῆθος πολὺ τοῦ λαοῦ ἀπὸ πάσης τῆς Ἰουδαίας καὶ Ἱερουσαλήμ, καὶ τῆς παραλίου Τύρου καὶ Σιδῶνος,

17And when he came down, he stopped at a level place with them, and with a large crowd of his disciples, and with a great multitude of the people from all of Judea and Jerusalem and from the coastal areas of Tyre and Sidon,

Lk 6:18 οἳ ἦλθον ἀκοῦσαι αὐτοῦ, καὶ ἰαθῆναι ἀπὸ τῶν νόσων αὐτῶν• καὶ οἱ ἐνοχλούμενοι ἀπὸ πνευμάτων ἀκαθάρτων, ἐθεραπεύοντο.

18who had come to hear him and to be healed of their diseases. And those oppressed by unclean spirits were being cured.

Lk 6:19 Καὶ πᾶς ὁ ὄχλος ἐζήτουν ἅπτεσθαι αὐτοῦ• ὅτι δύναμις παρ' αὐτοῦ ἐξήρχετο καὶ ἰᾶτο πάντας.

19And the entire crowd was trying to touch him, because power was going out from him, and curing everyone.

Lk 6:20 Καὶ αὐτὸς ἐπάρας τοὺς ὀφθαλμοὺς αὐτοῦ εἰς τοὺς μαθητὰς αὐτοῦ ἔλεγεν, Μακάριοι οἱ πτωχοί, ὅτι ὑμετέρα ἐστὶν ἡ βασιλεία τοῦ θεοῦ.

20And he lifted his eyes toward his disciples, and began to speak: "Blessed are you who are poor, for yours is the kingdom of God.

Lk 6:21 Μακάριοι οἱ πεινῶντες νῦν, ὅτι χορτασθήσεσθε. Μακάριοι οἱ κλαίοντες νῦν, ὅτι γελάσετε.

21Blessed are you who go hungry now, for you will be satisfied. Blessed are you who weep now, for you will laugh.

Lk 6:22 Μακάριοί ἐστε, ὅταν μισήσωσιν ὑμᾶς οἱ ἄνθρωποι, καὶ ὅταν ἀφορίσωσιν ὑμᾶς, καὶ ὀνειδίσωσιν, καὶ ἐκβάλωσιν τὸ ὄνομα ὑμῶν ὡς πονηρόν, ἕνεκα τοῦ υἱοῦ τοῦ ἀνθρώπου.

22Blessed are you when people hate you, excommunicate you and shame you and cast out your name as evil, because of the Son of Man.

Lk 6:23 Χάρητε ἐν ἐκείνῃ τῇ ἡμέρᾳ καὶ σκιρτήσατε• ἰδοὺ γάρ, ὁ μισθὸς ὑμῶν πολὺς ἐν τῷ οὐρανῷ• κατὰ ταῦτα τὰ αὐτὰ γὰρ ἐποίουν τοῖς προφήταις οἱ πατέρες αὐτῶν.

23"Rejoice in that day, and skip for joy! For behold, great is your reward in heaven, because the same things their ancestors did to the prophets.

Lk 6:24 Πλὴν οὐαὶ ὑμῖν τοῖς πλουσίοις, ὅτι ἀπέχετε τὴν παράκλησιν ὑμῶν.

24"But woe to you who are rich, because you have received your comfort.

Lk 6:25 Οὐαὶ ὑμῖν, ἐμπεπλησμένοι νῦν, ὅτι πεινάσετε. Οὐαὶ, οἱ γελῶντες νῦν, ὅτι πενθήσετε καὶ κλαύσετε.

25Woe to you who are well fed now, for you will go hungry. Woe to those who laugh now, for you will mourn and weep.

Lk 6:26 Οὐαὶ ὅταν ὑμᾶς καλῶς εἴπωσιν πάντες οἱ ἄνθρωποι• κατὰ τὰ αὐτὰ γὰρ ἐποίουν τοῖς ψευδοπροφήταις οἱ πατέρες αὐτῶν.
26Woe to you when all people[177] speak well of you, for the same their ancestors did to the false prophets.

Love Your Enemies

Lk 6:27 Ἀλλὰ ὑμῖν λέγω τοῖς ἀκούουσιν, Ἀγαπᾶτε τοὺς ἐχθροὺς ὑμῶν, καλῶς ποιεῖτε τοῖς μισοῦσιν ὑμᾶς,
27"But I say to you who are listening, love your enemies, treat well the ones hating you,
Lk 6:28 εὐλογεῖτε τοὺς καταρωμένους ὑμᾶς, προσεύχεσθε περὶ τῶν ἐπηρεαζόντων ὑμᾶς.
28bless the ones cursing you, pray for the ones insulting you.
Lk 6:29 Τῷ τύπτοντί σε ἐπὶ τὴν σιαγόνα, πάρεχε καὶ τὴν ἄλλην• καὶ ἀπὸ τοῦ αἴροντός σου τὸ ἱμάτιον, καὶ τὸν χιτῶνα μὴ κωλύσῃς.
29To the one striking you on the cheek, offer the other cheek also. And the person taking your jacket, do not prevent him from taking your shirt as well.
Lk 6:30 Παντὶ αἰτοῦντί σε δίδου• καὶ ἀπὸ τοῦ αἴροντος τὰ σὰ μὴ ἀπαίτει.
30To everyone asking you, give, and from the one forcefully taking your things, do not demand them back.
Lk 6:31 Καὶ καθὼς θέλετε ἵνα ποιῶσιν ὑμῖν οἱ ἄνθρωποι, ὑμεῖς ποιεῖτε αὐτοῖς ὁμοίως.
31And just as you wish people would do to you, do likewise to them.
Lk 6:32 Καὶ εἰ ἀγαπᾶτε τοὺς ἀγαπῶντας ὑμᾶς, ποία ὑμῖν χάρις ἐστίν; Καὶ γὰρ οἱ ἁμαρτωλοὶ τοὺς ἀγαπῶντας αὐτοὺς ἀγαπῶσιν.
32"And if you love the ones loving you, what credit is that to you? For the sinners also love the ones loving them.
Lk 6:33 Καὶ ἐὰν ἀγαθοποιῆτε τοὺς ἀγαθοποιοῦντας ὑμᾶς, ποία ὑμῖν χάρις ἐστίν; Καὶ οἱ ἁμαρτωλοὶ τὸ αὐτὸ ποιοῦσιν.
33And if you do good to the ones doing good to you, what credit is that to you? The sinners also do the same.
Lk 6:34 Καὶ ἐὰν δανίσητε παρ' ὧν ἐλπίζετε λαβεῖν, ποία ὑμῖν χάρις ἐστίν; Καὶ ἁμαρτωλοὶ ἁμαρτωλοῖς δανίζουσιν, ἵνα ἀπολάβωσιν τὰ ἴσα.
34And if you lend to the ones from whom you foresee repayment, what credit is that to you? Sinners also lend to sinners, in such a way they may receive the equal back.

---

177 **6:26** txt παντες οι ανθρωποι $\mathfrak{P}^{75}$ A B E H K M P Q R U X Θ Π Ξ Ψ 0135 0211 f^{1} 2^{c} 22 33 69 124 174 346 565 579 700 788 892^{mg} 1071 1241 1342 1424 1689 $\mathfrak{M}$-650 Lat cop^{sa,bomss} TR SBL TH NA28 {\} ‖ παντες ανθρωποι W 13 543 826 828 983 ‖ οι ανθρωποι παντες ℵ ‖ οι ανθρωποι D L S Y Γ Δ Ω 2* 28 157 892* $\mathfrak{M}$-997 vg^{CL} syr^{s,p} cop^{bomss} Marcion^{txt} RP ‖ *lac* C F G N T

Lk 6:35 Πλὴν ἀγαπᾶτε τοὺς ἐχθροὺς ὑμῶν, καὶ ἀγαθοποιεῖτε, καὶ δανίζετε, μηδὲν ἀπελπίζοντες· καὶ ἔσται ὁ μισθὸς ὑμῶν πολύς, καὶ ἔσεσθε υἱοὶ ὑψίστου· ὅτι αὐτὸς χρηστός ἐστιν ἐπὶ τοὺς ἀχαρίστους καὶ πονηρούς.

35But love your enemies, and do good and lend, expecting nothing, and great will be your reward, and you will be children of the Most High, for he is kind to the unthankful and evil.

Lk 6:36 Γίνεσθε οἰκτίρμονες, καθὼς ὁ πατὴρ ὑμῶν οἰκτίρμων ἐστίν.

36Be compassionate, just as your Father is compassionate.[178]

The Law of Reciprocity

Lk 6:37 Μὴ κρίνετε, καὶ οὐ μὴ κριθῆτε. Μὴ καταδικάζετε, καὶ οὐ μὴ καταδικασθῆτε· ἀπολύετε, καὶ ἀπολυθήσεσθε·

37"Do not be judgmental, and you will not be judged. Do not be condemning, and you will not be condemned. Be forgiving, and you will be forgiven.

Lk 6:38 δίδοτε, καὶ δοθήσεται ὑμῖν· μέτρον καλόν, πεπιεσμένον σεσαλευμένον ὑπερεκχυννόμενον δώσουσιν εἰς τὸν κόλπον ὑμῶν. Ὧι γὰρ μέτρῳ ᾧ μετρεῖτε ἀντιμετρηθήσεται ὑμῖν.

38"Be giving, and it will be given to you. A generous container: compacted, shaken[179] and running over they will hand into your arms. For with the standard you measure out, it will be measured back to you."

Correcting Others

Lk 6:39 Εἶπεν δὲ καὶ παραβολὴν αὐτοῖς, Μήτι δύναται τυφλὸς τυφλὸν ὁδηγεῖν; Οὐχὶ ἀμφότεροι εἰς βόθυνον ἐμπεσοῦνται;

39And he also spoke a parable to them: "Can a blind person lead a blind person? Will they not both fall into a ditch?

Lk 6:40 Οὐκ ἔστιν μαθητὴς ὑπὲρ τὸν διδάσκαλον κατηρτισμένος δὲ πᾶς ἔσται ὡς ὁ διδάσκαλος αὐτοῦ.

40A student is not above the teacher, but rather, every student when fully trained will be like his teacher.

Lk 6:41 Τί δὲ βλέπεις τὸ κάρφος τὸ ἐν τῷ ὀφθαλμῷ τοῦ ἀδελφοῦ σου, τὴν δὲ δοκὸν τὴν ἐν τῷ ἰδίῳ ὀφθαλμῷ οὐ κατανοεῖς;

41Why do you look at the speck in your brother's eye, but the log that is in your own eye you do not consider?

Lk 6:42 Πῶς δύνασαι λέγειν τῷ ἀδελφῷ σου, Ἀδελφέ, ἄφες ἐκβάλω τὸ κάρφος τὸ ἐν τῷ ὀφθαλμῷ σου, αὐτὸς τὴν ἐν τῷ ὀφθαλμῷ σου δοκὸν οὐ βλέπων; Ὑποκριτά, ἔκβαλε πρῶτον τὴν δοκὸν ἐκ τοῦ ὀφθαλμοῦ σου, καὶ τότε διαβλέψεις τὸ κάρφος τὸ ἐν τῷ ὀφθαλμῷ τοῦ ἀδελφοῦ σου ἐκβαλεῖν.

42How are you able to say to your brother, 'Brother, allow me to take out the speck that is in your eye,' while you are not seeing the log that is in your own

---

178 **6:36** Exodus 34:6-7; Psalm 103:8-14; Joel 2:13; Jonah 4:10-11

179 **6:38** In other words, settled. Along with being pressed down and compacted, the container would be holding the most it possibly could.

eye? You hypocrite, first get the log out of your own eye, and then you will see clearly the speck that is in your brother's eye, to remove it.[180]

A Tree and its Fruit

Lk 6:43 Οὐ γάρ ἐστιν δένδρον καλὸν ποιοῦν καρπὸν σαπρόν• οὐδὲ πάλιν δένδρον σαπρὸν ποιοῦν καρπὸν καλόν.

43"Now there is no good tree producing bad fruit, nor again a bad tree producing good fruit.

Lk 6:44 Ἕκαστον γὰρ δένδρον ἐκ τοῦ ἰδίου καρποῦ γινώσκεται. Οὐ γὰρ ἐξ ἀκανθῶν συλλέγουσιν σῦκα, οὐδὲ ἐκ βάτου σταφυλὴν τρυγῶσιν.

44For each tree is known by its own fruit. For they do not gather figs from thornbushes, neither do they pick a grape from a brier.

Lk 6:45 Ὁ ἀγαθὸς ἄνθρωπος ἐκ τοῦ ἀγαθοῦ θησαυροῦ τῆς καρδίας προφέρει τὸ ἀγαθόν, καὶ ὁ πονηρὸς ἐκ τοῦ πονηροῦ προφέρει τὸ πονηρόν• ἐκ γὰρ περισσεύματος καρδίας λαλεῖ τὸ στόμα αὐτοῦ.

45"The good person, out of the good stockpile of his heart, brings forth good, and the evil person out of the evil, brings forth evil. For out of the abundance of the heart one's mouth speaks.

The Two Kinds of Builders

Lk 6:46 Τί δέ με καλεῖτε, Κύριε, κύριε, καὶ οὐ ποιεῖτε ἃ λέγω;

46"And why do you keep calling me 'Lord, Lord,' and yet not do the things which I say?

Lk 6:47 Πᾶς ὁ ἐρχόμενος πρός με καὶ ἀκούων μου τῶν λόγων καὶ ποιῶν αὐτούς, ὑποδείξω ὑμῖν τίνι ἐστὶν ὅμοιος•

47Anyone who comes to me and hears my words and does them, I will show you what that person is like.

Lk 6:48 ὅμοιός ἐστιν ἀνθρώπῳ οἰκοδομοῦντι οἰκίαν, ὃς ἔσκαψεν καὶ ἐβάθυνεν, καὶ ἔθηκεν θεμέλιον ἐπὶ τὴν πέτραν• πλημμύρης δὲ γενομένης, προσέρηξεν ὁ ποταμὸς τῇ οἰκίᾳ ἐκείνῃ, καὶ οὐκ ἴσχυσεν σαλεῦσαι αὐτήν• διὰ τὸ καλῶς οἰκοδομῆσθαι αὐτήν.

48That person is like a man building a house, who dug and deepened and laid a foundation on the rock. And when a flood occurred, the river dashed against that house, but was not able to shake it, because it was well built.

---

[180] **6:42** Note that Jesus is not forbidding the correcting of others, nor telling us not to remove a speck from someone else's eye. But strangely enough, that is how many people interpret this passage. Rather, what this passage is saying is that we whould examine ourselves before we correct others. And then do correct others. See Luke 17:3, and several other passages in the New Testament.

Lk 6:49 Ὁ δὲ ἀκούσας καὶ μὴ ποιήσας ὅμοιός ἐστιν ἀνθρώπῳ οἰκοδομήσαντι οἰκίαν ἐπὶ τὴν γῆν χωρὶς θεμελίου• ᾗ προσέρηξεν ὁ ποταμός, καὶ εὐθὺς συνέπεσεν, καὶ ἐγένετο τὸ ῥῆγμα τῆς οἰκίας ἐκείνης μέγα.

49"But the one who has heard them and not done them, is like a man who built a house on the ground without a foundation, against which dashed the river, and very soon it collapsed, and the destruction of that house was great."

Chapter 7

One Centurion's Faith with Authority

Lk 7:1 Ἐπειδὴ δὲ ἐπλήρωσεν πάντα τὰ ῥήματα αὐτοῦ εἰς τὰς ἀκοὰς τοῦ λαοῦ, εἰσῆλθεν εἰς Καφαρναούμ.

1When he had finished all his sayings in the ears of the people, he entered Capernaum.

Lk 7:2 Ἑκατοντάρχου δέ τινος δοῦλος κακῶς ἔχων ἤμελλεν τελευτᾷν, ὃς ἦν αὐτῷ ἔντιμος.

2And the slave of a certain centurion,[181] who was very valuable to him, was sick and about to die.

Lk 7:3 Ἀκούσας δὲ περὶ τοῦ Ἰησοῦ, ἀπέστειλεν πρὸς αὐτὸν πρεσβυτέρους τῶν Ἰουδαίων, ἐρωτῶν αὐτὸν ὅπως ἐλθὼν διασώσῃ τὸν δοῦλον αὐτοῦ.

3And having heard about Jesus, he sent elders of the Jews to him, asking him to come and heal his slave.

Lk 7:4 Οἱ δέ, παραγενόμενοι πρὸς τὸν Ἰησοῦν, παρεκάλουν αὐτὸν σπουδαίως, λέγοντες ὅτι Ἄξιός ἐστιν ᾧ παρέξῃ τοῦτο•

4So when they came to Jesus, they were pleading earnestly with him, saying, "He is worthy that[182] you confer this upon him,

Lk 7:5 ἀγαπᾷ γὰρ τὸ ἔθνος ἡμῶν, καὶ τὴν συναγωγὴν αὐτὸς ᾠκοδόμησεν ἡμῖν.

5for he loves our nation, and he built us the synagogue."

Lk 7:6 Ὁ δὲ Ἰησοῦς ἐπορεύετο σὺν αὐτοῖς. Ἤδη δὲ αὐτοῦ οὐ μακρὰν ἀπέχοντος ἀπὸ τῆς οἰκίας, ἔπεμψεν φίλους ὁ ἑκατοντάρχης, λέγων αὐτῷ, Κύριε, μὴ σκύλλου• οὐ γάρ ἱκανός εἰμι ἵνα ὑπὸ τὴν στέγην μου εἰσέλθῃς•

6So Jesus went with them. And when he was not far from the house, the centurion sent friends saying to him as follows: "Lord, don't trouble yourself, for I am not fit that you should enter under my roof.

Lk 7:7 διὸ οὐδὲ ἐμαυτὸν ἠξίωσα πρός σε ἐλθεῖν•ἀλλὰ εἰπὲ λόγῳ, καὶ ἰαθήτω ὁ παῖς μου.

7So also neither did I consider myself worthy to come to you. But say with a word that my slave must be healed.[183]

---

181 **7:2** A Roman military officer commanding from 50 to 100 men, 100 if the cohort was a complete one. A full cohort— 1,000 men, would have ten *centurions*, each commanding 100 of the men.

182 **7:4** Interestingly, this message from the Roman centurion in Luke 7:4 contains a Latinism in the Greek. In the phrase Ἄξιός ἐστιν ᾧ παρεξῃ τοῦτο, the use of the relative pronoun instead of the customary ἵνα (hina) is a Latinism: *dignus qui* with the subjunctive.

Lk 7:8 Καὶ γὰρ ἐγὼ ἄνθρωπός εἰμι ὑπὸ ἐξουσίαν τασσόμενος, ἔχων ὑπ' ἐμαυτὸν στρατιώτας, καὶ λέγω τούτῳ, Πορεύθητι, καὶ πορεύεται• καὶ ἄλλῳ, Ἔρχου, καὶ ἔρχεται• καὶ τῷ δούλῳ μου, Ποίησον τοῦτο, καὶ ποιεῖ.

8For I too am a man stationed under authority, having soldiers under myself. And I say to this one, 'Go,' and he goes; and to another, 'Come,' and he comes; and to my slave, 'Do this,' and he does."

Lk 7:9 Ἀκούσας δὲ ταῦτα ὁ Ἰησοῦς ἐθαύμασεν αὐτόν, καὶ στραφεὶς τῷ ἀκολουθοῦντι αὐτῷ ὄχλῳ εἶπεν, Λέγω ὑμῖν, οὐδὲ ἐν τῷ Ἰσραὴλ τοσαύτην πίστιν εὗρον.

9And when Jesus heard these words, he was amazed at him, and turning to the crowd following him, he said, "I tell you, Not in Israel have I found such faith."

Lk 7:10 Καὶ ὑποστρέψαντεςεὶς τὸν οἶκον οἱ πεμφθέντες εὗρον τὸν δοῦλον ὑγιαίνοντα.

10And when the ones who had been sent returned to the house, they found the slave well.

Jesus Raises a Dead Man at Nain

Lk 7:11 Καὶ ἐγένετο ἐν τῇ ἑξῆς, ἐπορεύθη εἰς πόλιν καλουμένην Ναΐν• καὶ συνεπορεύοντο αὐτῷ οἱ μαθηταὶ αὐτοῦ καὶ ὄχλος πολύς.

11And it came about that on the next day, he went into a town called Nain, and his disciples and a large crowd went along with him.

---

183 **7:7** The Greek verb for heal here, ἰάομαι, is in the 3rd person, singular, aorist, imperative, passive form, ἰαθήτω. This is difficult to construe, and that is why later copyists changed it to the simple future indicative passive form ἰαθήσεται in conformity with the Matthew account in 8:8. Perhaps the copyists thought that the imperative form reflected badly on the centurion as being too demanding, as thus: "Say in a word, and let my servant be healed." And if the copyists felt a desire to do this, it is also very possible that here is an instance of Matthew making more palatable the Greek of a written Greek original *Spruchquelle* as compared to Luke's more conservative and word for word reproduction, rather than the scenario that Matthew translated the Aramaic of an Aramaic Spruchquelle into the future indicative in Greek, but Luke into the aorist imperative. As for the word 'and' here, καί, it is here used as an explicative καί and introducing a command in indirect quotation; in other words, to particularize the word to be spoken, as thus: "But say in a word, namely, that my slave be healed." This use of καί is not terribly uncommon in the New Testament, and this rendering preserves an imperative mood. Moreover, it is preceded here by εἶπον, which regularly precedes discourse. As for the centurion's peremptory tone, how remarkable is it that a soldier, and a commanding officer at that, would have that kind of personality? He was a bold man, but he humbled his tone well enough by twice stating that he was not worthy. It is commendable to be bold in this way, as indeed the Lord commended him for it. But how bold really was it? For after all, he had heard that Jesus was already doing such things as he was requesting, and was doing it for everybody who asked, and also some who did not ask. So it wasn't so bold and demanding after all, with the exception of expecting the same for a Gentile, which he covered by admitting his unfitness.

Lk 7:12 Ὡς δὲ ἤγγισεν τῇ πύλῃ τῆς πόλεως, καὶ ἰδού, ἐξεκομίζετο τεθνηκώς, μονογενὴς υἱὸς τῇ μητρὶ αὐτοῦ, καὶ αὐτὴ ἦν χήρα· καὶ ὄχλος τῆς πόλεως ἱκανὸς ἦν σὺν αὐτῇ.

12And as he approached the town gate, behold, a dead person was being carried out, the only son of his mother, and she was a widow. And a considerable crowd from the town was with her.

Lk 7:13 Καὶ ἰδὼν αὐτὴν ὁ κύριος ἐσπλαγχνίσθη ἐπ' αὐτῇ, καὶ εἶπεν αὐτῇ, Μὴ κλαῖε.

13When he saw her, the Lord was moved with pity for her, and he said to her, "Don't cry."

Lk 7:14 Καὶ προσελθὼν ἥψατο τῆς σοροῦ· οἱ δὲ βαστάζοντες ἔστησαν. Καὶ εἶπεν, Νεανίσκε, σοὶ λέγω, ἐγέρθητι.

14And he went up to the coffin and touched it, and the pallbearers stood still. And he said, "Young man, I say to you, rise up!"

Lk 7:15 Καὶ ἀνεκάθισεν ὁ νεκρός, καὶ ἤρξατο λαλεῖν. Καὶ ἔδωκεν αὐτὸν τῇ μητρὶ αὐτοῦ.

15And the dead man sat up, and began to speak. And he gave him back to his mother.

Lk 7:16 Ἔλαβεν δὲ φόβος πάντας, καὶ ἐδόξαζον τὸν θεόν, λέγοντες ὅτι Προφήτης μέγας ἠγέρθη ἐν ἡμῖν, καὶ ὅτι Ἐπεσκέψατο ὁ θεὸς τὸν λαὸν αὐτοῦ.

16And fear took hold of all, and they praised God, saying, "A great prophet has been raised up among us," and, "God has come to help his people."

Lk 7:17 Καὶ ἐξῆλθεν ὁ λόγος οὗτος ἐν ὅλῃ τῇ Ἰουδαίᾳ περὶ αὐτοῦ, καὶ πάσῃ τῇ περιχώρῳ.

17And this news about him spread throughout the land of the Jews and the surrounding country.

Jesus and John the Baptizer

Lk 7:18 Καὶ ἀπήγγειλαν Ἰωάννῃ οἱ μαθηταὶ αὐτοῦ περὶ πάντων τούτων. Καὶ προσκαλεσάμενος δύο τινὰς τῶν μαθητῶν αὐτοῦ ὁ Ἰωάννης

18And John's disciples reported to him about all these things. And after calling two of his disciples to him, John

Lk 7:19 ἔπεμψεν πρὸς τὸν κύριον, λέγων, Σὺ εἶ ὁ ἐρχόμενος, ἢ ἄλλον προσδοκῶμεν;

19sent word to the Lord, as follows: "Are you the one who was to come, or should we expect another?"

Lk 7:20 Παραγενόμενοι δὲ πρὸς αὐτὸν οἱ ἄνδρες εἶπαν, Ἰωάννης ὁ βαπτιστὴς ἀπέστειλεν ἡμᾶς πρός σε, λέγων, Σὺ εἶ ὁ ἐρχόμενος, ἢ ἄλλον προσδοκῶμεν;

20And when they had come to him, the men said, "John the Baptizer sent us to you saying, 'Are you the one who was to come, or should we expect another?'"

Lk 7:21 Ἐν ἐκείνῃ τῇ ὥρᾳ ἐθεράπευσεν πολλοὺς ἀπὸ νόσων καὶ μαστίγων καὶ πνευμάτων πονηρῶν, καὶ τυφλοῖς πολλοῖς ἐχαρίσατο βλέπειν.

21In that same hour he healed many *people* of diseases and sicknesses and evil spirits, and gave sight to many who were blind.

Lk 7:22 Καὶ ἀποκριθεὶς εἶπεν αὐτοῖς, Πορευθέντες ἀπαγγείλατε Ἰωάννῃ ἃ εἴδετε καὶ ἠκούσατε• τυφλοὶ ἀναβλέπουσιν, χωλοὶ περιπατοῦσιν, λεπροὶ καθαρίζονται, καὶ κωφοὶ ἀκούουσιν, νεκροὶ ἐγείρονται, πτωχοὶ εὐαγγελίζονται•

22And in answer, he said to them, "Go and report back to John what things you saw and heard: The blind see again, the lame walk, the lepers are cleansed, the deaf hear, the dead are raised, and good news is preached to the poor.

Lk 7:23 καὶ μακάριός ἐστιν, ὃς ἐὰν μὴ σκανδαλισθῇ ἐν ἐμοί.

23And *tell him*, 'Blessed be whoever is not offended on account of me.' "[184]

Lk 7:24 Ἀπελθόντων δὲ τῶν ἀγγέλων Ἰωάννου, ἤρξατο λέγειν τοῖς πρὸς τοὺς ὄχλους περὶ Ἰωάννου, Τί ἐξήλθατε εἰς τὴν ἔρημον θεάσασθαι; Κάλαμον ὑπὸ ἀνέμου σαλευόμενον;

24And as John's messengers were leaving, he began to speak to the crowd about John: "What did you go out into the desert to see? A reed getting swayed to and fro by the wind?

Lk 7:25 Ἀλλὰ τί ἐξήλθατε ἰδεῖν; Ἄνθρωπον ἐν μαλακοῖς ἱματίοις ἠμφιεσμένον; Ἰδού, οἱ ἐν ἱματισμῷ ἐνδόξῳ καὶ τρυφῇ ὑπάρχοντες ἐν τοῖς βασιλείοις εἰσίν.

25On the contrary, what did you go out to see? A man dressed in delicate clothes? Behold, those in expensive clothes and living in luxury are in royal palaces.

Lk 7:26 Ἀλλὰ τί ἐξήλθατε ἰδεῖν; Προφήτην; Ναί, λέγω ὑμῖν, καὶ περισσότερον προφήτου.

26On the contrary, what did you go out to see? A prophet? Yes indeed I tell you, and more than a prophet.

Lk 7:27 Οὗτός ἐστιν περὶ οὗ γέγραπται, Ἰδού, ἀποστέλλω τὸν ἄγγελόν μου πρὸ προσώπου σου, ὃς κατασκευάσει τὴν ὁδόν σου ἔμπροσθέν σου.

27This is the one about whom it is written: 'Behold, I am sending my messenger before your face, who will prepare your way before you.'[185]

---

[184] **7:23** Why did Jesus tell John this? Would John be offended by all the good works here recently listed? Not likely. It is more likely that what John would be offended by was Jesus' non-abstentious lifestyle, or even what in John the ascetic's view might be "shady" practices. John had already testified earlier, emphatically and with certainty, that Jesus was the Expected One. But now it appears, John was having his doubts about him. Jesus was apparently a contrast to John in the following: He did not worry too much about ceremonial washing (Diatess 5:45, 14:1-10; 5:25; Matt. 15:1-20; Mark 7:1-23; John 3:25,26, John 2:6). He de-emphasized the concept of clean v. unclean foods (Diatess 14:9; Matt. 15:11,17; Mark 7:15-19). He did not fast, or at least did not teach his disciples to fast (Diatess. 7:24; Matt. 9:14; Mark 2:18; Luke 5:33). He drank alcohol, enabling Pharisees to dare call him a "drunkard," (Luke 7:33, 34; Matt. 11:18-19; Diatess. 10:30). He associated with "shady" characters (Diatess 7:22, 10:30, 10:35-36, 21:1, 24:19; Matt. 9:11; Mark 2:16; Luke 5:30; Matt. 11:19; Luke 7:34, 7:39, 15:1-2, 19:7). He violated the Sabbath by allowing his disciples to husk grain (Mark 2:23-28; Matt. 12:1-8; Lk 6:1-5). He did not pay the two-drachma tax, except for only the 2 people who were discovered, out of the total of 13 in his party (Diatess. 17:22-26; Matt. 17:24-27. On this tax, which was voluntary at best, and illegal at worst, see the endnote in my translation of the gospel of Matthew). It remains today, that some who consider themselves righteous are offended by these truths about Jesus' lifestyle. But "Blessed be whoever is not offended on account of me." "For the kingdom of God is not a matter of eating and drinking, but of righteousness, peace, and joy in the Holy Spirit." Romans 14:17

[185] **7:27** This quote appears to be a blend of Exodus 23:20 and Malachi 3:1.

Lk 7:28 Λέγω ὑμῖν, μείζων ἐν γεννητοῖς γυναικῶν Ἰωάννου τοῦ βαπτιστοῦ οὐδείς ἐστιν• ὁ δὲ μικρότερος ἐν τῇ βασιλείᾳ τοῦ θεοῦ μείζων αὐτοῦ ἐστιν.

28I tell you, among those born of women, no one is greater than John the Baptizer. Yet the one who is least in the kingdom of God is greater than he."

Lk 7:29 Καὶ πᾶς ὁ λαὸς ἀκούσας καὶ οἱ τελῶναι ἐδικαίωσαν τὸν θεόν, βαπτισθέντες τὸ βάπτισμα Ἰωάννου•

29(And all the people who heard, even the revenue agents, vindicated God, having been baptized with the baptism of John.

Lk 7:30 οἱ δὲ Φαρισαῖοι καὶ οἱ νομικοὶ τὴν βουλὴν τοῦ θεοῦ ἠθέτησαν εἰς ἑαυτούς, μὴ βαπτισθέντες ὑπ' αὐτοῦ.

30But the Pharisees and the lawyers, not baptized by him, rejected the purpose of God for themselves.)

Lk 7:31 Τίνι οὖν ὁμοιώσω τοὺς ἀνθρώπους τῆς γενεᾶς ταύτης, καὶ τίνι εἰσὶν ὅμοιοι;

31"To what, then, shall I compare the people of this generation? And what are they like?

Lk 7:32 Ὅμοιοί εἰσιν παιδίοις τοῖς ἐν ἀγορᾷ καθημένοις, καὶ προσφωνοῦσιν ἀλλήλοις, καὶ λέγουσιν, Ηὐλήσαμεν ὑμῖν, καὶ οὐκ ὠρχήσασθε• ἐθρηνήσαμεν, καὶ οὐκ ἐκλαύσατε.

32They are like children sitting in the marketplace and calling out to one another and saying: 'We played the flute for you, and you didn't dance; we sang a dirge, and you didn't cry.'

Lk 7:33 Ἐλήλυθεν γὰρ Ἰωάννης ὁ βαπτιστὴς μὴ ἐσθίων ἄρτον μήτε πίνων οἶνον, καὶ λέγετε, Δαιμόνιον ἔχει•

33For John the Baptizer came neither eating bread nor drinking wine, and you say, 'He has a demon.'

Lk 7:34 ἐλήλυθεν ὁ υἱὸς τοῦ ἀνθρώπου ἐσθίων καὶ πίνων, καὶ λέγετε, Ἰδού, ἄνθρωπος φάγος καὶ οἰνοπότης, φίλος τελωνῶν καὶ ἁμαρτωλῶν.

34The Son of Man came eating and drinking, and you say, 'Behold a glutton and a drunkard, a friend of revenue agents and sinners.'

Lk 7:35 Καὶ ἐδικαιώθη ἡ σοφία ἀπὸ πάντων τῶν τέκνων αὐτῆς.

35Regardless, wisdom is vindicated by all her children."[186]

A Prostitute Washes Jesus' Feet with her Tears

Lk 7:36 Ἠρώτα δέ τις αὐτὸν τῶν Φαρισαίων ἵνα φάγῃ μετ' αὐτοῦ• καὶ εἰσελθὼν εἰς τὸν οἶκον τοῦ Φαρισαίου κατεκλίθη.

36But one of the Pharisees asked him to eat with him, and he went to the Pharisee's house and reclined.[187]

---

[186] **7:35** Greek: τέκνων; perhaps a misunderstanding of the Aramaic for "works." Which would make sense: emphasis on ALL. You have to look at ALL the works of a person, not judge on superficial things like eating and drinking, which in fact Paul says in Romans 14:17, but of righteousness, peace, and joy in the Holy Spirit.

[187] **7:36** In that time and culture, those eating a meal lay on a futon of sorts, on their sides and resting on an elbow, with their feet off the floor. That is how the woman could both stand behind him at his feet, and wipe his feet with her hair.

Lk 7:37 Καὶ ἰδού, γυνὴ ἥτις ἦν ἐν τῇ πόλει ἁμαρτωλός, καὶ ἐπιγνοῦσα ὅτι κατάκειται ἐν τῇ οἰκίᾳ τοῦ Φαρισαίου, κομίσασα ἀλάβαστρον μύρου,

37And behold, a woman who was being a sinner in that town came, who having learned that he is reclining at the Pharisee's house, had brought an alabaster bottle of perfume,

Lk 7:38 καὶ στᾶσα ὀπίσω παρὰ τοὺς πόδας αὐτοῦ κλαίουσα τοῖς δάκρυσιν ἤρξατο βρέχειν τοὺς πόδας αὐτοῦ καὶ ταῖς θριξὶν τῆς κεφαλῆς αὐτῆς ἐξέμασσεν, καὶ κατεφίλει τοὺς πόδας αὐτοῦ, καὶ ἤλειφεν τῷ μύρῳ.

38and appeared behind Jesus, weeping at his feet. And with the tears she began to bathe his feet. And with the hairs of her head she was wiping off, and earnestly kissing his feet, and anointing them with the perfume.

Lk 7:39 Ἰδὼν δὲ ὁ Φαρισαῖος ὁ καλέσας αὐτὸν εἶπεν ἐν ἑαυτῷ λέγων, Οὗτος, εἰ ἦν προφήτης, ἐγίνωσκεν ἂν τίς καὶ ποταπὴ ἡ γυνὴ ἥτις ἅπτεται αὐτοῦ, ὅτι ἁμαρτωλός ἐστιν.

39When the Pharisee who had invited him saw this, he thought to himself as follows, "If this man were a prophet, he would know who and of what sort is the woman touching him— that she is a sinner."

Lk 7:40 Καὶ ἀποκριθεὶς ὁ Ἰησοῦς εἶπεν πρὸς αὐτόν, Σίμων, ἔχω σοί τι εἰπεῖν. Ὁ δέ, Διδάσκαλε, εἰπέ, φησίν.

40And Jesus spoke up, and said to him, "Simon, I have something to tell you." "Tell me, teacher," he says.

Lk 7:41 Δύο χρεοφειλέται ἦσαν δανιστῇ τινι• ὁ εἷς ὤφειλεν δηνάρια πεντακόσια, ὁ δὲ ἕτερος πεντήκοντα.

41"Two men were debtors to a certain moneylender. One owed five hundred denarii,[188] and the other fifty.

Lk 7:42 Μὴ ἐχόντων δὲ αὐτῶν ἀποδοῦναι ἀμφοτέροις ἐχαρίσατο. Τίς οὖν αὐτῶν πλεῖον ἀγαπήσει αὐτόν;

42And as they did not have the money to pay him back, he freely forgave them both. Now which of them will love him more?"

Lk 7:43 Ἀποκριθεὶς Σίμων εἶπεν, Ὑπολαμβάνω ὅτι ᾧ τὸ πλεῖον ἐχαρίσατο. Ὁ δὲ εἶπεν αὐτῷ, Ὀρθῶς ἔκρινας.

43In answer Simon said, "I suppose the one whom he freely forgave more." And he said to him, "You have judged correctly."

Lk 7:44 Καὶ στραφεὶς πρὸς τὴν γυναῖκα, τῷ Σίμωνι ἔφη, Βλέπεις ταύτην τὴν γυναῖκα; Εἰσῆλθόν σου εἰς τὴν οἰκίαν, ὕδωρ μοι ἐπὶ πόδας οὐκ ἔδωκας• αὕτη δὲ τοῖς δάκρυσιν ἔβρεξέν μου τοὺς πόδας, καὶ ταῖς θριξὶν αὐτῆς ἐξέμαξεν.

44And turning toward the woman, he was saying to Simon, "Do you see this woman? Your house I entered. Water you did not give me for my feet, but this woman bathed my feet with her tears, and wiped them off with her hair.

Lk 7:45 Φίλημά μοι οὐκ ἔδωκας• αὕτη δέ, ἀφ' ἧς εἰσῆλθον, οὐ διέλιπεν καταφιλοῦσά μου τοὺς πόδας.

45A kiss you did not give me, but this woman, from the time I entered, has not stopped earnestly kissing my feet.

---

188 **7:41** A *denarius* was a coin worth about a day's wages.

Lk 7:46 Ἐλαίῳ τὴν κεφαλήν μου οὐκ ἤλειψας· αὕτη δὲ μύρῳ ἤλειψέν τοὺς πόδας μου.

46With oil you did not anoint my head, but this woman with perfume anointed my feet.

Lk 7:47 Οὗ χάριν, λέγω σοι, ἀφέωνται αἱ ἁμαρτίαι αὐτῆς αἱ πολλαί, ὅτι ἠγάπησεν πολύ· ᾧ δὲ ὀλίγον ἀφίεται, ὀλίγον ἀγαπᾷ.

47For which reason, I tell you, her many sins have been forgiven, that she loved much. But someone who has been forgiven little, loves little."[189]

Lk 7:48 Εἶπεν δὲ αὐτῇ, Ἀφέωνταί σου αἱ ἁμαρτίαι.

48And he said to her, "Your sins are forgiven."

Lk 7:49 Καὶ ἤρξαντο οἱ συνανακείμενοι λέγειν ἐν ἑαυτοῖς, Τίς οὗτός ἐστιν ὃς καὶ ἁμαρτίας ἀφίησιν;

49And those reclining with him began to say to themselves, "Who is this who even forgives sins?"

Lk 7:50 Εἶπεν δὲ πρὸς τὴν γυναῖκα, Ἡ πίστις σου σέσωκέν σε· πορεύου εἰς εἰρήνην.

50But he said to the woman, "Your faith has saved you. Go with peace."

Chapter 8

Jesus' Financiers

Lk 8:1 Καὶ ἐγένετο ἐν τῷ καθεξῆς, καὶ αὐτὸς διώδευεν κατὰ πόλιν καὶ κώμην, κηρύσσων καὶ εὐαγγελιζόμενος τὴν βασιλείαν τοῦ θεοῦ· καὶ οἱ δώδεκα σὺν αὐτῷ,

1And it came about after this that he traveled about through one city and village after another, proclaiming the good news of the kingdom of God. The Twelve were with him,

Lk 8:2 καὶ γυναῖκές τινες αἳ ἦσαν τεθεραπευμέναι ἀπὸ πνευμάτων πονηρῶν καὶ ἀσθενειῶν, Μαρία ἡ καλουμένη Μαγδαληνή, ἀφ' ἧς δαιμόνια ἑπτὰ ἐξεληλύθει,

2and also some women who had been cured of evil spirits and diseases: Mary, called the Magdalene,[190] from whom seven demons had come out;

---

189 **7:47** Verse 47 is difficult in terms of Greek exegesis, and a translator can't help but be influenced by one's own existing beliefs regarding sin and salvation. Are the woman's many sins forgiven because she loved much? Or does she love much because her many sins are forgiven? Consult the many English translations, and you will be surprised to see which falls on which side of this problem. Nevertheless, a few things are clear: Jesus means to point out that the woman loved more because she was forgiven more. And also clear is where Jesus declared in verse 50 that it was her faith that had saved her. And it was not faith without repentance. For her weeping and humility could indicate repentance, and since Jesus knew the hearts of all humans (John 2:24-25; Diatess. 5:36), he apparently knew that in her was true repentance.

190 **8:2** A *Magdalene is* someone who is from the town of *Magdala*, just as a Seattleite is someone who is from the city of Seattle.

Lk 8:3 καὶ Ἰωάννα γυνὴ Χουζᾶ ἐπιτρόπου Ἡρῴδου, καὶ Σουσάννα, καὶ ἕτεραι πολλαί, αἵτινες διηκόνουν αὐτοῖς ἀπὸ ἐκ τῶν ὑπαρχόντων αὐταῖς.

[3]and Joanna the wife of Kuza, the manager of Herod's household; and Susanna; plus many others; these women were providing for them out of their own means.

The Parable of the Sower

Lk 8:4 Συνιόντος δὲ ὄχλου πολλοῦ, καὶ τῶν κατὰ πόλιν ἐπιπορευομένων πρὸς αὐτόν, εἶπεν διὰ παραβολῆς,

[4]And when a great crowd was coming together, people from every one of those towns coming toward him, he spoke by means of a parable:

Lk 8:5 Ἐξῆλθεν ὁ σπείρων τοῦ σπεῖραι τὸν σπόρον αὐτοῦ. Καὶ ἐν τῷ σπείρειν αὐτόν, ὃ μὲν ἔπεσεν παρὰ τὴν ὁδόν, καὶ κατεπατήθη, καὶ τὰ πετεινὰ τοῦ οὐρανοῦ κατέφαγεν αὐτό.

[5]"The sower went out to sow his seed. And in the process of sowing, some seed fell beside the way and was trampled on, and the birds of the sky devoured it.

Lk 8:6 Καὶ ἕτερον κατέπεσεν ἐπὶ τὴν πέτραν, καὶ φυὲν ἐξηράνθη, διὰ τὸ μὴ ἔχειν ἰκμάδα.

[6]And other seed fell on rock, and after it grew, it withered, having no way to get moisture.

Lk 8:7 Καὶ ἕτερον ἔπεσεν ἐν μέσῳ τῶν ἀκανθῶν, καὶ συμφυεῖσαι αἱ ἄκανθαι ἀπέπνιξαν αὐτό.

[7]And other seed fell in the midst of thorns, and the thorns grew up and choked it.

Lk 8:8 Καὶ ἕτερον ἔπεσεν εἰς τὴν γῆν τὴν ἀγαθήν, καὶ φυὲν ἐποίησεν καρπὸν ἑκατονταπλασίονα. Ταῦτα λέγων ἐφώνει, Ὁ ἔχων ὦτα ἀκούειν ἀκουέτω.

[8]And other seed fell into good soil, and when grown it produced fruit a hundredfold." After he said these things, he called out, "Whoever has ears to hear, hear."

The Parable of the Sower Explained

Lk 8:9 Ἐπηρώτων δὲ αὐτὸν οἱ μαθηταὶ αὐτοῦ τίς αὕτη εἴη ἡ παραβολή,

[9]And his disciples asked him the intent[191] of this parable,

---

191 **8:9** The Greek word is the 3rd person, singular, present, optative form of the verb 'to be.' It says, literally, "What is the being of this parable?" Except in optative mood. "What is this parable supposed to be? Except there must be a word which encompasses both 'meaning' and 'reason for being.' Thus, "What is this parable meant to accomplish?" The word 'essence' comes to mind, but 'essence' does not include the "reason why you speak in parables" idea. The word 'intent' encompasses the meanings "import, significance, and meaning," and also the mood of potential. We know this 'why' meaning must be part of the meaning of the disciples' question, both because of Jesus' answer, explaining 'why' he used parables; and also from the parallel account in Matthew 13:10, where the disciples say simply, "Why do you speak to the people in parables." (In Mark it is very ambiguous.) Luke elsewhere in his Greek uses the word 'to be' for the meaning and intent of impersonal events.

Lk 8:10 ὁ δὲ εἶπεν, Ὑμῖν δέδοται γνῶναι τὰ μυστήρια τῆς βασιλείας τοῦ θεοῦ• τοῖς δὲ λοιποῖς ἐν παραβολαῖς, ἵνα βλέποντες μὴ βλέπωσιν, καὶ ἀκούοντες μὴ συνιῶσιν.

10and he said, "To you it is given such that you will know the mysteries of the kingdom of God, but to the rest in parables,[192] so that, "'Though seeing, they will not see, and though hearing, they will not understand.'[193]

Lk 8:11 Ἔστιν δὲ αὕτη ἡ παραβολή• Ὁ σπόρος ἐστὶν ὁ λόγος τοῦ θεοῦ.

11 "This, then, means the parable: The seed is the word of God.

Lk 8:12 Οἱ δὲ παρὰ τὴν ὁδὸν εἰσὶν οἱ ἀκούσαντες, εἶτα ἔρχεται ὁ διάβολος καὶ αἴρει τὸν λόγον ἀπὸ τῆς καρδίας αὐτῶν, ἵνα μὴ πιστεύσαντες σωθῶσιν.

12And the ones beside the way are those who when they hear, next comes the devil, and takes away the word from their heart, so that they will not believe and be saved.

Lk 8:13 Οἱ δὲ ἐπὶ τῆς πέτρας οἵ, ὅταν ἀκούσωσιν, μετὰ χαρᾶς δέχονται τὸν λόγον, καὶ οὗτοι ῥίζαν οὐκ ἔχουσιν, οἳ πρὸς καιρὸν πιστεύουσιν, καὶ ἐν καιρῷ πειρασμοῦ ἀφίστανται.

13And the ones on the rock are those who when they hear, receive the word with joy. They are also ones who have no root, and believe for a time, and in the time of trial shrink back.

Lk 8:14 Τὸ δὲ εἰς τὰς ἀκάνθας πεσόν, οὗτοί εἰσιν οἱ ἀκούσαντες, καὶ ὑπὸ μεριμνῶν καὶ πλούτου καὶ ἡδονῶν τοῦ βίου πορευόμενοι συμπνίγονται, καὶ οὐ τελεσφοροῦσιν.

14And the seed falling in the thorns, these are those who hear, and as they go, are choked by the worries and riches and pleasures of life, and do not bear fruit to the end.

Lk 8:15 Τὸ δὲ ἐν τῇ καλῇ γῇ, οὗτοί εἰσιν οἵτινες ἐν καρδίᾳ καλῇ καὶ ἀγαθῇ, ἀκούσαντες τὸν λόγον κατέχουσιν, καὶ καρποφοροῦσιν ἐν ὑπομονῇ.

15And the seed in good soil, these are those who when they hear the word, retain it in a good and worthy heart, and bear fruit with perseverance.

Lk 8:16 Οὐδεὶς δὲ λύχνον ἅψας καλύπτει αὐτὸν σκεύει, ἢ ὑποκάτω κλίνης τίθησιν, ἀλλ' ἐπὶ λυχνίας τίθησιν, ἵνα οἱ εἰσπορευόμενοι βλέπωσιν τὸ φῶς.

16Now no one after lighting a lamp covers it with a bucket, or puts it under a bed, but instead puts it on the lamp stand, so that those coming in may see the light.

See for example, Acts 2:12, where in reference to the disciples' speaking in dozens of languages simultaneously, the onlookers say, literally, "What does this wish to be?" But instead of the verb 'to be' in the optative mood, 'to be' is an infinitive, and the verb 'thelo' for 'wish, will' is used with it. However, Luke uses the exact same inflection of this same verb in Luke 3:15 as here in 8:9, where the crowd wonders if John the Baptizer might possibly be the Messiah.

192 **8:10a** Or, "To you it is granted (perfect tense) to know the mysteries of the kingdom of God, but to the rest in parables, so that..." The problem with this latter reading is determining what verb is to be implied or supplied for the phrase "but to the rest in parables." This is why I interpreted the infinitive as one of result: "such that you will know." Then the same idea, that is the idea, "in such a way," easily carries over to the "but to them in parables."

193 **8:10b** Isaiah 6:9

Lk 8:17 Οὐ γάρ ἐστιν κρυπτόν, ὃ οὐ φανερὸν γενήσεται• οὐδὲ ἀπόκρυφον, ὃ οὐ μὴ γνωσθῇ καὶ εἰς φανερὸν ἔλθῃ.

17For there is nothing hidden that will not be made manifest, nor secret, that will not become clearly known, and come into illumination.

Lk 8:18 Βλέπετε οὖν πῶς ἀκούετε• ὃς ἂν γὰρ ἔχῃ, δοθήσεται αὐτῷ• καὶ ὃς ἂν μὴ ἔχῃ, καὶ ὃ δοκεῖ ἔχειν ἀρθήσεται ἀπ' αὐτοῦ.

18Watch therefore how you listen, for whoever has, it will be granted him, and whoever has not, even what he seems to have will be taken away from him."

Jesus' Mother and Brothers

Lk 8:19 Παρεγένετο δὲ πρὸς αὐτὸν ἡ μήτηρ καὶ οἱ ἀδελφοὶ αὐτοῦ, καὶ οὐκ ἠδύναντο συντυχεῖν αὐτῷ διὰ τὸν ὄχλον.

19And his mother and brothers came to him, and were not able to get near him because of the crowd.

Lk 8:20 Ἀπηγγέλη δὲ αὐτῷ, Ἡ μήτηρ σου καὶ οἱ ἀδελφοί σου ἑστήκασιν ἔξω, ἰδεῖν θέλοντές σε.

20And it was reported to him, "Your mother and brothers are standing outside, wanting to see you."

Lk 8:21 Ὁ δὲ ἀποκριθεὶς εἶπεν πρὸς αὐτούς, Μήτηρ μου καὶ ἀδελφοί μου οὗτοί εἰσιν, οἱ τὸν λόγον τοῦ θεοῦ ἀκούοντες καὶ ποιοῦντες.

21But he in answer said to them, "These are my mother and brothers, the ones hearing and doing the word of God."

Jesus Commands the Elements

Lk 8:22 Ἐγένετο δὲ ἐν μιᾷ τῶν ἡμερῶν, καὶ αὐτὸς ἐνέβη εἰς πλοῖον καὶ οἱ μαθηταὶ αὐτοῦ, καὶ εἶπεν πρὸς αὐτούς, Διέλθωμεν εἰς τὸ πέραν τῆς λίμνης. Καὶ ἀνήχθησαν.

22And it came about during one of those days that he and his disciples had gotten into a boat, that he said to them, "Let's cross over to the other side of the lake." And they put out to sea.

Lk 8:23 Πλεόντων δὲ αὐτῶν ἀφύπνωσεν• καὶ κατέβη λαῖλαψ ἀνέμου εἰς τὴν λίμνην, καὶ συνεπληροῦντο, καὶ ἐκινδύνευον.

23And as they sailed, he fell asleep. And a storm of wind came down onto the lake, and they were being swamped, and in great danger.

Lk 8:24 Προσελθόντες δὲ διήγειραν αὐτόν, λέγοντες, Ἐπιστάτα, ἐπιστάτα, ἀπολλύμεθα. Ὁ δὲ διεγερθεὶς ἐπετίμησεν τῷ ἀνέμῳ καὶ τῷ κλύδωνι τοῦ ὕδατος• καὶ ἐπαύσαντο, καὶ ἐγένετο γαλήνη.

24And after approaching him, they roused him, saying, "Master, we are going to die!" And when he was awake, he rebuked the wind, and the roughness of the water, and they stopped, and it was calm.

Lk 8:25 Εἶπεν δὲ αὐτοῖς, Ποῦ ἡ πίστις ὑμῶν; Φοβηθέντες δὲ ἐθαύμασαν, λέγοντες πρὸς ἀλλήλους, Τίς ἄρα οὗτός ἐστιν, ὅτι καὶ τοῖς ἀνέμοις ἐπιτάσσει καὶ τῷ ὕδατι, καὶ ὑπακούουσιν αὐτῷ;
[25]And he said to them, "Where is your faith?" But they were amazed and fearful, saying to one another, "Who then is this? For he even commands the wind and the water, and they obey him!"

The Legion of Demons Near Gadara

Lk 8:26 Καὶ κατέπλευσαν εἰς τὴν χώραν τῶν Γαδαρηνῶν, ἥτις ἐστὶν ἀντιπέρα τῆς Γαλιλαίας.
[26]And they sailed down into the territory of the Gadarenes,[194] which is opposite Galilee.
Lk 8:27 Ἐξελθόντι δὲ αὐτῷ ἐπὶ τὴν γῆν, ὑπήντησεν ἀνήρ τις ἐκ τῆς πόλεως, ἔχων δαιμόνια καὶ χρόνῳ ἱκανῷ οὐκ ἐνεδύσατο ἱμάτιον, καὶ ἐν οἰκίᾳ οὐκ ἔμενεν, ἀλλ' ἐν τοῖς μνήμασιν.
[27]And as he was going on shore, a man from the town met him, demon-possessed, and not having put clothes on for quite some time, and who was living not in a house but in the tombs.
Lk 8:28 Ἰδὼν δὲ τὸν Ἰησοῦν, ἀνακράξας, προσέπεσεν αὐτῷ, καὶ φωνῇ μεγάλῃ εἶπεν, Τί ἐμοὶ καὶ σοί, Ἰησοῦ, υἱὲ τοῦ θεοῦ τοῦ ὑψίστου; Δέομαί σου, μή με βασανίσῃς.
[28]And when he saw Jesus, he fell down before him crying out, and in a loud voice he said: "What business is there between you and me, O Jesus, you son of the Most High God? I beg you, do not torture me!"
Lk 8:29 Παρήγγειλεν γὰρ τῷ πνεύματι τῷ ἀκαθάρτῳ ἐξελθεῖν ἀπὸ τοῦ ἀνθρώπου• πολλοῖς γὰρ χρόνοις συνηρπάκει αὐτόν, καὶ ἐδεσμεύετο ἁλύσεσιν καὶ πέδαις φυλασσόμενος, καὶ διαρρήσσων τὰ δεσμὰ ἠλαύνετο ὑπὸ τοῦ δαιμονίου εἰς τὰς ἐρήμους.
[29]For he was commanding the evil spirit to come out of the man. For many times it had possessed him, and he would be bound with chains and leg irons and guarded, but tearing the bonds apart, he would be driven by the demon into solitary places.
Lk 8:30 Ἐπηρώτησεν δὲ αὐτὸν ὁ Ἰησοῦς, Τί σοι ὄνομά ἐστιν; Ὁ δὲ εἶπεν, Λεγιών, ὅτι εἰσῆλθεν δαιμόνια πολλὰ εἰς αὐτόν.
[30]And Jesus questioned him: "What is your name?" And he said, "Legion.[195]" For many demons had entered into him.

---

194 **8:26** txt γαδαρηνων A E R W 𝔐 syr^{c,s,p,h} Diatess^{syr} mss$^{\text{acc to Or}}$ mss$^{\text{acc to Titus-Bostra}}$ TR RP ‖ γερασηνων 𝔓^{75} B D it$^{a,aur,b,d,e,f,ff^2,l,q,r^1}$ vg syr^{hmg} cop^{sa} mss$^{\text{acc to Or}}$ mss$^{\text{acc to Titus-Bostra}}$ SBL TH NA28 {C} ‖ γεργεσηνων ℵ L Ξ syr^{pal} arm eth geo Diatess^{arm} Or Titus-Bostra Epiph Cyr^{lem} Hesych ‖ *lac* C N P Q T. Note that both syr^{p,h} read Gadarenes in all 3 synoptic gospels. Topographically (the right cliffs, and the prepositional phrase of Lk 8:26, "down to the territory of...which is opposite Galilee"), and culturally (the raising of pigs), Gadarenes is the most likely. I am puzzled why any Bible translation would be content having different cities in different gospels in their version. I settle on Gadarenes for all 3 gospels.

Lk 8:31 Καὶ παρεκάλουν αὐτὸν ἵνα μὴ ἐπιτάξῃ αὐτοῖς εἰς τὴν ἄβυσσον ἀπελθεῖν.

31And they were pleading with him that he not order them to depart into the Abyss.

Lk 8:32 Ἦν δὲ ἐκεῖ ἀγέλη χοίρων ἱκανῶν βοσκομένων ἐν τῷ ὄρει• καὶ παρεκάλεσαν αὐτὸν ἵνα ἐπιτρέψῃ αὐτοῖς εἰς ἐκείνους εἰσελθεῖν. Καὶ ἐπέτρεψεν αὐτοῖς.

32And a considerable herd of pigs was feeding there on a hillside, and they begged him to allow them to enter into them, and he allowed them.

Lk 8:33 Ἐξελθόντα δὲ τὰ δαιμόνια ἀπὸ τοῦ ἀνθρώπου εἰσῆλθον εἰς τοὺς χοίρους• καὶ ὥρμησεν ἡ ἀγέλη κατὰ τοῦ κρημνοῦ εἰς τὴν λίμνην, καὶ ἀπεπνίγη.

33So coming out from the man, the demons entered into the pigs, and the herd rushed down the steep bank into the lake, and drowned.

Lk 8:34 Ἰδόντες δὲ οἱ βόσκοντες τὸ γεγονὸς ἔφυγον, καὶ ἀπήγγειλαν εἰς τὴν πόλιν καὶ εἰς τοὺς ἀγρούς.

34And seeing what had happened, the herders fled, and reported it to the town and to the farms.

Lk 8:35 Ἐξῆλθον δὲ ἰδεῖν τὸ γεγονός• καὶ ἦλθον πρὸς τὸν Ἰησοῦν, καὶ εὗρον καθήμενον τὸν ἄνθρωπον ἀφ' οὗ τὰ δαιμόνια ἐξῆλθεν, ἱματισμένον καὶ σωφρονοῦντα, παρὰ τοὺς πόδας τοῦ Ἰησοῦ• καὶ ἐφοβήθησαν.

35And they came out to see what had happened. And they came to Jesus, and found the man from whom the demons had gone out sitting at Jesus' feet, dressed, and in his right mind, and they were afraid.

Lk 8:36 Ἀπήγγειλαν δὲ αὐτοῖς οἱ ἰδόντες πῶς ἐσώθη ὁ δαιμονισθείς.

36And the ones who had seen reported to them how the demon-possessed man had been cured.

Lk 8:37 Καὶ ἠρώτησαν αὐτὸν ἅπαν τὸ πλῆθος τῆς περιχώρου τῶν Γαδαρηνῶν ἀπελθεῖν ἀπ' αὐτῶν, ὅτι φόβῳ μεγάλῳ συνείχοντο• αὐτὸς δὲ ἐμβὰς εἰς πλοῖον ὑπέστρεψεν.

37And all the population of the neighborhood of the Gadarenes asked him to go away from them, for they were overcome with great fear. So he got into the boat *and* turned back.

Lk 8:38 Ἐδέετο δὲ αὐτοῦ ὁ ἀνὴρ ἀφ' οὗ ἐξεληλύθει τὰ δαιμόνια εἶναι σὺν αὐτῷ. Ἀπέλυσεν δὲ αὐτὸν ὁ Ἰησοῦς λέγων,

38But the man from whom the demons had gone out was begging to accompany him. But Jesus sent him away, saying,

Lk 8:39 Ὑπόστρεφε εἰς τὸν οἶκόν σου, καὶ διηγοῦ ὅσα ἐποίησέν σοι ὁ θεός. Καὶ ἀπῆλθεν, καθ' ὅλην τὴν πόλιν κηρύσσων ὅσα ἐποίησεν αὐτῷ ὁ Ἰησοῦς.

39"Return to your house, and recount all the things God has done for you." And he went, throughout the whole town, proclaiming what things Jesus had done for him.

---

195 **8:30** Among the Romans a *legion* was a select body of soldiers— a complete army of cavalry and infantry, numbering from 4,200 to 6,000 men, usually with approximately an equal number of auxiliary troops, thus totaling about 10,000. The *legion* was divided into ten cohorts of 1,000 each. In this case, a more general meaning of the word *legion* probably applies: a very large number.

A Dead Damsel and a Sick Woman

Lk 8:40 Ἐγένετο δὲ ἐν τῷ ὑποστρέψαι τὸν Ἰησοῦν, ἀπεδέξατο αὐτὸν ὁ ὄχλος• ἦσαν γὰρ πάντες προσδοκῶντες αὐτόν.

40And it came about that upon his return, a crowd was welcoming him, for they were all expecting him.

Lk 8:41 Καὶ ἰδού, ἦλθεν ἀνὴρ ᾧ ὄνομα Ἰάϊρος, καὶ οὗτος ἄρχων τῆς συναγωγῆς ὑπῆρχεν, καὶ πεσὼν παρὰ τοὺς πόδας Ἰησοῦ παρεκάλει αὐτὸν εἰσελθεῖν εἰς τὸν οἶκον αὐτοῦ•

41And behold, a man had come whose name was Jairus, and this man was a synagogue ruler. And falling at Jesus' feet, he begged him to come to his house,

Lk 8:42 ὅτι θυγάτηρ μονογενὴς ἦν αὐτῷ ὡς ἐτῶν δώδεκα, καὶ αὐτὴ ἀπέθνῃσκεν. Ἐν δὲ τῷ ὑπάγειν αὐτὸν οἱ ὄχλοι συνέπνιγον αὐτόν.

42because he had an only daughter, about twelve years of age, and she was dying. And as he was on his way, the crowds were pinching him in.

Lk 8:43 Καὶ γυνὴ οὖσα ἐν ῥύσει αἵματος ἀπὸ ἐτῶν δώδεκα, ἥτις ἰατροῖς προσαναλώσασα ὅλον τὸν βίον οὐκ ἴσχυσεν ἀπ' οὐδενὸς θεραπευθῆναι,

43And a woman suffering a flow of blood since twelve years, who had spent everything she owned on doctors and not been able to get healing from[196] anyone,

Lk 8:44 προσελθοῦσα ὄπισθεν, ἥψατο τοῦ κρασπέδου τοῦ ἱματίου αὐτοῦ• καὶ παραχρῆμα ἔστη ἡ ῥύσις τοῦ αἵματος αὐτῆς.

44came up behind and touched the tassel[197] of his cloak, and immediately her flow of blood stopped.

Lk 8:45 Καὶ εἶπεν ὁ Ἰησοῦς, Τίς ὁ ἁψάμενός μου; Ἀρνουμένων δὲ πάντων, εἶπεν ὁ Πέτρος, Ἐπιστάτα, οἱ ὄχλοι συνέχουσίν σε καὶ ἀποθλίβουσιν.

45And Jesus said, "Who was it touching me?" When everyone denied it, Peter said, "Master, the crowds are pushing in together and jostling you."

Lk 8:46 Ὁ δὲ Ἰησοῦς εἶπεν, Ἥψατό μού τις• ἐγὼ γὰρ ἔγνων δύναμιν ἐξελθοῦσαν ἀπ' ἐμοῦ.

46But Jesus said, "Someone touched me, for I sensed power go out from me."

Lk 8:47 Ἰδοῦσα δὲ ἡ γυνὴ ὅτι οὐκ ἔλαθεν, τρέμουσα ἦλθεν, καὶ προσπεσοῦσα αὐτῷ, δι' ἣν αἰτίαν ἥψατο αὐτοῦ ἀπήγγειλεν ἐνώπιον παντὸς τοῦ λαοῦ, καὶ ὡς ἰάθη παραχρῆμα.

47Then the woman, seeing that she was not going unnoticed, came, trembling.[198] And falling at his feet, she related before all the people the reason she had touched him, and how she had been instantly healed.

---

196 **8:43** ἀπ' οὐδενὸς θεραπευθῆναι - literally, *from anyone to receive to heal.* For the verb θεραπεύω – therapeúō is in the passive infinitive form, the same ablative construction as in Acts 17:25, where it is said God need not receive any help or service from (ἀπό) human hands.

197 **8:44** See Numbers 15:38, Deut. 22:12

198 **8:47** The reason for her fear was probably because she knew she had violated the Rabbi's cleanness. As a woman with a flow of blood, she was perpetually unclean ceremonially (Leviticus 15:25-31), and the others in the crowd, were they to touch her, would be unclean as well.

Lk 8:48 Ὁ δὲ εἶπεν αὐτῇ, Θυγάτηρ ἡ πίστις σου σέσωκέν σε• πορεύου εἰς εἰρήνην.

48And he said to her, "Daughter, your faith has healed you. Go with peace."

Lk 8:49 ¶ Ἔτι αὐτοῦ λαλοῦντος, ἔρχεταί τις παρὰ τοῦ ἀρχισυναγώγου, λέγων ὅτι Τέθνηκεν ἡ θυγάτηρ σου• μηκέτι σκύλλε τὸν διδάσκαλον.

49While he was still speaking, someone comes from the synagogue ruler's, saying, "Your daughter has died. Don't trouble the teacher any more."

Lk 8:50 Ὁ δὲ Ἰησοῦς ἀκούσας ἀπεκρίθη αὐτῷ, Μὴ φοβοῦ• μόνον πίστευσον, καὶ σωθήσεται.

50But having heard, Jesus responded to him, "Don't be afraid. Only believe, and she will be healed."

Lk 8:51 Ἐλθὼν δὲ εἰς τὴν οἰκίαν, οὐκ ἀφῆκεν εἰσελθεῖν οὐδένα τινα σὺν αὐτῷ εἰ μὴ Πέτρον καὶ Ἰωάννην καὶ Ἰάκωβον, καὶ τὸν πατέρα τῆς παιδὸς καὶ τὴν μητέρα.

51And when he went into the house, he did not allow anyone to enter with him except Peter and John and James, and the father of the maiden and the mother.

Lk 8:52 Ἔκλαιον δὲ πάντες, καὶ ἐκόπτοντο αὐτήν. Ὁ δὲ εἶπεν, Μὴ κλαίετε• οὐκ ἀπέθανεν, ἀλλὰ καθεύδει.

52And all were weeping and wailing for her. But he said, "Do not weep. She is not dead but sleeping."

Lk 8:53 Καὶ κατεγέλων αὐτοῦ, εἰδότες ὅτι ἀπέθανεν.

53And they laughed scornfully at him, knowing that she had died.

Lk 8:54 Αὐτὸς δὲ κρατήσας τῆς χειρὸς αὐτῆς, ἐφώνησεν λέγων, Ἡ παῖς, ἔγειρε.

54Then, holding her hand, he called out, as follows: "Damsel, wake up!"[199]

Lk 8:55 Καὶ ἐπέστρεψεν τὸ πνεῦμα αὐτῆς, καὶ ἀνέστη παραχρῆμα• καὶ διέταξεν αὐτῇ δοθῆναι φαγεῖν.

55And her spirit returned, and she stood up at once, and he ordered that she be given something to eat.

Lk 8:56 Καὶ ἐξέστησαν οἱ γονεῖς αὐτῆς• ὁ δὲ παρήγγειλεν αὐτοῖς μηδενὶ εἰπεῖν τὸ γεγονός.

56And her parents were astonished. Then he charged them not to tell anyone what had happened.

Chapter 9

Jesus Sends Out the Twelve

Lk 9:1 Συγκαλεσάμενος δὲ τοὺς δώδεκα, ἔδωκεν αὐτοῖς δύναμιν καὶ ἐξουσίαν ἐπὶ πάντα τὰ δαιμόνια, καὶ νόσους θεραπεύειν.

1And having called the Twelve together, he gave them power and authority over all the demons and diseases, in order to heal.

---

199 **8:54** The Greek verb ἐγείρω would generally mean "rouse yourself; wake up; get up." In figurative use it means, "wake up from death," or in the passive, "be raised from the dead." So also with the Greek word ἀνίστημι , which means "stand up," but which spiritually means "rise from the dead."

Lk 9:2 Καὶ ἀπέστειλεν αὐτοὺς κηρύσσειν τὴν βασιλείαν τοῦ θεοῦ, καὶ ἰᾶσθαι.
2And he sent them to proclaim the kingdom of God and to cure,[200]
Lk 9:3 Καὶ εἶπεν πρὸς αὐτούς, Μηδὲν αἴρετε εἰς τὴν ὁδόν• μήτε ῥάβδους, μήτε πήραν, μήτε ἄρτον, μήτε ἀργύριον, μήτε ἀνὰ δύο χιτῶνας ἔχειν.
3and said to them: "Take nothing for the journey— neither staffs,[201] nor knapsack, nor bread, nor silver, neither have two[202] tunics each.
Lk 9:4 Καὶ εἰς ἣν ἂν οἰκίαν εἰσέλθητε, ἐκεῖ μένετε, καὶ ἐκεῖθεν ἐξέρχεσθε.
4"And into whatever house you might enter, there remain, and from there go forward.

---

200 **9:2** txt ἰᾶσθαι B 2206 syr^{c,s} WH NA25 ‖ ἀσθενοῦντας θεραπεύειν 1424 ‖ ἰᾶσθαι τοὺς ἀσθενεῖς ℵ A D L Ξ Ψ f^{1} 33 38 157 205 579 1071 1241 1612 2786 it$^{a,aur,b,c,d,e,ff2,l,q,r^1}$ vg arm (eth) geo SBL TH [NA28] {C} ‖ ἰάσασθαι τοὺς ἀσθενεῖς 070 ‖ ἰάσασθαι τοὺς ἀσθενοῦντας F W ‖ ἰᾶσθαι τοὺς ἀσθενοῦντας C E H K M U X Γ Δ Θ Λ Π 0211 f^{13} 28 69 180 565 597 700 892 1006 1009 1010 1079 1195 1216 1230 1242 1243 1253 1292 1342 1344 1365 1505 1546 1646 2148 2174^{vid} 2882 𝔐 *Lect* slav TR RP ‖ ἰᾶσθαι πάντας τοὺς ἀσθενοῦντας 407 435 it^{f} ‖ *lac* 𝔓^{45} 𝔓^{75} G N P Q T. I think the additions were only natural and that the variety of them betrays their spuriousness.

201 **9:3a** txt μήτε ῥάβδους A C^{2} K U Γ Δ Θ Λ Π 28 565 700 2882 𝔐 TR RP ‖ μὴ ῥάβδους 2 ‖ μὴ πήραν μήτε ῥάβδον 579 ‖ μήτε ῥάβδον ℵ B C* D E* F L M W Ψ f^{1} f^{13} 33 157 1071 1424 TH NA28 {\} ‖ *lac* 𝔓^{45} 𝔓^{75} G N P Q T. The UBS (singular) reading would mean Jesus is saying, "Take nothing for the journey, neither a staff..." Whereas in Mark 6:8, both Greek texts say that Jesus instructed them "that they should take nothing for the trip except a staff only." Did an Alexandrian copyist accidentally change the number of this word to the singular in conformity with the surrounding subjects in the phrase? Or did a later copyist that gave us the Byzantine tradition change it to the plural in an attempt to eliminate the contradiction with Mark 6:8? Some interpreters say that the plural of staffs is similar to how Jesus tells them, later in the same verse of Luke 9:3, not to take more than one tunic. So let us suppose that that is true, that Jesus told them to take only one staff each, instead of more than one staff each. Then the question arises: why would anyone take more than one staff anyway? And have you ever seen anyone use more than one staff at a time? I think I have seen that once or twice in my lifetime, and that was because the person was lame or injured. (Actually, in 2007 I just met a guy who does use two walking sticks; he is not injured. They are metal, somewhat like ski poles. It seemed ridiculous to me; he is apt to catch one on something and trip over it.) But we have no reason to think here that any of the disciples was lame or injured. The only other reason that I could come up with as a reason why the disciples might take more than one staff each, was to carry a spare staff. To do that would not make much sense to me though, as someone who has done a lot of hiking in my lifetime (for lack of automobile roads in my part of New Guinea). I would not want to carry the extra weight or bulk for insufficient reason. But then again, I hiked in rain forest, where I could cut myself a new walking stick at any time without any trouble finding one. The disciples, on the other hand, were hiking in a place much more arid, where it would not be near as easy to find another walking stick after the rocky surface had worn down their first one.

202 **9:3b** txt ἀνὰ δύο A C^{3} D E* H K M W X Γ Δ Θ Λ Π Ψ f^{1} f^{13} 2 28 33 157 180 205 565 597 700 892 1006 1010 1071 1243 1292 1424 1505 2786 2882 *Lect* it^{d} syr^{h} Basil TR RP SBL (NA28: [ἀνὰ] δύο) {C} ‖ δύο ℵ B C* F L Ξ 070 0202 0211 372 494 579 1241 1342 1513 2411 2737 2796 ℓ547 it^{a,aur,b,c,e,f,ff2,l,q,r1} vg syr^{s,c,p,pal} cop^{sa,bo} arm eth geo slav WH TH ‖ "and not even two" syr^{s} ‖ *lac* 𝔓^{45} 𝔓^{75} G N P Q T.

Lk 9:5 Καὶ ὅσοι ἂν μὴ δέξωνται ὑμᾶς, ἐξερχόμενοι ἀπὸ τῆς πόλεως ἐκείνης τὸν κονιορτὸν ἀπὸ τῶν ποδῶν ὑμῶν ἀποτινάσσετε εἰς μαρτύριον ἐπ' αὐτούς.

5And all the *places* that do not welcome you, going forth from that town, shake the dust off your feet, as a testimony against them."

Lk 9:6 Ἐξερχόμενοι δὲ διήρχοντο κατὰ τὰς κώμας, εὐαγγελιζόμενοι καὶ θεραπεύοντες πανταχοῦ.

6And going forth they went throughout all the villages, preaching the good news, and healing everywhere.

Herod Hears of Jesus

Lk 9:7 Ἤκουσεν δὲ Ἡρῴδης ὁ τετράρχης τὰ γινόμενα πάντα• καὶ διηπόρει, διὰ τὸ λέγεσθαι ὑπό τινων ὅτι Ἰωάννης ἠγέρθη ἐκ νεκρῶν•

7Now Herod the tetrarch heard about all that was going on, and kept becoming perplexed, because it was said by some that John had been raised from the dead,

Lk 9:8 ὑπό τινων δὲ ὅτι Ἠλίας ἐφάνη• ἄλλων δὲ ὅτι Προφήτης τις τῶν ἀρχαίων ἀνέστη.

8and by some that Elijah had appeared, and still others that a prophet, one of the Ancients, had come back to life.

Lk 9:9 Εἶπεν δὲ Ἡρῴδης, Ἰωάννην ἐγὼ ἀπεκεφάλισα• τίς δέ ἐστιν οὗτος, περὶ οὗ ἀκούω τοιαῦτα; Καὶ ἐζήτει ἰδεῖν αὐτόν.

9But Herod said, "John, I beheaded. Who, then, is this I hear such things about?" And he tried to see him.

Jesus Feeds the Five Thousand

Lk 9:10 Καὶ ὑποστρέψαντες οἱ ἀπόστολοι διηγήσαντο αὐτῷ ὅσα ἐποίησαν. Καὶ παραλαβὼν αὐτούς, ὑπεχώρησεν κατ' ἰδίαν εἰς πόλιν καλουμένην Βηθσαϊδά.

10And when the apostles returned, they reported to him what things they had done. Then he took them, and retreated in private toward a town called Bethsaida.[203]

---

203 **9:10** txt

εἰς πολιν καλουμενην Βδα. 𝔓75 א1 B L Ξ* 33 (syrs) copsa,bo TH NA28 {B}

εἰς κωμην λεγομενην Βδα. D (itd)

εἰς τοπον ερημον א*,2 157 syrc copbomss

εἰς ερημον τοπον 1241

εἰς κωμην καλουμενην Βδα. εἰς τοπον ερημον Θ itr1

εἰς τοπον καλουμενον Βδα. Ψ

εἰς τοπον ερημον καλουμενον Βδα. ita,aur,b,c,e,f,ff2,l,q vg

εἰς ερημον τοπον πολεως κλουμενης Βδα(ν). A *f*13 565

εἰς τοπον πολεως κλουμενης Βδα(ν). *f*1 205 700

εἰς τοπον ερημον πολεως κλουμενης Βδα(ν). C E G H K M N U W Γ Δ Π Ξc 2 28 180 597 700 892 1006 1071 1243 1292 1424 1505 𝔐 syr(p),h (arm) (eth) (geo) TR RP

lac 𝔓45 F P Q T

Lk 9:11 Οἱ δὲ ὄχλοι γνόντες ἠκολούθησαν αὐτῷ· καὶ ἀποδεξάμενος αὐτούς, ἐλάλει αὐτοῖς περὶ τῆς βασιλείας τοῦ θεοῦ, καὶ τοὺς χρείαν ἔχοντας θεραπείας ἰᾶτο.

11But the crowds who knew, followed him. So, welcoming them, he spoke to them about the kingdom of God, and the ones having need of healing, he cured.

Lk 9:12 Ἡ δὲ ἡμέρα ἤρξατο κλίνειν· προσελθόντες δὲ οἱ δώδεκα εἶπαν αὐτῷ, Ἀπόλυσον τὸν ὄχλον, ἵνα πορευθέντες εἰς τὰς κύκλῳ κώμας καὶ ἀγροὺς καταλύσωσιν, καὶ εὕρωσιν ἐπισιτισμόν· ὅτι ὧδε ἐν ἐρήμῳ τόπῳ ἐσμέν.

12But the daylight began to decline, and the twelve approached *and* said to him, "Dismiss the crowd, so they can go to the surrounding villages and farms to sleep and find supplies. Because here, we are in a remote place."

Lk 9:13 Εἶπεν δὲ πρὸς αὐτούς, Δότε αὐτοῖς ὑμεῖς φαγεῖν. Οἱ δὲ εἶπαν, Οὐκ εἰσὶν ἡμῖν πλεῖον ἢ ἄρτοι πέντε καὶ ἰχθύες δύο, εἰ μήτι πορευθέντες ἡμεῖς ἀγοράσωμεν εἰς πάντα τὸν λαὸν τοῦτον βρώματα.

13And he said to them, "You give them something to eat." But they said, "We have no more than five loaves and two fish, unless we were to go and buy food for all this crowd."

Lk 9:14 Ἦσαν γὰρ ὡσεὶ ἄνδρες πεντακισχίλιοι. Εἶπεν δὲ πρὸς τοὺς μαθητὰς αὐτοῦ, Κατακλίνατε αὐτοὺς κλισίας ὡσεὶ ἀνὰ πεντήκοντα.

14For there were about five thousand men. And he said to his disciples, "Get them to recline in groups of about fifty each."

Lk 9:15 Καὶ ἐποίησαν οὕτως, καὶ κατέκλιναν ἅπαντας.

15And they did so, and got them all to recline.

Lk 9:16 Λαβὼν δὲ τοὺς πέντε ἄρτους καὶ τοὺς δύο ἰχθύας, ἀναβλέψας εἰς τὸν οὐρανόν, εὐλόγησεν αὐτούς, καὶ κατέκλασεν, καὶ ἐδίδου τοῖς μαθηταῖς παραθεῖναι τῷ ὄχλῳ.

16And taking the loaves and the two fish, *and* looking up to heaven, he blessed them and broke them, and gave to the disciples to set before the people.

Lk 9:17 Καὶ ἔφαγον καὶ ἐχορτάσθησαν πάντες· καὶ ἤρθη τὸ περισσεῦσαν αὐτοῖς κλασμάτων, κόφινοι δώδεκα.

17And they all ate and were satisfied, and their leftovers picked up were twelve large baskets of fragments.

I think the great variety of readings in the Greek manuscripts here arose from many scribes' simplistic understanding of the preposition εἰς having to mean "into Bethsaida," or "in Bethsaida," and then changing the text in order to eliminate a perceived contradiction. But Luke in his gospel and Acts often uses the preposition εἰς to mean "toward," "in the direction of." There is no contradiction here in the UBS/NA28 text with other gospels, since the rendering, "retreated toward Bethsaida" allows them to have stopped before reaching Bethsaida, stopped in a deserted place. The reading in the UBS text best explains the rise of all the other readings, and is original. The usual renderings of the Majority Text, such as "retreated into a deserted place belonging to the city of Bethsaida" sound concocted and unnatural do they not?

Peter's Confession of Messiah

Lk 9:18 Καὶ ἐγένετο ἐν τῷ εἶναι αὐτὸν προσευχόμενον κατὰ μόνας, συνῆσαν αὐτῷ οἱ μαθηταί• καὶ ἐπηρώτησεν αὐτούς, λέγων, Τίνα με λέγουσιν οἱ ὄχλοι εἶναι;

18And it came about that, when he was praying in private, the disciples were with him, and he queried them, saying, "Who do the crowds maintain me to be?"

Lk 9:19 Οἱ δὲ ἀποκριθέντες εἶπαν, Ἰωάννην τὸν βαπτιστήν• ἄλλοι δὲ Ἠλίαν• ἄλλοι δὲ ὅτι Προφήτης τις τῶν ἀρχαίων ἀνέστη.

19And they in answer said, "John the Baptizer; and others, Elijah; and others that a prophet, one of the Ancients, has risen again."

Lk 9:20 Εἶπεν δὲ αὐτοῖς, Ὑμεῖς δὲ τίνα με λέγετε εἶναι; Πέτρος δὲ ἀποκριθεὶς εἶπεν, Τὸν χριστὸν τοῦ θεοῦ.

20And he said to them, "But you, who do you maintain me to be?" And Peter in answer said, "The Christ of God."

Jesus Predicts His Death

Lk 9:21 Ὁ δὲ ἐπιτιμήσας αὐτοῖς παρήγγειλεν μηδενὶ λέγειν τοῦτο,

21But he, admonishing them, charged them to tell this to no one,

Lk 9:22 εἰπὼν ὅτι Δεῖ τὸν υἱὸν τοῦ ἀνθρώπου πολλὰ παθεῖν, καὶ ἀποδοκιμασθῆναι ἀπὸ τῶν πρεσβυτέρων καὶ ἀρχιερέων καὶ γραμματέων, καὶ ἀποκτανθῆναι, καὶ τῇ τρίτῃ ἡμέρᾳ ἐγερθῆναι.

22saying, "The Son of Man must suffer many things and be rejected by the elders, the chief priests, and Torah scholars, and be killed, and on the third day be raised again."

Lk 9:23 Ἔλεγεν δὲ πρὸς πάντας, Εἴ τις θέλει ὀπίσω μου ἔρχεσθαι, ἀρνησάσθω ἑαυτόν, καὶ ἀράτω τὸν σταυρὸν αὐτοῦ καθ' ἡμέραν, καὶ ἀκολουθείτω μοι.

23Then toward everyone he was saying, "If someone wants to come after me, he must deny himself, and take up his cross daily,[204] and follow me.

Lk 9:24 Ὃς γὰρ ἂν θέλῃ τὴν ψυχὴν αὐτοῦ σῶσαι, ἀπολέσει αὐτήν• ὃς δ' ἂν ἀπολέσῃ τὴν ψυχὴν αὐτοῦ ἕνεκεν ἐμοῦ, οὗτος σώσει αὐτήν.

24For whoever wants to save his life will lose it; but whoever loses his life for my sake, this one will save it.

Lk 9:25 Τί γὰρ ὠφελεῖται ἄνθρωπος, κερδήσας τὸν κόσμον ὅλον, ἑαυτὸν δὲ ἀπολέσας ἢ ζημιωθείς;

25For how does it benefit a human being when he has gained the whole world, but has lost or been forfeited his very self?

---

204 **9:23** txt καθ' ἡμέραν 𝔓^{75} ℵ^{*,2b} A B K L M R W Y Θ Π Ξ Ψ *f*^{1} *f*^{13} 33 69 157 700 892 1071 1241 1342 2542 it^{aur,f} vg syr^{c,p,h**} cop^{samss,bo} Did TR TH NA28 {/} ‖ *omit* ℵ^{*,2a} C D U X Γ Δ Λ 2 28 565 579 1424 𝔐 it syr^{s,hmg} cop^{sams} Or? RP ‖ *lac* 𝔓^{45} F N P Q T 13

Lk 9:26 Ὃς γὰρ ἂν ἐπαισχυνθῇ με καὶ τοὺς ἐμοὺς λόγους, τοῦτον ὁ υἱὸς τοῦ ἀνθρώπου ἐπαισχυνθήσεται, ὅταν ἔλθῃ ἐν τῇ δόξῃ αὐτοῦ καὶ τοῦ πατρὸς καὶ τῶν ἁγίων ἀγγέλων.

26For whoever is ashamed of me and of my words, that person the Son of Man will be ashamed of, when he comes in his glory, and of the Father, and of the holy angels.

Lk 9:27 Λέγω δὲ ὑμῖν ἀληθῶς, εἰσίν τινες τῶν αὐτοῦ ἑστηκότων οἳ οὐ μὴ γεύσωνται θανάτου, ἕως ἂν ἴδωσιν τὴν βασιλείαν τοῦ θεοῦ.

27But truly I say to you: There are some, of the ones standing here, who will certainly not taste death until they see the kingdom of God."

The Transfiguration

Lk 9:28 Ἐγένετο δὲ μετὰ τοὺς λόγους τούτους ὡσεὶ ἡμέραι ὀκτώ, καὶ παραλαβὼν Πέτρον καὶ Ἰωάννην καὶ Ἰάκωβον, ἀνέβη εἰς τὸ ὄρος προσεύξασθαι.

28And it came about, something like eight days after these words, that having taken Peter and John and James, he went up into the mountain, to pray.

Lk 9:29 Καὶ ἐγένετο, ἐν τῷ προσεύχεσθαι αὐτόν, τὸ εἶδος τοῦ προσώπου αὐτοῦ ἕτερον, καὶ ὁ ἱματισμὸς αὐτοῦ λευκὸς ἐξαστράπτων.

29And it came about that as he prayed, the appearance of his face was different, and his clothes were a glistening white.

Lk 9:30 Καὶ ἰδού, ἄνδρες δύο συνελάλουν αὐτῷ, οἵτινες ἦσαν Μωϋσῆς καὶ Ἠλίας,

30And behold, two men were conversing with him, who were Moses and Elijah,

Lk 9:31 οἳ ὀφθέντες ἐν δόξῃ ἔλεγον τὴν ἔξοδον αὐτοῦ ἣν ἤμελλεν πληροῦν ἐν Ἰερουσαλήμ.

31who, having been made visible in glory, were relating about the exodus[205] of him, which was soon to be coming true in Jerusalem.

Lk 9:32 Ὁ δὲ Πέτρος καὶ οἱ σὺν αὐτῷ ἦσαν βεβαρημένοι ὕπνῳ• διαγρηγορήσαντες δὲ εἶδον τὴν δόξαν αὐτοῦ, καὶ τοὺς δύο ἄνδρας τοὺς συνεστῶτας αὐτῷ.

32But Peter and the ones with him were heavy-eyed with sleepiness. But when they had fully waken up, they saw his glory, and the two men standing with him.

Lk 9:33 Καὶ ἐγένετο, ἐν τῷ διαχωρίζεσθαι αὐτοὺς ἀπ' αὐτοῦ, εἶπεν ὁ Πέτρος πρὸς τὸν Ἰησοῦν, Ἐπιστάτα, καλόν ἐστιν ἡμᾶς ὧδε εἶναι• καὶ ποιήσωμεν σκηνὰς τρεῖς, μίαν σοί, καὶ μίαν Μωϋσεῖ καὶ μίαν Ἠλίᾳ• μὴ εἰδὼς ὃ λέγει.

33And it came about that as those were moving off from Jesus, Peter said to him, "O Master, it is good for us to be here, and we should make three shelters, one for you and one for Moses and one for Elijah." (Not knowing what he is saying.)

Lk 9:34 Ταῦτα δὲ αὐτοῦ λέγοντος, ἐγένετο νεφέλη καὶ ἐπεσκίαζεν αὐτούς• ἐφοβήθησαν δὲ ἐν τῷ εἰσελθεῖν αὐτοὺς εἰς τὴν νεφέλην.

34And as he was saying these things, a cloud came, and it began to overshadow them. And they were afraid as they went into the cloud.

---

205 **9:31** A euphemism for death, like our phrase, "passing on."

Lk 9:35 Καὶ φωνὴ ἐγένετο ἐκ τῆς νεφέλης, λέγουσα, Οὗτός ἐστιν ὁ υἱός μου ὁ ἐκλελεγμένος· αὐτοῦ ἀκούετε.

35And a voice came from the cloud, saying, "This is my Son, the Chosen One;[206] listen to him."

Lk 9:36 Καὶ ἐν τῷ γενέσθαι τὴν φωνήν, εὑρέθη Ἰησοῦς μόνος. Καὶ αὐτοὶ ἐσίγησαν, καὶ οὐδενὶ ἀπήγγειλαν ἐν ἐκείναις ταῖς ἡμέραις οὐδὲν ὧν ἑώρακαν.

36And when the voice happened, they found Jesus alone. And they kept quiet and told no one in those days anything that they had seen.

The Disciples Accused of Impotence to Heal

Lk 9:37 Ἐγένετο δὲ τῇ ἑξῆς ἡμέρᾳ, κατελθόντων αὐτῶν ἀπὸ τοῦ ὄρους, συνήντησεν αὐτῷ ὄχλος πολύς.

37And it came about that during the following day, as they were coming down from the mountain, a large crowd met him.

Lk 9:38 Καὶ ἰδού, ἀνὴρ ἀπὸ τοῦ ὄχλου ἐβόησεν, λέγων, Διδάσκαλε, δέομαί σου, ἐπίβλεψαι ἐπὶ τὸν υἱόν μου, ὅτι μονογενής μοί ἐστιν,

38And behold, a man in the crowd shouted out, saying, "Teacher, I beg of you to look at my son; because he is my only born,

Lk 9:39 καὶ ἰδού, πνεῦμα λαμβάνει αὐτόν, καὶ ἐξαίφνης κράζει, καὶ σπαράσσει αὐτὸν μετὰ ἀφροῦ, καὶ μόγις ἀποχωρεῖ ἀπ' αὐτοῦ, συντρῖβον αὐτόν.

39and behold, a spirit takes over him and he suddenly cries out, and it convulses him with foaming *at the mouth.* And it hardly goes away from him, wearing him out.

Lk 9:40 Καὶ ἐδεήθην τῶν μαθητῶν σου ἵνα ἐκβάλωσιν αὐτό, καὶ οὐκ ἠδυνήθησαν.

40And I pleaded with your disciples that they cast it out, and they were not able to."

Lk 9:41 Ἀποκριθεὶς δὲ ὁ Ἰησοῦς εἶπεν, Ὦ γενεὰ ἄπιστος καὶ διεστραμμένη, ἕως πότε ἔσομαι πρὸς ὑμᾶς, καὶ ἀνέξομαι ὑμῶν; Προσάγαγε ὧδε τὸν υἱόν σου.

41And in response Jesus said, "O unbelieving and perverted generation, how long must I be with you, and put up with you? Bring your son here."

---

206 **9:35** txt ἐκλελεγμένος 𝔓45 𝔓75 ℵ B L Ξ 892 1241 1342 it^a,aur,ff2,l vg^st syr^s,hmg cop^sa,bo arm (eth) TH NA28 {B} ‖ ἐκλεγμένος 579 ‖ ἐκλεκτός Θ 1 1582* ℓ547 ‖ ἀγαπητός (Mk 9:7) A C* E G H K N P U W Γ Δ Λ Π f13 2 28 33 69 118 124 157 180 346 565 579 597 700 788 892 1010 1071 1243 1292 1424 1582c 1505 2882 ℓ253 ℓ292 ℓ1552 𝔐 it^b,c,e,f,q vg^cl,ww syr^(c),p,h,pal geo slav Marcion^T,E Cyril Tertullian Ambrose TR RP ‖ ἀγαπητός, ἐν ᾧ ηὐδόκησα D Ψ ‖ ἀγαπητός, ἐν ᾧ εὐδόκησα C3 M *Lect* it^d (cop^boms) ‖ *lac* F Q T 13. It is much easier to explain why copyists would change it to "beloved," than why they would change it to "chosen." This is an example of "scribal assimilation," where the copyists, whether deliberately, or merely because they were more familiar with the other gospels, changed the reading to harmonize it with Matthew's gospel, or even Luke's account of the baptism of Jesus, where God says, "My beloved Son." Or perhaps the concept of "chosen son," since God had only one son, was too difficult, leading copyists to change it to agree with Matthew.

Lk 9:42 Ἔτι δὲ προσερχομένου αὐτοῦ, ἔρρηξεν αὐτὸν τὸ δαιμόνιον καὶ συνεσπάραξεν· ἐπετίμησεν δὲ ὁ Ἰησοῦς τῷ πνεύματι τῷ ἀκαθάρτῳ, καὶ ἰάσατο τὸν παῖδα, καὶ ἀπέδωκεν αὐτὸν τῷ πατρὶ αὐτοῦ.

42And even as he was approaching Him, the demon dashed him to the ground, and thrashed him back and forth. But Jesus rebuked the unclean spirit, and the child was restored to wholeness, and He gave him back to his father.

Lk 9:43 Ἐξεπλήσσοντο δὲ πάντες ἐπὶ τῇ μεγαλειότητι τοῦ θεοῦ. Πάντων δὲ θαυμαζόντων ἐπὶ πᾶσιν οἷς ἐποίει, εἶπεν πρὸς τοὺς μαθητὰς αὐτοῦ,

43And all were struck by the majesty of God. And while everyone marvelled at all that he was doing, he said to his disciples,

Lk 9:44 Θέσθε ὑμεῖς εἰς τὰ ὦτα ὑμῶν τοὺς λόγους τούτους· ὁ γὰρ υἱὸς τοῦ ἀνθρώπου μέλλει παραδίδοσθαι εἰς χεῖρας ἀνθρώπων.

44"You place into your ears these words. For the Son of Man is about to be transferred into[207] the hands of human beings."

Lk 9:45 Οἱ δὲ ἠγνόουν τὸ ῥῆμα τοῦτο, καὶ ἦν παρακεκαλυμμένον ἀπ' αὐτῶν, ἵνα μὴ αἴσθωνται αὐτό· καὶ ἐφοβοῦντο ἐρωτῆσαι αὐτὸν περὶ τοῦ ῥήματος τούτου.

45But they were not understanding this statement, and *the meaning* was being kept hidden from them, with the result that they did not see it.[208] And they were afraid to ask him about this statement.

Who Is the Greatest?

Lk 9:46 Εἰσῆλθεν δὲ διαλογισμὸς ἐν αὐτοῖς, τὸ τίς ἂν εἴη μείζων αὐτῶν.

46So[209] contention came into[210] them, as to who of them was greatest.[211]

---

207 **9:44** Turned over to, delivered into the custody or jurisdiction of.

208 **9:45** The verb "to see" in the Greek is in the infinitive form, which DeBrunner [§391(5)] says is an "infinitive of result." This would mean that, instead of the meaning being hidden "with the intended purpose that they would not see it," the sense would be a little weaker, that it was hidden from them, "and the result was that they did not see it."

209 **9:46a** Verse 46 begins with the conjunctive or transitional particle δε. The sense seems to be still connected to v. 45, in that there, Jesus admonished them to be sure to understand that he was soon going to be apparently defeated, but they did not understand this, and indeed, as illustration that they did not understand, a contention next arose in them as to who of them is greatest in Jesus' imminent (so they thought) rising to rule over Israel.

210 **9:46b** The Greek phrase is the verb εἰσέρχομαι combined with the prepositional phrase ἐν αὐτοῖς. Εἰσέρχομαι means "enter into," and the preposition ἐν would usually mean "in," but speaking of a group, as here, could mean "among." The BAG lexicon gives two possibilities for εἰσέρχομαι, both "entered into them," 1 b β on p. 232d, and "arose among them," 2 b on p. 233b. The BDF Greek Grammar in §202 under "Eis-" says the preposition "en" here is used as "eis," or "into." And in §218, Blass is adamant that the ἐν here in Luke 9:46 is an example of the "hyper-correct use of "en" (in) for "eis" (into), the most obvious and certain of which are Lk 9:46 'came into them, into their hearts' (cf. v. 47)..." The thing for Blass that re-inforces in his mind that the debate "entered their hearts," is that in the next verse, it says Jesus "knew what was in their hearts." This makes much sense. Yet no English translation that I possess follows Blass in this. But for me, the combination of Bauer and Blass are authorities too great to controvert.

Lk 9:47 Ὁ δὲ Ἰησοῦς εἰδὼς τὸν διαλογισμὸν τῆς καρδίας αὐτῶν, ἐπιλαβόμενος παιδίον, ἔστησεν αὐτὸ παρ' ἑαυτῷ,

47And Jesus, knowing[212] the contention of their hearts, took a child by the hand, *and* stood him next to himself.

Lk 9:48 καὶ εἶπεν αὐτοῖς, Ὃς ἐὰν δέξηται τοῦτο τὸ παιδίον ἐπὶ τῷ ὀνόματί μου ἐμὲ δέχεται• καὶ ὃς ἂν ἐμὲ δέξηται δέχεται τὸν ἀποστείλαντά με• ὁ γὰρ μικρότερος ἐν πᾶσιν ὑμῖν ὑπάρχων οὗτος ἐστιν μέγας.

48And he said to them, "Whoever welcomes this child on the basis of my name, is welcoming me, and whoever welcomes me, is welcoming the one who sent me. For the person who is smallest among you all, that is who is great."

Do Not Hinder Other Camps of God's People

Lk 9:49 Ἀποκριθεὶς δὲ Ἰωάννης εἶπεν, Ἐπιστάτα, εἴδομέν τινα ἐπὶ ἐν τῷ ὀνόματί σου ἐκβάλλοντα δαιμόνια• καὶ ἐκωλύομεν αὐτόν, ὅτι οὐκ ἀκολουθεῖ μεθ' ἡμῶν.

49And in response, John said, "Master, we saw someone casting out demons in your name, and we tried to stop[213] him; for he is not following *you* together with us."[214]

Lk 9:50 Εἶπεν δὲ πρὸς αὐτὸν ὁ Ἰησοῦς, Μὴ κωλύετε• ὃς γὰρ οὐκ ἔστιν καθ' ὑμῶν, ὑπὲρ ὑμῶν ἐστιν.

50But Jesus said to him, "Do not stop *such*, for someone who is not against you is for you."

Jesus Rejected by a Samaritan Village

Lk 9:51 Ἐγένετο δὲ ἐν τῷ συμπληροῦσθαι τὰς ἡμέρας τῆς ἀναλήμψεως αὐτοῦ, καὶ αὐτὸς τὸ πρόσωπον ἐστήρισεν τοῦ πορεύεσθαι εἰς Ἱερουσαλήμ,

51And it came about that the days leading to his being taken up were running out, and he set his face to head toward Jerusalem.

Lk 9:52 καὶ ἀπέστειλεν ἀγγέλους πρὸ προσώπου αὐτοῦ• καὶ πορευθέντες εἰσῆλθον εἰς κώμην Σαμαριτῶν ὡς ἑτοιμάσαι αὐτῷ.

52And he sent out messengers before his face. And when they proceeded forth they went into a Samaritan village, so as to prepare *it* for him.

---

211 **9:46c** The Greek verb "to be" here is in the optative mood, which DeBrunner says is an example of Luke's use of the optative when following a secondary tense, to introduce indirect discourse.

212 **9:47** txt ειδως ℵ B F K Λ Π 124 597 700 1424 2542 cop^{sa} arm eth geo slav TH NA28 {C} ‖ γνους f^1 205 ‖ ιδων A C D E G H L M W Γ Δ Θ Ξ Ψ 0115 2 28 33 69 157 180 346 565 579 788 892 1006 1010 1071 1241 1243 1292 1342 1505 𝔐 latt cop^{bo} (Or) Jer TR RP ‖ *lac* 𝔓^{45} 𝔓^{75} N P Q T 13.

213 **9:49a** The Greek verb for "stop" or "bar," κωλύω, is in the imperfect form, which DeBrunner in §326 says is a "conative imperfect," which means "tried to prevent." A little over half of my English translations agree, and render this as "tried to" stop, or something similar.

214 **9:49b** According to DeBrunner, BDF §193(1), this is an "associative (commitative) dative," thus, not meaning "following us," but rather, "following [you] together with us."

Lk 9:53 Καὶ οὐκ ἐδέξαντο αὐτόν, ὅτι τὸ πρόσωπον αὐτοῦ ἦν πορευόμενον εἰς Ἱερουσαλήμ.

53And they did not welcome him, because his face was heading toward Jerusalem.

Lk 9:54 Ἰδόντες δὲ οἱ μαθηταὶ Ἰάκωβος καὶ Ἰωάννης εἶπαν, Κύριε, θέλεις εἴπωμεν πῦρ καταβῆναι ἀπὸ τοῦ οὐρανοῦ, καὶ ἀναλῶσαι αὐτούς;

54And when they saw *this*, the disciples James and John said, "Lord, do you will that we command fire to come down from heaven and consume them?"[215]

Lk 9:55 Στραφεὶς δὲ ἐπετίμησεν αὐτοῖς.

55But when he turned *to them*, he rebuked them.[216] [217]

Lk 9:56 Καὶ ἐπορεύθησαν εἰς ἑτέραν κώμην.

56And they moved on, to a different village.

---

215 **9:54** txt 𝔓45 𝔓75 ℵ B L Ξ 17 157 579 700* 854 1241 1342 1612 1627 1675 2735 2786 it^{aur,e,l} vg syr^{c,s} cop^{sa,bopt} eth^{mss} arm geo^{1} Diatess Cyril Jerome TH NA28 {B} ‖ *add* αὐτοὺς ὡς καὶ Ἠλίας ἐποίησεν "even as Elijah did?" A C D E G H K M U W Γ Δ Θ Λ Π Ψ 0211 f^{1} f^{13} 2 28 33 69 124 180 205 346 565 597 700^{c} 788 1006 1009 1010 1071 1079 1195 1216 1230 1242 1243 1253 1292 1344 1365 1424 1505 1546 1646 2148 2174 2882 𝔐 *Lect* it^{d,f} syr^{p,h,pal} cop^{bopt} geo^{2} slav Basil (Chrysostom) TR [HF] RP ‖ *add* αὐτοὺς ὡς Ἠλίας ἐποίησεν 892 it$^{a,b,(c),q,r1}$ vg^{mss} (Ambrosiaster) Gaudentius Augustine.

216 **9:55** txt 𝔓45 𝔓75 ℵ A B C E G H L S V W Δ Ξ Ψ Ω 047 0211 28 33 157 565 892 1009 1010 1071 1241 1342 1424 1675 2786 *Lect*$^{pt, AD 1/3}$ it^{aur,e,l} vgst syr^{c,s} cop^{sa,bopt} eth^{pt} slav^{mss} Basil Cyril-Jerusalem Jerome TH NA28 {A} ‖ *add* καὶ εἶπεν, Οὐκ οἴδατε ποίου πνεύματός ἐστε D 700 1216 2174 it^{d} geo (Epiphanius) Chrysostom Theodoret^{vid} ‖ *add* καὶ εἶπεν, Οὐκ οἴδατε οἵου πνεύματός ἐστε U Γ Λ 69 124 788 ‖ *add* καὶ εἶπεν, Οὐκ οἴδατε ποίου πνεύματός ἔσται Θ ‖ *add* καὶ εἶπεν, Οὐκ οἴδατε ποίου πνεύματός ἐστε ὑμεῖς f^{1} 1365 2148 2882 ℓ69^{m} ‖ *add* καὶ εἶπεν, Οὐκ οἴδατε οἵου πνεύματός ἐστε ὑμεῖς M Y Π f^{13} 2 346 669 1675 it^{a,b,c,f,q,r1} vg^{cl,ww} syr^{p,h,pal} cop^{bopt} arm goth slav^{pt} Ambrosiaster Ambrose Clement? Chrysostom Epiphanius Didymus TR HF RP ‖ *add* καὶ εἶπεν, Οὐκ οἴδατε οἵου πνεύματός ἔσται ὑμεῖς K ‖ *add* καὶ εἶπεν, καὶ πορευομένων αὐτῶν εἶπεν τίς προς αὐτόν· Οὐκ οἴδατε ποίου πνεύματός (ἔσται Swanson) (ἐστε UBS4) 579. Not counting the latter MS, the main additions are: "...and said, 'You do not know what spirit you are of / will be.'" Following are other witnesses for the TR/RP reading, which are not listed in Swanson or UBS3, so I don't know which of the minor variants they have: 180 205 597 1006 1079 1230 1242 1243 1253 1292 1344 1505 1546 1646 2542.

217 **9:55-56** txt 𝔓45 𝔓75 ℵ A B C D E G H L S V W Δ Ξ Ψ Ω 047 0211 28 33 157 565 669 892 1009 1010 1071 1241 1342 1424 1675 2786 *Lect*$^{pt, AD 1/3}$ it^{l} vgst syr^{s} cop^{sa,bopt} eth^{pt} slav^{mss} Basil Cyril-Jerusalem Epiphanius Jerome Marcion Chrysostom Didymus TH NA28 {A} ‖ *add* Ὁ γὰρ Υἱὸς τοῦ Ἀνθρώπου οὐκ ἦλθεν ψυχὰς ἀνθρώπων ἀπολέσαι, ἀλλὰ σῶσαι K M Y Π f^{13} 2 346 2542 2882 it^{c,f,q} syr^{c,p,h,pal} cop^{bopt} arm (goth *omit* ἀνθρώπων) Clement? Ambrose TR HF RP ‖ *add* Ὁ Υἱὸς τοῦ Ἀνθρώπου ἦλθεν ψυχὰς ἀνθρώπων ἀποκτεῖναι, ἀλλὰ σῶσαι. U 124 700 1216 1230 1253 1646 ‖ *add* Ὁ Υἱὸς τοῦ Ἀνθρώπου ἦλθεν ψυχὴν ἀνθρώπων ἀποκτεῖναι, ἀλλὰ σῶσαι. Γ ‖ *add* Ὁ Υἱὸς τοῦ Ἀνθρώπου ἦλθεν ψυχὰς ἀνθρώπων ἀπολέσαι, ἀλλὰ σῶσαι Θ Λ f^{1} 69 579 788 1195 it^{a,b,r1} ‖ *add* Ὁ Υἱὸς τοῦ Ἀνθρώπου ἦλθεν ψυχὰς ἀπολέσαι, ἀλλὰ σῶσαι it^{aur,e} vg ‖ These are other witnesses for the TR/HF reading, which are not listed in Swanson or UBS3, so I don't know which of the minor variants they have:. 180 205 597 1006 1243 1292 1365 1505.

The Cost of Following Jesus

Lk 9:57 Καὶ πορευομένων αὐτῶν ἐν τῇ ὁδῷ, εἶπέν τις πρὸς αὐτόν, Ἀκολουθήσω σοι ὅπου ἐὰν ἀπέρχῃ.

57And as they were proceeding on the way, someone said to him, "I will follow you, wherever you might go."

Lk 9:58 Καὶ εἶπεν αὐτῷ ὁ Ἰησοῦς, Αἱ ἀλώπεκες φωλεοὺς ἔχουσιν, καὶ τὰ πετεινὰ τοῦ οὐρανοῦ κατασκηνώσεις• ὁ δὲ υἱὸς τοῦ ἀνθρώπου οὐκ ἔχει ποῦ τὴν κεφαλὴν κλίνῃ.

58And Jesus said to him, "The foxes have dens, and the birds of the sky, nestling places, but the Son of Man has nowhere he can lay his head."

Lk 9:59 Εἶπεν δὲ πρὸς ἕτερον, Ἀκολούθει μοι. Ὁ δὲ εἶπεν, Κύριε, ἐπίτρεψόν μοι ἀπελθόντι πρῶτον θάψαι τὸν πατέρα μου.

59And to another *man*, he said, "Follow me." But he said, "Lord, give me leave to first go and bury my father."

Lk 9:60 Εἶπεν δὲ αὐτῷ ὁ Ἰησοῦς, Ἄφες τοὺς νεκροὺς θάψαι τοὺς ἑαυτῶν νεκρούς• σὺ δὲ ἀπελθὼν διάγγελλε τὴν βασιλείαν τοῦ θεοῦ.

60But Jesus said to him, "Leave those who are dead to bury their dead themselves; and you, after you have come away,[218] you publicize the kingdom of God."

Lk 9:61 Εἶπεν δὲ καὶ ἕτερος, Ἀκολουθήσω σοι, κύριε• πρῶτον δὲ ἐπίτρεψόν μοι ἀποτάξασθαι τοῖς εἰς τὸν οἶκόν μου.

61And another also said, "I will follow you, Lord. But first give me leave to say farewell to my household."

Lk 9:62 Εἶπεν δὲ ὁ Ἰησοῦς· Οὐδείς, ἐπιβαλὼν τὴν χεῖρα ἐπ' ἄροτρον, καὶ βλέπων εἰς τὰ ὀπίσω, εὔθετός ἐστιν τῇ βασιλείᾳ τοῦ θεοῦ.

62But Jesus said, "No one putting hand to plow and looking back to the things behind, is cut out for the kingdom of God."

Chapter 10

Jesus Sends Out the Seventy-Two

Lk 10:1 Μετὰ δὲ ταῦτα ἀνέδειξεν ὁ κύριος ἑτέρους ἑβδομήκοντα δύο, καὶ ἀπέστειλεν αὐτοὺς ἀνὰ δύο πρὸ προσώπου αὐτοῦ εἰς πᾶσαν πόλιν καὶ τόπον οὗ ἤμελλεν αὐτὸς ἔρχεσθαι.

1And after these things, the Lord appointed another seventy-two,[219] and sent them out two by two before his face, into every town and place where he himself was about to go.

---

218 **9:60** Or, "after you have gone away." It could mean, either after the man leaves Jesus, or after the man leaves (comes away from) the dead. In Greek, the word for "come" was the same as the word for "go." The context here allows the possibility of either. Something else to think about is that in this one conversation between Jesus and the man who wanted to bury his father, three different Greek words are used that could be translated "leave" in English: ἐπιτρέπω ("give me leave"), ἀπέρχομαι (twice, "go off" and "come away"), and ἀφίημι ("leave").

Lk 10:2 Ἔλεγεν δὲ πρὸς αὐτούς, Ὁ μὲν θερισμὸς πολύς, οἱ δὲ ἐργάται ὀλίγοι• δεήθητε οὖν τοῦ κυρίου τοῦ θερισμοῦ, ὅπως ἐργάτας ἐκβάλῃ εἰς τὸν θερισμὸν αὐτοῦ.

2And he was saying to them, "The crop is large, but the workers are few. Request therefore of the lord of the harvest, that he send out workers into his harvest.

Lk 10:3 Ὑπάγετε• ἰδού, ἀποστέλλω ὑμᾶς ὡς ἄρνας ἐν μέσῳ λύκων.

3Be on your way. Behold, I am sending you out like sheep in the midst of wolves.

Lk 10:4 Μὴ βαστάζετε βαλλάντιον, μὴ πήραν, μὴ ὑποδήματα• καὶ μηδένα κατὰ τὴν ὁδὸν ἀσπάσησθε.

4You must carry no moneybag, no knapsack, no sandals, and greet no one along the way.[220]

Lk 10:5 Εἰς ἣν δ' ἂν εἰσέλθητε οἰκίαν, πρῶτον λέγετε, Εἰρήνη τῷ οἴκῳ τούτῳ.

5And into whatever house you enter, first you say, 'Peace to this house.'

Lk 10:6 Καὶ ἐὰν ἐκεῖ ᾖ υἱὸς εἰρήνης, ἐπαναπαήσεται ἐπ' αὐτὸν ἡ εἰρήνη ὑμῶν• εἰ δὲ μή γε, ἐφ' ὑμᾶς ἀνακάμψει.

6And if a child of peace is there, your peace will settle upon him. Otherwise, it will bounce back onto you.

Lk 10:7 Ἐν αὐτῇ δὲ τῇ οἰκίᾳ μένετε, ἐσθίοντες καὶ πίνοντες τὰ παρ' αὐτῶν• ἄξιος γὰρ ὁ ἐργάτης τοῦ μισθοῦ αὐτοῦ. Μὴ μεταβαίνετε ἐξ οἰκίας εἰς οἰκίαν.

7And in that same house you are to remain, eating and drinking the things belonging to them; for the worker is worthy of his pay; you are not to be moving from house to house.

Lk 10:8 Καὶ εἰς ἣν ἂν πόλιν εἰσέρχησθε, καὶ δέχωνται ὑμᾶς, ἐσθίετε τὰ παρατιθέμενα ὑμῖν,

8And into whatever town you enter that[221] they welcome you, eat the things being set before you,

Lk 10:9 καὶ θεραπεύετε τοὺς ἐν αὐτῇ ἀσθενεῖς, καὶ λέγετε αὐτοῖς, Ἤγγικεν ἐφ' ὑμᾶς ἡ βασιλεία τοῦ θεοῦ.

9and heal the sick in it, and say to them, 'The kingdom of God has drawn over you.'

Lk 10:10 Εἰς ἣν δ' ἂν πόλιν εἰσέλθητε, καὶ μὴ δέχωνται ὑμᾶς, ἐξελθόντες εἰς τὰς πλατείας αὐτῆς εἴπατε,

10But into whatever town you enter that they do not welcome you, go out into the streets of it, and say,

---

219 **10:1** txt ἑβδομήκοντα δύο 𝔓^{75} B D M 0181 372 it^{a,aur,b,c,d,e,l} vg syr^{c,s} cop^{sa,boms} arm geo Diatess Adam AposCon Ambrosiaster Aug Marcion^{A} SBL (NA28 [δύο]) {C} ‖ ἑβδομήκοντα ℵ A C E G H K L U W X Γ Δ Θ Λ Ξ Π Ψ *f*^{1} *f*^{13} 28 69 157 180 205 565 579 700 892 1006 1010 1071 1241 1243 1292 1342 1424 1505 𝔐 it$^{f,q,r1?}$ syr^{p,h} cop^{bo} eth slav MarcionT Ir-lat Clem Or Eus Bas Cyr Thodoret; Tert Ambrose^{vid} Jer TR RP TH ‖ ἑβδομήκοντα μαθητάς *Lect* (syr^{pal}) ‖ *lac* 𝔓^{45} F N P Q T 33. See Endnote #2 at the end of this document, which more fully discusses this question.

220 **10:4** The meaning of the Greek is such that these commands and prohibitions are generally valid, for the whole campaign, and not just right now as they are first leaving.

221 **10:8** A Hebraism, the substituting of καί for ὅτι. Also in verse 10.

Lk 10:11 Καὶ τὸν κονιορτὸν τὸν κολληθέντα ἡμῖν ἐκ τῆς πόλεως ὑμῶν εἰς τοὺς πόδας ἀπομασσόμεθα ὑμῖν• πλὴν τοῦτο γινώσκετε, ὅτι ἤγγικεν ἡ βασιλεία τοῦ θεοῦ.

11'Even the dust sticking to us from your town onto our feet, we are shaking off to you. Even so, know this, that the kingdom of God has drawn near.'

Lk 10:12 Λέγω ὑμῖν ὅτι Σοδόμοις ἐν τῇ ἡμέρᾳ ἐκείνῃ ἀνεκτότερον ἔσται, ἢ τῇ πόλει ἐκείνῃ.

12I assure you, it will be more bearable for Sodom in That Day, than for that town.

Lk 10:13 Οὐαί σοι, Χοραζίν, οὐαί σοι, Βηθσαϊδά• ὅτι εἰ ἐν Τύρῳ καὶ Σιδῶνι ἐγενήθησαν αἱ δυνάμεις αἱ γενόμεναι ἐν ὑμῖν, πάλαι ἂν ἐν σάκκῳ καὶ σποδῷ καθήμενοι μετενόησαν.

13Woe to you, Khorazin! Woe to you, Bethsaida! For if the miracles that took place in you took place in Tyre and Sidon, they would have repented long ago, sitting in sackcloth and ashes.

Lk 10:14 Πλὴν Τύρῳ καὶ Σιδῶνι ἀνεκτότερον ἔσται ἐν τῇ κρίσει, ἢ ὑμῖν.

14In any case, it will be more bearable in the judgment for Tyre and Sidon than for you.

Lk 10:15 Καὶ σύ, Καπερναούμ, μὴ ἕως οὐρανοῦ ὑψωθήσῃ; ἕως τοῦ Ἅιδου καταβήσῃ.

15And you, Capernaum, will you be exalted up to heaven? You will go down to Hades![222]

Lk 10:16 Ὁ ἀκούων ὑμῶν ἐμοῦ ἀκούει• καὶ ὁ ἀθετῶν ὑμᾶς ἐμὲ ἀθετεῖ• ὁ δὲ ἐμὲ ἀθετῶν ἀθετεῖ τὸν ἀποστείλαντά με.

16The person who listens to you is listening to me, and the one rejecting you, is rejecting me. And the one rejecting me, is rejecting the one who sent me."

Lk 10:17 Ὑπέστρεψαν δὲ οἱ ἑβδομήκοντα δύο μετὰ χαρᾶς λέγοντες, Κύριε, καὶ τὰ δαιμόνια ὑποτάσσεται ἡμῖν ἐν τῷ ὀνόματί σου.

17And the seventy-two[223] returned, with joy, saying, "Lord, even the demons submit themselves to us in your name."

---

222 **10:15** This sentence is quite different in the Majority Text, as also Matthew 11:23. It appears that what I have above, is the original reading. But various transcriptional factors involving the way Greek was written without spaces between words (see the UBS Textual Commentary) and also seemingly a better contextual sense, caused copyists to change the verbs from "will you be exalted" to "you who are exalted," and from "you will go down," to "you will be brought down." Regarding the "You Capernaum, you who are exalted to heaven," the context speaks of what chance each city had to see the light, and experience the kingdom of God having drawn near over them. It does make sense to me, as perhaps to some of the manuscript copyists, that the point Jesus is making is that Capernaum, having been Jesus' base of operations, and his "own town," had already been lifted up to heaven, compared to any other town, in terms of the kingdom of heaven having drawn near. But the UBS textual commentary says, "The unexpected expression, 'And you, Capernaum, will you be exalted to heaven?' is a sharp and startling interrogation, entirely in the manner of Jesus' use of vivid language."

223 **10:17** txt ἑβδομήκοντα δύο 𝔓^{75} B D R 0181 372 it^{a,aur,b,c,d,e,l} vg syr^{s,hmg} cop^{sa,boms} arm geo Diatess Adam AposCon (Ambrosiaster) Aug SBL (NA28 [δύο]) {C} ‖ ἑβδομήκοντα 𝔓^{45} ℵ A C E F G K L M N S W X Γ Δ Θ Λ Ξ Π Ψ 0115 f^1 f^{13} 28 33 69 157 180 205 565 579 700 892 1006 1010 1071

Lk 10:18 Εἶπεν δὲ αὐτοῖς, Ἐθεώρουν τὸν Σατανᾶν ὡς ἀστραπὴν ἐκ τοῦ οὐρανοῦ πεσόντα.

18And he said to them, "I was watching as Satan fell from heaven like lightning.

Lk 10:19 Ἰδού, δέδωκα ὑμῖν τὴν ἐξουσίαν τοῦ πατεῖν ἐπάνω ὄφεων καὶ σκορπίων, καὶ ἐπὶ πᾶσαν τὴν δύναμιν τοῦ ἐχθροῦ• καὶ οὐδὲν ὑμᾶς οὐ μὴ ἀδικήσῃ.

19"Behold, I have given you authority to tread upon snakes and scorpions, and over all the power of the enemy; and nothing will by any means harm you.

Lk 10:20 Πλὴν ἐν τούτῳ μὴ χαίρετε ὅτι τὰ πνεύματα ὑμῖν ὑποτάσσεται• χαίρετε δὲ ὅτι τὰ ὀνόματα ὑμῶν ἐγγέγραπται ἐν τοῖς οὐρανοῖς.

20Nevertheless, do not rejoice in this, that the spirits submit to you; but rejoice that your names are written down in heaven."

Lk 10:21 Ἐν αὐτῇ τῇ ὥρᾳ ἠγαλλιάσατο τῷ πνεύματι, καὶ εἶπεν, Ἐξομολογοῦμαί σοι, πάτερ, κύριε τοῦ οὐρανοῦ καὶ τῆς γῆς, ὅτι ἀπέκρυψας ταῦτα ἀπὸ σοφῶν καὶ συνετῶν, καὶ ἀπεκάλυψας αὐτὰ νηπίοις. Ναί, ὁ πατήρ, ὅτι οὕτως εὐδοκία ἐγένετο ἔμπροσθέν σου.

21In that same hour, he exulted in the Holy Spirit, and said, "I praise you, Father, O Lord of heaven and earth, that you have hidden these things from the learned and intelligent, and revealed them to babes. Yes, O Father, for that is what was pleasing in your sight.

Lk 10:22 Πάντα μοι παρεδόθη ὑπὸ τοῦ πατρός μου• καὶ οὐδεὶς γινώσκει τίς ἐστιν ὁ υἱός, εἰ μὴ ὁ πατήρ, καὶ τίς ἐστιν ὁ πατήρ, εἰ μὴ ὁ υἱός, καὶ ᾧ ἐὰν βούληται ὁ υἱὸς ἀποκαλύψαι.

22"Everything has been turned over to me by my Father, and no one knows who the Son is, except the Father; and who the Father is, except the Son, and those to whom the Son decides to reveal *it*."

Lk 10:23 Καὶ στραφεὶς πρὸς τοὺς μαθητὰς κατ' ἰδίαν εἶπεν, Μακάριοι οἱ ὀφθαλμοὶ οἱ βλέποντες ἃ βλέπετε.

23And after he had turned toward his disciples privately, he said, "Blessed are the eyes that see what you see.

Lk 10:24 Λέγω γὰρ ὑμῖν ὅτι πολλοὶ προφῆται καὶ βασιλεῖς ἠθέλησαν ἰδεῖν ἃ ὑμεῖς βλέπετε, καὶ οὐκ εἶδαν• καὶ ἀκοῦσαι ἃ ἀκούετε, καὶ οὐκ ἤκουσαν.

24For I tell you, many prophets and kings wanted to see what you are seeing, and did not see it, and to hear what you are hearing, and did not hear it."

The Good Samaritan

Lk 10:25 Καὶ ἰδού, νομικός τις ἀνέστη, ἐκπειράζων αὐτόν, λέγων, Διδάσκαλε, τί ποιήσας ζωὴν αἰώνιον κληρονομήσω;

25And behold, a lawyer arose, testing him, saying, "Teacher, what must I do to inherit eternal life?"

1241 1292 1342 1424 1505 𝔐 it[f,i,q] syr[c,p,h,pal] cop[bo] eth slav Ir-lat Hipp[Arab] Clem Or Eus Chrys TR RP TH ‖ ἑβδομήκοντα μαθηταί 1243 ‖ *lac* H P Q T. See Endnote #2 at the end of this document, which more fully discusses this question.

Lk 10:26 Ὁ δὲ εἶπεν πρὸς αὐτόν, Ἐν τῷ νόμῳ τί γέγραπται; Πῶς ἀναγινώσκεις;

26 And he said to him, "What is written in the law? What is your reading of it?"[224]

Lk 10:27 Ὁ δὲ ἀποκριθεὶς εἶπεν, Ἀγαπήσεις κύριον τὸν θεόν σου ἐξ ὅλης τῆς καρδίας σου καὶ ἐν ὅλῃ τῇ ψυχῇ σου καὶ ἐν ὅλῃ τῇ ἰσχύϊ σου καὶ ἐν ὅλῃ τῇ διανοίᾳ σου, καὶ τὸν πλησίον σου ὡς σεαυτόν.

27 And he in answer said, "You shall love Yahweh your God from your whole heart, and with all your soul, and with all your strength, and with all your mind, and your neighbor as yourself."

Lk 10:28 Εἶπεν δὲ αὐτῷ, Ὀρθῶς ἀπεκρίθης• τοῦτο ποίει, καὶ ζήσῃ.

28 And He said, "You have answered correctly. Do this, and you will live."

Lk 10:29 Ὁ δὲ θέλων δικαιῶσαι ἑαυτὸν εἶπεν πρὸς τὸν Ἰησοῦν, Καὶ τίς ἐστίν μου πλησίον;

29 But wanting to justify himself, he said to Jesus, "And who is my neighbor?"

Lk 10:30 Ὑπολαβὼν ὁ Ἰησοῦς εἶπεν, Ἄνθρωπός τις κατέβαινεν ἀπὸ Ἱερουσαλὴμ εἰς Ἰεριχώ, καὶ λῃσταῖς περιέπεσεν, οἳ καὶ ἐκδύσαντες αὐτὸν καὶ πληγὰς ἐπιθέντες ἀπῆλθον, ἀφέντες ἡμιθανῆ.

30 In reply, Jesus said, "A man was going down from Jerusalem to Jericho, and he fell among bandits. And they, when they had stripped him and inflicted wounds, went away, leaving him half dead.[225]

Lk 10:31 Κατὰ συγκυρίαν δὲ ἱερεύς τις κατέβαινεν ἐν τῇ ὁδῷ ἐκείνῃ• καὶ ἰδὼν αὐτὸν ἀντιπαρῆλθεν.

31 And by chance a priest was going down that road, and when he saw him, he avoided *him*.

---

224 **10:26** The Greek says literally, "How do you read it?" The BDAG lexicon says this means "What does it say."

225 **10:30** txt ἡμιθανῆ 𝔓45 𝔓75 ℵ B D L Θ Ξ f^{1} 22 33 579 700 1241 TH NA28 {/} ‖ ἡμιθανῆ τυγχάνοντα A C E G H K M N S U X W Y Γ Δ Λ Π Ψ 070 f^{13} 2 28 157 565 892 1071 1342 1424 2542 𝔐 TR RP ‖ *lac* F P Q T. The BDAG lexicon says this 𝔐 reading means "leaving him for half dead, as indeed he was." The BDF grammar §414(1) glosses the word τυγχάνειν as "happen to be." Thus: the bandits supposed that he was half dead without knowing for sure, but it so happens that he was indeed half dead.

Lk 10:32 Ὁμοίως δὲ καὶ Λευίτης κατὰ τὸν τόπον ἐλθὼν καὶ ἰδὼν ἀντιπαρῆλθεν.

32And likewise also a Levite, when he came near that place and saw,[226] passed on around.

Lk 10:33 Σαμαρίτης δέ τις ὁδεύων ἦλθεν κατ' αὐτόν, καὶ ἰδὼν ἐσπλαγχνίσθη,

33But a Samaritan came traveling by him, and when he saw, was moved with pity.

Lk 10:34 καὶ προσελθὼν κατέδησεν τὰ τραύματα αὐτοῦ, ἐπιχέων ἔλαιον καὶ οἶνον• ἐπιβιβάσας δὲ αὐτὸν ἐπὶ τὸ ἴδιον κτῆνος, ἤγαγεν αὐτὸν εἰς πανδοχεῖον, καὶ ἐπεμελήθη αὐτοῦ.

34And he approached *and* stopped up his wounds, after first applying olive oil and wine. And mounting him on his own animal, he took him to an inn and took care of him.

Lk 10:35 Καὶ ἐπὶ τὴν αὔριον, ἐκβαλὼν ἔδωκεν δύο δηνάρια τῷ πανδοχεῖ, καὶ εἶπεν, Ἐπιμελήθητι αὐτοῦ• καὶ ὅ τι ἂν προσδαπανήσῃς, ἐγὼ ἐν τῷ ἐπανέρχεσθαί με ἀποδώσω σοι.

35And on the morrow, he took out two denarii,[227] gave *them* to the innkeeper, and said, 'Take care of him, and whatever you spend beyond *this*, I will reimburse you when I return.'

Lk 10:36 Τίς τούτων τῶν τριῶν πλησίον δοκεῖ σοι γεγονέναι τοῦ ἐμπεσόντος εἰς τοὺς λῃστάς;

36"Which of these three seems to you a neighbor for the one who fell among bandits?"

Lk 10:37 Ὁ δὲ εἶπεν, Ὁ ποιήσας τὸ ἔλεος μετ' αὐτοῦ. Εἶπεν δὲ αὐτῷ ὁ Ἰησοῦς, Πορεύου, καὶ σὺ ποίει ὁμοίως.

37And he said, "The one who did the mercy with him." And Jesus said to him, "Go yourself and do likewise."

Jesus At Mary and Martha's House

Lk 10:38 Ἐν δὲ τῷ πορεύεσθαι αὐτούς αὐτὸς εἰσῆλθεν εἰς κώμην τινά• γυνὴ δέ τις ὀνόματι Μάρθα ὑπεδέξατο αὐτόν.

38And when he moved on, he entered a certain village. And a woman by the name of Martha hosted him for dinner.

---

226 **10:32** txt

	κατα τον	τοπον ελθων	και ιδων	𝔓[75] ℵ[2] B L Ξ 070 *f*[1] 33 700 892 1241 SBL TH
γενομενος	κατα τον	τοπον	και ιδων	𝔓[45]
γενομενος	κατα τον	τοπον	και ιδων αυτον	D Π lat
γενομενος	κατα τον αυτον	τοπον ελθων	και ιδων	Ψ
[γενομενος]	κατα τον	τοπον ελθων	και ιδων	NA28 {/}
γενομενος	κατα τον	τοπον ιδων αυτον		syr[s,c,p] arm
γενομενος	κατα τον	τοπον ελθων	και ιδων αυτον	A Y Γ Δ 124 157 892 1071 syr[h] cop
γενομενος	κατα τον	τοπον ελθων	και ιδων	C K N W Θ *f*[13] 2 565 2542 𝔐 TR RP
γενομενος	κατα την	οδον ελθων	και ιδων	28
		omit (h.t.)		ℵ*
		lac		F P Q T

227 **10:35** One denarius was worth a day's wage.

Lk 10:39 Καὶ τῇδε ἦν ἀδελφὴ καλουμένη Μαριάμ, καὶ παρακαθεσθεῖσα πρὸς τοὺς πόδας τοῦ κυρίου ἤκουεν τὸν λόγον αὐτοῦ.

39There was also a sister to that one, named Mary, and she having sat down at the Lord's feet, was listening to his word.

Lk 10:40 Ἡ δὲ Μάρθα περιεσπᾶτο περὶ πολλὴν διακονίαν• ἐπιστᾶσα δὲ εἶπεν, Κύριε, οὐ μέλει σοι ὅτι ἡ ἀδελφή μου μόνην με κατέλιπεν διακονεῖν; Εἰπὲ οὖν αὐτῇ ἵνα μοι συναντιλάβηται.

40But Martha was being drawn away by many chores of hospitality. But when she did come over, she said, "Lord, doesn't it concern you that my sister has left me to serve alone? Tell her therefore that she should help carry the load with me."

Lk 10:41 Ἀποκριθεὶς δὲ εἶπεν αὐτῇ ὁ Ἰησοῦς, Μάρθα, Μάρθα, μεριμνᾷς καὶ θορυβάζῃ περὶ πολλά•

41But in answer, Jesus said to her, "Martha, Martha. You are getting concerned and agitated over many things.

Lk 10:42 ἑνὸς δέ ἐστιν χρεία• Μαριὰμ γὰρ δὲ τὴν ἀγαθὴν μερίδα ἐξελέξατο, ἥτις οὐκ ἀφαιρεθήσεται αὐτῆς.

42But there is only one thing that warrants it. For Mary has selected the good portion, which will not be taken away from her."

Chapter 11

Prayer

Lk 11:1 Καὶ ἐγένετο ἐν τῷ εἶναι αὐτὸν ἐν τόπῳ τινὶ προσευχόμενον, ὡς ἐπαύσατο, εἶπέν τις τῶν μαθητῶν αὐτοῦ πρὸς αὐτόν, Κύριε, δίδαξον ἡμᾶς προσεύχεσθαι, καθὼς καὶ Ἰωάννης ἐδίδαξεν τοὺς μαθητὰς αὐτοῦ.

1And it came about when he was praying in a certain place, that as he was finishing, one of his disciples said to him, "Lord, teach us to pray, even as John taught his disciples."

Lk 11:2 Εἶπεν δὲ αὐτοῖς, Ὅταν προσεύχησθε, λέγετε, Πάτερ, ἁγιασθήτω τὸ ὄνομά σου. Ἐλθέτω ἡ βασιλεία σου.

2And he said to them, "When you pray, say: "'Father,[228] hallowed be your name. May your kingdom come.[229]

---

[228] **11:2a** txt 𝔓^{75} ℵ B (L arm +ἡμῶν) f^{1} 700 1342 it^{aur} vg syr^{s} Marcion Tert Or Cyr SBL TH NA28 {A} ‖ *add* ἡμῶν ὁ ἐν τοῖς οὐρανοῖς (*harmonization to Mt 6:9*) A C D K M P U W Γ Δ Θ Λ Π Ψ f^{13} 2 28 118 157 346 565^{sup} 579 700 788 892 1009 1010 1071 1079 1195 1216 1230 1241 1242 1253 1344 1365 1424 (1546) 1582^{c} 1646 2148 2174 2882 𝔐 *Lect* it$^{(a),b,(c),d,e,f,(ff2,i)l,q,r1*}$ syr^{c,p,h} cop^{sa,bo} eth geo Diatess Orig TR RP ‖ *lac* 𝔓^{45} 33 N Q T 565.

[229] **11:2b** txt σου 𝔓^{75} B L 1 1342 vg syr^{c,s} arm Diatess^{syr} (Marcion$^{acc. to Tertullian}$) Or; Tertullian^{vid} Aug^{vid} SBL TH NA28 {A} ‖ σου· γενηθήτω τὸ θέλημά σου it^{a} vg^{mss} cop^{sa,bomss} geo ‖ σου· γενηθήτω τὸ θέλημὰ σου, ὡς ἐν οὐρανῷ, οὕτω καί ἐπὶ τῆς γῆς ℵ* ‖ σου· γενηθήτω τὸ θέλημὰ σου, ὡς οὐρανῷ, καὶ ἐπὶ τῆς γῆς F ‖ σου· γενηθήτω τὸ θέλημὰ σου, ὡς ἐν οὐρανῷ, καὶ ἐπὶ γῆς ℵ^{3} 070^{vid} A C D P W Δ Θ 892 1079 1195 ℓ48 it$^{aur,b,c,d,e,f, ff2,i,(l),q,r1}$ vg^{mss} syr^{p,h}

Lk 11:3 Τὸν ἄρτον ἡμῶν τὸν ἐπιούσιον δίδου ἡμῖν τὸ καθ' ἡμέραν.
3Give us each day our daily bread.
Lk 11:4 Καὶ ἄφες ἡμῖν τὰς ἁμαρτίας ἡμῶν, καὶ γὰρ αὐτοὶ ἀφίομεν παντὶ ὀφείλοντι
ἡμῖν. Καὶ μὴ εἰσενέγκῃς ἡμᾶς εἰς πειρασμόν.
4And forgive us our sins, for we ourselves also forgive everyone who is
indebted to us. And lead us not into temptation.' "[230]
Lk 11:5 Καὶ εἶπεν πρὸς αὐτούς, Τίς ἐξ ὑμῶν ἕξει φίλον, καὶ πορεύσεται πρὸς αὐτὸν
μεσονυκτίου, καὶ εἴπῃ αὐτῷ, Φίλε, χρῆσόν μοι τρεῖς ἄρτους,
5And he said to them, "Suppose one of you shall have a friend, and will go to
him at midnight and say to him, 'Friend, lend me three loaves,
Lk 11:6 ἐπειδὴ φίλος μου παρεγένετο ἐξ ὁδοῦ πρός με, καὶ οὐκ ἔχω ὃ παραθήσω
αὐτῷ•
6because a friend of mine has shown up, from a journey toward me, and I have
nothing to set before him.'
Lk 11:7 κἀκεῖνος ἔσωθεν ἀποκριθεὶς εἴπῃ, Μή μοι κόπους πάρεχε• ἤδη ἡ θύρα
κέκλεισται, καὶ τὰ παιδία μου μετ' ἐμοῦ εἰς τὴν κοίτην εἰσίν• οὐ δύναμαι ἀναστὰς
δοῦναί σοι.
7That one inside may say in answer, 'Do not cause me hassles. The door is
already shut up, and my children are in bed with me. I can't get up to give you
something.'
Lk 11:8 Λέγω ὑμῖν, εἰ καὶ οὐ δώσει αὐτῷ ἀναστάς, διὰ τὸ εἶναι φίλον αὐτοῦ, διά
γε τὴν ἀναίδειαν αὐτοῦ ἐγερθεὶς δώσει αὐτῷ ὅσων χρῄζει.
8I tell you, even if he will not get up and give you[231] something because of
being your friend, yet because of brash persistence on your part he will get up,
and give you as much as you need.
Lk 11:9 Κἀγὼ ὑμῖν λέγω, αἰτεῖτε, καὶ δοθήσεται ὑμῖν• ζητεῖτε, καὶ εὑρήσετε•
κρούετε, καὶ ἀνοιγήσεται ὑμῖν.
9So I say to you: Keep asking, and it will be given to you; keep seeking, and
you will find; keep knocking, and it will be opened to you.

---

cop^{bo} eth ‖ σου· γενηθήτω τὸ θέλημά, ὡς ἐν οὐρανῷ, καὶ ἐπὶ γῆς 1230 ‖ σου· γενηθήτω τὸ θέλημά, ὡς ἐν οὐρανῷ, καὶ ἐπὶ τῆς γῆς 565^{sup} ‖ σου· γενηθήτω τὸ θέλημά σου, ὡς ἐν οὐρανῷ, καὶ ἐπὶ τῆς γῆς ℵ^{2} E G H K U X Γ Λ Π Ψ *f*^{13} 2 28 33^{vid} 118 157 180 205 579 597 700 1006 1009 1010 1071 1216 1241 1242 1243 1253 1292 1344 1365 1424 1505 1546 1646 2148 2174 2882 𝔐 *Lect* it$^{aur,b,c,d,e,f, ff2,i,(l),q,r1}$ vg^{mss} syr^{p,h} cop^{bo} eth slav (Titus-Bostra) Cyril TR RP ‖ lac 𝔓^{45} N Q T 565.

[230] **11:4** *txt* 𝔓^{75} ℵ^{*,3} B L *f*^{1} 700 1342 it^{aur} vg syr^{s} cop^{sa,bopt} arm geo Marcion Tertullian Or Cyril Aug NA28 ‖ *add* ἀλλὰ ῥῦσαι ἡμᾶς ἀπὸ τοῦ πονηροῦ (*harmonization to Mt 6:13*) ℵ^{2} A C D E F G H K M U W Γ Δ Θ Λ Π Ψ *f*^{13} 2 28 33 118 157 180 205 565 579 597 892 1006 1010 1071 1241 1243 1292 1424 1505 2882 𝔐 *Lect* it^{aur,b,c,d,e,f,ff2,i,l,q,r1*} vg^{mss} syr^{c,p,h} cop^{bopt} eth slav Diatess^{syr} (Titus-Bostra) TR HF RP ‖ *lac* 𝔓^{45} N P Q T. (Swanson erroneously cites P here where in fact it is lacunose, acc. to McFall.) The first corrector of Codex Sinaiticus transposes the words to after "earth" in another addition to the text earlier.

[231] **11:8** The Greek says, "being *his* friend, and give *him* as much as *he* needed." But Jesus starts out the parable, "Suppose one of *you*..." And using "you" accomplishes gender inclusiveness.

Lk 11:10 Πᾶς γὰρ ὁ αἰτῶν λαμβάνει• καὶ ὁ ζητῶν εὑρίσκει• καὶ τῷ κρούοντι ἀνοιγήσεται.

[10]For everyone who keeps asking, receives; and the person who keeps seeking, finds; and to the one who keeps on knocking, it will be opened.[232]

Lk 11:11 Τίνα δὲ ἐξ ὑμῶν τὸν πατέρα αἰτήσει ὁ υἱὸς ἰχθῦν, καὶ ἀντὶ ἰχθύος ὄφιν αὐτῷ ἐπιδώσει;

[11]"And which father among you, if his child will ask for a fish, will hand him a snake instead?[233]

Lk 11:12 Ἢ καὶ αἰτήσει ᾠόν, μὴ ἐπιδώσει αὐτῷ σκορπίον;

[12]Or again, if he asks for an egg, will hand him a scorpion?

Lk 11:13 Εἰ οὖν ὑμεῖς πονηροὶ ὑπάρχοντες οἴδατε δόματα ἀγαθὰ διδόναι τοῖς τέκνοις ὑμῶν, πόσῳ μᾶλλον ὁ πατὴρ ὁ ἐξ οὐρανοῦ δώσει πνεῦμα ἅγιον τοῖς αἰτοῦσιν αὐτόν;

[13]If you, then, though you are evil, know how to give good gifts to your children, how much more will the Father from heaven give the Holy Spirit to those who ask him?"

Jesus and Baalzibbul

Lk 11:14 Καὶ ἦν ἐκβάλλων δαιμόνιον κωφόν. Ἐγένετο δέ, τοῦ δαιμονίου ἐξελθόντος, ἐλάλησεν ὁ κωφός• καὶ ἐθαύμασαν οἱ ὄχλοι.

[14]And he was casting out a demon of muteness.[234] And it came about that after the demon went out, the mute man spoke. And the crowd was amazed.

Lk 11:15 Τινὲς δὲ ἐξ αὐτῶν εἶπον, Ἐν Βεελζεβοὺλ τῷ ἄρχοντι τῶν δαιμονίων ἐκβάλλει τὰ δαιμόνια.

[15]But some of them said, "It is by Ba'al-zibbul,[235] the prince of demons, that he drives out demons."

---

[232] **11:10** The "continuous" aspect of the Greek verbs here is a part of their meaning that is essential to this passage. In fact, the whole point of the parable is persistence, verse 8. So to translate verse 9 as, "Ask, and it will be given to you," would be incorrect and misleading. Someone might interpret it to mean that you will only have to ask once. See my endnote at the end of this document, entitled, "Continuous Aspect," which discusses this and other pertinent passages more fully.

[233] **11·11** ιχθυν και αντι ιχθυος οφιν 𝔓^{45} 𝔓^{75C} B it^{ff2,i,l} syr^{s} cop^{sa} arm Marc^{Ep} Or SBL TH NA28 {B} ‖ ιχθυν και αντι ιχθυος ισχυν 𝔓^{75*} ‖ αρτον μη λιθον επιδωσει αυτω η ιχθυν μη αντι ιχθυος οφιν ℵ L it$^{aur,b,c,(d),f,r1}$ vg Aug ‖ αρτον μη λιθον επιδωσει αυτω η και ιχθυν μη αντι ιχθυος οφινA E R W 𝔐 it^{q} syr$^{(c,p),h}$ (cop^{bo}) eth (geo) (Adam) (Sev) RP ‖ αρτον μη λιθον αυτω επιδωσει η και ιχθυν αιτησει μη αντι ιχθυος οφιν D ‖ αρτον μη λιθον επιδωσει αυτω ει και ιχθυν μη αντι ιχθυος οφιν TR ‖ αρτον μη λιθον επιδωσει αυτω και εαν αιτησι ωον μη επιδωσει αυτω σκορπιον η και ιχθυν μη αντι ιχθυος οφιν C ‖ *lac* N P Q T
Editors opposing the Byz reading say it is a harmonization to Matthew 7:9.

[234] **11:14** txt δαιμονιον κωφον 𝔓^{45} 𝔓^{75} ℵ A* B (D) L syr^{c,s} cop^{sa,bo} arm SBL TH ‖ δαιμονιον [και αυτο ην] κωφον NA28 {C} ‖ κωθον δαιμονιον και αυτο ην κωθον A^{c} C E R W 𝔐 lat syr^{p,h} eth geo Cyr^{lem} TR RP ‖ *lac* N P Q T Ξ

[235] **11:15** The Greek manuscripts say Beelzeboul. The KJV and NKJV say Beelzebub, even though there is not one Greek manuscript that says that, not even the Textus Receptus; but only a few Latin and Syriac. Beelzeboul comes from the Hebrew Ba'al-zibbul. "Ba'al" means

Lk 11:16 Ἕτεροι δὲ πειράζοντες σημεῖον ἐξ οὐρανοῦ ἐζήτουν παρ' αὐτοῦ.

16And others, testing him, wanted from him a sign out of heaven.

Lk 11:17 Αὐτὸς δὲ εἰδὼς αὐτῶν τὰ διανοήματα εἶπεν αὐτοῖς, Πᾶσα βασιλεία ἐφ' ἑαυτὴν διαμερισθεῖσα ἐρημοῦται• καὶ οἶκος ἐπὶ οἶκον, πίπτει.

17But he, knowing their thoughts, said to them, "Every kingdom divided against itself is desolated, and a house divided against itself falls.

Lk 11:18 Εἰ δὲ καὶ ὁ Σατανᾶς ἐφ' ἑαυτὸν διεμερίσθη, πῶς σταθήσεται ἡ βασιλεία αὐτοῦ; Ὅτι λέγετε, Ἐν Βεελζεβοὺλ ἐκβάλλειν με τὰ δαιμόνια.

18So also, if Satan was divided against himself, how will his kingdom stand? I say this because you claim I drive out demons by Baal-zibbul.

Lk 11:19 Εἰ δὲ ἐγὼ ἐν Βεελζεβοὺλ ἐκβάλλω τὰ δαιμόνια, οἱ υἱοὶ ὑμῶν ἐν τίνι ἐκβάλλουσιν; Διὰ τοῦτο αὐτοὶ ὑμῶν κριταὶ ἔσονται.

19Now if I drive out demons by Baal-zibbul, by whom do your followers drive them out? So then, they will be your judges.

Lk 11:20 Εἰ δὲ ἐν δακτύλῳ θεοῦ ἐκβάλλω τὰ δαιμόνια, ἄρα ἔφθασεν ἐφ' ὑμᾶς ἡ βασιλεία τοῦ θεοῦ.

20But if I am driving out demons by the finger of God, then the kingdom of God has come upon you.

Lk 11:21 Ὅταν ὁ ἰσχυρὸς καθωπλισμένος φυλάσσῃ τὴν ἑαυτοῦ αὐλήν, ἐν εἰρήνῃ ἐστὶν τὰ ὑπάρχοντα αὐτοῦ•

21"When a strong man, fully armed, guards his own castle, his possessions are safe.

Lk 11:22 ἐπὰν δὲ ἰσχυρότερος αὐτοῦ ἐπελθὼν νικήσῃ αὐτόν, τὴν πανοπλίαν αὐτοῦ αἴρει ἐφ' ᾗ ἐπεποίθει, καὶ τὰ σκῦλα αὐτοῦ διαδίδωσιν.

22But when a stronger one than he comes and overpowers him, he takes away the armor upon which his confidence was based, and divides out the spoils.

Lk 11:23 Ὁ μὴ ὢν μετ' ἐμοῦ κατ' ἐμοῦ ἐστιν• καὶ ὁ μὴ συνάγων μετ' ἐμοῦ σκορπίζει.

23"The person who is not with me is against me, and the one not gathering with me is scattering."

Lk 11:24 Ὅταν τὸ ἀκάθαρτον πνεῦμα ἐξέλθῃ ἀπὸ τοῦ ἀνθρώπου, διέρχεται δι' ἀνύδρων τόπων, ζητοῦν ἀνάπαυσιν• καὶ μὴ εὑρίσκον τότε λέγει, Ὑποστρέψω εἰς τὸν οἶκόν μου ὅθεν ἐξῆλθον.

24"When an evil spirit comes out of a human being, it goes through waterless places, seeking rest. And not finding it, at that time[236] it says, 'I will return to the house from which I came out.'

Lord or Prince. Ba'al was a Canaanite god, the son of Dagon, the god of grain. Baal was the bull prince, the bull being a symbol of fertility. Ba'alzebub, as in the Hebrew text of II Kings 1:2, is a derisive alteration of Ba'alzibbul meaning "Prince of flies." In this way the followers of Yahweh made fun of Ba'al. Later the name Baalzebub became associated with the Aramaic Beeldebaba, "enemy."

236 **11:24** txt τοτε λεγει 𝔓^{75} ℵ^{2} B L Ξ 070 it^{b,l} syr^{h} cop^{sa,bo} Or^{lat} [NA28] {C} ‖ λεγει 𝔓^{45} ℵ* A C D E R W it$^{a^2,aur,d,f,ff^2,i,q,r^1}$ vg syr^{c,s,p} arm eth geo TR SBL TH RP ‖ *lac* N P Q T. The NA28 has the word τοτε in square brackets because it is suspect as a scribal assimilation to the parallel in Matthew 12:44.

Lk 11:25 Καὶ ἐλθὸν εὑρίσκει σεσαρωμένον καὶ κεκοσμημένον.

25And when it arrives, it finds the house unoccupied, swept clean and put in order.

Lk 11:26 Τότε πορεύεται καὶ παραλαμβάνει ἕτερα πνεύματα πονηρότερα ἑαυτοῦ ἑπτά, καὶ ἐλθόντα κατοικεῖ ἐκεῖ• καὶ γίνεται τὰ ἔσχατα τοῦ ἀνθρώπου ἐκείνου χείρονα τῶν πρώτων.

26Then it goes and brings with it seven other spirits more wicked than itself, and they come inside and live there. And the final condition of that human is worse than the first."

Lk 11:27 Ἐγένετο δὲ ἐν τῷ λέγειν αὐτὸν ταῦτα, ἐπάρασά τις φωνὴν γυνὴ ἐκ τοῦ ὄχλου εἶπεν αὐτῷ, Μακαρία ἡ κοιλία ἡ βαστάσασά σε, καὶ μαστοὶ οὓς ἐθήλασας.

27And it came about that as Jesus was saying these things, a woman in the crowd lifted up her voice and said to him, "Blessed are the womb that bore you, and the breasts on which you sucked."

Lk 11:28 Αὐτὸς δὲ εἶπεν, Μενοῦν μακάριοι οἱ ἀκούοντες τὸν λόγον τοῦ θεοῦ καὶ φυλάσσοντες.

28But he replied, "Blessed rather[237] are those who hear the word of God and obey it."

The Sign of Jonah

Lk 11:29 Τῶν δὲ ὄχλων ἐπαθροιζομένων ἤρξατο λέγειν, Ἡ γενεὰ αὕτη γενεὰ πονηρά ἐστιν• σημεῖον ζητεῖ, καὶ σημεῖον οὐ δοθήσεται αὐτῇ, εἰ μὴ τὸ σημεῖον Ἰωνᾶ.

29And as the crowds were pressing together upon him, he began to say, "This generation is a wicked generation; it asks for a sign. And no sign will be given it except the sign of Jonah.[238]

Lk 11:30 Καθὼς γὰρ ἐγένετο Ἰωνᾶς τοῖς Νινευίταις σημεῖον, οὕτως ἔσται καὶ ὁ υἱὸς τοῦ ἀνθρώπου τῇ γενεᾷ ταύτῃ.

30For just as Jonah was a sign to the Ninevites, so also the Son of Man will be to this generation.

Lk 11:31 Βασίλισσα νότου ἐγερθήσεται ἐν τῇ κρίσει μετὰ τῶν ἀνδρῶν τῆς γενεᾶς ταύτης, καὶ κατακρινεῖ αὐτούς• ὅτι ἦλθεν ἐκ τῶν περάτων τῆς γῆς ἀκοῦσαι τὴν σοφίαν Σολομῶνος, καὶ ἰδού, πλεῖον Σολομῶνος ὧδε.

31The Queen of the South will be raised at the judgment with the men of this generation and condemn them, for she came from the ends of the earth to listen to the wisdom of Solomon, and behold, one greater than Solomon is here.

---

237 **11:28** Or possibly, "Well yes, but blessed more are those who..."

238 **11:29** Matthew 12:40 (DRP) says, "For as Jonah was three days and three nights in the belly of the huge sea creature, so the Son of Man will be three days and three nights in the heart of the earth." And further, according to II Kings 14:25, the prophet Jonah was from Gath Hepher, in Galilee, in the territory of the tribe of Zebulun (Joshua 19:13), only one hill over from Nazareth, if not the same hill. Jonah volunteered to be killed in order to save the rest of the souls on the boat, would be dead for 3 days, and then would come back to life. Jonah said about himself that he was in Sheol / Hades (Jonah 2:2). This is yet another way in which Jonah was a sign of Jesus Christ.

Lk 11:32 Ἄνδρες Νινευῖται ἀναστήσονται ἐν τῇ κρίσει μετὰ τῆς γενεᾶς ταύτης καὶ κατακρινοῦσιν αὐτήν• ὅτι μετενόησαν εἰς τὸ κήρυγμα Ἰωνᾶ, καὶ ἰδού, πλεῖον Ἰωνᾶ ὧδε.

32The men of Nineveh will rise at the judgment with this generation and condemn it, for they repented at the preaching of Jonah, and behold, one greater than Jonah is here.

The Light of the Body

Lk 11:33 Οὐδεὶς λύχνον ἅψας εἰς κρύπτην τίθησιν, οὐδὲ ὑπὸ τὸν μόδιον, ἀλλ' ἐπὶ τὴν λυχνίαν, ἵνα οἱ εἰσπορευόμενοι τὸ φέγγος φῶς βλέπωσιν.

33"No one after lighting a lamp puts it out of view, or under a basket,[239] but rather on the lamp stand, so that those who come in may see the light.

Lk 11:34 Ὁ λύχνος τοῦ σώματός ἐστιν ὁ ὀφθαλμός σου• ὅταν οὖν ὁ ὀφθαλμός σου ἁπλοῦς ᾖ, καὶ ὅλον τὸ σῶμά σου φωτεινόν ἐστιν• ἐπὰν δὲ πονηρὸς ᾖ, καὶ τὸ σῶμά σου σκοτεινόν.

34The lamp of the body is your eye. When your eye is open and generous, your entire body is brightly lit also. But when your eye is suspicious and stingy,[240] your body is in darkness also.

Lk 11:35 Σκόπει οὖν μὴ τὸ φῶς τὸ ἐν σοὶ σκότος ἐστίν.

35See to it, therefore, that the light in you is not darkness.

Lk 11:36 Εἰ οὖν τὸ σῶμά σου ὅλον φωτεινόν, μὴ ἔχον μέρος τι σκοτεινόν, ἔσται φωτεινὸν ὅλον, ὡς ὅταν ὁ λύχνος τῇ ἀστραπῇ φωτίζῃ σε.

36If then your whole body is brightly lit, not having any part dark, it will all be lighted, like when the lamp by its brightness illumines you."

Six Woes

Lk 11:37 Ἐν δὲ τῷ λαλῆσαι, ἐρωτᾷ αὐτὸν Φαρισαῖος ὅπως ἀριστήσῃ παρ' αὐτῷ• εἰσελθὼν δὲ ἀνέπεσεν.

37And as he was speaking, a Pharisee asks him to have lunch with him; so having gone inside, he reclined.

---

239 **11:33** The reading that includes the words "or under a basket" is that of ℵ A B C D W Δ Θ Ψ f^{13} 28 33 it^{a} syr$^{(c)}$ cop^{bo} *al.* However, those words are absent from 𝔓^{45,75} L Ξ 070 f^{1} 205 syr^{s} cop^{sa} arm geo *al.* The UBS textual commentary says, "Since Luke preferred not to use μόδιον in 8:16, a word which is present in the parallel in Mark (and Matthew), it may well be that the word, with its clause, was absent from the original form of the present passage also. On the other hand, since the clause is attested by weighty and diversified external evidence, a majority of the Committee was unwilling to drop it altogether and compromised by enclosing the words within square brackets."

240 **11:34** Literally, "if your eye is evil." From the Hebrew, עַיִן הָרַע - 'ayin ha'ra; see the endnote at the end of my translation of the gospel of Mark, for a full discussion of this concept:
https:||www.bibletranslation.ws/trans/markwgrk.pdf

Lk 11:38 Ὁ δὲ Φαρισαῖος ἰδὼν ἐθαύμασεν ὅτι οὐ πρῶτον ἐβαπτίσθη πρὸ τοῦ ἀρίστου.

38And the Pharisee when he saw, was shocked that he did not first baptize before the meal.[241]

Lk 11:39 Εἶπεν δὲ ὁ κύριος πρὸς αὐτόν, Νῦν ὑμεῖς οἱ Φαρισαῖοι τὸ ἔξωθεν τοῦ ποτηρίου καὶ τοῦ πίνακος καθαρίζετε, τὸ δὲ ἔσωθεν ὑμῶν γέμει ἁρπαγῆς καὶ πονηρίας.

39And the Lord said to him, "As it is, you Pharisees clean the outside of the cup and platter, but the inside of you is loaded with acquisitiveness[242] and wickedness.

Lk 11:40 Ἄφρονες, οὐχ ὁ ποιήσας τὸ ἔξωθεν καὶ τὸ ἔσωθεν ἐποίησεν;

40O foolish ones! Did not the one who made the outside, make the inside also?

Lk 11:41 Πλὴν τὰ ἐνόντα δότε ἐλεημοσύνην• καὶ ἰδού, πάντα καθαρὰ ὑμῖν ἐστιν.

41But the things lying within[243] give to the poor, and behold, all things are now clean for you.[244]

Lk 11:42 Ἀλλὰ οὐαὶ ὑμῖν τοῖς Φαρισαίοις, ὅτι ἀποδεκατοῦτε τὸ ἡδύοσμον καὶ τὸ πήγανον καὶ πᾶν λάχανον, καὶ παρέρχεσθε τὴν κρίσιν καὶ τὴν ἀγάπην τοῦ θεοῦ• ταῦτα δὲ ἔδει ποιῆσαι, κἀκεῖνα μὴ παρεῖναι.

42But woe to you, Pharisees! For you tithe the mint, and even the rue[245] and every kind of garden herb, and neglect the justice and the love of God. But these latter things you ought to practice, without leaving the former undone.

---

241 **11:38** The Greek word βαπτίζω was used for the ceremonial dunking of not only human beings' bodies (vessels), but for the ceremonial dunking of dishes and hands as well. But because the word has been transliterated into English only in the case of dunking the human body, English speakers have not acquired a full understanding of what it means. This translator therefore thought it best to transliterate the word in every instance.

242 **11:39** Acquisitiveness means continuously acquiring things, always wanting more things. This is wickedness, both because it makes an idol of possessions over and above God, and also because there are so many people who have little. It has already been established earlier in Luke's gospel, 3:11, that one fruit characteristic of repentance was to give away your extra possessions to the poor.

243 **11:41a** Somewhat a play on words. Their inside is "loaded up" with wickedness, and Jesus segues from that to the idea of the inside of their warehouse, or perhaps their platter, being loaded up with goods, which is evil in itself; but if they give what is lying inside to the poor, the inside of their vessel will be clean. Another play on words is that in New Testament Greek, "vessel" sometimes means your body, which is your container or dish, so to speak.

244 **11:41b** A variable here is the dative case of the words meaning "for you" in the phrase πάντα καθαρὰ ὑμῖν ἐστιν. Some translations say "for you," others "to you," and others leave it untranslated altogether. The rendering "clean for you" is easy enough to understand. Clean "to you" could be an "ethical dative," meaning "clean in your sight." For the N.T. teaches that some things are clean to some people, but unclean to others, depending on their conscience. Perhaps here, the giving to charity changes the evil conscience of the rich. When a rich person is rich selfishly, he has an evil conscience, and his wealth can be unclean in his own eyes, whereas if he is generous, he no longer feels guilty? Something to think about. Paul said in Romans 14:14, "to him that thinks any thing to be unclean, to him it is unclean."

Lk 11:43 Οὐαὶ ὑμῖν τοῖς Φαρισαίοις, ὅτι ἀγαπᾶτε τὴν πρωτοκαθεδρίαν ἐν ταῖς συναγωγαῖς, καὶ τοὺς ἀσπασμοὺς ἐν ταῖς ἀγοραῖς.

43Woe to you, Pharisees! For you love the prominent seats in the synagogues, and the greetings in the marketplaces.

Lk 11:44 Οὐαὶ ὑμῖν, ὅτι ἐστὲ ὡς τὰ μνημεῖα τὰ ἄδηλα, καὶ οἱ ἄνθρωποι οἱ περιπατοῦντες ἐπάνω οὐκ οἴδασιν.

44Woe to you! [246] For you are like graves that are not marked, and the people when walking over them do not know it."[247]

Lk 11:45 Ἀποκριθεὶς δέ τις τῶν νομικῶν λέγει αὐτῷ, Διδάσκαλε, ταῦτα λέγων καὶ ἡμᾶς ὑβρίζεις.

45And in response, someone from the class of lawyers says to him, "Teacher, in saying these things, you are insulting us also."

Lk 11:46 Ὁ δὲ εἶπεν, Καὶ ὑμῖν τοῖς νομικοῖς οὐαί, ὅτι φορτίζετε τοὺς ἀνθρώπους φορτία δυσβάστακτα, καὶ αὐτοὶ ἑνὶ τῶν δακτύλων ὑμῶν οὐ προσψαύετε τοῖς φορτίοις.

46But he said, "And to you lawyers also, woe! For you make people carry loads oppressive to bear, and you yourselves, not one of your fingers do you touch to such loads.

Lk 11:47 Οὐαὶ ὑμῖν, ὅτι οἰκοδομεῖτε τὰ μνημεῖα τῶν προφητῶν, οἱ δὲ πατέρες ὑμῶν ἀπέκτειναν αὐτούς.

47Woe to you! For you build mausoleums for the prophets, and it was your forefathers who murdered them.

Lk 11:48 Ἄρα μάρτυρές ἐστε καὶ συνευδοκεῖτε τοῖς ἔργοις τῶν πατέρων ὑμῶν• ὅτι αὐτοὶ μὲν ἀπέκτειναν αὐτούς, ὑμεῖς δὲ οἰκοδομεῖτε.

48So then, approving witnesses you are, to the deeds of your forefathers; for they do the killing of them, and you do the building.

Lk 11:49 Διὰ τοῦτο καὶ ἡ σοφία τοῦ θεοῦ εἶπεν, Ἀποστελῶ εἰς αὐτοὺς προφήτας καὶ ἀποστόλους, καὶ ἐξ αὐτῶν ἀποκτενοῦσιν καὶ διώξουσιν•

49For this reason also the wisdom of God has said, 'I am sending to them prophets and apostles; and some of them they will kill, and some of them they will persecute,'

Lk 11:50 ἵνα ἐκζητηθῇ τὸ αἷμα πάντων τῶν προφητῶν τὸ ἐκκεχυμένον ἀπὸ καταβολῆς κόσμου ἀπὸ τῆς γενεᾶς ταύτης,

50with the result that the blood of all the prophets spilled since the founding of the world will be demanded of this generation,

---

245 **11:42** Another garden herb, *ruta graveolens.* Deuteronomy 14:22 commands the Israelites to give God a tithe from all their crops. But according to the Mishna (Shebi'ith IX 1; cf. Billerb. II 189) it was not necessary to tithe the rue. Hence Jesus' words, "even" the rue.

246 **11:44a** *omit* 𝔓^{45} 𝔓^{75} ℵ B C L it$^{a,aur,e,ff^2,l}$ vg syr^{s,c} cop^{sa,bopt} arm geo TH NA28 {\} ‖ γραμματεις και φαρισαιοι D it$^{d,i,r^1}$ ‖ γραμματεις και φαρισαιοι υποκριται A E W 𝔐 it^{b,f,q} syr^{p,h} cop^{bopt} TR RP ‖ *lac* N P Q T

247 **11:44b** Jesus is bringing up an analogy much more grave than is apparent, unless one is familiar with Numbers 19:16-22. At stake is whether someone remained an Israelite, or was cut off from Israel. If an Israelite touched a grave, he was unclean for seven days. If after he touched a grave, he did not do the prescribed cleansing process, he was to be cut off from Israel.

Lk 11:51 ἀπὸ αἵματος Ἄβελ ἕως αἵματος Ζαχαρίου τοῦ ἀπολομένου μεταξὺ τοῦ θυσιαστηρίου καὶ τοῦ οἴκου. Ναί, λέγω ὑμῖν, ἐκζητηθήσεται ἀπὸ τῆς γενεᾶς ταύτης.

51from the blood of Abel, up until the blood of Zechariah, who perished between the altar and the sanctuary; yes, I tell you, *all* will be demanded of this generation.

Lk 11:52 Οὐαὶ ὑμῖν τοῖς νομικοῖς, ὅτι ἤρατε τὴν κλεῖδα τῆς γνώσεως· αὐτοὶ οὐκ εἰσήλθατε, καὶ τοὺς εἰσερχομένους ἐκωλύσατε.

52Woe to you, lawyers! For you have taken away the key *to the door* of knowledge. You yourselves have not gone in, and the ones going in you have barred."[248]

Lk 11:53 Κἀκεῖθεν ἐξελθόντος αὐτοῦ ἤρξαντο οἱ γραμματεῖς καὶ οἱ Φαρισαῖοι δεινῶς ἐνέχειν καὶ ἀποστοματίζειν αὐτὸν περὶ πλειόνων,

53And then as he went forth from there,[249] the Torah scholars and Pharisees began to be extremely hostile, and to provoke him to speak unpreparedly[250] about a great variety of topics,

Lk 11:54 ἐνεδρεύοντες αὐτόν, θηρεῦσαί τι ἐκ τοῦ στόματος αὐτοῦ.

54ambushing him, to pounce on something coming from his mouth.[251]

---

248 **11:52** The Greek verb I translated "barred" is κωλύω, which is related to the word for "limb" of the body, κώλον. Thus we get a picture of someone blocking the way by putting their arm across the way, like a bar. So even after someone figured out how to enter, in spite of the key being withheld, the lawyers would still further block the way, probably by passing a law against it, and enforcing that law. Even as the international pictogram for something which is forbidden by law, is the picture of the activity, with a bar across it. Even when not making it illegal, the "clergy" down through the ages to the present time, have in other ways led the "laity" to believe that the Bible is either too hard to understand or translate without their key, without being initiated into their clergy club, or else it is against church policy, or something like that.

249 **11:53a** txt κακειθεν εξελθοντος αυτου 𝔓75 (-ντες) א B C L syrhmg copsa,bo TH NA28 {\} ‖ κακειθεν εξελθοντος 𝔓45*vid* ‖ λεγοντος δε αυτου ταυτα προς αυτους A E W 𝔐 syrp,h TR RP ‖ λεγοντος δε ταυτα προς αυτους ενωπιον παντος του λαου D (it) (syrs,c,hmg) arm ‖ *lac* N P Q T. Wieland Willker suggests that perhaps the reading "as he went forth from there" was deemed unacceptable since the place where Jesus was speaking was not stated.

250 **11:53b** The Greek verb I translated "to provoke to speak unpreparedly" is ἀποστοματίζω, of which we do not have a large sampling in Greek literature. You will find a great variety of renderings of it in the English translations. I have stuck with the most ancient and traditional interpretation.

251 **11:54** txt *omit* 𝔓45 𝔓75 א B L syrs copsa,bo TH NA28 {\} ‖ ινα ευρωσιν κατηγορησαι αυτου D ‖ ινα κατηγορησουσιν αυτου A W* ‖ ινα κατηγορησωσιν αυτου C E Wc 𝔐 lat vg syr(c,p),h TR RP ‖ *lac* N P Q T

Chapter 12

Warnings and Encouragements

Lk 12:1 Ἐν οἷς ἐπισυναχθεισῶν τῶν μυριάδων τοῦ ὄχλου, ὥστε καταπατεῖν ἀλλήλους, ἤρξατο λέγειν πρὸς τοὺς μαθητὰς αὐτοῦ πρῶτον, Προσέχετε ἑαυτοῖς ἀπὸ τῆς ζύμης τῶν Φαρισαίων, ἥτις ἐστὶν ὑπόκρισις.

1When a vast multitude had gathered, such that they were trampling on one another, he bagan to say to his disciples first, "Be on your guard against the yeast of the Pharisees, which is hypocrisy.

Lk 12:2 Οὐδὲν δὲ συγκεκαλυμμένον ἐστὶν ὃ οὐκ ἀποκαλυφθήσεται, καὶ κρυπτὸν ὃ οὐ γνωσθήσεται.

2But[252] there is nothing covered up that will not be revealed, and *nothing* secret that will not be made known.

Lk 12:3 Ἀνθ' ὧν ὅσα ἐν τῇ σκοτίᾳ εἴπατε, ἐν τῷ φωτὶ ἀκουσθήσεται• καὶ ὃ πρὸς τὸ οὖς ἐλαλήσατε ἐν τοῖς ταμείοις, κηρυχθήσεται ἐπὶ τῶν δωμάτων.

3Therefore, what things you have said in the darkness, will be heard in the light, and what you have spoken close to an ear in the cellars, will be proclaimed on the housetops.

Lk 12:4 Λέγω δὲ ὑμῖν τοῖς φίλοις μου, Μὴ φοβηθῆτε ἀπὸ τῶν ἀποκτεινόντων τὸ σῶμα, καὶ μετὰ ταῦτα μὴ ἐχόντων περισσότερόν τι ποιῆσαι.

4I tell you, my friends, do not be afraid of the ones killing the body, and after that having nothing worse left to do.

Lk 12:5 Ὑποδείξω δὲ ὑμῖν τίνα φοβηθῆτε• φοβήθητε τὸν μετὰ τὸ ἀποκτεῖναι ἔχοντα ἐξουσίαν ἐμβαλεῖν εἰς τὴν γέενναν• ναί, λέγω ὑμῖν, τοῦτον φοβήθητε.

5But I will suggest to you whom you should fear. Fear the one who after the killing, has the power to cast into Gehenna. Yes, I tell you, fear him.

Lk 12:6 Οὐχὶ πέντε στρουθία πωλοῦνται ἀσσαρίων δύο; Καὶ ἓν ἐξ αὐτῶν οὐκ ἔστιν ἐπιλελησμένον ἐνώπιον τοῦ θεοῦ.

6Are not five sparrows sold for a penny?[253] And not one of them is forgotten before God.

Lk 12:7 Ἀλλὰ καὶ αἱ τρίχες τῆς κεφαλῆς ὑμῶν πᾶσαι ἠρίθμηνται. Μὴ φοβεῖσθε• πολλῶν στρουθίων διαφέρετε.

7But in your case, even the hairs of your head, each is numbered. You should not be afraid. You matter more than many sparrows.

---

252 **12:2** The particle δέ is meant to make a contrast here, between hypocrisy, in v. 1, and the disclosure of v. 2. For hypocrisy entails a covering up of one's true inner motives, a pretention. A hypocrite has a secret life.

253 **12:6** Literally, "two assarion," which were little fragments of brass coin. It means, practically, "a pittance, a trifle, a doit." We say, "I sold it for peanuts." We don't say exactly how many peanuts, like "I sold it for three peanuts." That is not the point.

Lk 12:8 Λέγω δὲ ὑμῖν, Πᾶς ὃς ἂν ὁμολογήσῃ ἐν ἐμοὶ ἔμπροσθεν τῶν ἀνθρώπων, καὶ ὁ υἱὸς τοῦ ἀνθρώπου ὁμολογήσει ἐν αὐτῷ ἔμπροσθεν τῶν ἀγγέλων τοῦ θεοῦ·

8"But I tell you, whoever stands up for me before human beings, the Son of Man also will stand up for him before the angels of God.[254]

Lk 12:9 ὁ δὲ ἀρνησάμενός με ἐνώπιον τῶν ἀνθρώπων ἀπαρνηθήσεται ἐνώπιον τῶν ἀγγέλων τοῦ θεοῦ.

9Whereas the one disowning me before human beings, will be disowned before the angels of God.

Lk 12:10 Καὶ πᾶς ὃς ἐρεῖ λόγον εἰς τὸν υἱὸν τοῦ ἀνθρώπου, ἀφεθήσεται αὐτῷ· τῷ δὲ εἰς τὸ ἅγιον πνεῦμα βλασφημήσαντι οὐκ ἀφεθήσεται.

10And everyone who will speak a word against the Son of Man, it will be forgiven him. But to the person who blasphemes against the Holy Spirit, it will not be forgiven.

Lk 12:11 Ὅταν δὲ εἰσφέρωσιν ὑμᾶς ἐπὶ τὰς συναγωγὰς καὶ τὰς ἀρχὰς καὶ τὰς ἐξουσίας, μὴ μεριμνήσητε πῶς ἢ τί ἀπολογήσησθε, ἢ τί εἴπητε·

11And when they deliver you over to the synagogues, and to the rulers and to the authorities, do not worry how or what you should defend, or what you should say.

Lk 12:12 τὸ γὰρ ἅγιον πνεῦμα διδάξει ὑμᾶς ἐν αὐτῇ τῇ ὥρᾳ, ἃ δεῖ εἰπεῖν.

12For the Holy Spirit will instruct you in that very hour what needs to be said."

False Financial Security

Lk 12:13 Εἶπεν δέ τις ἐκ τοῦ ὄχλου αὐτῷ, Διδάσκαλε, εἰπὲ τῷ ἀδελφῷ μου μερίσασθαι μετ' ἐμοῦ τὴν κληρονομίαν.

13And someone in the crowd said, "Teacher, tell my brother to divide the inheritance with me."

Lk 12:14 Ὁ δὲ εἶπεν αὐτῷ, Ἄνθρωπε, τίς με κατέστησεν κριτὴν ἢ μεριστὴν ἐφ' ὑμᾶς;

14But he said to him, "Man, who appointed me judge or arbiter over you *two*?"

Lk 12:15 Εἶπεν δὲ πρὸς αὐτούς, Ὁρᾶτε καὶ φυλάσσεσθε ἀπὸ πάσης πλεονεξίας· ὅτι οὐκ ἐν τῷ περισσεύειν τινὶ ἡ ζωὴ αὐτοῦ ἐστιν ἐκ τῶν ὑπαρχόντων αὐτῷ.

15And he said to them, "Watch out, and be on your guard against every form of covetousness.[255] For the life of one is not in the abundance of one's possessions."[256]

---

[254] **12:8** This is not a standard Greek sentence, but "Biblical Greek," like that in the Septuagint, which is to say, Greek influenced strongly by the Semitic languages. Here we have a very unusual use of the Greek preposition ἐν, the lexical gloss of which is "in" in English; thus: "Whoever confesses in me before humans, I will also confess in him before the angels of God." It is a Semitic principle of, "You do something in my advantage, something 'for' me, and I will do something in your advantage, something 'for' you, in exchange." Blass, §220(2), and Bauer, IV 5, say it means "whoever acknowledges me before men, him also I will acknowledge before the angels of God."

Lk 12:16 Εἶπεν δὲ παραβολὴν πρὸς αὐτούς, λέγων, Ἀνθρώπου τινὸς πλουσίου εὐφόρησεν ἡ χώρα•

16And he spoke a parable to them as follows: "The land of a certain rich man yielded abundantly,

Lk 12:17 καὶ διελογίζετο ἐν ἑαυτῷ λέγων, Τί ποιήσω, ὅτι οὐκ ἔχω ποῦ συνάξω τοὺς καρπούς μου;

17and he was thinking to himself, 'What shall I do? For I have no place where I can stack my produce.'

Lk 12:18 Καὶ εἶπεν, Τοῦτο ποιήσω• καθελῶ μου τὰς ἀποθήκας, καὶ μείζονας οἰκοδομήσω, καὶ συνάξω ἐκεῖ πάντα τὸν σῖτον καὶ τὰ ἀγαθά μου.

18And he said, 'This is what I will do. I will pull down my warehouses, and build bigger ones, and there I will stack all my wheat, and all my goods.

Lk 12:19 Καὶ ἐρῶ τῇ ψυχῇ μου, Ψυχή, ἔχεις πολλὰ ἀγαθὰ κείμενα εἰς ἔτη πολλά• ἀναπαύου, φάγε, πίε, εὐφραίνου.

19And I will say to my soul, "Soul, you have much goods sitting there into many years. Relax, eat, drink, be merry." '

Lk 12:20 Εἶπεν δὲ αὐτῷ ὁ θεός, Ἄφρων, ταύτῃ τῇ νυκτὶ τὴν ψυχήν σου ἀπαιτοῦσιν ἀπὸ σοῦ• ἃ δὲ ἡτοίμασας, τίνι ἔσται;

20But God said to him, 'You fool, this very night they are demanding your soul back from you,[257] and the provisions you have made, whose will they be?'

---

255 **12:15a** txt πασης πλεονεξιας $\mathfrak{P}^{75}$ ℵ A B D H K L M N Q R U W X Θ Π Ψ 070 0153 0211 f^1 $f^{13 (exc\ 124)}$ 22 33 157 579 892 1071 1241 latt syr cop TH NA28 {\} ‖ της πλεονεξιας E Γ Δ Λ 2 28 124 565 700 1424 𝔐 TR RP ‖ *lac* $\mathfrak{P}^{45}$ C P T

256 **12:15b** Greek: οὐκ ἐστιν ἐκ τῶν ὑπαρχόντων αὐτῷ. The preposition ἐκ (from) is the word posing some difficulty. Bauer, 3 f, says this means, "He does not live because of..." For the whole 3 f section he gives the meaning, "of the reason which is a presupposition for something: *by reason of, as a result of, because of.* This calls to my mind the verse in Proverbs where it says, "Guard your heart, for out of it are the issues of life."

257 **12:20** Bauer says this is a figure of speech, found in other writers such as Cicero, and Epictetus, using the concept of a human being's life as a loan. And that now, "they," the creditors, are demanding payment in full, of the loan, "calling in the loan." The Greek verb for "demand back," ἀπαιτέω, is used only twice in the N.T., both times by Luke, one time here, and the other time being in the Sermon on the Mount in Luke 6:30b, "...from the one forcefully taking your things, do not demand *them* back." It is used nine times in the Septuagint: four times for the demanding of repayment of loans, twice for extortion; once for the demand by Pharaoh for all the gold and silver of the land; and finally, one time in Isaiah 30:33, very much like Luke's use here. That occurrence is also for God's demanding of someone's life prematurely, the life of the king of Assyria. The exact phrase there is Σὺ γὰρ πρὸ ἡμερῶν ἀπαιτηθήσῃ, the same 3rd person, singular, passive inflection on ἀπαιτέω as on the verb ἐκζητέω in Luke 11:50, "so that the blood of all the prophets that has been spilled from the foundation of the world, would be demanded of this generation." However, here in Luke 12:20 we have 3rd person plural, and active voice: "they are demanding." Apart from Bauer's explanation, this reminds me of the place in the prophet Daniel, in chapter 4 verses 13 & 17, where it says, "This sentence is by the decree of the angelic watchers, and the decision is the command of the holy ones, in order that the living may know that the Most High is ruler over the realm of mankind..." It implies in v. 17 that there exists a council of some sort, composed of "holy ones," that is, angels, who make decisions on behalf of God. See also Psalm 82:1, "God stands in the assembly of gods, and in their midst, he judges gods." Sometimes angels are referred to as gods, or "sons of god." But the point I am making is that

Lk 12:21 Οὕτως ὁ θησαυρίζων ἑαυτῷ, καὶ μὴ εἰς θεὸν πλουτῶν.
21Such is the person saving up for himself, and not becoming rich to God."[258]

True Financial Security

Lk 12:22 Εἶπεν δὲ πρὸς τοὺς μαθητὰς αὐτοῦ, Διὰ τοῦτο λέγω ὑμῖν, μὴ μεριμνᾶτε τῇ ψυχῇ, τί φάγητε• μηδὲ τῷ σώματι, τί ἐνδύσησθε.
22And to his disciples, he said, "Because of this I say to you, do not worry about life, what you will eat, nor about the body, what you will wear.
Lk 12:23 γὰρ ψυχὴ πλεῖόν ἐστιν τῆς τροφῆς, καὶ τὸ σῶμα τοῦ ἐνδύματος.
23For life means more than food, and the body more than clothes.
Lk 12:24 Κατανοήσατε τοὺς κόρακας, ὅτι οὐ σπείρουσιν, οὐδὲ θερίζουσιν, οἷς οὐκ ἔστιν ταμεῖον οὐδὲ ἀποθήκη, καὶ ὁ θεὸς τρέφει αὐτούς• πόσῳ μᾶλλον ὑμεῖς διαφέρετε τῶν πετεινῶν;
24Consider the ravens, that they neither sow nor reap, and God feeds them. How much higher priority you are than birds!

---

such a council of angels, like the group who decided when Nebuchadnezzar was to die, are a "they," plural, like when God told the rich man here in Luke, "they are demanding your soul back from you." So in this instance, it would make sense to render it "This very night they are demanding your soul back from you." Most English translations render this as a passive with an unexpressed subject or agent, i.e., "your soul is being demanded of you." This is because in Indo-European languages this syntax is a phenomenon called the "3rd person plural with unexpressed indefinite subject used to form a passive." It should be noted that this is not an Aramaism or Semitism. In the long list of Semitisms in Koine Greek in the BDF grammar on p. 273, this "3rd person plural with unexpressed indefinite subject" is not to be found. Indeed, examples of this syntax may be found in classical Greek writings, in Latin, German, Spanish and French etc. as well. In fact, in Indo-European languages in general, a passive sentence may be formed with a third person plural verb form with or without an impersonal subject. But in the Greek New Testament, this is not consistently rendered as passive in English by Greek scholars. For example, in Revelation 12:6: ἵνα ἐκεῖ τρέφωσιν αὐτὴν is rendered in the KJV as " that they should feed her there." Though most do, such as the NASB: "so that there she would be nourished." But why should Greek do that, when it has the common passive verb forms? In Revelation 12:14, just 8 verses later, and even talking about the same subject, the Greek in Revelation uses the passive form of the same verb: τρέφεται!

258 **12:21** Though he was rich in his own eyes, and rich to his neighbors, he was not rich to God. To God, he was "wretched, pathetic, poor, blind, and naked," Revelation 3:17-18. It is preposterous for a human being to think he is rich, when his very life he possesses only as a loan. The Greek word translated "to" in the phrase "to God," is the preposition εἰς, used with the accusative form of the word God. Luke also uses this preposition with the accusavit as meaning "in." Thus Tyndale translated this, "and is not rich in God." His rendering may well be right. It is perhaps possible this could alternatively mean, "becoming rich with God as the goal, becoming rich for the sake of God," as opposed to becoming rich for oneself. Scripture elsewhere teaches us that there exists a very rare breed: a rich believer, who makes much money for the purpose of giving it away for the cause of spreading the gospel, or otherwise advancing the kingdom of God. And in the lists of spiritual gifts, there is a gift called "the gift of giving." Certainly, people cannot keep giving as their full-time ministry, unless they keep earning. Though it is naturally impossible for a camel to go through the eye of a needle, with God it is possible.

Lk 12:25 Τίς δὲ ἐξ ὑμῶν μεριμνῶν δύναται ἐπὶ τὴν ἡλικίαν αὐτοῦ προσθεῖναι πῆχυν ἕνα;

25Now which of you by worrying is able to add onto his lifespan one foot?[259]

Lk 12:26 Εἰ οὖν οὐδὲ ἐλάχιστον δύνασθε, τί περὶ τῶν λοιπῶν μεριμνᾶτε;

26If therefore you cannot accomplish even this very little thing, why do you worry about the rest?

Lk 12:27 Κατανοήσατε τὰ κρίνα πῶς αὐξάνει• οὐ κοπιᾷ, οὐδὲ νήθει• λέγω δὲ ὑμῖν, οὐδὲ Σολομὼν ἐν πάσῃ τῇ δόξῃ αὐτοῦ περιεβάλετο ὡς ἓν τούτων.

27Consider the lilies, how they grow. They neither labor nor weave. But I tell you, not even Solomon in all his splendor, was bedecked like one of these.

Lk 12:28 Εἰ δὲ ἐν ἀγρῷ τὸν χόρτον ὄντα σήμερον, καὶ αὔριον εἰς κλίβανον βαλλόμενον, ὁ θεὸς οὕτως ἀμφιέζει, πόσῳ μᾶλλον ὑμᾶς, ὀλιγόπιστοι;

28Now if God thus clothes the wild grass, which is here this day and the next is thrown into the stove, how much more would he rather clothe you, O you of little faith?

Lk 12:29 Καὶ ὑμεῖς μὴ ζητεῖτε τί φάγητε καὶ τί πίητε• καὶ μὴ μετεωρίζεσθε.

29And you also should not seek after how you will eat and how you will drink; that is, do not be anxious.

Lk 12:30 Ταῦτα γὰρ πάντα τὰ ἔθνη τοῦ κόσμου ἐπιζητοῦσιν• ὑμῶν δὲ ὁ πατὴρ οἶδεν ὅτι χρῄζετε τούτων.

30Because all these things, the nations of the world are striving for. But your Father knows that you have need of these things.

Lk 12:31 Πλὴν ζητεῖτε τὴν βασιλείαν αὐτοῦ, καὶ ταῦτα προστεθήσεται ὑμῖν.

31Only seek instead his kingdom, and these things will be included for you.

Lk 12:32 Μὴ φοβοῦ, τὸ μικρὸν ποίμνιον• ὅτι εὐδόκησεν ὁ πατὴρ ὑμῶν δοῦναι ὑμῖν τὴν βασιλείαν.

32Do not be afraid, little flock; for it has given your Father pleasure to give you the kingdom.

Lk 12:33 Πωλήσατε τὰ ὑπάρχοντα ὑμῶν καὶ δότε ἐλεημοσύνην. Ποιήσατε ἑαυτοῖς βαλλάντια μὴ παλαιούμενα, θησαυρὸν ἀνέκλειπτον ἐν τοῖς οὐρανοῖς, ὅπου κλέπτης οὐκ ἐγγίζει, οὐδὲ σὴς διαφθείρει•

33Sell your possessions, and give to the poor: make for yourselves money bags unfailing, a stockpile not shrinking; in the heavens, where neither a thief ever gets close, nor a moth ever destroys.

Lk 12:34 ὅπου γάρ ἐστιν ὁ θησαυρὸς ὑμῶν, ἐκεῖ καὶ ἡ καρδία ὑμῶν ἔσται.

34For where your treasure is, there your heart will be also.

Be Ready

Lk 12:35 Ἔστωσαν ὑμῶν αἱ ὀσφύες περιεζωσμέναι, καὶ οἱ λύχνοι καιόμενοι•

35"You must keep your waists girded and your lamps burning,

---

259 **12:25** Literally, one cubit. There was an expression in classical Greek, πήχυιον ἐπὶ χρόνον = "only one cubit of time." It is legitimate therefore to translate this as "a single hour to his life."

Lk 12:36 καὶ ὑμεῖς ὅμοιοι ἀνθρώποις προσδεχομένοις τὸν κύριον ἑαυτῶν, πότε ἀναλύσῃ ἐκ τῶν γάμων, ἵνα, ἐλθόντος καὶ κρούσαντος, εὐθέως ἀνοίξωσιν αὐτῷ.

36and you must be like people waiting for their own master, *waiting* for when he returns from the wedding celebrations, so that when he arrives and is knocking, they may immediately open for him.

Lk 12:37 Μακάριοι οἱ δοῦλοι ἐκεῖνοι, οὓς ἐλθὼν ὁ κύριος εὑρήσει γρηγοροῦντας• ἀμὴν λέγω ὑμῖν ὅτι περιζώσεται καὶ ἀνακλινεῖ αὐτούς, καὶ παρελθὼν διακονήσει αὐτοῖς.

37Happy are those slaves who when the master arrives, he finds watching. Truly I tell you, he will gird himself and bid them recline, and after coming in, he will serve them.

Lk 12:38 Κἂν ἐν τῇ δευτέρᾳ κἂν ἐν τῇ δευτέρᾳ φυλακῇ, καὶ ἐν τῇ τρίτῃ φυλακῇ ἔλθῃ, καὶ εὕρῃ οὕτως, μακάριοί εἰσιν οἱ δοῦλοι ἐκεῖνοι.

38Those slaves are happy, whether he arrives and finds them so in the second, or even in the third watch.

Lk 12:39 Τοῦτο δὲ γινώσκετε, ὅτι εἰ ᾔδει ὁ οἰκοδεσπότης ποίᾳ ὥρᾳ ὁ κλέπτης ἔρχεται, καὶ οὐκ ἂν ἀφῆκεν διορυχθῆναι τὸν οἶκον αὐτοῦ.

39And this you know, that if the manager of the household knew what hour the thief was coming, he would not have allowed his house to be broken into.

Lk 12:40 Καὶ ὑμεῖς γίνεσθε ἕτοιμοι• ὅτι ᾗ ὥρᾳ οὐ δοκεῖτε ὁ υἱὸς τοῦ ἀνθρώπου ἔρχεται.

40You also must be the same, because the Son of Man is coming at an hour you would not think he would."

Lk 12:41 Εἶπεν δὲ ὁ Πέτρος, Κύριε, πρὸς ἡμᾶς τὴν παραβολὴν ταύτην λέγεις, ἢ καὶ πρὸς πάντας;

41Then Peter said, "Lord, are you saying this parable to us, or to everyone else as well?"

Lk 12:42 Καὶ εἶπεν ὁ κύριος, Τίς ἄρα ἐστὶν ὁ πιστὸς οἰκονόμος ὁ φρόνιμος,[260] ὃν καταστήσει ὁ κύριος ἐπὶ τῆς θεραπείας αὐτοῦ, τοῦ διδόναι ἐν καιρῷ σιτομέτριον;

42And the Lord said, "So who is the faithful and sensible steward, whom the master will place over his domestic service, to be giving out rations in due time?

Lk 12:43 Μακάριος ὁ δοῦλος ἐκεῖνος, ὃν ἐλθὼν ὁ κύριος αὐτοῦ εὑρήσει ποιοῦντα οὕτως.

43Happy will be that slave who when his lord comes, he finds doing so.

Lk 12:44 Ἀληθῶς λέγω ὑμῖν ὅτι ἐπὶ πᾶσιν τοῖς ὑπάρχουσιν αὐτοῦ καταστήσει αὐτόν.

44Truly I tell you, he will place him over all his possessions.

---

260 **12:42** txt οικονομος ο φρονιμος 𝔓75 B E G H K N P Q S W Δ Λ Ψ Ω 28 565 579 1424 TH NA28 {\} ‖ οικονομος ο φρονιμος ο αγαθος D 157 ‖ δουλος και φρονιμος א* ‖ οικονομος και φρονιμος א2 A L M U Y Γ Π *f*1 *f*13 2 33 700 1071 TR RP ‖ οικονομος και ο φρονιμος Θ ‖ *lac* 𝔓45 C F T

Lk 12:45 Ἐὰν δὲ εἴπῃ ὁ δοῦλος ἐκεῖνος ἐν τῇ καρδίᾳ αὐτοῦ, Χρονίζει ὁ κύριός μου ἔρχεσθαι, καὶ ἄρξηται τύπτειν τοὺς παῖδας καὶ τὰς παιδίσκας, ἐσθίειν τε καὶ πίνειν καὶ μεθύσκεσθαι•

45But if that slave says in his heart, 'My master is taking his time to come,' and he begins to slap around the workboys and the workgirls, and to eat and drink and get drunk,

Lk 12:46 ἥξει ὁ κύριος τοῦ δούλου ἐκείνου ἐν ἡμέρᾳ ᾗ οὐ προσδοκᾷ, καὶ ἐν ὥρᾳ ᾗ οὐ γινώσκει, καὶ διχοτομήσει αὐτόν, καὶ τὸ μέρος αὐτοῦ μετὰ τῶν ἀπίστων θήσει.

46the master of that slave will come at an hour he is not expecting, and at a time he does not know, and will cut him in two, and appoint him his inheritance with the unbelieving.

Lk 12:47 Ἐκεῖνος δὲ ὁ δοῦλος ὁ γνοὺς τὸ θέλημα τοῦ κυρίου αὐτοῦ, καὶ μὴ ἑτοιμάσας ἢ ποιήσας πρὸς τὸ θέλημα αὐτοῦ, δαρήσεται πολλάς•

47And that slave, knowing the will of his master, and not having prepared or done in accordance with his will, he will be lashed many times.

Lk 12:48 ὁ δὲ μὴ γνούς, ποιήσας δὲ ἄξια πληγῶν, δαρήσεται ὀλίγας. Παντὶ δὲ ᾧ ἐδόθη πολύ, πολὺ ζητηθήσεται παρ' αὐτοῦ• καὶ ᾧ παρέθεντο πολύ, περισσότερον αἰτήσουσιν αὐτόν.

48Whereas the one not knowing, and having done things deserving of scourging, he will be lashed few times. So then, anyone to whom much has been given, much will be required of him, and from him to whom much has been entrusted, that much more will be demanded.

Jesus Causes Division

Lk 12:49 Πῦρ ἦλθον βαλεῖν ἐπὶ τὴν γῆν, καὶ τί θέλω εἰ ἤδη ἀνήφθη;

49"I have come to cast fire upon the earth, and how I wish it were already kindled!

Lk 12:50 Βάπτισμα δὲ ἔχω βαπτισθῆναι, καὶ πῶς συνέχομαι ἕως ὅτου τελεσθῇ.

50But I have a baptism to be baptized, and how tormented I am until that has been accomplished.

Lk 12:51 Δοκεῖτε ὅτι εἰρήνην παρεγενόμην δοῦναι ἐν τῇ γῇ; Οὐχί, λέγω ὑμῖν, ἀλλ' ἢ διαμερισμόν.

51You think that I have come to provide peace upon the earth. Not at all, I tell you, but rather division.

Lk 12:52 Ἔσονται γὰρ ἀπὸ τοῦ νῦν πέντε ἐν ἑνὶ οἴκῳ διαμεμερισμένοι, τρεῖς ἐπὶ δυσίν, καὶ δύο ἐπὶ τρισίν.

52For from now on, five in one household will be divided: three against two, and two against three.

Lk 12:53 Διαμερισθήσονται πατὴρ ἐπὶ υἱῷ, καὶ υἱὸς ἐπὶ πατρί• μήτηρ ἐπὶ τὴν θυγατέρα καὶ θυγάτηρ ἐπὶ τὴν μητέρα• πενθερὰ ἐπὶ τὴν νύμφην αὐτῆς, καὶ νύμφη ἐπὶ τὴν πενθεράν.

53Father will be divided against son, and son against father; mother against daughter and daughter against mother; mother-in-law against her daughter-in-law, and daughter-in-law against mother-in-law."

Judge For Yourselves

Lk 12:54 Ἔλεγεν δὲ καὶ τοῖς ὄχλοις, Ὅταν ἴδητε νεφέλην ἀνατέλλουσαν ἐπὶ δυσμῶν, εὐθέως λέγετε ὅτι Ὄμβρος ἔρχεται• καὶ γίνεται οὕτως.

54And he was also saying to the crowds, "When you see a cloud rising in the west, right away you say, 'A rainstorm is coming,' and it happens so.

Lk 12:55 Καὶ ὅταν νότον πνέοντα, λέγετε ὅτι Καύσων ἔσται• καὶ γίνεται.

55And when the south wind blows, you say, 'It will be hot,' and it happens.

Lk 12:56 Ὑποκριταί, τὸ πρόσωπον τῆς γῆς καὶ τοῦ οὐρανοῦ οἴδατε δοκιμάζειν• τὸν καιρὸν δὲ τοῦτον πῶς οὐκ οἴδατε δοκιμάζειν;

56Hypocrites! The face of the earth and sky you know how to interpret, but this present time you do not know how to interpret?

Lk 12:57 Τί δὲ καὶ ἀφ' ἑαυτῶν οὐ κρίνετε τὸ δίκαιον;

57And why also do you not judge equity yourselves?

Lk 12:58 Ὡς γὰρ ὑπάγεις μετὰ τοῦ ἀντιδίκου σου ἐπ' ἄρχοντα, ἐν τῇ ὁδῷ δὸς ἐργασίαν ἀπηλλάχθαι ἀπ' αὐτοῦ• μήποτε κατασύρῃ σε πρὸς τὸν κριτήν, καὶ ὁ κριτής σε παραδώσει τῷ πράκτορι, καὶ ὁ πράκτωρ σε βαλεῖ εἰς φυλακήν.

58For as you are going with your adversary to court, on the way make every effort to be free of him,[261] lest he drag you before the judge, and the judge hand you over to the officer, and the officer throw you in prison.

Lk 12:59 Λέγω σοι, οὐ μὴ ἐξέλθῃς ἐκεῖθεν, ἕως καὶ τὸ ἔσχατον λεπτὸν ἀποδῷς.

59I tell you, no way will you come out of that place, until you have paid back the very last penny."

Chapter 13

Repent or Perish

Lk 13:1 Παρῆσαν δέ τινες ἐν αὐτῷ τῷ καιρῷ ἀπαγγέλλοντες αὐτῷ περὶ τῶν Γαλιλαίων, ὧν τὸ αἷμα Πιλάτος ἔμιξεν μετὰ τῶν θυσιῶν αὐτῶν.

1And some who were present at that time, were reporting to him about the Galileans whose blood Pilate had mingled with the blood of their sacrifices.[262]

Lk 13:2 Καὶ ἀποκριθεὶς εἶπεν αὐτοῖς, Δοκεῖτε ὅτι οἱ Γαλιλαῖοι οὗτοι ἁμαρτωλοὶ παρὰ πάντας τοὺς Γαλιλαίους ἐγένοντο, ὅτι ταῦτα πεπόνθασιν;

2And in response he said to them, "Do you think that because they suffered these things, those Galileans were sinners, more so than all the rest of the Galileans?

---

[261] **12:58** That is, by satisfying him, coming to a settlement with him.

[262] **13:1** Bauer says this means, "whom Pilate ordered to be slain even as they were sacrificing." And so, their own blood would mingle on the ground with the blood of the animal they were sacrificing. A literal rendering of this is a vivid and grabbing figure of speech, and it is a shame to turn this into a bland dynamic equivalent in English.

Lk 13:3 Οὐχί, λέγω ὑμῖν• ἀλλ' ἐὰν μὴ μετανοῆτε, πάντες ὁμοίως ἀπολεῖσθε.

3Not at all, I tell you; but on the other hand, if you do not repent, you shall all likewise perish.

Lk 13:4 Ἢ ἐκεῖνοι οἱ δεκαοκτώ, ἐφ' οὓς ἔπεσεν ὁ πύργος ἐν τῷ Σιλωὰμ καὶ ἀπέκτεινεν αὐτούς, δοκεῖτε ὅτι αὐτοὶ ὀφειλέται ἐγένοντο παρὰ πάντας τοὺς ἀνθρώπους τοὺς κατοικοῦντας Ἱερουσαλήμ;

4Or those eighteen, on whom the tower in Siloam fell and killed them, do you think they were debtors worse than all the rest of the people living in Jerusalem?

Lk 13:5 Οὐχί, λέγω ὑμῖν• ἀλλ' ἐὰν μὴ μετανοῆτε, πάντες ὡσαύτως ἀπολεῖσθε.

5Not at all, I tell you; but on the other hand, if you do not repent, you shall all likewise perish."

Lk 13:6 Ἔλεγεν δὲ ταύτην τὴν παραβολήν• Συκῆν εἶχέν τις πεφυτευμένην ἐν τῷ ἀμπελῶνι αὐτοῦ πεφυτευμένην• καὶ ἦλθεν ζητῶν καρπὸν ἐν αὐτῇ, καὶ οὐχ εὗρεν.

6And he continued with this parable: "A man had a fig tree planted in his vineyard. And he came seeking fruit on it, and did not find any.

Lk 13:7 Εἶπεν δὲ πρὸς τὸν ἀμπελουργόν, Ἰδού, τρία ἔτη ἀφ' οὗ ἔρχομαι ζητῶν καρπὸν ἐν τῇ συκῇ ταύτῃ, καὶ οὐχ εὑρίσκω• ἔκκοψον αὐτήν• ἱνατί καὶ τὴν γῆν καταργεῖ;

7And he said to the vine dresser, 'Look, it has been three years already I have been coming, seeking fruit on this fig tree and not finding it. Cut it down. Why is it still using up the soil?'

Lk 13:8 Ὁ δὲ ἀποκριθεὶς λέγει αὐτῷ, Κύριε, ἄφες αὐτὴν καὶ τοῦτο τὸ ἔτος, ἕως ὅτου σκάψω περὶ αὐτήν, καὶ βάλω κόπρια•

8"But in answer, he says to him, 'Sir, leave it for this year also, until such time I have dug and put manure around it;

Lk 13:9 κἂν μὲν ποιήσῃ καρπὸν εἰς τὸ μέλλον• εἰ δὲ μή γε, ἐκκόψεις αὐτήν.

9and if in the future it does produce fruit, so much the better.[263] But if not, then you would cut it down.'"

A Crippled Woman Healed on the Sabbath

Lk 13:10 Ἦν δὲ διδάσκων ἐν μιᾷ τῶν συναγωγῶν ἐν τοῖς σάββασιν•

10And he was teaching in one of the synagogues during the Sabbath.

Lk 13:11 καὶ ἰδού, γυνὴ πνεῦμα ἔχουσα ἀσθενείας ἔτη δεκαοκτώ, καὶ ἦν συγκύπτουσα, καὶ μὴ δυναμένη ἀνακύψαι εἰς τὸ παντελές.

11And behold, a woman having had a spirit of disability for eighteen years was there. And she was bent over double, and not able to look up at all.

Lk 13:12 Ἰδὼν δὲ αὐτὴν ὁ Ἰησοῦς προσεφώνησεν, καὶ εἶπεν αὐτῇ, Γύναι, ἀπολέλυσαι τῆς ἀσθενείας σου.

12And when Jesus saw her, he called to her and said to her, "Woman, be set free from your disability."

---

263 **13:9** The words "so much the better" are not in the Greek text, but we have to put something there. This is a legitimate ellipsis. The Greek says only, "And if indeed in the future it does produce fruit– but if not, then you would cut it down."

Lk 13:13 Καὶ ἐπέθηκεν αὐτῇ τὰς χεῖρας• καὶ παραχρῆμα ἀνωρθώθη, καὶ ἐδόξαζεν τὸν θεόν.

13And he laid hands on her; and she became erect at once, and was praising God.

Lk 13:14 Ἀποκριθεὶς δὲ ὁ ἀρχισυνάγωγος, ἀγανακτῶν ὅτι τῷ σαββάτῳ ἐθεράπευσεν ὁ Ἰησοῦς, ἔλεγεν τῷ ὄχλῳ ὅτι Ἓξ ἡμέραι εἰσὶν ἐν αἷς δεῖ ἐργάζεσθαι• ἐν αὐταῖς οὖν ἐρχόμενοι θεραπεύεσθε, καὶ μὴ τῇ ἡμέρᾳ τοῦ σαββάτου.

14But in response, the synagogue ruler, being indignant that Jesus had healed during the Sabbath, was saying to the crowd, "There are six days in which *you are* supposed to work; you should therefore be coming during those to be healed, and not during the day of rest."

Lk 13:15 Ἀπεκρίθη δὲ αὐτῷ ὁ κύριος, καὶ εἶπεν, Ὑποκριταί,[264] ἕκαστος ὑμῶν τῷ σαββάτῳ οὐ λύει τὸν βοῦν αὐτοῦ ἢ τὸν ὄνον ἀπὸ τῆς φάτνης, καὶ ἀπαγαγὼν ποτίζει;

15But the Lord answered him, and said, "You hypocrites! Who among you on the Sabbath does not free his ox or his donkey from its stall, and after leading it out, give it drink?

Lk 13:16 Ταύτην δέ, θυγατέρα Ἀβραὰμ οὖσαν, ἣν ἔδησεν ὁ Σατανᾶς, ἰδού, δέκα καὶ ὀκτὼ ἔτη, οὐκ ἔδει λυθῆναι ἀπὸ τοῦ δεσμοῦ τούτου τῇ ἡμέρᾳ τοῦ σαββάτου;

16But this woman, a daughter of Abraham, whom Satan has kept bound lo these eighteen years, she should not be freed from this bondage on the day of rest?!"[265]

Lk 13:17 Καὶ ταῦτα λέγοντος αὐτοῦ, κατῃσχύνοντο πάντες οἱ ἀντικείμενοι αὐτῷ• καὶ πᾶς ὁ ὄχλος ἔχαιρεν ἐπὶ πᾶσιν τοῖς ἐνδόξοις τοῖς γινομένοις ὑπ' αὐτοῦ.

17And with his saying these things, all his opponents were being humiliated, and the whole crowd was cheering, for all the glorious things being accomplished by him.

The Parables of the Mustard Seed and the Yeast

Lk 13:18 Ἔλεγεν οὖν, Τίνι ὁμοία ἐστὶν ἡ βασιλεία τοῦ θεοῦ; Καὶ τίνι ὁμοιώσω αὐτήν;

18Then he was saying, "What is the kingdom of God like? And to what may I compare it?

---

264 **13:15** txt υποκριται $\mathfrak{P}^{75}$ ℵ A B E F G H K L M N S U Y Γ Δ Θ Λ Π Ψ Ω f^{13} 2 28 565 700 1071 1424 latt syr^{h} $cop^{sa,bo}$ eth arm Hipp Ir RP TH NA28 {/} ‖ υποκριτα $\mathfrak{P}^{45}$ D W f^{1} 157 579 2542 $it^{f,l}$ $syr^{s,c,p,hmg}$ TR ‖ *omit vv. 15,16* 33 ‖ *lac* C P Q T

265 **13:16** The number six signifies human effort, which falls short of seven, God's perfection or completion. This woman was enslaved for eighteen years, three times six, three times the normal human effort. What better day than the seventh, the day of rest, for someone to be set free from the slavery of working six days three times? See Deuteronomy 15:1, "Every seventh year you must cancel debts." And 15:12, "If a fellow Hebrew, a man or a woman, sells himself to you and serves you six years, in the seventh year you must let him go free." This woman was kept in bondage three sets of six years, and not being set free.

Lk 13:19 Ὁμοία ἐστὶν κόκκῳ σινάπεως, ὃν λαβὼν ἄνθρωπος ἔβαλεν εἰς κῆπον ἑαυτοῦ• καὶ ηὔξησεν, καὶ ἐγένετο εἰς δένδρον, καὶ τὰ πετεινὰ τοῦ οὐρανοῦ κατεσκήνωσεν ἐν τοῖς κλάδοις αὐτοῦ.

19It is like a mustard seed, which a man took *and* cast into his garden, and it grew and became a tree, and the birds of the sky nested in its branches."

Lk 13:20 Καὶ πάλιν εἶπεν, Τίνι ὁμοιώσω τὴν βασιλείαν τοῦ θεοῦ;

20And again he said, "To what may I compare the kingdom of God?

Lk 13:21 Ὁμοία ἐστὶν ζύμῃ, ἣν λαβοῦσα γυνὴ ἐνέκρυψεν εἰς ἀλεύρου σάτα τρία, ἕως οὗ ἐζυμώθη ὅλον.

21It is like yeast that a woman took and folded into three measures[266] of dough until the whole *of it* was leavened."

The Narrow Door

Lk 13:22 Καὶ διεπορεύετο κατὰ πόλεις καὶ κώμας διδάσκων, καὶ πορείαν ποιούμενος εἰς Ἱεροσόλυμα.

22And he was going through every city and village teaching, even as he was making his journey toward Jerusalem.

Lk 13:23 Εἶπεν δέ τις αὐτῷ, Κύριε, εἰ ὀλίγοι οἱ σῳζόμενοι; Ὁ δὲ εἶπεν πρὸς αὐτούς,

23And someone said to him, "Lord, are those being saved going to be few?" And he said to him,

Lk 13:24 Ἀγωνίζεσθε εἰσελθεῖν διὰ τῆς στενῆς θύρας• ὅτι πολλοί, λέγω ὑμῖν, ζητήσουσιν εἰσελθεῖν, καὶ οὐκ ἰσχύσουσιν.

24"Make every effort to go in through the narrow door. For many, I tell you, will try to enter, and not be able to.

Lk 13:25 Ἀφ' οὗ ἂν ἐγερθῇ ὁ οἰκοδεσπότης καὶ ἀποκλείσῃ τὴν θύραν, καὶ ἄρξησθε ἔξω ἑστάναι καὶ κρούειν τὴν θύραν, λέγοντες, Κύριε, ἄνοιξον ἡμῖν• καὶ ἀποκριθεὶς ἐρεῖ ὑμῖν, Οὐκ οἶδα ὑμᾶς, πόθεν ἐστέ•

25Once the master of the house has gotten up and closed the door, after that you may begin to stand outside, and knock *on* the door, saying, 'Lord, open to us,' and in answer he will say to you, 'I don't know where you are from.'

Lk 13:26 τότε ἄρξεσθε λέγειν, Ἐφάγομεν ἐνώπιόν σου καὶ ἐπίομεν, καὶ ἐν ταῖς πλατείαις ἡμῶν ἐδίδαξας.

26At that time you will begin to say, "We ate and drank in your presence, and you taught in our streets."

Lk 13:27 Καὶ ἐρεῖ λέγων ὑμῖν, οὐκ οἶδα ὑμᾶς όθεν ἐστέ• ἀπόστητε ἀπ' ἐμοῦ πάντες ἐργάται ἀδικίας.

27And then at that time he will say to you as follows: 'I don't know where you are from. Get away from me, all you workers of unrighteousness.'

---

266 **13:21** Greek: three *sata,* about 5 gallons, or 22 liters.

Lk 13:28 Ἐκεῖ ἔσται ὁ κλαυθμὸς καὶ ὁ βρυγμὸς τῶν ὀδόντων, ὅταν ὄψησθε Ἀβραὰμ καὶ Ἰσαὰκ καὶ Ἰακὼβ καὶ πάντας τοὺς προφήτας ἐν τῇ βασιλείᾳ τοῦ θεοῦ, ὑμᾶς δὲ ἐκβαλλομένους ἔξω.

28In that place there will be weeping, and gnashing of teeth, when you see Abraham and Isaac and Jacob and all the prophets in the kingdom of God, and you are being cast outside,

Lk 13:29 Καὶ ἥξουσιν ἀπὸ ἀνατολῶν καὶ δυσμῶν, καὶ ἀπὸ βορρᾶ καὶ νότου, καὶ ἀνακλιθήσονται ἐν τῇ βασιλείᾳ τοῦ θεοῦ.

29and *people* will have come from the east and the west, and from the north and the south, and be reclined in the kingdom of God.

Lk 13:30 Καὶ ἰδού, εἰσὶν ἔσχατοι οἳ ἔσονται πρῶτοι, καὶ εἰσὶν πρῶτοι οἳ ἔσονται ἔσχατοι.

30And behold, there are those who are last, who will be first; and there are those who are first who will be last."

Jesus Laments Jerusalem

Lk 13:31 Ἐν αὐτῇ τῇ ὥρᾳ προσῆλθάν τινες Φαρισαῖοι, λέγοντες αὐτῷ, Ἔξελθε καὶ πορεύου ἐντεῦθεν, ὅτι Ἡρῴδης θέλει σε ἀποκτεῖναι.

31In that hour, some Pharisees came up to him, saying to him, "You should move on, and get out of this place, because Herod is trying to kill you."

Lk 13:32 Καὶ εἶπεν αὐτοῖς, Πορευθέντες εἴπατε τῇ ἀλώπεκι ταύτῃ, Ἰδού, ἐκβάλλω δαιμόνια καὶ ἰάσεις ἀποτελῶ σήμερον καὶ αὔριον, καὶ τῇ τρίτῃ τελειοῦμαι.

32And he said to them, "Go tell that fox: 'Behold, I am casting out demons and accomplishing healings today and tomorrow, and on the third day I will reach my goal.'[267]

Lk 13:33 Πλὴν δεῖ με σήμερον καὶ αὔριον καὶ τῇ ἐχομένῃ πορεύεσθαι• ὅτι οὐκ ἐνδέχεται προφήτην ἀπολέσθαι ἔξω Ἱερουσαλήμ.

33Regardless, I would have to be continuing on today and tomorrow and the next day. For it is not possible for a prophet to be killed outside Jerusalem!

Lk 13:34 Ἱερουσαλήμ, Ἱερουσαλήμ, ἡ ἀποκτείνουσα τοὺς προφήτας καὶ λιθοβολοῦσα τοὺς ἀπεσταλμένους πρὸς αὐτήν, ποσάκις ἠθέλησα ἐπισυνάξαι τὰ τέκνα σου, ὃν τρόπον ὄρνις τὴν ἑαυτῆς νοσσιὰν ὑπὸ τὰς πτέρυγας, καὶ οὐκ ἠθελήσατε.

34O Jerusalem, Jerusalem, that kills the prophets, and stones those sent to it! How often I have wished to gather your children, as a hen does her brood under her wings, and you were not willing.

---

[267] **13:32** The Greek for the last phrase, καὶ τῇ τρίτῃ τελειοῦμαι could also possibly be translated, "and on the third day I will be finished." But this saying of Jesus seems related to verse 22 of this same chapter, that he was making his way to Jerusalem. The verb τελειόω can also mean to reach the end of something, like a journey, so it makes sense to translate it that way in view of what he says in verse 33. That verse implies that he will reach Jerusalem in three days. Reaching his goal of arriving in Jerusalem, he says, is essential, because it is not possible for a prophet to be killed outside of Jerusalem.

Lk 13:35 Ἰδού, ἀφίεται ὑμῖν ὁ οἶκος ὑμῶν. Λέγω ὑμῖν, οὐ μή ἴδητέ με ἕως ἥξει ὅτε εἴπητε, Εὐλογημένος ὁ ἐρχόμενος ἐν ὀνόματι κυρίου.

35Behold, your[268] house is now abandoned to you.[269] I tell you, you will not see me, until the day when you say,[270] 'Blessed is he who comes in the name of the Lord.'"[271]

Chapter 14

Jesus at a Pharisee's House

Lk 14:1 Καὶ ἐγένετο ἐν τῷ ἐλθεῖν αὐτὸν εἰς οἶκόν τινος τῶν ἀρχόντων τῶν Φαρισαίων σαββάτῳ φαγεῖν ἄρτον, καὶ αὐτοὶ ἦσαν παρατηρούμενοι αὐτόν.

1And it came about that when he went into the house of a certain ruler of the Pharisees on a Sabbath, to eat bread, they were watching him closely.

Lk 14:2 Καὶ ἰδού, ἄνθρωπός τις ἦν ὑδρωπικὸς ἔμπροσθεν αὐτοῦ.

2And behold, a man with dropsy was right in front of him.[272]

---

268 **13:35a** The Greek pronoun for "you" is plural, as also the "you" all three times in this same verse.

269 **13:35b** txt {A} ὑμῶν 𝔓^{75} א A B K L S W Y Γ Λ Π Ω *f*^{1} 124 565 579 597 788 1006 1010 1243 1292 1582* 2542 Byz^{pt} *Lect*^{pt} it^{aur,e,ff2,i} vg^{ww,st} syr^{s} cop^{sa,bopt} arm slav Ir$^{lat v.l.}$ Epiphanius; Aug TH NA28 {B} ‖ ὑμῶν ἔρημος D E G H M N U Δ Θ Ψ *f*^{13} 2 28 33 118 157 180 205 346 700 892 1071 1241 1342 1424 1505 1582^{c} Byz^{pt} *Lect*^{pt,AD} it^{a,b,c,d,f,l,q,r1} vg^{cl} syr^{c,p,h} cop^{bopt} geo Ir^{lat} TR RP ‖ *lac* 𝔓^{45} C F P Q T. Many manuscripts add the word ἔρημος, "desolate." This is may be to harmonize Luke with Matthew 23:38. But this was not necessary, since the word ἀφίημι, translated "left" in most translations, also can mean "abandon." The meaning seems to be, that their house, whether it means their temple, or their lineage, or their houses, will be abandoned by Jesus, since he tells them they will not see him again until he fulfills Psalm 118:26. Abandoned to them alone without him. What is their temple without the high priest? What is their lineage without the Lion of Judah? What are their homes without the Light of Humankind?

270 **13:35c** txt ἕως [ἥξει ὅτε] εἴπητε (ἥξει ἡ ἡμέρα it^{a,b,f} syr^{c,h}) D WH NA28 {C} ‖ ἕως ἂν ἥξῃ ὅτε εἴπητε E G (H ℓ76 ὅτι) U Γ Ψ 124^{c} 180 565 597 700 788 1006 1195 1230 1292 1344 1365 1505 1646 2174 Byz^{pt} *Lect*^{pt,AD} it$^{aur,(d),d,(ff2),l,q,r1}$ vg slav^{mss} Aug TR RP ‖ ἕως ἂν ἥξει (itacism for ἥξῃ?) ὅτε εἴπητε A N S W Λ Ω 2 28 (579 ἥξει ὅταν) 1009 1216 1242^{Z} 1243 1253 1342 1424 Byz^{pt} *Lect*^{pt} Cyril^{lem} ‖ ἕως εἴπητε 𝔓^{75} B L 892 1242^{txt} TH ‖ ἕως ὅτε εἴπητε K Π 1079 1546 ‖ ἕως ἂν εἴπητε 𝔓^{45} א M X *f*^{13} 1 124* 157 205 346 1010 1071 ℓ292$^{1/2}$ ℓ514 ℓ1552 (Epiphanius) (ἕως or ἕως ἂν it^{c,i} vg^{ms} cop^{samss,fay} arm eth geo slav^{mss}) ‖ ἀπ' ἄρτι ἕως ἂν εἴπητε Θ 1241 ℓ950 cop^{samss,bo} ‖ ἀπ' ἄρτι ἕως ἂν ἥξει ὅτε εἴπητε Δ ‖ *lac* C F P Q T. According to the UBS textual commentary, there was apparently an effort to smooth over a very rare usage on Luke's part of ὅτε with the subjunctive mood, as found in Codex D. Or they may have succumbed to the temptation to assimilate Luke to Matthew 23:39. Note that the footnote in the UBS4 Greek New Testament is in error in its citation of 𝔓^{75} and 𝔓^{45}, having them switched.

271 **13:35d** Psalm 118:26 בָּרוּךְ הַבָּא. בְּשֵׁם יְהוָה;
http://www.mechon-mamre.org/p/pt/pt26b8.htm

272 **14:2** Perhaps the "behold" could mean similar to the exclamation, "what do you know." Like this: "And what do you know, there was a man with dropsy right in front of him." At any rate, it looks like it was a set-up.

Lk 14:3 Καὶ ἀποκριθεὶς ὁ Ἰησοῦς εἶπεν πρὸς τοὺς νομικοὺς καὶ Φαρισαίους,
λέγων, Ἔξεστιν τῷ σαββάτῳ θεραπεῦσαι ἢ οὔ;

3And in response, Jesus said to the lawyers and Pharisees as follows: "Is it
permissible during a Sabbath to heal, or is it not?"

Lk 14:4 Οἱ δὲ ἡσύχασαν. Καὶ ἐπιλαβόμενος ἰάσατο αὐτόν, καὶ ἀπέλυσεν.

4But they kept quiet. And after grasping him, he healed him, and dismissed
him.

Lk 14:5 Καὶ πρὸς αὐτοὺς εἶπεν, Τίνος ὑμῶν υἱὸς ἢ βοῦς εἰς φρέαρ πεσεῖται, καὶ
οὐκ εὐθέως ἀνασπάσει αὐτὸν ἐν ἡμέρᾳ τοῦ σαββάτου;

5And he said to them, "Who among you whose son[273] or ox should fall into a
pit during the Sabbath day, would not immediately pull him out?"

Lk 14:6 Καὶ οὐκ ἴσχυσαν ἀνταποκριθῆναι αὐτῷ πρὸς ταῦτα.

6And they were not able to rebut these *words*.

Lk 14:7 Ἔλεγεν δὲ πρὸς τοὺς κεκλημένους παραβολήν, ἐπέχων πῶς τὰς
πρωτοκλισίας ἐξελέγοντο, λέγων πρὸς αὐτούς,

7And toward those who had been invited, he was speaking a parable, referring
to how they were claiming the most prestigious seats, saying to them as follows:

Lk 14:8 Ὅταν κληθῇς ὑπό τινος εἰς γάμους, μὴ κατακλιθῇς εἰς τὴν
πρωτοκλισίαν• μήποτε ἐντιμότερός σου ᾖ κεκλημένος ὑπ' αὐτοῦ,

8"When you are invited by someone to a banquet, do not recline at the place
of honor, in case someone more distinguished than you is invited by him,

Lk 14:9 καὶ ἐλθὼν ὁ σὲ καὶ αὐτὸν καλέσας ἐρεῖ σοι, Δὸς τούτῳ τόπον• καὶ τότε
ἄρξῃ μετὰ αἰσχύνης τὸν ἔσχατον τόπον κατέχειν.

9and the one who invited both you and him comes and says to you, 'Yield
place to this person.' And then you would proceed with embarrassment to
make for[274] the last seat.

Lk 14:10 Ἀλλ' ὅταν κληθῇς, πορευθεὶς ἀνάπεσε εἰς τὸν ἔσχατον τόπον• ἵνα, ὅταν
ἔλθῃ ὁ κεκληκώς σε, ἐρεῖ σοι, Φίλε, προσανάβηθι ἀνώτερον• τότε ἔσται σοι δόξα
ἐνώπιον πάντων τῶν συνανακειμένων σοι.

10Instead, when you are invited, make your way to the least desirable place
and recline, so that when the one who invited you comes, he will say to you,
'Friend, move up to a better place.' Then, there will be honor for you in front of
all your fellow dinner guests.

---

273 **14:5** txt υιος η βους $\mathfrak{P}^{75}$ B E G H M N W Γ Δ Λ Ω 2 28 180 565 1009 1010 1195 1216 1242 1243 1342 1365 1424 1505 2148 𝔐 *Lect* it^{e,f,q} syr^{p,h} cop^{sa} geo RP SBL NA28 {B} ‖ η υιος η βους $\mathfrak{P}^{45}$ ‖ ονος η βους ℵ K L X Y Π Ψ f^{1} f^{13} 33 157 205 579 597 892 1071 1079 1230 1241 1253 1292 1546 1646 ℓ524 ℓ547 it$^{a,aur,b,c,ff^2,i,l,r^1}$ vg syr$^{(s),pal}$ cop^{bo,fay} arm (eth) slav TR ‖ ο υιος η βους A S U 700 1006 ‖ ονος υιος η βους Θ ‖ υιος η βους η ονος syr^{c} ‖ προβατον η βους D it^{d} ‖ ορος η βους 69 ‖ *lac* C F P Q T. TCGNT: John Mill conjectured that υἱός is a corruption of the old Greek word ὄϊς ("a sheep"); see John Mill, *Novum Testamentum Graecum*, 2nd ed. (Leipzig, 1723), p. 44, § 423.

274 **14:9** The Greek verb κατέχω - katéchō, which I translated "make your way toward," generally means to take, to occupy. But the verb also was a nautical term meaning "head for, make for, steer toward." I chose that shade of meaning here, because the emphasis seems to be the embarrassment you would feel the whole time you are picking your way, in front of everyone, toward the back seat all the way from the front one. The emphasis seems to be on the long, embarrassing process, rather than on the point of taking the seat.

Lk 14:11 Ὅτι πᾶς ὁ ὑψῶν ἑαυτὸν ταπεινωθήσεται, καὶ ὁ ταπεινῶν ἑαυτὸν ὑψωθήσεται.

11For anyone who exalts himself will be humbled; and the one who humbles himself will be exalted."

Lk 14:12 Ἔλεγεν δὲ καὶ τῷ κεκληκότι αὐτόν, Ὅταν ποιῇς ἄριστον ἢ δεῖπνον, μὴ φώνει τοὺς φίλους σου, μηδὲ τοὺς ἀδελφούς σου, μηδὲ τοὺς συγγενεῖς σου, μηδὲ γείτονας πλουσίους• μήποτε καὶ αὐτοί ἀντικαλέσωσίν σε, καὶ γένηταί ἀνταπόδομά σοι.

12And he was also saying to the man who had invited him, "When you make a breakfast or dinner, do not call your friends, or your siblings or relatives or rich neighbors, lest they also invite you back in return, and that would be repayment for you.

Lk 14:13 Ἀλλ' ὅταν δοχὴν ποιῇς, κάλει πτωχούς, ἀναπείρους, χωλούς, τυφλούς•

13Instead, when you make a banquet, invite the poor, the crippled, the lame, the blind;

Lk 14:14 καὶ μακάριος ἔσῃ, ὅτι οὐκ ἔχουσιν ἀνταποδοῦναί σοι• ἀνταποδοθήσεται γάρ σοι ἐν τῇ ἀναστάσει τῶν δικαίων.

14and you will be blessed, because they do not have the means to repay you. For it will be repaid to you, you see, at the resurrection of the righteous."

The Parable of the Great Banquet

Lk 14:15 Ἀκούσας δέ τις τῶν συνανακειμένων ταῦτα εἶπεν αὐτῷ, Μακάριος, ὅστις φάγεται ἄρτον ἐν τῇ βασιλείᾳ τοῦ θεοῦ.

15And after hearing these things, one of the dinner guests said to him, "Blessed is the person who will eat bread[275] in the kingdom of God."

Lk 14:16 Ὁ δὲ εἶπεν αὐτῷ, Ἄνθρωπός τις ἐποίει δεῖπνον μέγα, καὶ ἐκάλεσεν πολλούς•

16And Jesus[276] said to him, "A man was holding a great banquet, and invited many people.

Lk 14:17 καὶ ἀπέστειλεν τὸν δοῦλον αὐτοῦ τῇ ὥρᾳ τοῦ δείπνου εἰπεῖν τοῖς κεκλημένοις, Ἔρχεσθε, ὅτι ἤδη ἕτοιμά ἐστιν.

17And at the hour of the banquet, he sent his slave out to tell those who were invited, 'Come, for it is now ready.'

Lk 14:18 Καὶ ἤρξαντο ἀπὸ μιᾶς πάντες παραιτεῖσθαι. Ὁ πρῶτος εἶπεν αὐτῷ, Ἀγρὸν ἠγόρασα, καὶ ἔχω ἀνάγκην ἐξελθὼν ἰδεῖν αὐτόν• ἐρωτῶ σε, ἔχε με παρῃτημένον.

18And they all alike began to ask to be excused. The first one said to him, 'I have bought a field, and I urgently have to go out and see it. I ask you, consider me excused.'

---

275 **14:15** txt αρτον 𝔓^{75} ℵ^{1} A^{c} B D G H* K* L N P R Δ Θ Λ Ψ 1 157 579 892 1241 2542 latt syr^{p,h} cop^{sa,bo} Cl Eus Epiph TR TH NA28 {/} ‖ αριστον A* E H^{c} K^{c} M S U W Y Γ Π Ω 047 0211 *f*^{13} 28 124 565 700 788 1424 1582 𝔐 syr^{s,c} Cyr^{lem} RP ‖ *lac* 𝔓^{45} C F Q T 33

276 **14:16** The Greek says "he," not "Jesus."

Lk 14:19 Καὶ ἕτερος εἶπεν, Ζεύγη βοῶν ἠγόρασα πέντε, καὶ πορεύομαι δοκιμάσαι αὐτά• ἐρωτῶ σε, ἔχε με παρῃτημένον.

19And another one said, 'I have bought five yoke of oxen, and I'm on my way to try them out. I ask you, consider me excused.'

Lk 14:20 Καὶ ἕτερος εἶπεν, Γυναῖκα ἔγημα, καὶ διὰ τοῦτο οὐ δύναμαι ἐλθεῖν.

20And another one said, 'I have married a wife, and for this reason I am not able to come.'

Lk 14:21 Καὶ παραγενόμενος ὁ δοῦλος ἀπήγγειλεν τῷ κυρίῳ αὐτοῦ ταῦτα. Τότε ὀργισθεὶς ὁ οἰκοδεσπότης εἶπεν τῷ δούλῳ αὐτοῦ, Ἔξελθε ταχέως εἰς τὰς πλατείας καὶ ῥύμας τῆς πόλεως, καὶ τοὺς πτωχοὺς καὶ ἀναπείρους καὶ τυφλοὺς καὶ χωλοὺς εἰσάγαγε ὧδε.

21And when he came back, the slave reported these things to his master. Angered then, the master of the house said to his slave, 'Quick, go out into the boulevards and lanes of the town. And the poor, the crippled, the blind, the lame, lead them here.'

Lk 14:22 Καὶ εἶπεν ὁ δοῦλος, Κύριε, γέγονεν ὃ ἐπέταξας, καὶ ἔτι τόπος ἐστίν.

22And the slave said, 'Master, what you have commanded has been done, and still there is room.'

Lk 14:23 Καὶ εἶπεν ὁ κύριος πρὸς τὸν δοῦλον, Ἔξελθε εἰς τὰς ὁδοὺς καὶ φραγμούς, καὶ ἀνάγκασον εἰσελθεῖν, ἵνα γεμισθῇ μου ὁ οἶκος.

23And the master said to the slave, 'Go out into the trails and the fence lines, and urgently invite them to come in, so that my house will be filled.

Lk 14:24 Λέγω γὰρ ὑμῖν ὅτι οὐδεὶς τῶν ἀνδρῶν ἐκείνων τῶν κεκλημένων γεύσεταί μου τοῦ δείπνου.[277]

24You can be sure, I tell you, that not one of those men who were invited, will taste of my banquet!'"

Jesus Qualifies the Crowds

Lk 14:25 Συνεπορεύοντο δὲ αὐτῷ ὄχλοι πολλοί• καὶ στραφεὶς εἶπεν πρὸς αὐτούς,

25And great crowds were going along with him, and he turned around, and said to them,

Lk 14:26 Εἴ τις ἔρχεται πρός με, καὶ οὐ μισεῖ τὸν πατέρα αὐτοῦ, καὶ τὴν μητέρα, καὶ τὴν γυναῖκα, καὶ τὰ τέκνα, καὶ τοὺς ἀδελφούς, καὶ τὰς ἀδελφάς, ἔτι τε καὶ τὴν ψυχὴν ἑαυτοῦ, οὐ δύναταί εἶναί μου μαθητής.

26"If someone is coming with me, and does not spurn his father, and mother, and wife, and children, and brothers, and sisters, and yes, even his own life, he cannot be my disciple.

Lk 14:27 Ὅστις οὐ βαστάζει τὸν σταυρὸν ἑαυτοῦ καὶ ἔρχεται ὀπίσω μου, οὐ δύναται εἶναί μου μαθητής.

27Anyone that does not take up his own cross and follow after me, cannot be my disciple.

---

277 **14:24** txt δειπνου 𝔓^{45} 𝔓^{75} ℵ A B D E* L N P R W 047 latt syr cop TR TH NA28 {/} ‖ δειπνου. πολλοι γαρ εισιν κλητοι ολιγοι δε εκλεκτοι syr^{palms} geo^{mss} RP ‖ δειπνου. προσθες πολλοι γαρ εισιν κλητοι ολιγοι δε εκλεκτοι E^{c} ‖ *lac* C Q T. (Showing only 8th century and earlier witnesses.) The extra phrase is probably from lectionary influence.

Lk 14:28 Τίς γὰρ ἐξ ὑμῶν θέλων πύργον οἰκοδομῆσαι, οὐχὶ πρῶτον καθίσας ψηφίζει τὴν δαπάνην, εἰ ἔχει εἰς ἀπαρτισμόν;

28For who of you wishing to build a tower, does not first sit down and count the cost, whether he has enough for completion?

Lk 14:29 Ἵνα μήποτε, θέντος αὐτοῦ θεμέλιον καὶ μὴ ἰσχύοντος ἐκτελέσαι, πάντες οἱ θεωροῦντες ἄρξωνται αὐτῷ ἐμπαίζειν,

29It would be no good if he lays the foundation, and not being able to finish, all those observing start to ridicule him,

Lk 14:30 λέγοντες, ὅτι Οὗτος ὁ ἄνθρωπος ἤρξατο οἰκοδομεῖν, καὶ οὐκ ἴσχυσεν ἐκτελέσαι.

30saying, 'This fellow began to build, and was not able to finish.'

Lk 14:31 Ἢ τίς βασιλεὺς πορευόμενος ἑτέρῳ βασιλεῖ συμβαλεῖν εἰς πόλεμον οὐχὶ καθίσας πρῶτον βουλεύεται εἰ δυνατός ἐστιν ἐν δέκα χιλιάσιν ὑπαντῆσαι τῷ μετὰ εἴκοσι χιλιάδων ἐρχομένῳ ἐπ' αὐτόν;

31Or what king, going out to another king to meet in battle, does not first sit down to consider whether he is strong enough with ten thousand, to match the one who is coming against him with twenty thousand?

Lk 14:32 Εἰ δὲ μή γε, ἔτι αὐτοῦ πόρρω ὄντος, πρεσβείαν ἀποστείλας ἐρωτᾷ τὰ πρὸς εἰρήνην.

32For indeed if not, while he is still at a distance he sends out a delegation, and asks what are the conditions for peace.[278]

Lk 14:33 Οὕτως οὖν πᾶς ἐξ ὑμῶν ὃς οὐκ ἀποτάσσεται πᾶσιν τοῖς ἑαυτοῦ ὑπάρχουσιν, οὐ δύναταί εἶναί μου μαθητής.

33In the same way, then, any of you who does not say goodbye to everything that he has, cannot be my disciple.

Lk 14:34 Καλὸν οὖν τὸ ἅλας• ἐὰν δὲ καὶ τὸ ἅλας μωρανθῇ, ἐν τίνι ἀρτυθήσεται;

34Salt then is a good thing; but if the salt itself becomes bland, what will it be spiced with?

Lk 14:35 Οὔτε εἰς γῆν οὔτε εἰς κοπρίαν εὔθετόν ἐστιν• ἔξω βάλλουσιν αὐτό. Ὁ ἔχων ὦτα ἀκούειν ἀκουέτω.

35It is fit neither for the soil, nor for the manure pile;[279] they throw it out. Whoever has ears to hear, hear."

---

278 **14:32** DeBrunner, §155(2), regarding double accusatives, says this phrase ἐρωτᾷ τὰ πρὸς εἰρήνην, with both τὰ and εἰρήνην being accusative case, is equivalent to the Hebrew שָׁאַל לְשָׁלוֹם - šāʾal ləšālôm, and that it means "he inquires after his well-being." He says there are several examples in the Septuagint, and refers us to R. Helbing, "Die Kasussyntax der Verba bei den Septuaginta," 40. Another possibility according to DeBrunner, is: "he greets him (and pays homage to him)." He then refers us to Foerster. This translator does not have access to Helbing's or Foerster's works, so looked for LXX examples himself, and the closest thing he found was Psalm 122:6, Ερωτήσατε δὴ τὰ εἰς εἰρήνην Ἱερουσαλὴμ, "Pray now for the things that lead to the peace of Jerusalem."

279 **14:35** For salt at that time, do not picture purely refined, white, fine-grained sodium chloride like we use now. There are many speculations as to what this verse implies about the salt of that day. Bauer says that salt was sometimes used as fertilizer. Another scholar says that salt was sometimes used to make the soil of one's enemies **in**fertile! And why would someone put salt on a dung heap? To preserve it? Or was it to amend it, stretch it? The best explanation I have heard is that the word salt would have been understood to mean any

Chapter 15

The Parable of the Lost Sheep

Lk 15:1 Ἦσαν δὲ αὐτῷ ἐγγίζοντες πάντες οἱ τελῶναι καὶ οἱ ἁμαρτωλοί, ἀκούειν αὐτοῦ.

1And all the revenue agents and the sinners were coming up next to him, to listen to him.

Lk 15:2 Καὶ διεγόγγυζον οἵ τε Φαρισαῖοι καὶ οἱ γραμματεῖς λέγοντες ὅτι Οὗτος ἁμαρτωλοὺς προσδέχεται, καὶ συνεσθίει αὐτοῖς.

2And both the Pharisees and the Torah scholars were complaining, saying, "This fellow welcomes sinners, and eats with them."

Lk 15:3 Εἶπεν δὲ πρὸς αὐτοὺς τὴν παραβολὴν ταύτην, λέγων,

3But he spoke this parable to them, as follows:

Lk 15:4 Τίς ἄνθρωπος ἐξ ὑμῶν ἔχων ἑκατὸν πρόβατα, καὶ ἀπολέσας ἐξ αὐτῶν ἓν οὐ καταλείπει τὰ ἐνενήκοντα ἐννέα ἐν τῇ ἐρήμῳ, καὶ πορεύεται ἐπὶ τὸ ἀπολωλός, ἕως εὕρῃ αὐτό;

4"What man among you who has a hundred sheep and is missing one of them, does not leave behind the ninety-nine in the desert, and go out after the lost one, until he finds it?

Lk 15:5 Καὶ εὑρὼν ἐπιτίθησιν ἐπὶ τοὺς ὤμους αὐτοῦ χαίρων.

5And when he has found it, he places it on his shoulders, rejoicing.

Lk 15:6 Καὶ ἐλθὼν εἰς τὸν οἶκον, συγκαλεῖ τοὺς φίλους καὶ τοὺς γείτονας, λέγων αὐτοῖς, Συγχάρητέ μοι, ὅτι εὗρον τὸ πρόβατόν μου τὸ ἀπολωλός.

6And upon returning home he calls his friends and neighbors together, saying to them, 'Rejoice with me; for I have found my sheep that was lost.'

Lk 15:7 Λέγω ὑμῖν ὅτι οὕτως χαρὰ ἐν τῷ οὐρανῷ ἔσται ἐπὶ ἑνὶ ἁμαρτωλῷ μετανοοῦντι, ἢ ἐπὶ ἐνενήκοντα ἐννέα δικαίοις, οἵτινες οὐ χρείαν ἔχουσιν μετανοίας.

7I tell you, in just the same way, there will be more joy in heaven over one sinner repenting, than over ninety-nine righteous persons having no need of repentance.

---

substance that tasted salty, including, say, potassium nitrate, which could be used for fertilizer. And Ben Crick of England says that the word salt would have been used of any chemical salt, which would include a whole range of substances called "halides" (the Greek word for salt here is "halas"), such as fluorine, chlorine, bromine, iodine and astatine. Fortunately, the moral of the parable remains clear: unless you give up all your possessions, and take up your cross and follow like Jesus, you are salt that is not salty, so is not useful for anything.

The Parable of the Lost Coin

Lk 15:8 Ἢ τίς γυνὴ δραχμὰς ἔχουσα δέκα, ἐὰν ἀπολέσῃ δραχμὴν μίαν, οὐχὶ ἅπτει λύχνον, καὶ σαροῖ τὴν οἰκίαν, καὶ ζητεῖ ἐπιμελῶς ἕως οὗ εὕρῃ;

8 Or what woman having ten drachmas,[280] if she loses one drachma, does not light a lamp and sweep the house clean, and search diligently until such time she finds it?

Lk 15:9 Καὶ εὑροῦσα συγκαλεῖ τὰς φίλας καὶ γείτονας, λέγουσα, Συγχάρητέ μοι, ὅτι εὗρον τὴν δραχμὴν ἣν ἀπώλεσα.

9 And when she has found it, she calls her friends and neighbors together, saying, 'Rejoice with me; for I have found the drachma that was lost.'

Lk 15:10 Οὕτως, λέγω ὑμῖν, γίνεται χαρὰ ἐνώπιον τῶν ἀγγέλων τοῦ θεοῦ ἐπὶ ἑνὶ ἁμαρτωλῷ μετανοοῦντι.

10 In just the same way, I tell you, rejoicing breaks out among the angels of God over one sinner repenting."

The Parable of the Lost Son

Lk 15:11 Εἶπεν δέ, Ἄνθρωπός τις εἶχεν δύο υἱούς•

11 And he said, "A certain man had two sons.

Lk 15:12 καὶ εἶπεν ὁ νεώτερος αὐτῶν τῷ πατρί, Πάτερ, δός μοι τὸ ἐπιβάλλον μέρος τῆς οὐσίας. Ὁ δὲ διεῖλεν αὐτοῖς τὸν βίον.

12 And the younger of them said to the father, 'Father, pay out to me the applicable share of the holdings.' So he divided to them the life savings.

Lk 15:13 Καὶ μετ' οὐ πολλὰς ἡμέρας συναγαγὼν πάντα ὁ νεώτερος υἱὸς ἀπεδήμησεν εἰς χώραν μακράν, καὶ ἐκεῖ διεσκόρπισεν τὴν οὐσίαν αὐτοῦ, ζῶν ἀσώτως.

13 And not many days later, having gathered everything together, the younger son journeyed off, to a far away country, and there he wasted his estate, living indulgently.

Lk 15:14 Δαπανήσαντος δὲ αὐτοῦ πάντα, ἐγένετο λιμὸς ἰσχυρὰ κατὰ τὴν χώραν ἐκείνην, καὶ αὐτὸς ἤρξατο ὑστερεῖσθαι.

14 And after he had spent everything he had, a severe famine took place over that whole country, and he himself began to be without.

Lk 15:15 Καὶ πορευθεὶς ἐκολλήθη ἑνὶ τῶν πολιτῶν τῆς χώρας ἐκείνης• καὶ ἔπεμψεν αὐτὸν εἰς τοὺς ἀγροὺς αὐτοῦ βόσκειν χοίρους.

15 And so going forth, he joined on with one of the citizens of that country, who sent him into his fields to tend swine.

Lk 15:16 Καὶ ἐπεθύμει χορτασθῆναι ἐκ τὴν κοιλίαν αὐτοῦ ἀπὸ τῶν κερατίων ὧν ἤσθιον οἱ χοῖροι• καὶ οὐδεὶς ἐδίδου αὐτῷ.

16 And he was craving to be fed of[281] the carob pods[282] that the swine were eating, and no one gave him any.

---

280 **15:8** A *drachma* was worth about a day's wage.

281 **15:16a** txt χορτασθηναι εκ 𝔓^{75} א B D L R it^{d,e,f} syr$^{(c),pal}$ cop^{sa} eth (Cyr) Aug TH NA28 {B} ‖ γεμισαι την κοιλιαν αυτου απο A N P Q 𝔐 it$^{(a),aur,b,ff^2,i,q,r^1}$ vg syr^{s,p,h} cop^{bo} arm geo$^{(2)}$ Cyr^{lem} Ambrose Chrom Jer TR RP ‖ γεμισαι την κοιλιαν και χορτασθηναι απο W ‖ *lac* 𝔓^{45} C E T. Some

Lk 15:17 Εἰς ἑαυτὸν δὲ ἐλθὼν ἔφη, Πόσοι μίσθιοι τοῦ πατρός μου περισσεύονται ἄρτων, ἐγὼ δὲ λιμῷ ὧδε ἀπόλλυμαι•

17 And when he came to himself,[283] he was saying, 'How many hired men of my father's have more than enough food, and here I am,[284] perishing with hunger.

Lk 15:18 ἀναστὰς πορεύσομαι πρὸς τὸν πατέρα μου, καὶ ἐρῶ αὐτῷ, Πάτερ, ἥμαρτον εἰς τὸν οὐρανὸν καὶ ἐνώπιόν σου•

18 I will arise and go to my father, and I will say to him, "Father, I have sinned against heaven, and before you.

Lk 15:19 οὐκέτι εἰμὶ ἄξιος κληθῆναι υἱός σου• ποίησόν με ὡς ἕνα τῶν μισθίων σου.

19 I am no longer worthy to be called your son; make me as one of your hired men." '

Lk 15:20 Καὶ ἀναστὰς ἦλθεν πρὸς τὸν πατέρα αὐτοῦ. Ἔτι δὲ αὐτοῦ μακρὰν ἀπέχοντος, εἶδεν αὐτὸν ὁ πατὴρ αὐτοῦ, καὶ ἐσπλαγχνίσθη, καὶ δραμὼν ἐπέπεσεν ἐπὶ τὸν τράχηλον αὐτοῦ, καὶ κατεφίλησεν αὐτόν.

20 And he arose and went to his father. But while he was still a long way off, his father saw him, and was moved with pity. And he ran out, flung his arms around him and kissed him.

Lk 15:21 Εἶπεν δὲ ὁ υἱὸς αὐτῷ, Πάτερ, ἥμαρτον εἰς τὸν οὐρανὸν καὶ ἐνώπιόν σου, οὐκέτι εἰμὶ ἄξιος κληθῆναι υἱός σου.

21 But the son said to him, 'Father, I have sinned against heaven, and before you. I am no longer worthy to be called your son.'

Lk 15:22 Εἶπεν δὲ ὁ πατὴρ πρὸς τοὺς δούλους αὐτοῦ, Ταχὺ ἐξενέγκατε στολὴν τὴν πρώτην καὶ ἐνδύσατε αὐτόν, καὶ δότε δακτύλιον εἰς τὴν χεῖρα αὐτοῦ, καὶ ὑποδήματα εἰς τοὺς πόδας•

22 But the father said to his servants, 'Quick, bring out the best robe and drape it on him, and put a ring on his hand, and shoes to his feet,

---

people think the NA28 reading is a harmonization to Lk 16:21. Some major translations that are usually based on the NA text follow the BYZ here instead, such as the NASB and the NIV.

282 **15:16b** Greek, κεράτιον, meaning "little horn,' so named because of the shape of the pods of the species *Ceratonia siliqua*, Arabic "kharrubah," meaning bean pod; aka. Cods of Syria, aka. St. John's Bread, alluding to an erroneous notion, based on folk etymological comparisons of the Greek for "husk" and "locust", that the locusts John the Baptizer lived on were instead carob pods; from a leguminous tree having pods 9 inches long and 1 inch broad, once common in the forests of Galilee (Arthur Penrhyn Stanley, Sinai & Palestine in connection with their history, ii 146, **1858**), and considered a food grain of lower grade; the pods that the Prodigal Son eyed longingly in the pig pens, Luke 15:16; cf. Lychophron, from 675 to 678, **III BC**. For further examples showing that "carob pod" was the meaning of the Greek word *keration*, see Aristotle, Polybius, 26, 1, 4, **II BC**; Dioscurides 1, 114, **I AD**; Aëtius, Treatment of Diseases of the Eye, 160, 3, **VI AD**; F. G. Kenyon & H. I. Bell, Greek Papyri in the British Museum I-V, 131, 7, 1893-1917.

283 **15:17a** That is, "came to his senses." There was another expression as antonym, "he was beside himself," said of Jesus in Mark 3:21, that is, "he is out of his senses" or "out of his right mind."

284 **15:17b** txt λιμω ωδε 𝔓^{75} ℵ B L it^{e,ff2} syr^{pal,h} NA28 {/} ‖ ωδε λιμω D N R lat syr^{s,c,p} cop arm geo ‖ λιμω A P Q W 𝔐 cop^{sams} TR RP ‖ *lac* 𝔓^{45} C E T

Lk 15:23 καὶ φέρετε τὸν μόσχον τὸν σιτευτὸν θύσατε, καὶ φαγόντες εὐφρανθῶμεν•
23and bring the fattened calf, and slaughter it, and let us feast and celebrate;
Lk 15:24 ὅτι οὗτος ὁ υἱός μου νεκρὸς ἦν, καὶ ἀνέζησεν• ἦν ἀπολωλώς, καὶ εὑρέθη. Καὶ ἤρξαντο εὐφραίνεσθαι.
24for this my son was dead and is alive again; was lost and has been found!' And they proceeded to celebrate.
Lk 15:25 Ἦν δὲ ὁ υἱὸς αὐτοῦ ὁ πρεσβύτερος ἐν ἀγρῷ• καὶ ὡς ἐρχόμενος ἤγγισεν τῇ οἰκίᾳ, ἤκουσεν συμφωνίας καὶ χορῶν.
25But his elder son was in the fields. And as he was getting close to the house, he heard the sound of music and of dancing.
Lk 15:26 Καὶ προσκαλεσάμενος ἕνα τῶν παίδων, ἐπυνθάνετο τί ἂν εἴη ταῦτα.
26And calling over one of the workboys, he was asking what it was all about.
Lk 15:27 Ὁ δὲ εἶπεν αὐτῷ ὅτι Ὁ ἀδελφός σου ἥκει• καὶ ἔθυσεν ὁ πατήρ σου τὸν μόσχον τὸν σιτευτόν, ὅτι ὑγιαίνοντα αὐτὸν ἀπέλαβεν.
27And he told him, 'Your brother has returned, and your father has slaughtered the fattened calf, because he has him back safe and sound.'
Lk 15:28 Ὠργίσθη δέ, καὶ οὐκ ἤθελεν εἰσελθεῖν• ὁ δὲ πατὴρ αὐτοῦ ἐξελθὼν παρεκάλει αὐτόν.
28Then he was angry, and refused to go inside. And his father, after coming out, was pleading with him.
Lk 15:29 Ὁ δὲ ἀποκριθεὶς εἶπεν τῷ πατρὶ αὐτοῦ, Ἰδοὺ τοσαῦτα ἔτη δουλεύω σοι, καὶ οὐδέποτε ἐντολήν σου παρῆλθον, καὶ ἐμοὶ οὐδέποτε ἔδωκας ἔριφον, ἵνα μετὰ τῶν φίλων μου εὐφρανθῶ.
29But in response he said to his father, 'All these years I have been serving you, and not once did I ever deviate from your instructions. Yet to me, you have never given so much as a baby goat so I could celebrate with my friends.
Lk 15:30 Ὅτε δὲ ὁ υἱός σου οὗτος ὁ καταφαγών σου τὸν βίον μετὰ πορνῶν ἦλθεν, ἔθυσας αὐτῷ τὸν σιτευτὸν μόσχον.
30But when this son of yours comes who ate up your life savings with prostitutes, you slaughter for him the fattened calf!'
Lk 15:31 Ὁ δὲ εἶπεν αὐτῷ, Τέκνον, σὺ πάντοτε μετ' ἐμοῦ εἶ, καὶ πάντα τὰ ἐμὰ σά ἐστιν.
31But he said to him, 'Dear child, you are always with me, and everything that is mine is yours.
Lk 15:32 Εὐφρανθῆναι δὲ καὶ χαρῆναι ἔδει• ὅτι ὁ ἀδελφός σου οὗτος νεκρὸς ἦν καὶ ἔζησεν, καὶ ἀπολωλὼς καὶ εὑρέθη.
32But to celebrate, and be cheered up, is only right; for this your brother was dead and is alive again; was lost, and has been found!' "

Chapter 16

The Shrewd Money Manager

Lk 16:1 Ἔλεγεν δὲ καὶ πρὸς τοὺς μαθητάς, Ἄνθρωπός τις ἦν πλούσιος, ὃς εἶχεν οἰκονόμον• καὶ οὗτος διεβλήθη αὐτῷ ὡς διασκορπίζων τὰ ὑπάρχοντα αὐτοῦ.

1And then toward his disciples he was saying: "There was a rich man, who had a business manager. And accusations were brought to him against this man, that he was wasting his property.

Lk 16:2 Καὶ φωνήσας αὐτὸν εἶπεν αὐτῷ, Τί τοῦτο ἀκούω περὶ σοῦ; Ἀπόδος τὸν λόγον τῆς οἰκονομίας σου• οὐ γὰρ δύνῃ ἔτι οἰκονομεῖν.

2So having summoned him, he said to him, 'What is this I am hearing about you? Surrender the records of your management; for you can no longer be manager.'

Lk 16:3 Εἶπεν δὲ ἐν ἑαυτῷ ὁ οἰκονόμος, Τί ποιήσω, ὅτι ὁ κύριός μου ἀφαιρεῖται τὴν οἰκονομίαν ἀπ' ἐμοῦ; Σκάπτειν οὐκ ἰσχύω, ἐπαιτεῖν αἰσχύνομαι.

3And the manager said to himself, 'What will I do, now that my master is taking away the management from me? I am not strong enough to dig. I am ashamed to beg.

Lk 16:4 Ἔγνων τί ποιήσω, ἵνα, ὅταν μετασταθῶ ἐκ τῆς οἰκονομίας, δέξωνταί με εἰς τοὺς οἴκους αὐτῶν.

4I know what I will do, so that after I am removed from my management, people will welcome me into their homes.'

Lk 16:5 Καὶ προσκαλεσάμενος ἕνα ἕκαστον τῶν χρεοφειλετῶν τοῦ κυρίου ἑαυτοῦ, ἔλεγεν τῷ πρώτῳ, Πόσον ὀφείλεις τῷ κυρίῳ μου;

5And calling in each and every one of his master's debtors, he said to the first one, 'How much do you owe my master?'

Lk 16:6 Ὁ δὲ εἶπεν, Ἑκατὸν βάτους ἐλαίου. Ὁ δὲ εἶπεν αὐτῷ, Δέξαι σου τὰ γράμματα, καὶ καθίσας ταχέως γράψον πεντήκοντα.

6And he said, 'A hundred baths of olive oil.' And he told him, 'Take your bill, and sit down quickly and write "fifty." '

Lk 16:7 Ἔπειτα ἑτέρῳ εἶπεν, Σὺ δὲ πόσον ὀφείλεις; Ὁ δὲ εἶπεν, Ἑκατὸν κόρους σίτου. Λέγει αὐτῷ, Δέξαι σου τὰ γράμματα, καὶ γράψον ὀγδοήκοντα.

7Then, to another one he said, 'And you, how much do you owe?' And he said, 'A hundred kors of wheat.' He says to him, 'Take your bill and write "eighty." '

Lk 16:8 Καὶ ἐπῄνεσεν ὁ κύριος τὸν οἰκονόμον τῆς ἀδικίας ὅτι φρονίμως ἐποίησεν• ὅτι οἱ υἱοὶ τοῦ αἰῶνος τούτου φρονιμώτεροι ὑπὲρ τοὺς υἱοὺς τοῦ φωτὸς εἰς τὴν γενεὰν τὴν ἑαυτῶν εἰσίν.

8And that master gave credit to the unrighteous manager, in that he had acted shrewdly. For the children of this age are more shrewd toward their own generation than are the children of light.

Lk 16:9 Καὶ ἐγὼ ὑμῖν λέγω, Ἑαυτοῖς ποιήσατε φίλους ἐκ τοῦ μαμωνᾶ τῆς ἀδικίας, ἵνα, ὅταν ἐκλίπητε, δέξωνται ὑμᾶς εἰς τὰς αἰωνίους σκηνάς.

9And as for me, I say to you, make friends for yourselves by means of the undependable[285] wealth, so that when it fails, they may welcome you into perpetual dwellings.

Lk 16:10 Ὁ πιστὸς ἐν ἐλαχίστῳ καὶ ἐν πολλῷ πιστός ἐστιν, καὶ ὁ ἐν ἐλαχίστῳ ἄδικος καὶ ἐν πολλῷ ἄδικός ἐστιν.

10The person who is faithful with little is also faithful with much, and the one who is undependable with little is also undependable with much.

Lk 16:11 Εἰ οὖν ἐν τῷ ἀδίκῳ μαμωνᾷ πιστοὶ οὐκ ἐγένεσθε, τὸ ἀληθινὸν τίς ὑμῖν πιστεύσει;

11If therefore you do not prove faithful with the undependable wealth, who will trust you with the true?

Lk 16:12 Καὶ εἰ ἐν τῷ ἀλλοτρίῳ πιστοὶ οὐκ ἐγένεσθε, τὸ ὑμέτερον τίς ὑμῖν δώσει;

12And if with someone else's property you have not turned out to be faithful, who will grant you property of your own?

Lk 16:13 Οὐδεὶς οἰκέτης δύναται δυσὶν κυρίοις δουλεύειν• ἢ γὰρ τὸν ἕνα μισήσει, καὶ τὸν ἕτερον ἀγαπήσει• ἢ ἑνὸς ἀνθέξεται, καὶ τοῦ ἑτέρου καταφρονήσει. Οὐ δύνασθε θεῷ δουλεύειν καὶ μαμωνᾷ.

13No house slave is able to serve two masters; for he would either spurn the one and love the other, or devote himself to the one and despise the other. You cannot serve both God and Wealth."

Lk 16:14 Ἤκουον δὲ ταῦτα πάντα οἱ Φαρισαῖοι φιλάργυροι ὑπάρχοντες, καὶ ἐξεμυκτήριζον αὐτόν.

14And the Pharisees had been listening to all this and, being moneylovers, were sneering at him.

Lk 16:15 Καὶ εἶπεν αὐτοῖς, Ὑμεῖς ἐστε οἱ δικαιοῦντες ἑαυτοὺς ἐνώπιον τῶν ἀνθρώπων, ὁ δὲ θεὸς γινώσκει τὰς καρδίας ὑμῶν• ὅτι τὸ ἐν ἀνθρώποις ὑψηλὸν βδέλυγμα ἐνώπιον τοῦ θεοῦ.

15And he said to them, "You are ones who justify yourselves before human beings, but God knows your hearts. For what is highly esteemed among human beings, is detestable in God's sight.

---

285 **16:9** The Greek word "adikos" here is usually rendered "unrighteous, but can also mean "untrustworthy, undependable," as indeed Jesus uses it here and in vv. 10-11 with that meaning. Jesus is also making a play on words, on the word Mammon (here rendered Wealth), which word is based on a Semitic root for "dependable, reliable." The idea of mammon was a wealth to such an extent that one could relax and feel secure and confident financially. But Jesus here is saying that it will fail. Jesus calls it the wealth that is ἀδικίας, which means "unrighteous, unreliable, fraudulent, false, untrustworthy." When Jesus says "unrighteous Mammon," he is saying something like "insecure security." And this is the same word he used to describe the manager. A false manager, an undependable manager. Another play is the contrast of the undependable property with the "true" or "real" property. Wherever I have the word "undependable," you can substitute the word "false, dishonest" as in whoever is false with little, is also false with much;" and, "false wealth."

Lk 16:16 Ὁ νόμος καὶ οἱ προφῆται μέχρι Ἰωάννου• ἀπὸ τότε ἡ βασιλεία τοῦ θεοῦ εὐαγγελίζεται, καὶ πᾶς εἰς αὐτὴν βιάζεται.

16The law and the prophets were[286] until John; from that time on the kingdom of God is being proclaimed, and everyone is pushing their way into it.

Lk 16:17 Εὐκοπώτερον δέ ἐστιν τὸν οὐρανὸν καὶ τὴν γῆν παρελθεῖν, ἢ τοῦ νόμου μίαν κεραίαν πεσεῖν.

17But it is easier for sky and earth to pass away, than for one serif of the law to fall.

Lk 16:18 Πᾶς ὁ ἀπολύων τὴν γυναῖκα αὐτοῦ καὶ γαμῶν ἑτέραν μοιχεύει• καὶ ὁ ἀπολελυμένην ἀπὸ ἀνδρὸς γαμῶν μοιχεύει.

18Anyone who dismisses his wife and marries another is committing adultery, and he who marries her who has been dismissed by a husband, is committing adultery.[287]

The Rich Man and Lazarus

Lk 16:19 Ἄνθρωπος δέ τις ἦν πλούσιος, καὶ ἐνεδιδύσκετο πορφύραν καὶ βύσσον, εὐφραινόμενος καθ' ἡμέραν λαμπρῶς.

19Now a certain man was rich, and used to put on a purple robe and fine linen, and live it up splendidly every day.

Lk 16:20 Πτωχὸς δέ τις ὀνόματι Λάζαρος ἐβέβλητο πρὸς τὸν πυλῶνα αὐτοῦ εἱλκωμένος

20But a beggar, Lazarus by name, was laid at his gate, covered with sores;

Lk 16:21 καὶ ἐπιθυμῶν χορτασθῆναι ἀπὸ τῶν ψιχίων τῶν πιπτόντων ἀπὸ τῆς τραπέζης τοῦ πλουσίου• ἀλλὰ καὶ οἱ κύνες ἐρχόμενοι ἐπέλειχον τὰ ἕλκη αὐτοῦ.

21and he kept longing in vain to eat the scraps dropping from that rich man's table. In contrast, the dogs would at least come and lick his sores.

Lk 16:22 Ἐγένετο δὲ ἀποθανεῖν τὸν πτωχόν, καὶ ἀπενεχθῆναι αὐτὸν ὑπὸ τῶν ἀγγέλων εἰς τὸν κόλπον Ἀβραάμ• ἀπέθανεν δὲ καὶ ὁ πλούσιος, καὶ ἐτάφη.

22"Now the beggar came to die, and was carried off by the angels to Abraham's bosom. And the rich man also died, and was buried.

Lk 16:23 Καὶ ἐν τῷ Ἅιδῃ ἐπάρας τοὺς ὀφθαλμοὺς αὐτοῦ, ὑπάρχων ἐν βασάνοις, ὁρᾷ Ἀβραὰμ ἀπὸ μακρόθεν, καὶ Λάζαρον ἐν τοῖς κόλποις αὐτοῦ.

23And in Hades, when he lifted up his eyes, from being in torment, he sees Abraham far away, and Lazarus in his bosom.[288]

---

[286] **16:16** There is no verb in this sentence in the Greek. But the only word in Greek customarily allowed to be omitted but implied, is the simple copula. That is, the verb "is." And since it is talking about something that was in the past, and plural, therefore we supply the word "were."

[287] **16:18** Why is this said here, at this time? The context is Jesus scolding the Pharisees for being apparently righteous, but being detestable in God's sight. Therefore I believe that what is happening here is that the Pharisees commonly divorced and remarried, and would justify it somehow. But Jesus was known to have taught a stricter view of divorce than even the strictest school of the Pharisees.

[288] **16:23** Also in v. 22, εἰς τὸν κόλπον Ἀβραάμ "Abraham's side." Compare John 13:23, where John's place at the Passover meal was ἐν τῷ κόλπῳ τοῦ Ἰησοῦ "in the bosom of Jesus," and

Lk 16:24 Καὶ αὐτὸς φωνήσας εἶπεν, Πάτερ Ἀβραάμ, ἐλέησόν με, καὶ πέμψον Λάζαρον, ἵνα βάψῃ τὸ ἄκρον τοῦ δακτύλου αὐτοῦ ὕδατος, καὶ καταψύξῃ τὴν γλῶσσάν μου• ὅτι ὀδυνῶμαι ἐν τῇ φλογὶ ταύτῃ.

24So after calling out to him, he said, 'Father Abraham, have pity on me, and send Lazarus to dip the tip of his finger in water, to cool my tongue, because I am in agony in this fire.'

Lk 16:25 Εἶπεν δὲ Ἀβραάμ, Τέκνον, μνήσθητι ὅτι ἀπέλαβες τὰ ἀγαθά σου ἐν τῇ ζωῇ σου, καὶ Λάζαρος ὁμοίως τὰ κακά• νῦν δὲ ὧδε παρακαλεῖται, σὺ δὲ ὀδυνᾶσαι.

25"But Abraham said, 'Son, recall that in your lifetime, you received your good things, while Lazarus likewise received his bad; so now here, he is comforted, and you are suffering.

Lk 16:26 Καὶ ἐν πᾶσιν τούτοις, μεταξὺ ἡμῶν καὶ ὑμῶν χάσμα μέγα ἐστήρικται, ὅπως οἱ θέλοντες διαβῆναι ἔνθεν πρὸς ὑμᾶς μὴ δύνωνται, μηδὲ ἐκεῖθεν πρὸς ἡμᾶς διαπερῶσιν.

26And besides all this, between us and you a great chasm has been fixed, such that those who want to go from here to you are not able to, neither can anyone cross over from there to us.'

Lk 16:27 Εἶπεν δέ, Ἐρωτῶ σε οὖν, πάτερ, ἵνα πέμψῃς αὐτὸν εἰς τὸν οἶκον τοῦ πατρός μου,

27"And he said, 'Then I beg you, father, please send him to my father's house,

Lk 16:28 ἔχω γὰρ πέντε ἀδελφούς, ὅπως διαμαρτύρηται αὐτοῖς, ἵνα μὴ καὶ αὐτοὶ ἔλθωσιν εἰς τὸν τόπον τοῦτον τῆς βασάνου.

28since I have five brothers, in order that he solemnly warn them not to also come to this place of torment.'

Lk 16:29 Λέγει δὲ Ἀβραάμ, Ἔχουσιν Μωϋσέα καὶ τοὺς προφήτας• ἀκουσάτωσαν αὐτῶν.

29"But Abraham says, 'They have Moses and the Prophets; let them take heed to them.'

Lk 16:30 Ὁ δὲ εἶπεν, Οὐχί, πάτερ Ἀβραάμ• ἀλλ' ἐάν τις ἀπὸ νεκρῶν πορευθῇ πρὸς αὐτούς, μετανοήσουσιν.

30"And he said, 'Hardly, father Abraham; but if someone from the dead goes to them, they will repent.'

Lk 16:31 Εἶπεν δὲ αὐτῷ, Εἰ Μωϋσέως καὶ τῶν προφητῶν οὐκ ἀκούουσιν, οὐδ' ἐάν τις ἐκ νεκρῶν ἀναστῇ, πεισθήσονται.

31"And he said to him, 'If they are not taking heed to Moses and the Prophets, neither will they be persuaded if someone rises from the dead.'"

John 1:18, where Jesus Christ the Son is said to be εἰς τὸν κόλπον τοῦ πατρὸς "in the bosom of the Father."

Chapter 17

A Brother Who Sins

Lk 17:1 Εἶπεν δὲ πρὸς τοὺς μαθητὰς αὐτοῦ, Ἀνένδεκτόν ἐστιν τοῦ τὰ σκάνδαλα
μὴ ἐλθεῖν• πλὴν οὐαὶ δι' οὗ ἔρχεται.
1And he said to his disciples, "It is not possible for there not to come things that cause people to fall. Nevertheless, woe to that person by whom such comes!
Lk 17:2 Λυσιτελεῖ αὐτῷ εἰ λίθος μυλικὸς περίκειται περὶ τὸν τράχηλον αὐτοῦ,
καὶ ἔρριπται εἰς τὴν θάλασσαν, ἢ ἵνα σκανδαλίσῃ τῶν μικρῶν τούτων ἕνα.
2It would be better for him if a mill stone is lying around his neck and he is thrown into the sea, than that he cause one of these little ones to fall.
Lk 17:3 Προσέχετε ἑαυτοῖς. Ἐὰν ἁμάρτῃ ὁ ἀδελφός σου, ἐπιτίμησον αὐτῷ• καὶ
ἐὰν μετανοήσῃ, ἄφες αὐτῷ.
3Watch yourselves. If your brother sins,[289] rebuke him, and if he repents, forgive him.

---

289 **17:3** txt ἁμάρτῃ ℵ A B L W it$^{a,aur,b,f,ff^2,l}$ vg^{ww,st} syr^{c,s,p,h,pal} cop^{sa,b}o arm geo^1 Clem Bas SBL TH NA28 {A} ‖ ἁμάρτῃ εἰς σε E N 𝔐 it$^{d,e,q,r^1}$ vg^{cl} cop^{bomss} eth geo^2 Ambrose Aug TR RP ‖ ἁμαρτήσῃ εἰς σε D ‖ *lac* 𝔓^{75} C P Q T Ξ. See also Matt 18:15.

Lk 17:4 Καὶ ἐὰν ἑπτάκις τῆς ἡμέρας ἁμαρτήσῃ εἰς σέ, καὶ ἑπτάκις ἐπιστρέψῃ πρὸς σέ, λέγων, Μετανοῶ, ἀφήσεις αὐτῷ.

4And if he sins against you seven times in a day,[290] and seven times he turns toward you,[291] saying, 'I repent,' you must forgive him."

Faith and Duty

Lk 17:5 Καὶ εἶπαν οἱ ἀπόστολοι τῷ κυρίῳ, Πρόσθες ἡμῖν πίστιν.

5And the apostles said to the Lord, "Give us more faith."

Lk 17:6 Εἶπεν δὲ ὁ κύριος, Εἰ ἔχετε πίστιν ὡς κόκκον σινάπεως, ἐλέγετε ἂν τῇ συκαμίνῳ ταύτῃ, Ἐκριζώθητι, καὶ φυτεύθητι ἐν τῇ θαλάσσῃ• καὶ ὑπήκουσεν ἂν ὑμῖν.

6But the Lord said, "If you have faith as *small as* a mustard seed, you could say to this mulberry tree, 'Be uprooted and planted in the sea,' and it would obey you.

Lk 17:7 Τίς δὲ ἐξ ὑμῶν δοῦλον ἔχων ἀροτριῶντα ἢ ποιμαίνοντα, ὃς εἰσελθόντι ἐκ τοῦ ἀγροῦ ἐρεῖ αὐτῷ, Εὐθέως παρελθὼν ἀνάπεσε•

7Now who of you having a servant plowing or tending the sheep, when he comes in from the field would say to him, 'Come right over here and recline'?

Lk 17:8 ἀλλ' οὐχὶ ἐρεῖ αὐτῷ, Ἑτοίμασον τί δειπνήσω, καὶ περιζωσάμενος διακόνει μοι, ἕως φάγω καὶ πίω• καὶ μετὰ ταῦτα φάγεσαι καὶ πίεσαι σύ;

8Would he not instead say to him, 'Fix something I can eat, and after you have girded yourself, serve me while I eat and drink, and after these things, you shall eat and drink'?

Lk 17:9 Μὴ ἔχει χάριν τῷ δούλῳ ὅτι ἐποίησεν τὰ διαταχθέντα.

9Neither does he thank the servant, that he has done what he has been told.

Lk 17:10 Οὕτως καὶ ὑμεῖς, ὅταν ποιήσητε πάντα τὰ διαταχθέντα ὑμῖν, λέγετε ὅτι Δοῦλοι ἀχρεῖοί ἐσμεν• ὃ ὠφείλομεν ποιῆσαι πεποιήκαμεν.

10In the same way, you also, when you have done all the things that were prescribed for you, you should say, 'We are unprofitable servants; we have done what we are supposed to have done.'"

---

[290] **17:4a** Or possibly, as some translations say, "seven times a day." This latter reading would be a great deal more forgiving to do. Yet, Jesus in another place said we must forgive someone "seventy times seven" times, or perhaps "seventy-seven times." It seems to me, that the spirit of the teaching would also apply if someone sins against you seven times every day, but does turn to you seven times each day, saying, "I repent." Because really, that about describes our relationship with God, how many times he has to forgive us. And most of us don't even repent that many times a day, though we have need of it.

[291] **17:4b** txt

	επιστρεψη προς σε	ℵ B D L Ψ 892 1241 it syr^{s,c,pal} cop^{bopt} arm geo Clem SBL TH NA28 {/}
	επιστρεψη επι σε	2542
	επιστρεψη	E
της ημερας	επιστρεψη προς σε	A Λ 157 579 1071 it^{aur,e} vg syr^{p,h} cop^{sa,bopt}
της ημερας	επιστρεψη επι σε	f^{1} TR
της ημερας	επιστρεψη	F G H K M N S U W Y Γ Δ Θ Π Ω f^{13} 2 28 565 700 1424 it^{f} RP
lac		𝔓^{75} C P Q T Ξ

Ten Healed of Leprosy

Lk 17:11 Καὶ ἐγένετο ἐν τῷ πορεύεσθαι εἰς Ἱερουσαλήμ, καὶ αὐτὸς διήρχετο διὰ μέσον Σαμαρείας καὶ Γαλιλαίας.

11And it came about that as he was on his way to Jerusalem, he was passing through the middle of Samaria and Galilee.

Lk 17:12 Καὶ εἰσερχομένου αὐτοῦ εἴς τινα κώμην, ἀπήντησαν αὐτῷ δέκα λεπροὶ ἄνδρες, οἳ ἔστησαν πόρρωθεν•

12And as he was coming into a village, ten men who had leprosy met him, who stopped and stood at a distance.

Lk 17:13 καὶ αὐτοὶ ἦραν φωνήν, λέγοντες, Ἰησοῦ, ἐπιστάτα, ἐλέησον ἡμᾶς.

13And they called out loudly, saying, "Jesus, Master, have pity on us!"

Lk 17:14 Καὶ ἰδὼν εἶπεν αὐτοῖς, Πορευθέντες ἐπιδείξατε ἑαυτοὺς τοῖς ἱερεῦσιν. Καὶ ἐγένετο ἐν τῷ ὑπάγειν αὐτούς, ἐκαθαρίσθησαν.

14And when he saw this, he said to them, "Go show yourselves to the priests." And it came about that as they went, they were cleansed.

Lk 17:15 Εἷς δὲ ἐξ αὐτῶν, ἰδὼν ὅτι ἰάθη, ὑπέστρεψεν, μετὰ φωνῆς μεγάλης δοξάζων τὸν θεόν•

15And one of them, when he saw that he had been healed, turned and came back, praising God with a very loud voice.

Lk 17:16 καὶ ἔπεσεν ἐπὶ πρόσωπον παρὰ τοὺς πόδας αὐτοῦ, εὐχαριστῶν αὐτῷ• καὶ αὐτὸς ἦν Σαμαρίτης.

16And he fell on his face at Jesus' feet, thanking him. And he was a Samaritan.

Lk 17:17 Ἀποκριθεὶς δὲ ὁ Ἰησοῦς εἶπεν, Οὐχὶ οἱ δέκα ἐκαθαρίσθησαν; Οἱ δὲ ἐννέα ποῦ;

17So in response Jesus said, "Were there not ten cleansed? Where then are the other nine?

Lk 17:18 Οὐχ εὑρέθησαν ὑποστρέψαντες δοῦναι δόξαν τῷ θεῷ, εἰ μὴ ὁ ἀλλογενὴς οὗτος;

18Were none found to have come back to give glory to God, except this foreigner?"

Lk 17:19 Καὶ εἶπεν αὐτῷ, Ἀναστὰς πορεύου• ἡ πίστις σου σέσωκέν σε.

19And he said to him, "Get up and go your way; your faith has saved you."

The Coming of the Kingdom of God

Lk 17:20 Ἐπερωτηθεὶς δὲ ὑπὸ τῶν Φαρισαίων, πότε ἔρχεται ἡ βασιλεία τοῦ θεοῦ, ἀπεκρίθη αὐτοῖς καὶ εἶπεν, Οὐκ ἔρχεται ἡ βασιλεία τοῦ θεοῦ μετὰ παρατηρήσεως•

20And when he was questioned by the Pharisees as to when the kingdom of God was coming, he answered them as follows: "The kingdom of God does not show with careful observation,

Lk 17:21 οὐδὲ ἐροῦσιν, Ἰδοὺ ὧδε, ἤ, Ἐκεῖ. Ἰδοὺ γάρ, ἡ βασιλεία τοῦ θεοῦ ἐντὸς ὑμῶν ἐστίν.

21neither will people say, 'Behold, here;' or 'Behold, there.' For behold, the kingdom of God is within you."

Lk 17:22 Εἶπεν δὲ πρὸς τοὺς μαθητάς, Ἐλεύσονται ἡμέραι ὅτε ἐπιθυμήσετε μίαν τῶν ἡμερῶν τοῦ υἱοῦ τοῦ ἀνθρώπου ἰδεῖν, καὶ οὐκ ὄψεσθε.

22And he said to the disciples, "Days are coming, when it is one of the days of the Son of Man you will long to see, and you will not have that experience.

Lk 17:23 Καὶ ἐροῦσιν ὑμῖν, Ἰδοὺ ἐκεῖ ἤ Ἰδοὺ ὧδε• μὴ ἀπέλθητε, μηδὲ διώξητε.

23And people will say to you, 'Behold, there!' or 'Behold, here!' Do not go, neither follow after *them*.

Lk 17:24 Ὥσπερ γὰρ ἡ ἀστραπὴ ἀστράπτουσα ἐκ τῆς ὑπὸ τὸν οὐρανὸν εἰς τὴν ὑπ' οὐρανὸν λάμπει, οὕτως ἔσται ὁ υἱὸς τοῦ ἀνθρώπου ἐν τῇ ἡμέρᾳ αὐτοῦ.

24For just as lightning shines forth flashing from one end of the sky to the other, so shall it be with the Son of Man in his day.

Lk 17:25 Πρῶτον δὲ δεῖ αὐτὸν πολλὰ παθεῖν καὶ ἀποδοκιμασθῆναι ἀπὸ τῆς γενεᾶς ταύτης.

25But first he must suffer much at the hands of this generation and be rejected.

Lk 17:26 Καὶ καθὼς ἐγένετο ἐν ταῖς ἡμέραις Νῶε, οὕτως ἔσται καὶ ἐν ταῖς ἡμέραις τοῦ υἱοῦ τοῦ ἀνθρώπου.

26And just as it was in the days of Noah, so shall it be also in the days of the Son of Man.

Lk 17:27 Ἤσθιον, ἔπινον, ἐγάμουν, ἐγαμίζοντο, ἄχρι ἧς ἡμέρας εἰσῆλθεν Νῶε εἰς τὴν κιβωτόν, καὶ ἦλθεν ὁ κατακλυσμός, καὶ ἀπώλεσεν πάντας.

27People were eating, drinking, marrying, being given in marriage, up until the day that Noah entered into the ark, and the flood came, and destroyed them all.

Lk 17:28 Ὁμοίως καθὼς ἐγένετο ἐν ταῖς ἡμέραις Λώτ• ἤσθιον, ἔπινον, ἠγόραζον, ἐπώλουν, ἐφύτευον, ᾠκοδόμουν•

28It was just the same in the days of Lot. People were eating, drinking, buying, selling, planting, building,

Lk 17:29 ᾗ δὲ ἡμέρᾳ ἐξῆλθεν Λὼτ ἀπὸ Σοδόμων, ἔβρεξεν πῦρ καὶ θεῖον ἀπ' οὐρανοῦ, καὶ ἀπώλεσεν πάντας•

29but the day that Lot left Sodom, fire and sulphur rained down from heaven, and destroyed them all.

Lk 17:30 κατὰ τὰ αὐτὰ ἔσται ᾗ ἡμέρᾳ ὁ υἱὸς τοῦ ἀνθρώπου ἀποκαλύπτεται.

30Along those lines will be the day in which the Son of Man is being revealed.

Lk 17:31 Ἐν ἐκείνῃ τῇ ἡμέρᾳ, ὃς ἔσται ἐπὶ τοῦ δώματος, καὶ τὰ σκεύη αὐτοῦ ἐν τῇ οἰκίᾳ, μὴ καταβάτω ἆραι αὐτά• καὶ ὁ ἐν ἀγρῷ ὁμοίως μὴ ἐπιστρεψάτω εἰς τὰ ὀπίσω.

31In that day, if someone is on the roof, and his stuff is in the house, he should not go down to get it, and the one in the field should likewise not turn back around.

Lk 17:32 Μνημονεύετε τῆς γυναικὸς Λώτ.

32Remember Lot's wife.

Lk 17:33 Ὃς ἐὰν ζητήσῃ τὴν ψυχὴν αὐτοῦ περιποιήσασθαι ἀπολέσει αὐτήν• ὃς δ' ἂν ἀπολέσῃ ζῳογονήσει αὐτήν.

33Whoever tries to save his life will lose it, and whoever loses it will keep it alive.

Lk 17:34 Λέγω ὑμῖν, ταύτῃ τῇ νυκτὶ ἔσονται δύο ἐπὶ κλίνης μιᾶς• ὁ εἷς παραλημφθήσεται, καὶ ὁ ἕτερος ἀφεθήσεται.

34I tell you, in that night there will be two men on one couch; one will be taken, and the other left.

Lk 17:35 Ἔσονται δύο ἀλήθουσαι ἐπὶ τὸ αὐτό• ἡ μία παραλημφθήσεται, ἡ δὲ ἑτέρα ἀφεθήσεται.

35There will be two women together grinding grain; one will be taken, and the other left."

Lk 17:36 [292]

Lk 17:37 Καὶ ἀποκριθέντες λέγουσιν αὐτῷ, Ποῦ, κύριε; Ὁ δὲ εἶπεν αὐτοῖς, Ὅπου τὸ σῶμα, ἐκεῖ καὶ οἱ ἀετοὶ ἐπισυναχθήσονται.

37And they in response are saying to him, "Where, Lord?" And he said to them, "Where the body is, there also the eagles[293] will be gathered."

Chapter 18

The Parable of the Persistent Widow

Lk 18:1 Ἔλεγεν δὲ παραβολὴν αὐτοῖς πρὸς τὸ δεῖν πάντοτε προσεύχεσθαι αὐτοὺς καὶ μὴ ἐγκακεῖν,

1And he was speaking a parable to them, to the end that they ought always to pray, and not to lose heart,

Lk 18:2 λέγων, Κριτής τις ἦν ἔν τινι πόλει, τὸν θεὸν μὴ φοβούμενος, καὶ ἄνθρωπον μὴ ἐντρεπόμενος•

2as follows: "There was a judge in a certain city, who had no fear of God, and no regard for man.

---

292 **17:36** The King James Version has verse 36, "Two *men* shall be in the field; the one shall be taken, and the other left." But if you read an original 1611 King James Version, you will find a marginal note that says that the verse 17:36 was absent from most of their Greek manuscripts. You can view an actual scan of this marginal note, from just such a KJV, at: https://www.bibletranslation.ws/gfx/luke17-36.jpg

293 **17:37** Greek: ὁ αετος - **ho aetós**, a word used for both eagles and vultures. Yet this is apparently a quote by Jesus of the parable in Job 39:30, where the parallel in the Septuagint to ὁ αετος is ἱεραξ - **hiérax**, a hawk, v. 26. Both Aristotle and Pliny in their Histories class the vulture among the eagles. Both eagles and vultures are classified as unclean in the law of Moses, Lev. 11:13, Deut. 14:12, in that they both eat carrion (in Job 39:30 **ho aetós** is eating carrion). Yet generally speaking, where **ho aetós** is eating carrion, vultures may be assumed to be meant. Now T.W. Manson, in "Sayings of Jesus," says the eagle would emphasize the swiftness of the coming of the Day of the Son of man. It is true that the eagle in passages such as Job 9:26, and Rev. 12:14, is a symbol of swiftness. I also get some amount of meaning in this verse that the eagles are acting as a form of messenger, which again, the eagle sometimes symbolizes, but not vultures as much. But the main emphasis here about the bird is not that of messenger, but that of a clear sign in the sky. Still, either 'eagles' or 'vultures' would be an acceptable rendering here.

Lk 18:3 χήρα δὲ ἦν ἐν τῇ πόλει ἐκείνῃ, καὶ ἤρχετο πρὸς αὐτόν, λέγουσα, Ἐκδίκησόν με ἀπὸ τοῦ ἀντιδίκου μου.

3But there was a widow in that city, and she kept on coming to him, saying, 'Give me redress from my adversary.'

Lk 18:4 Καὶ οὐκ ἤθελεν ἐπὶ χρόνον• μετὰ δὲ ταῦτα εἶπεν ἐν ἑαυτῷ, Εἰ καὶ τὸν θεὸν οὐ φοβοῦμαι, οὐδὲ ἄνθρωπον ἐντρέπομαι•

4And for some time he had been refusing, but after all this, he said to himself, 'Even if I don't fear God, nor have regard for man,

Lk 18:5 διά γε τὸ παρέχειν μοι κόπον τὴν χήραν ταύτην, ἐκδικήσω αὐτήν, ἵνα μὴ εἰς τέλος ἐρχομένη ὑπωπιάζῃ με.

5just because this widow is causing me trouble, I will avenge her, lest all her coming in the end wears me out.' "

Lk 18:6 Εἶπεν δὲ ὁ κύριος, Ἀκούσατε τί ὁ κριτὴς τῆς ἀδικίας λέγει.

6And the Lord said, "Listen to what the unjust kind of judge was saying.

Lk 18:7 Ὁ δὲ θεὸς οὐ μὴ ποιήσῃ τὴν ἐκδίκησιν τῶν ἐκλεκτῶν αὐτοῦ τῶν βοώντων αὐτῷ ἡμέρας καὶ νυκτός, καὶ μακροθυμεῖ ἐπ' αὐτοῖς;

7So God, would he not bring about the avenging of his elect, who keep crying out to him day and night? And is he slow to respond to them?

Lk 18:8 Λέγω ὑμῖν ὅτι ποιήσει τὴν ἐκδίκησιν αὐτῶν ἐν τάχει. Πλὴν ὁ υἱὸς τοῦ ἀνθρώπου ἐλθὼν ἆρα εὑρήσει τὴν πίστιν ἐπὶ τῆς γῆς;

8I tell you, he would bring about justice for them, in short order. However, when the Son of Man comes, will he find any faith on the earth at all?"[294]

The Parable of the Pharisee and the Revenue Agent

Lk 18:9 Εἶπεν δὲ καὶ πρός τινας τοὺς πεποιθότας ἐφ' ἑαυτοῖς ὅτι εἰσὶν δίκαιοι, καὶ ἐξουθενοῦντας τοὺς λοιπούς, τὴν παραβολὴν ταύτην•

9And also, to some, who were convinced within themselves that they were righteous, and looking down on everyone else, he told this parable:

Lk 18:10 Ἄνθρωποι δύο ἀνέβησαν εἰς τὸ ἱερὸν προσεύξασθαι• ὁ εἷς Φαρισαῖος, καὶ ὁ ἕτερος τελώνης.

10"Two men went up to the temple to pray, one a Pharisee, and the other a revenue agent.

Lk 18:11 Ὁ Φαρισαῖος σταθεὶς πρὸς ἑαυτὸν ταῦτα προσηύχετο, Ὁ θεός, εὐχαριστῶ σοι ὅτι οὐκ εἰμὶ ὥσπερ οἱ λοιποὶ τῶν ἀνθρώπων, ἅρπαγες, ἄδικοι, μοιχοί, ἢ καὶ ὡς οὗτος ὁ τελώνης.

11When the Pharisee stood, he was praying inside himself as follows: 'O God, I thank you that I am not like other people, who are swindlers, dishonest, adulterers, or indeed, like this revenue agent.

Lk 18:12 Νηστεύω δὶς τοῦ σαββάτου, ἀποδεκατῶ πάντα ὅσα κτῶμαι.

12I fast twice a week, I tithe of everything I get.'

---

294 **18:8** "any at all" is from the Greek ἆρα, a particle not directly translatable, but which indicates irritatedness or impatience or displeasure.

Lk 18:13 Ὁ δὲ τελώνης μακρόθεν ἑστὼς οὐκ ἤθελεν οὐδὲ τοὺς ὀφθαλμοὺς ἐπᾶραι εἰς τὸν οὐρανόν, ἀλλ' ἔτυπτεν τὸ στῆθος αὐτοῦ, λέγων, Ὁ θεός, ἱλάσθητί μοι τῷ ἁμαρτωλῷ.

13But the revenue agent, standing a distance off, was not even willing to lift his eyes toward heaven, but was beating his chest, saying, 'O God, be merciful to me, a sinner.'

Lk 18:14 Λέγω ὑμῖν, κατέβη οὗτος δεδικαιωμένος εἰς τὸν οἶκον αὐτοῦ παρ' ἐκεῖνον• ὅτι πᾶς ὁ ὑψῶν ἑαυτὸν ταπεινωθήσεται, ὁ δὲ ταπεινῶν ἑαυτὸν ὑψωθήσεται.

14I tell you, this latter went down to his house justified, rather than the former. For all who exalt themselves will be humbled, and those who humble themselves will be exalted."[295]

The Little Children and Jesus

Lk 18:15 Προσέφερον δὲ αὐτῷ καὶ τὰ βρέφη, ἵνα αὐτῶν ἅπτηται• ἰδόντες δὲ οἱ μαθηταὶ ἐπετίμων αὐτοῖς.

15And people were bringing little children to him, so that he would touch them. But when the disciples saw this, they started rebuking them.

Lk 18:16 Ὁ δὲ Ἰησοῦς προσεκαλέσατο αὐτὰ λέγων, Ἄφετε τὰ παιδία ἔρχεσθαι πρός με, καὶ μὴ κωλύετε αὐτά• τῶν γὰρ τοιούτων ἐστὶν ἡ βασιλεία τοῦ θεοῦ.

16But Jesus called them over to him, saying, "Allow the children to come to me and stop preventing them, for of such is the kingdom of God.

Lk 18:17 Ἀμὴν λέγω ὑμῖν, ὃς ἂν μὴ δέξηται τὴν βασιλείαν τοῦ θεοῦ ὡς παιδίον, οὐ μὴ εἰσέλθῃ εἰς αὐτήν.

17Truly I tell you, whoever does not receive the kingdom of God like a child will certainly not enter it."

The Rich Young Ruler

Lk 18:18 Καὶ ἐπηρώτησέν τις αὐτὸν ἄρχων, λέγων, Διδάσκαλε ἀγαθέ, τί ποιήσας ζωὴν αἰώνιον κληρονομήσω;

18And a certain ruler queried him as follows: "Good teacher, with what done will I inherit eternal life?"

Lk 18:19 Εἶπεν δὲ αὐτῷ ὁ Ἰησοῦς, Τί με λέγεις ἀγαθόν; Οὐδεὶς ἀγαθός, εἰ μὴ εἷς, ὁ θεός.

19And Jesus said to him, "Why are you calling me good? No one is good, except God alone.

Lk 18:20 Τὰς ἐντολὰς οἶδας, Μὴ μοιχεύσῃς, μὴ φονεύσῃς, μὴ κλέψῃς, μὴ ψευδομαρτυρήσῃς, τίμα τὸν πατέρα σου καὶ τὴν μητέρα.

20The commandments you know: Do not commit adultery, Do not murder, Do not steal, Do not give false testimony, Honor your father and mother."

---

295 **18:14** Though the Greek pronouns and articles in this sentence are singular, I have felt free to generalize and neuterize to the plural, in view of the fact that the sentence begins with the Greek word πᾶς - pâs, which means "all" or "everyone." This is a general and plural subject.

Lk 18:21 Ὁ δὲ εἶπεν, Ταῦτα πάντα ἐφύλαξα ἐκ νεότητός.

21And he said, "All these I have kept since childhood."

Lk 18:22 Ἀκούσας δὲ ὁ Ἰησοῦς εἶπεν αὐτῷ, Ἔτι ἕν σοι λείπει• πάντα ὅσα ἔχεις πώλησον, καὶ διάδος πτωχοῖς, καὶ ἕξεις θησαυρὸν ἐν οὐρανοῖς• καὶ δεῦρο, ἀκολούθει μοι.

22And when Jesus heard this, he said to him, "There is till one thing lacking with you. Everything you have, sell and hand out to the poor, and you will have treasure in heaven, and then come follow me."

Lk 18:23 Ὁ δὲ ἀκούσας ταῦτα περίλυπος ἐγενήθη• ἦν γὰρ πλούσιος σφόδρα.

23But hearing these *words* made him very sad, for he was extremely wealthy.

Lk 18:24 Ἰδὼν δὲ αὐτὸν ὁ Ἰησοῦς εἶπεν, Πῶς δυσκόλως οἱ τὰ χρήματα ἔχοντες εἰς τὴν βασιλείαν τοῦ θεοῦ εἰσπορεύονται.

24And when Jesus saw this, he said, "How hard it is for those who have wealth to go into the kingdom of God.

Lk 18:25 Εὐκοπώτερον γάρ ἐστιν κάμηλον διὰ τρήματος βελόνης εἰσελθεῖν, ἢ πλούσιον εἰς τὴν βασιλείαν τοῦ θεοῦ εἰσελθεῖν.

25Indeed, it is easier for a camel[296] to go through the eye of a needle, than for the rich to enter into the kingdom of God."

Lk 18:26 Εἶπαν δὲ οἱ ἀκούσαντες, Καὶ τίς δύναται σωθῆναι;

26And those who heard said, "Who then CAN be saved?"

Lk 18:27 Ὁ δὲ εἶπεν, Τὰ ἀδύνατα παρὰ ἀνθρώποις δυνατὰ παρὰ τῷ θεῷ ἐστιν.

27And he said, "Things impossible with human beings are possible with God."

Lk 18:28 Εἶπεν δὲ ὁ Πέτρος, Ἰδού, ἡμεῖς ἀφέντες τὰ ἴδια ἠκολουθήσαμέν σοι.

28And Peter said, "Behold, we have left behind our own things to follow you."

Lk 18:29 Ὁ δὲ εἶπεν αὐτοῖς, Ἀμὴν λέγω ὑμῖν ὅτι οὐδείς ἐστιν ὃς ἀφῆκεν οἰκίαν ἢ γυναῖκα ἢ ἀδελφοὺς ἢ γονεῖς ἢ τέκνα ἕνεκεν τῆς βασιλείας τοῦ θεοῦ,

29And he said to them, "Truly I say to you, there is no one who has left house or wife or siblings or parents or children, for the sake of the kingdom of God,

Lk 18:30 ὃς οὐχὶ μὴ ἀπολάβῃ πολλαπλασίονα ἐν τῷ καιρῷ τούτῳ, καὶ ἐν τῷ αἰῶνι τῷ ἐρχομένῳ ζωὴν αἰώνιον.

30who will not receive back many times as much in this present time; and in the coming age, eternal life."

---

296 **18:25** Just as it is impossible, humanly speaking, for a camel to go through the eye of a needle, Jesus says in v. 27 that it is "impossible" for a rich man to enter the kingdom of God. Some people teach that Jesus really instead said "rope to go through the eye of a needle," because he was speaking in the Aramaic language, and the Aramaic word for camel was also the word for a kind of rope. Regardless, Jesus would want to invent a simile that was in line with his main point: "something impossible." His illustration must demonstrate something that is impossible, naturally speaking. "Camel" is more impossible than "rope," so at worst, camel works just fine, and at best, camel is the best rendering because it is more impossible.

Jesus Again Predicts His Death

Lk 18:31 Παραλαβὼν δὲ τοὺς δώδεκα, εἶπεν πρὸς αὐτούς, Ἰδού, ἀναβαίνομεν εἰς Ἱερουσαλήμ, καὶ τελεσθήσεται πάντα τὰ γεγραμμένα διὰ τῶν προφητῶν τῷ υἱῷ τοῦ ἀνθρώπου.

31And after having taken the twelve aside, he told them, "Behold, we are going up to Jerusalem, and everything that is written by the prophets about the Son of Man will be carried out.

Lk 18:32 Παραδοθήσεται γὰρ τοῖς ἔθνεσιν, καὶ ἐμπαιχθήσεται, καὶ ὑβρισθήσεται, καὶ ἐμπτυσθήσεται,

32For he will be handed over to the Gentiles, and be made fun of and mistreated and spit upon,

Lk 18:33 καὶ μαστιγώσαντες ἀποκτενοῦσιν αὐτόν• καὶ τῇ ἡμέρᾳ τῇ τρίτῃ ἀναστήσεται.

33and after scourging him they will kill him, and on the third day he will rise again."

Lk 18:34 Καὶ αὐτοὶ οὐδὲν τούτων συνῆκαν, καὶ ἦν τὸ ῥῆμα τοῦτο κεκρυμμένον ἀπ' αὐτῶν, καὶ οὐκ ἐγίνωσκον τὰ λεγόμενα.

34And they understood none of these things. Indeed, this statement was hidden from them, and they did not realize the things being said.

An Obnoxious Beggar Gets His Wish

Lk 18:35 Ἐγένετο δὲ ἐν τῷ ἐγγίζειν αὐτὸν εἰς Ἱεριχώ, τυφλός τις ἐκάθητο παρὰ τὴν ὁδὸν ἐπαιτῶν•

35And it came about that when he was drawing near to Jericho, a blind man was sitting beside the road, begging.

Lk 18:36 ἀκούσας δὲ ὄχλου διαπορευομένου, ἐπυνθάνετο τί εἴη τοῦτο.

36And when he heard the crowd going through, he was inquiring what this was all about.

Lk 18:37 Ἀπήγγειλαν δὲ αὐτῷ ὅτι Ἰησοῦς ὁ Ναζωραῖος παρέρχεται.

37And they informed him that Jesus the Nazarene was passing by.

Lk 18:38 Καὶ ἐβόησεν, λέγων, Ἰησοῦ, υἱὲ Δαυίδ, ἐλέησόν με.

38Then he cried out, saying, "Jesus, son of David, have mercy on me!"

Lk 18:39 Καὶ οἱ προάγοντες ἐπετίμων αὐτῷ ἵνα σιγήσῃ• αὐτὸς δὲ πολλῷ μᾶλλον ἔκραζεν, Υἱὲ Δαυίδ, ἐλέησόν με.

39And those leading the way were rebuking him, that he should be quiet. But he was shouting that much more, "Son of David, have mercy on me!"

Lk 18:40 Σταθεὶς δὲ ὁ Ἰησοῦς ἐκέλευσεν αὐτὸν ἀχθῆναι πρὸς αὐτόν• ἐγγίσαντος δὲ αὐτοῦ ἐπηρώτησεν αὐτόν,

40And after stopping, Jesus ordered that he be brought to him. And when he had come near, he asked him,

Lk 18:41 Τί σοι θέλεις ποιήσω; Ὁ δὲ εἶπεν, Κύριε, ἵνα ἀναβλέψω.

41"What do you want me to do for you?" And he said, "Lord, that I could see again."

Lk 18:42 Καὶ ὁ Ἰησοῦς εἶπεν αὐτῷ, Ἀνάβλεψον• ἡ πίστις σου σέσωκέν σε.

42And Jesus said to him, "See again; your faith has saved you."[297]

Lk 18:43 Καὶ παραχρῆμα ἀνέβλεψεν, καὶ ἠκολούθει αὐτῷ, δοξάζων τὸν θεόν• καὶ πᾶς ὁ λαὸς ἰδὼν ἔδωκεν αἶνον τῷ θεῷ.

43And at once he saw again, and he was following him, giving glory to God. And all the people also, when they saw, gave praise to God.

Chapter 19

Zacchaeus the Revenue Officer

Lk 19:1 Καὶ εἰσελθὼν διήρχετο τὴν Ἰεριχώ.

1And he entered, passing on through Jericho.

Lk 19:2 Καὶ ἰδού, ἀνὴρ ὀνόματι καλούμενος Ζακχαῖος, καὶ αὐτὸς ἦν ἀρχιτελώνης, καὶ αὐτὸς πλούσιος.

2And behold, there was a man called by the name of Zacchaeus, and he was a revenue officer, and he was rich.

Lk 19:3 Καὶ ἐζήτει ἰδεῖν τὸν Ἰησοῦν τίς ἐστιν, καὶ οὐκ ἠδύνατο ἀπὸ τοῦ ὄχλου, ὅτι τῇ ἡλικίᾳ μικρὸς ἦν.

3And he was trying to see who Jesus was, but was prevented by the crowd, since he was short in stature.

Lk 19:4 Καὶ προδραμὼν εἰς τὸ ἔμπροσθεν ἀνέβη ἐπὶ συκομορέαν ἵνα ἴδῃ αὐτόν• ὅτι ἐκείνης ἤμελλεν διέρχεσθαι.

4And after running on forward ahead, he climbed up onto a sycamore tree, so that he could see him, for he was about to pass that way.

Lk 19:5 Καὶ ὡς ἦλθεν ἐπὶ τὸν τόπον, ἀναβλέψας ὁ Ἰησοῦς εἶπεν πρὸς αὐτόν, Ζακχαῖε, σπεύσας κατάβηθι• σήμερον γὰρ ἐν τῷ οἴκῳ σου δεῖ με μεῖναι.

5And when Jesus arrived to the place, he looked up and said to him, "Hurry down, Zacchaeus, for today I need to stay at your house."

Lk 19:6 Καὶ σπεύσας κατέβη, καὶ ὑπεδέξατο αὐτὸν χαίρων.

6And he hurried down, and took him in gladly.

Lk 19:7 Καὶ ἰδόντες πάντες διεγόγγυζον, λέγοντες ὅτι Παρὰ ἁμαρτωλῷ ἀνδρὶ εἰσῆλθεν καταλῦσαι.

7And all who had seen this were complaining, saying, "He has gone in to stay the night with a sinful man."

Lk 19:8 Σταθεὶς δὲ Ζακχαῖος εἶπεν πρὸς τὸν κύριον, Ἰδού, τὰ ἡμίσιά μου τῶν ὑπαρχόντων, κύριε, τοῖς πτωχοῖς δίδωμι• καὶ εἴ τινός τι ἐσυκοφάντησα, ἀποδίδωμι τετραπλοῦν.

8And Zacchaeus stood up,[298] *and* said to the Lord, "Look, one half of all I possess, Lord, I am giving to the poor, and where I have defrauded anyone of anything, I am making restitution threefold.

---

[297] **18:42** Or, "your faith has *healed* you." As also in many other places in Luke.

[298] **19:8** Some translators interpret ἵστημι here as "stopped," seeing the situation as the grumblers grumbling while Zacchaeus and Jesus were still in their presence. So then

Lk 19:9 Εἶπεν δὲ πρὸς αὐτὸν ὁ Ἰησοῦς ὅτι Σήμερον σωτηρία τῷ οἴκῳ τούτῳ ἐγένετο, καθότι καὶ αὐτὸς υἱὸς Ἀβραάμ ἐστιν.

9And Jesus said in reference to him, "Today, salvation has come to this house, in view of the fact that this man too is a son of Abraham.

Lk 19:10 Ἦλθεν γὰρ ὁ υἱὸς τοῦ ἀνθρώπου ζητῆσαι καὶ σῶσαι τὸ ἀπολωλός.

10For the Son of Man came to seek and to save that which was lost."[299]

The Parable of the Ten Servants

Lk 19:11 Ἀκουόντων δὲ αὐτῶν ταῦτα, προσθεὶς εἶπεν παραβολήν, διὰ τὸ ἐγγὺς εἶναι Ἰερουσαλὴμ αὐτόν, καὶ δοκεῖν αὐτοὺς ὅτι παραχρῆμα μέλλει ἡ βασιλεία τοῦ θεοῦ ἀναφαίνεσθαι.

11And as they were listening to these things, he included *and* spoke another parable, because he was drawing near to Jerusalem, and they thought that the kingdom of God was about to be appearing shortly.

Lk 19:12 Εἶπεν οὖν, Ἄνθρωπός τις εὐγενὴς ἐπορεύθη εἰς χώραν μακράν, λαβεῖν ἑαυτῷ βασιλείαν, καὶ ὑποστρέψαι.

12He said therefore, "A certain man well born journeyed off to a far country, to receive for himself a kingdom and then return.

Lk 19:13 Καλέσας δὲ δέκα δούλους ἑαυτοῦ, ἔδωκεν αὐτοῖς δέκα μνᾶς, καὶ εἶπεν πρὸς αὐτούς, Πραγματεύσασθε ἐν ᾧ ἔρχομαι.

13Now after calling ten of his servants, he had given them ten minas,[300] and said to them, 'Do business, until such time I return.'

Lk 19:14 Οἱ δὲ πολῖται αὐτοῦ ἐμίσουν αὐτόν, καὶ ἀπέστειλαν πρεσβείαν ὀπίσω αὐτοῦ, λέγοντες, Οὐ θέλομεν τοῦτον βασιλεῦσαι ἐφ' ἡμᾶς.

14But his subjects hated him, and they sent ambassadors behind him saying, 'We do not want this man to be king over us.'

Zacchaeus would have stopped and said the things he said in response to those complaining. I do not see it that way. I think that Jesus and Zacchaeus had already gone into Zack's house and were reclined, when Zack stood up to say what he says in verse eight. I could be wrong.

299 **19:10** Jesus is the Good Shepherd of Ezekiel 34:16, and not a false shepherd of Ezekiel 34:4, and does search for that which was lost, as in Ezekiel 34:11. The exact same form of the Greek article and noun for "the lost,"τὸ ἀπολωλός, occurs also in the Septuagint in Ezekiel 34:4, 16. The translator should word the Ezekiel passages and here exactly the same way, so that the readers get the connection.

300 **19:13** That is, he gave the ten servants one mina each. The mina, which was originally a Semitic word that the Greek language had long since borrowed, was equivalent to 100 drachmas. One drachma was not insignificant in purchasing power. Culling Greek literature, you can find quite a variance: some times and places, one drachma could buy you one sheep, but was only one-fifth the price of an ox. Other times, one drachma could buy you an ox. Either way, a mina was worth at least 100 sheep. That is a lot of money. Anyone could take that amount of money and by investing, turn it into more.

Lk 19:15 Καὶ ἐγένετο ἐν τῷ ἐπανελθεῖν αὐτὸν λαβόντα τὴν βασιλείαν, καὶ εἶπεν φωνηθῆναι αὐτῷ τοὺς δούλους τούτους, οἷς δεδώκει τὸ ἀργύριον, ἵνα γνοῖ τί διεπραγματεύσαντο.

15And it came about that when he returned, he had received the kingship. And he ordered his servants to be summoned to him, those to whom he had given the money, in order to find out what they had earned.

Lk 19:16 Παρεγένετο δὲ ὁ πρῶτος, λέγων, Κύριε, ἡ μνᾶ σου δέκα προσηργάσατο μνᾶς.

16So the first one came, reporting as follows: 'Lord, your mina has grown to ten minas.'

Lk 19:17 Καὶ εἶπεν αὐτῷ, Εὖγε, ἀγαθὲ δοῦλε• ὅτι ἐν ἐλαχίστῳ πιστὸς ἐγένου, ἴσθι ἐξουσίαν ἔχων ἐπάνω δέκα πόλεων.

17And he said to him, 'Well *done*, good servant. Since with a little you have proven faithful, be therefore ruler over ten cities.'

Lk 19:18 Καὶ ἦλθεν ὁ δεύτερος, λέγων, Ἡ μνᾶ σου κύριε ἐποίησεν πέντε μνᾶς.

18And the second one came, saying, 'Your mina, Lord, has become five minas.'

Lk 19:19 Εἶπεν δὲ καὶ τούτῳ, Καὶ σὺ ἐπάνω γίνου πέντε πόλεων.

19So he said to that one, 'And you, you shall be over five cities.'

Lk 19:20 Καὶ ὁ ἕτερος ἦλθεν, λέγων, Κύριε, ἰδού, ἡ μνᾶ σου, ἣν εἶχον ἀποκειμένην ἐν σουδαρίῳ•

20And the other one[301] came, saying, "Lord, here is your mina, which I have been keeping laid away in a napkin.

Lk 19:21 ἐφοβούμην γάρ σε, ὅτι ἄνθρωπος αὐστηρὸς εἶ• αἴρεις ὃ οὐκ ἔθηκας, καὶ θερίζεις ὃ οὐκ ἔσπειρας.

21For I was afraid of you, since you are a demanding man; you collect what you did not deposit, and reap what you did not sow.'

Lk 19:22 Λέγει αὐτῷ, Ἐκ τοῦ στόματός σου κρινῶ σε, πονηρὲ δοῦλε. Ἤιδεις ὅτι ἐγὼ ἄνθρωπος αὐστηρός εἰμι, αἴρων ὃ οὐκ ἔθηκα, καὶ θερίζων ὃ οὐκ ἔσπειρα•

22He says to him, 'By your own mouth I judge you, you wicked servant. You knew, did you, that I am a demanding man, collecting what I did not deposit, and reaping what I did not sow?

Lk 19:23 καὶ διὰ τί οὐκ ἔδωκας μου τὸ ἀργύριον ἐπὶ τράπεζαν, κἀγὼ ἐλθὼν σὺν τόκῳ ἂν αὐτὸ ἔπραξα;

23Why then did you not put my money in the bank, and I having returned would collect it with interest?'

---

301 **19:20** Or, "another one," or, "a different one." There is a theory that this parable of the Ten Minas is drawn from Matthew's parable of the Ten Talants of 25:14-30, in which there are only three servants, and here Luke has "fatigued" of maintaining his version's uniqueness from Matthew, and reverted back to following Matthew's version exactly. On the other hand, Jesus may well have used modified versions of the parable at various times. Still, there are things about this Lukan version that do not add up, literally. The first servant is given one mina, and then in most translations, he says, "Your mina has made ten minas more." Then Jesus says in verse 24, 'Take the mina away from him, and give it to the one who has ten minas.' But, if he started with one mina, and made ten minas more, wouldn't he have eleven minas, and not ten? So, perhaps the aforementioned theory is true; or else, the phrase usually translated, "made ten minas more," can be translated something like I have it: "increased to ten minas." Note also that the "western text" omits v. 25.

Lk 19:24 Καὶ τοῖς παρεστῶσιν εἶπεν, Ἄρατε ἀπ' αὐτοῦ τὴν μνᾶν, καὶ δότε τῷ τὰς δέκα μνᾶς ἔχοντι.

24And to some standing there he said, 'Take the mina away from him, and give it to the one who has ten minas.'

Lk 19:25 Καὶ εἶπαν αὐτῷ, Κύριε, ἔχει δέκα μνᾶς.

25And they said to him, 'Lord, he **has** ten minas!'

Lk 19:26 Λέγω ὑμῖν ὅτι παντὶ τῷ ἔχοντι δοθήσεται• ἀπὸ δὲ τοῦ μὴ ἔχοντος, καὶ ὃ ἔχει ἀρθήσεται ἀπ' αὐτοῦ.

26'I tell you,[302] to everyone who has, it will be given, but the one who has not, even such that he has will be taken away from him.

Lk 19:27 Πλὴν τοὺς ἐχθρούς μου τούτους, τοὺς μὴ θελήσαντάς με βασιλεῦσαι ἐπ' αὐτούς, ἀγάγετε ὧδε, καὶ κατασφάξατε αὐτοὺς ἔμπροσθέν μου.

27But as for my enemies, those who had not wanted me to be king over them, bring them here, and slay them in front of me.'"

The Triumphal Entry

Lk 19:28 Καὶ εἰπὼν ταῦτα, ἐπορεύετο ἔμπροσθεν, ἀναβαίνων εἰς Ἱεροσόλυμα.

28And having said these things, he was pressing his way onward, going up to Jerusalem.

Lk 19:29 Καὶ ἐγένετο ὡς ἤγγισεν εἰς Βηθσφαγὴ καὶ Βηθανίαν πρὸς τὸ ὄρος τὸ καλούμενον Ἐλαιῶν, ἀπέστειλεν δύο τῶν μαθητῶν,

29And it came about that as he drew near to Bethphage and Bethany at the hill called the Mount of Olives, he sent away two of his disciples,

Lk 19:30 λέγων, Ὑπάγετε εἰς τὴν κατέναντι κώμην• ἐν ᾗ εἰσπορευόμενοι εὑρήσετε πῶλον δεδεμένον, ἐφ' ὃν οὐδεὶς πώποτε ἀνθρώπων ἐκάθισεν• καὶ λύσαντες αὐτὸν ἀγάγετε.

30saying, "Go into the village ahead of you, in which as you are entering you will find a colt[303] tethered, upon which no one has ever yet sat, and you are to untie it and bring it.

Lk 19:31 Καὶ ἐάν τις ὑμᾶς ἐρωτᾷ, Διὰ τί λύετε; οὕτως ἐρεῖτε ὅτι Ὁ κύριος αὐτοῦ χρείαν ἔχει.

31And if someone asks you, 'Why are you untying it,' say this, 'The Lord needs it.'

Lk 19:32 Ἀπελθόντες δὲ οἱ ἀπεσταλμένοι εὗρον καθὼς εἶπεν αὐτοῖς.

32And when the ones who were sent went, they found things just as he had told them.

Lk 19:33 Λυόντων δὲ αὐτῶν τὸν πῶλον, εἶπαν οἱ κύριοι αὐτοῦ πρὸς αὐτούς, Τί λύετε τὸν πῶλον;

33And as they were untying the colt, the owners of it said to them, "Why are you untying the colt?"

---

302 **19:26** txt λεγω ℵ B L it^{a} syr^{p} $cop^{sa,bo}$ arm TH NA28 {\} ‖ λεγω γαρ A D E N W 𝔐 ($it^{b,e,f}$ vg: *dico autem*) $syr^{h,s}$ TR RP ‖ *lac* $𝔓^{75}$ C P Q T Ξ. There seems to be confusion as to whether the lord speaking is the lord character within the parable, or the Lord himself outside the parable.

303 **19:30** πῶλος, a young mount animal, a word used for the foals of both donkeys and horses. But we know from the other accounts that this was the foal of a donkey.

Lk 19:34 Οἱ δὲ εἶπαν ὅτι Ὁ κύριος αὐτοῦ χρείαν ἔχει.

34And they said, "The Lord needs it."

Lk 19:35 Καὶ ἤγαγον αὐτὸν πρὸς τὸν Ἰησοῦν• καὶ ἐπιρίψαντες αὐτῶν τὰ ἱμάτια ἐπὶ τὸν πῶλον, ἐπεβίβασαν τὸν Ἰησοῦν.

35And they brought it to Jesus, and after throwing garments of theirs on the colt, they mounted Jesus upon it.

Lk 19:36 Πορευομένου δὲ αὐτοῦ, ὑπεστρώννυον τὰ ἱμάτια αὐτῶν ἐν τῇ ὁδῷ.

36And as he was proceeding along, people were spreading their cloaks in the road beneath.

Lk 19:37 Ἐγγίζοντος δὲ αὐτοῦ ἤδη πρὸς τῇ καταβάσει τοῦ ὄρους τῶν Ἐλαιῶν, ἤρξαντο ἅπαν τὸ πλῆθος τῶν μαθητῶν χαίροντες αἰνεῖν τὸν θεὸν φωνῇ μεγάλῃ περὶ πασῶν ὧν εἶδον δυνάμεων,

37And having come near now to the descent of the Mount of Olives, the whole company of disciples started rejoicing, to lift God up with a loud voice for all the miracles that they had seen.

Lk 19:38 λέγοντες, Εὐλογημένος ὁ ἐρχόμενος ὁ βασιλεὺς ἐν ὀνόματι κυρίου• ἐν οὐρανῷ εἰρήνη, καὶ δόξα ἐν ὑψίστοις.

38They were saying, "Blessed is the king who comes in the name of the Lord![304] Peace in heaven, and glory in the highest!"

Lk 19:39 Καί τινες τῶν Φαρισαίων ἀπὸ τοῦ ὄχλου εἶπαν πρὸς αὐτόν, Διδάσκαλε, ἐπιτίμησον τοῖς μαθηταῖς σου.

39And some Pharisees in the crowd said to him, "Teacher, rebuke your disciples!"

Lk 19:40 Καὶ ἀποκριθεὶς εἶπεν, Λέγω ὑμῖν ἐὰν οὗτοι σιωπήσουσιν, οἱ λίθοι κράξουσιν.

40And he in answer said, "I tell you, if these go silent, the stones will cry out."[305]

Lk 19:41 Καὶ ὡς ἤγγισεν, ἰδὼν τὴν πόλιν, ἔκλαυσεν ἐπ' αὐτήν,

41And as he drew near and saw the city, he wept over it,

Lk 19:42 λέγων ὅτι Εἰ ἔγνως ἐν τῇ ἡμέρᾳ ταύτῃ καὶ σὺ τὰ πρὸς εἰρήνην• νῦν δὲ ἐκρύβη ἀπὸ ὀφθαλμῶν σου.

---

304 **19:38** Psalm 118:26

305 **19:40** A few manuscripts (Γ Δ al.) have the verbs "be quiet" and "cry out" in the subjunctive mood, which in English would be, "If these were to keep silent, the stones would cry out." But the original reading is so certainly with the verbs in the future inflection, that this difference is not noted at all in the apparatus of the United Bible Societies' Greek New Testament, nor in their textual commentary. I have been translating the gospels long enough to have seen a trend, that copyists sometimes thought the future awkward, and changed it to the subjunctive. Because indeed the rule was, according to BDF §373, when the clause begins with ἐὰν as here, a subjunctive verb is expected. Thus, it is far more likely that copyists would have corrected an original future reading to a subjunctive one, than the other way around. But the future indicative here makes Jesus' statement that much more emphatic.

42saying, "If you, yes ironically you,[306] [307] had only known what would bring you peace[308] on this very day![309] But now it is hidden from your eyes.

Lk 19:43 Ὅτι ἥξουσιν ἡμέραι ἐπὶ σέ, καὶ παρεμβαλοῦσιν οἱ ἐχθροί σου χάρακά σοι, καὶ περικυκλώσουσίν σε, καὶ συνέξουσίν σε πάντοθεν,

43For the days will come upon you that your enemies will throw a palisade up against you, and encircle you, and press in on you from every side,

Lk 19:44 καὶ ἐδαφιοῦσίν σε καὶ τὰ τέκνα σου ἐν σοί, καὶ οὐκ ἀφήσουσιν λίθον ἐπὶ λίθον ἐν σοί, ἀνθ' ὧν οὐκ ἔγνως τὸν καιρὸν τῆς ἐπισκοπῆς σου.

44and throw you to the ground,[310] you and your children within you, and there will not be left within you a stone upon a stone, in retribution for the fact you did not recognize the time of your gracious visitation."[311]

Jesus Clears the Temple

Lk 19:45 Καὶ εἰσελθὼν εἰς τὸ ἱερόν, ἤρξατο ἐκβάλλειν τοὺς πωλοῦντας,

45And when he had entered the temple, he proceeded to drive out the vendors,[312]

---

306 **19:42a** txt

εν τη ημερα ταυτη και συ	ℵ B L eth^{pp} Or SBL TH NA28 {B}
και συ εν τη ημερα ταυτη	D it^{d,f,q} cop^{sa} ethTH (geo) (Marcus Ir^{lat}) Or^{lat}
και συ και γε εν τη ημερα ταυτη	A it^{i} (arm) Basil
συ και γε εν τη ημερα σου ταυτη	it^{a,ff2,l,r1}
και συ και γε εν τη ημερα σου ταυτη	E N R W 𝔐 it^{aur} vg syr$^{(p),h}$ (Diatess^{syr,arm}) (Eus) TR RP
lac	𝔓^{75} C P Q T

307 **19:42b** Jesus says, "yes, even you," because of the irony that the city of Jerusalem, whose name includes the Semitic root word for peace, did not recognize what would bring it peace, and did not recognize the Prince of Peace.

308 **19:42c** txt ειρηνην ℵ B L cop^{sa,boms} (Diatess^{syr}) Marcus Ir^{lat} Or½ Did TH NA28 {B} ‖ ειρηνην σου A E N W 𝔐 it^{a} syr^{c,s,p,h,palms} cop^{bo} arm eth geo (Diatess^{arm}) Or½ Eus⅘ Basil Cyr TR RP ‖ ειρηνην σοι D it^{aur,d,e,f,ff2,i,l,q,r1} vg Or^{lat} Eus⅕ Jer ‖ *lac* 𝔓^{75} C P Q T

309 **19:42d** This exact phrase, τὰ πρὸς εἰρήνην appeared also in Luke 14:32, where I translated it, "the conditions for peace."

310 **19:44a** The Greek verb for "dash to the ground," ἐδαφίζω, in reference to a city, means both "raze to the ground," as in the Septuagint in Isaiah 3:26, and also "dash to the ground," as in Psalm 136:9, Hosea 10:14, 14:1 and others. Here both meanings have to apply for the one instance of the word: you, referring to Jerusalem, the city, will be razed to the ground, and her children will be dashed to the ground.

311 **19:44b** The Greek words usually translated "because," here, "because you did not recognize," are the words ἀντι followed by the relative pronoun. A literal translation of this would be, "in exchange for the fact that you did not recognize your gracious visitation." For the previously mentioned disasters were also a visitation. A visitation, rendered in Greek by the word ἐπισκοπη, could be both a negative one, or a positive one. A gracious visitation was predicted for them and offered many times in the Hebrew scriptures, and earlier in the gospel of Luke, in Zechariah's song in Luke 1:78, where he said "because of the tender feelings of our God with which he Sunrise from on high will look over - ἐπισκέπτομαι us. Since they forfeited their gracious ἐπισκοπη, God would give them a calamitous one in exchange, in repayment, in retribution, instead.

Lk 19:46 λέγων αὐτοῖς, Γέγραπται, Καὶ ἔσται ὁ οἶκός μου οἶκος προσευχῆς• ὑμεῖς δὲ αὐτὸν ἐποιήσατε σπήλαιον λῃστῶν.

46telling them, "It is written, 'And my house shall be a house of prayer,'[313] but you have made it a haunt of bandits.'[314]"

Lk 19:47 Καὶ ἦν διδάσκων τὸ καθ' ἡμέραν ἐν τῷ ἱερῷ• οἱ δὲ ἀρχιερεῖς καὶ οἱ γραμματεῖς ἐζήτουν αὐτὸν ἀπολέσαι, καὶ οἱ πρῶτοι τοῦ λαοῦ•

47And he was teaching daily in the temple. And the chief priests and the Torah scholars, along with the leaders of the people, were trying to kill him.

Lk 19:48 καὶ οὐχ εὕρισκον τὸ τί ποιήσωσιν, ὁ λαὸς γὰρ ἅπας ἐξεκρέματο αὐτοῦ ἀκούων.

48Yet they were not finding any way they could do it, because the entire crowd was hanging on him, listening to him.

Chapter 20

The Authorities Question Jesus' Authority

Lk 20:1 Καὶ ἐγένετο ἐν μιᾷ τῶν ἡμερῶν διδάσκοντος αὐτοῦ τὸν λαὸν ἐν τῷ ἱερῷ καὶ εὐαγγελιζομένου, ἐπέστησαν οἱ ἀρχιερεῖς καὶ οἱ γραμματεῖς σὺν τοῖς πρεσβυτέροις,

1And it came about during one of those days of his teaching the crowd in the temple and preaching the good news, that the high priests and Torah scholars and elders came up,

Lk 20:2 καὶ εἶπαν λέγοντες πρὸς αὐτόν, Εἰπὸν ἡμῖν, ἐν ποίᾳ ἐξουσίᾳ ταῦτα ποιεῖς, ἢ τίς ἐστιν ὁ δούς σοι τὴν ἐξουσίαν ταύτην;

2and they said to him as follows: "Tell us, by what authority are you doing these things? Or, who is the one who gave you the authority for these things?"

Lk 20:3 Ἀποκριθεὶς δὲ εἶπεν πρὸς αὐτούς, Ἐρωτήσω ὑμᾶς κἀγὼ λόγον, καὶ εἴπατέ μοι•

3And in answer Jesus said to them, "I will also ask you something, that you must tell me:

Lk 20:4 Τὸ βάπτισμα Ἰωάννου ἐξ οὐρανοῦ ἦν, ἢ ἐξ ἀνθρώπων;

4John's baptism, was it from heaven, or from human beings?"

Lk 20:5 Οἱ δὲ συνελογίσαντο πρὸς ἑαυτούς, λέγοντες ὅτι Ἐὰν εἴπωμεν, Ἐξ οὐρανοῦ, ἐρεῖ, Διὰ τί οὐκ ἐπιστεύσατε αὐτῷ;

5So they discussed it among themselves, saying, "If we say, 'From heaven,' he will say, 'Then why didn't you believe him?'

---

312 **19:45** txt τους πωλουντας ℵ B L syr^{pal} cop geo TH NA28 {/} ‖ τους πωλουντας και αγοραζοντας N ‖ τους πωλουντας και τους αγοραζοντας ‖ τους πωλουντας εν αυτω και αγοραζοντας A E R W 𝔐 latt syr$^{(s,c,p),hmg}$ TR RP ‖ τους πωλουντας εν αυτω και αγοραζοντας και τας τραπεζας των κολυβιστων εξεχεεν και τας καθεδρας D ‖ *lac* 𝔓^{75} P Q T

313 **19:46a** Isaiah 56:7

314 **19:46b** Jeremiah 7:11

Lk 20:6 Ἐὰν δὲ εἴπωμεν, Ἐξ ἀνθρώπων, ὁ λαὸς ἅπας καταλιθάσει ἡμᾶς• πεπεισμένος γάρ ἐστιν Ἰωάννην προφήτην εἶναι.

6 But if we say, 'From human beings,' all the people will stone us, because they are convinced that John was a prophet.'"

Lk 20:7 Καὶ ἀπεκρίθησαν μὴ εἰδέναι πόθεν.

7 And they professed not to know where it was from.

Lk 20:8 Καὶ ὁ Ἰησοῦς εἶπεν αὐτοῖς, Οὐδὲ ἐγὼ λέγω ὑμῖν ἐν ποίᾳ ἐξουσίᾳ ταῦτα ποιῶ.

8 And Jesus said to them, "Neither am I telling you by what authority I do these things."

The Parable of the Tenants

Lk 20:9 Ἤρξατο δὲ πρὸς τὸν λαὸν λέγειν τὴν παραβολὴν ταύτην• Ἄνθρωπος ἐφύτευσεν ἀμπελῶνα, καὶ ἐξέδετο αὐτὸν γεωργοῖς, καὶ ἀπεδήμησεν χρόνους ἱκανούς•

9 And he began to speak this parable to the crowd: "A man planted a vineyard, and leased it out to tenant-farmers, and journeyed away for quite some time.

Lk 20:10 καὶ καιρῷ ἀπέστειλεν πρὸς τοὺς γεωργοὺς δοῦλον, ἵνα ἀπὸ τοῦ καρποῦ τοῦ ἀμπελῶνος δώσουσιν αὐτῷ. Οἱ δὲ γεωργοὶ ἐξαπέστειλαν αὐτὸν δείραντες κενόν.

10 And in the time *of harvest*, he sent a servant to the tenants, so they could pay him rent out of the fruit of the vineyard. But the tenants, after beating him, sent him away empty-handed.

Lk 20:11 Καὶ προσέθετο ἕτερον πέμψαι δοῦλον• οἱ δὲ κἀκεῖνον δείραντες καὶ ἀτιμάσαντες ἐξαπέστειλαν κενόν.

11 And he proceeded to send a another servant; and that one also, after beating and insulting him, they sent away empty-handed.

Lk 20:12 Καὶ προσέθετο τρίτον πέμψαι• οἱ δὲ καὶ τοῦτον τραυματίσαντες ἐξέβαλον.

12 And he proceeded to send a third; and that one also they threw out, after injuring him.

Lk 20:13 Εἶπεν δὲ ὁ κύριος τοῦ ἀμπελῶνος, Τί ποιήσω; Πέμψω τὸν υἱόν μου τὸν ἀγαπητόν• ἴσως τοῦτον ἐντραπήσονται.

13 So the owner of the vineyard said, 'What should I do? I will send my beloved son; maybe him, they will respect.'[315]

Lk 20:14 Ἰδόντες δὲ αὐτὸν οἱ γεωργοὶ διελογίζοντο πρὸς ἑαυτούς, λέγοντες, Οὗτός ἐστιν ὁ κληρονόμος• ἀποκτείνωμεν αὐτόν, ἵνα ἡμῶν γένηται ἡ κληρονομία.

14 But when they saw him, the tenants discussed it among themselves, saying, 'This is the heir. Let us kill him, so that the inheritance will be ours.'

---

315 **20:13** txt εντραπησονται א B C D L Q it syr^{s,c,hmg} cop arm geo TH NA28 {/} ∥ ιδοντες εντραπησονται A E N R W 𝔐 vg it^{aur,f} syr^{p,h} TR RP ∥ *lac* 𝔓^{75} P T

Lk 20:15 Καὶ ἐκβαλόντες αὐτὸν ἔξω τοῦ ἀμπελῶνος, ἀπέκτειναν. Τί οὖν ποιήσει αὐτοῖς ὁ κύριος τοῦ ἀμπελῶνος;

15And they threw him outside the vineyard *and* killed him. What then will the owner of the vineyard do to them?

Lk 20:16 Ἐλεύσεται καὶ ἀπολέσει τοὺς γεωργοὺς τούτους, καὶ δώσει τὸν ἀμπελῶνα ἄλλοις. Ἀκούσαντες δὲ εἶπαν, Μὴ γένοιτο.

16He will come, and he will kill those tenants, and he will give the vineyard to others." And those who heard this said, "May it never be!"

Lk 20:17 Ὁ δὲ ἐμβλέψας αὐτοῖς εἶπεν, Τί οὖν ἐστιν τὸ γεγραμμένον τοῦτο, Λίθον ὃν ἀπεδοκίμασαν οἱ οἰκοδομοῦντες, οὗτος ἐγενήθη εἰς κεφαλὴν γωνίας;

17But he, after looking at them, said, "Why then is this written: 'A stone which the builders rejected, this one has become the chief cornerstone'?[316]

Lk 20:18 Πᾶς ὁ πεσὼν ἐπ' ἐκεῖνον τὸν λίθον συνθλασθήσεται• ἐφ' ὃν δ' ἂν πέσῃ, λικμήσει αὐτόν.

18Everyone who trips over that stone will be broken into pieces; upon whomever the stone falls, it will turn him into powder."

Lk 20:19 Καὶ ἐζήτησαν οἱ γραμματεῖς καὶ οἱ ἀρχιερεῖς ἐπιβαλεῖν ἐπ' αὐτὸν τὰς χεῖρας ἐν αὐτῇ τῇ ὥρᾳ, καὶ ἐφοβήθησαν τὸν λαόν• ἔγνωσαν γὰρ ὅτι πρὸς αὐτοὺς εἶπεν τὴν παραβολὴν ταύτην.

19And at that time, the Torah scholars and high priests wanted to lay their hands on him, yet they were afraid of the people. For they knew that he had spoken this parable in reference to them.

Paying the Tribute Tax to Caesar

Lk 20:20 Καὶ παρατηρήσαντες ἀπέστειλαν ἐγκαθέτους, ὑποκρινομένους ἑαυτοὺς δικαίους εἶναι, ἵνα ἐπιλάβωνται αὐτοῦ λόγου, ὥστε τὸ παραδοῦναι αὐτὸν τῇ ἀρχῇ καὶ τῇ ἐξουσίᾳ τοῦ ἡγεμόνος.

20And beginning to watch him closely, they sent spies presenting themselves as sincere, in order to catch some statement of his, such that they could hand him over to the jurisdiction and authority of the governor.

Lk 20:21 Καὶ ἐπηρώτησαν αὐτόν, λέγοντες, Διδάσκαλε, οἴδαμεν ὅτι ὀρθῶς λέγεις καὶ διδάσκεις• καὶ οὐ λαμβάνεις πρόσωπον, ἀλλ' ἐπ' ἀληθείας τὴν ὁδὸν τοῦ θεοῦ διδάσκεις.

21And they questioned him as follows: "Teacher, we know that you talk straight, and you teach straight; that is, you do not acknowledge personage, but only on the basis of truth you teach the way of God.

Lk 20:22 Ἔξεστιν ἡμᾶς Καίσαρι φόρον δοῦναι, ἢ οὔ;

22Is it permissible for us to pay the tribute tax[317] to Caesar, or not?"

---

316 **20:17** Psalm 118:22

317 **20:22** The Greek word translated "tribute" is φόρος. The Roman Caesar would charge a head tax (capita tax) based on a head count or census. The Latin root word for head is *cap*. Thus, this tax was a *per capita* tax, or a *capitation*. It was a flat tax, having no relation to graduated percentages, or ability to pay. It was not an *income* tax. Every head had to cough up the same amount. Black's Law Dictionary, Sixth Ed., defines a Capitation tax thusly: "A poll tax. A tax or imposition upon the person. It is a very ancient kind of tribute, and

Lk 20:23 Κατανοήσας δὲ αὐτῶν τὴν πανουργίαν, εἶπεν πρὸς αὐτούς,

23But he perceived their trickery, *and* said to them,[318]

Lk 20:24 Δείξατέ μοι δηνάριον• τίνος ἔχει εἰκόνα καὶ ἐπιγραφήν; Οἱ δὲ εἶπαν, Καίσαρος.

24"Show me a denarius. Whose image does it bear, and whose inscription?" And they said, "Caesar's."

Lk 20:25 Ὁ δὲ εἶπεν πρὸς αὐτούς, Τοίνυν ἀπόδοτε τὰ Καίσαρος Καίσαρι, καὶ τὰ τοῦ θεοῦ τῷ θεῷ.

25And he said to them, "Well then, Caesar's things give back to Caesar, and God's things to God."

Lk 20:26 Καὶ οὐκ ἴσχυσαν ἐπιλαβέσθαι αὐτοῦ ῥήματος ἐναντίον τοῦ λαοῦ• καὶ θαυμάσαντες ἐπὶ τῇ ἀποκρίσει αὐτοῦ, ἐσίγησαν.

26And they were not able to catch him in a saying in the presence of the people; and having been astonished by his answer, they remained silent.

Marriage at the Resurrection

Lk 20:27 Προσελθόντες δέ τινες τῶν Σαδδουκαίων, οἱ λέγοντες ἀνάστασιν μὴ εἶναι, ἐπηρώτησαν αὐτόν,

27Then some of the Sadducees approached (Sadducees say there is no resurrection), and they questioned him

Lk 20:28 λέγοντες, Διδάσκαλε, Μωϋσῆς ἔγραψεν ἡμῖν, Ἐάν τινος ἀδελφὸς ἀποθάνῃ ἔχων γυναῖκα, καὶ οὗτος ἄτεκνος ᾖ, ἵνα λάβῃ ὁ ἀδελφὸς αὐτοῦ τὴν γυναῖκα, καὶ ἐξαναστήσῃ σπέρμα τῷ ἀδελφῷ αὐτοῦ.

28as follows: "Teacher, Moses wrote for us, 'If a man's brother dies having a wife, and that *deceased* is childless, that the man should take the wife of his brother, and raise up descendants for his brother.'[319]

Lk 20:29 Ἑπτὰ οὖν ἀδελφοὶ ἦσαν• καὶ ὁ πρῶτος λαβὼν γυναῖκα, ἀπέθανεν ἄτεκνος•

29Well, there were seven brothers. And the first one, who had taken a wife, died childless.

---

answers to what the Latins called '*tributum*,' by which taxes on persons are distinguished from taxes on merchandise, called '*vectigalia*.'" Remember, a census was forbidden by God, and King David incurred God's wrath when he numbered the people. (A census tax or capita tax is also the kind expressly prohibited by the Constitution for the United States of America.) Black's Law Dictionary defines Tribute in turn as: "A contribution which is raised by a prince or sovereign from his subjects to sustain the expenses of the state. A sum of money paid by an inferior sovereign or state to a superior potentate, to secure the friendship or protection of the latter." Now as for coinage, Jesus obviously knew some principles of law. When he said in verse 25, "Caesar's things give back to Caesar," he recognized that every single coin circulated that bore Caesar's portrait and inscription, already belonged to Caesar. The Jewish religious taxes, on the other hand, were paid in weight of silver– shekels, or even drachmas, but not in Roman coins.

318 **20:23** txt αυτους ℵ B L 0266^{vid} it^{e} cop arm TH NA28 {/} ‖ αυτους τι με πειραζετε A D E N P W 𝔐 lat syr TR RP ‖ αυτους τι με πειραζετε υποκριται C ‖ *lac* $\mathfrak{P}^{75}$ Q T

319 **20:28** Deuteronomy 25:5; Genesis 38:8

Lk 20:30 καὶ ὁ δεύτερος
30And the second one [320]
Lk 20:31 καὶ ὁ τρίτος ἔλαβεν αὐτήν, ὡσαύτως δὲ καὶ οἱ ἑπτὰ οὐ κατέλιπον τέκνα,
καὶ ἀπέθανον.
31took her, and the third one, and in fact all seven in the same way left behind
no child, and died.
Lk 20:32 Ὕστερον καὶ ἡ γυνὴ ἀπέθανεν.
32Last of all, the woman also died.
Lk 20:33 Ἡ γυνὴ οὖν ἐν τῇ ἀναστάσει, τίνος αὐτῶν γίνεται γυνή; Οἱ γὰρ ἑπτὰ
ἔσχον αὐτὴν γυναῖκα.
33So the woman, in the resurrection, whose wife is she going to be? For all
seven had her as wife."
Lk 20:34 Καὶ εἶπεν αὐτοῖς ὁ Ἰησοῦς, Οἱ υἱοὶ τοῦ αἰῶνος τούτου γαμοῦσιν καὶ
γαμίσκονται,
34And Jesus said to them, "The children of this age marry and are given in
marriage;
Lk 20:35 οἱ δὲ καταξιωθέντες τοῦ αἰῶνος ἐκείνου τυχεῖν καὶ τῆς ἀναστάσεως τῆς
ἐκ νεκρῶν οὔτε γαμοῦσιν οὔτε γαμίζονται•
35but those considered worthy to taste of that age and of the resurrection
from the dead, will neither marry nor be given in marriage,
Lk 20:36 οὐδὲ γὰρ ἀποθανεῖν ἔτι δύνανται• ἰσάγγελοι γάρ εἰσιν, καὶ υἱοί εἰσιν
θεοῦ, τῆς ἀναστάσεως υἱοὶ ὄντες.
36nor will they be able to die any more, for they will be like the angels and be
children of God, since they are children of the resurrection.
Lk 20:37 Ὅτι δὲ ἐγείρονται οἱ νεκροί, καὶ Μωϋσῆς ἐμήνυσεν ἐπὶ τῆς βάτου, ὡς
λέγει, Κύριον τὸν θεὸν Ἀβραὰμ καὶ θεὸν Ἰσαὰκ καὶ θεὸν Ἰακώβ.
37But that the dead are rising, even Moses intimated so, at the part about the
bush, the way he says Yahweh is the God of Abraham, and the God of Isaac, and
the God of Jacob.
Lk 20:38 Θεὸς δὲ οὐκ ἔστιν νεκρῶν, ἀλλὰ ζώντων• πάντες γὰρ αὐτῷ ζῶσιν.
38Now God is not the God of dead people, but of living, for to him all *of those*
are alive."
Lk 20:39 Ἀποκριθέντες δέ τινες τῶν γραμματέων εἶπαν, Διδάσκαλε, καλῶς εἶπας.
39And one of the Torah scholars said in response, " Teacher, well said."

Whose Son Is the Messiah

Lk 20:40 Οὐκέτι ἐτόλμων ἐπερωτᾶν αὐτὸν οὐδέν.
40Indeed, no longer did any of them dare to question him.
Lk 20:41 Εἶπεν δὲ πρὸς αὐτούς, Πῶς λέγουσιν τὸν χριστὸν εἶναι Δαυὶδ υἱόν;
41So he said in reference to them, "How do they maintain the Messiah to be
the son of David?

---

[320] **20:30** txt και ο δευτερος ℵ B D L 0266 it^{d,e} cop geo TH NA28 {/} ‖ και ελαβεν ο δευτερος την γυναικα και ουτος απεθανεν ατεκνος A E P W 𝔐 lat syr$^{(c)}$ (cop^{boms}) TR RP ‖ και ε....... *lac* N ‖ *lac* 𝔓^{75} C Q T

Lk 20:42 Αὐτὸς γὰρ Δαυὶδ λέγει ἐν βίβλῳ ψαλμῶν, Εἶπεν κύριος τῷ κυρίῳ μου, Κάθου ἐκ δεξιῶν μου,

42For David himself says in the scroll of the Psalms, "Yahweh[321] said to my Lord: "Sit at my right hand

Lk 20:43 ἕως ἂν θῶ τοὺς ἐχθρούς σου ὑποπόδιον τῶν ποδῶν σου.

43until such time I make your enemies a footstool for your feet.'[322]"

Lk 20:44 Δαυὶδ οὖν κύριον αὐτὸν καλεῖ, καὶ πῶς αὐτοῦ υἱός ἐστιν;

44So, David calls him Lord. How then is he his son?"

Jesus Denounces the Torah Scholars

Lk 20:45 Ἀκούοντος δὲ παντὸς τοῦ λαοῦ, εἶπεν τοῖς μαθηταῖς,

45And with the entire crowd listening, he said to the disciples,

Lk 20:46 Προσέχετε ἀπὸ τῶν γραμματέων τῶν θελόντων περιπατεῖν ἐν στολαῖς, καὶ φιλούντων ἀσπασμοὺς ἐν ταῖς ἀγοραῖς, καὶ πρωτοκαθεδρίας ἐν ταῖς συναγωγαῖς, καὶ πρωτοκλισίας ἐν τοῖς δείπνοις•

46"Beware of the Torah scholars, wanting to walk around in robes, and loving the greetings in the marketplaces, and chief seats in the synagogues, and places of honor at banquets;

Lk 20:47 οἳ κατεσθίουσιν τὰς οἰκίας τῶν χηρῶν, καὶ προφάσει μακρὰ προσεύχονται. Οὗτοι λήμψονται περισσότερον κρίμα.

47they devour the houses of widows, and for a front, make lengthy prayers. These will receive greater condemnation."

Chapter 21

The Widow's Offering

Lk 21:1 Ἀναβλέψας δὲ εἶδεν τοὺς βάλλοντας εἰς τὸ γαζοφυλάκιον τὰ δῶρα αὐτῶν πλουσίους•

1And when he looked up, he saw rich people putting their gifts into the donation chest.

Lk 21:2 εἶδεν δέ τινα καὶ χήραν πενιχρὰν βάλλουσαν ἐκεῖ λεπτὰ δύο,

2Then he saw a penniless widow dropping there two lepta,[323]

---

321 **20:42** Εἶπεν κύριος τῷ κυρίῳ, "The LORD said to my Lord," from the Hebrew נְאֻם יְהוָה, לַאדֹנִי - nəʾum Yəhōvah laʾḏōnōî of Psalm 110:1. In this verse, both the Tetragrammaton יהוה (YHVH) and Adonai are found, together. But one could hardly say, "Adonai said to Adonai." In an attempt to avoid this, the Masoretes inserted a paseq in between, one of these: | , to make them be in separate phrases, and thus the Masoretic text reads: נְאֻם יְהוָה | לַאדֹנִי.

322 **20:43** Psalm 110:1

323 **21:2** Two small, thin copper coins, totaling about one fourth of one cent.

Lk 21:3 καὶ εἶπεν, Ἀληθῶς λέγω ὑμῖν ὅτι ἡ χήρα αὕτη ἡ πτωχὴ πλεῖον πάντων ἔβαλεν•

3and he said, "Truly I tell you, this poor widow has put in more than all the rest.

Lk 21:4 πάντες γὰρ οὗτοι ἐκ τοῦ περισσεύοντος αὐτοῖς ἔβαλον εἰς τὰ δῶρα• αὕτη δὲ ἐκ τοῦ ὑστερήματος αὐτῆς πάντα τὸν βίον ὃν εἶχεν ἔβαλεν.

4For they all put in their gifts out of the extra they had, but she out of her lack put in all she had to live on."

Signs of the Times

Lk 21:5 Καί τινων λεγόντων περὶ τοῦ ἱεροῦ, ὅτι λίθοις καλοῖς καὶ ἀναθήμασιν κεκόσμηται, εἶπεν,

5And as some of them were talking about the temple, how with such beautiful stones and gifts it was adorned, he said:

Lk 21:6 Ταῦτα ἃ θεωρεῖτε, ἐλεύσονται ἡμέραι ἐν αἷς οὐκ ἀφεθήσεται λίθος ἐπὶ λίθῳ, ὃς οὐ καταλυθήσεται.

6"These things that you are looking at, days will come in which there will not be left a stone upon a stone that will not be thrown down."

Lk 21:7 Ἐπηρώτησαν δὲ αὐτόν, λέγοντες, Διδάσκαλε, πότε οὖν ταῦτα ἔσται; Καὶ τί τὸ σημεῖον ὅταν μέλλῃ ταῦτα γίνεσθαι;

7And they questioned him as follows, "Teacher, so when will these things be, and what sign will happen when they are all about to take place?"

Lk 21:8 Ὁ δὲ εἶπεν, Βλέπετε μὴ πλανηθῆτε• πολλοὶ γὰρ ἐλεύσονται ἐπὶ τῷ ὀνόματί μου, λέγοντες Ἐγώ εἰμι• καί, Ὁ καιρὸς ἤγγικεν, μὴ πορευθῆτε ὀπίσω αὐτῶν.

8And he said, "See to it that you are not led astray. For many will come in my name, saying, 'I am He,' and, 'The Lord is near.' Do not go off after them.

Lk 21:9 Ὅταν δὲ ἀκούσητε πολέμους καὶ ἀκαταστασίας, μὴ πτοηθῆτε• δεῖ γὰρ ταῦτα γενέσθαι πρῶτον, ἀλλ' οὐκ εὐθέως τὸ τέλος.

9So when you hear of wars and unrest, do not be alarmed; for these things need to happen first, but the end does not come immediately."

Lk 21:10 Τότε ἔλεγεν αὐτοῖς, Ἐγερθήσεται ἔθνος ἐπ'ἔθνος, καὶ βασιλεία ἐπὶ βασιλείαν•

10Then, he was saying to them, "Nation will rise up against nation, and kingdom against kingdom,

Lk 21:11 σεισμοί τε μεγάλοι καὶ κατὰ τόπους λιμοὶ καὶ λοιμοὶ ἔσονται, φόβητρά τε καὶ σημεῖα ἀπ' οὐρανοῦ μεγάλα ἔσται.

11and there will be mega-quakes, and famines and epidemics in various places, and frightful and awesome signs from heaven.

Lk 21:12 Πρὸ δὲ τούτων πάντων ἐπιβαλοῦσιν ἐφ' ὑμᾶς τὰς χεῖρας αὐτῶν, καὶ διώξουσιν, παραδιδόντες εἰς τὰς συναγωγὰς καὶ φυλακάς, ἀπαγομένους ἐπὶ βασιλεῖς καὶ ἡγεμόνας, ἕνεκεν τοῦ ὀνόματός μου.

12But before all these things, they will lay their hands on you and will persecute you, handing you over to synagogues and prisons, being led all the way up to kings and governors for the sake of my name;

Lk 21:13 Ἀποβήσεται ὑμῖν εἰς μαρτύριον.
13it will work out for you to be a testimony.
Lk 21:14 Θέτε οὖν ἐν ταῖς καρδίαις ὑμῶν μὴ προμελετᾷν ἀπολογηθῆναι•
14Put it in your hearts therefore, not to be practicing *how* to answer in defense;
Lk 21:15 ἐγὼ γὰρ δώσω ὑμῖν στόμα καὶ σοφίαν, ᾗ οὐ δυνήσονται ἀντιστῆναι ἢ ἀντειπεῖν πάντες οἱ ἀντικείμενοι ὑμῖν.
15for I will give you utterance and wisdom that none of those opposing you will be able to stand against or rebut.
Lk 21:16 Παραδοθήσεσθε δὲ καὶ ὑπὸ γονέων καὶ ἀδελφῶν καὶ συγγενῶν καὶ φίλων, καὶ θανατώσουσιν ἐξ ὑμῶν.
16But you will also be turned in by parents and siblings and relatives and friends, and they will put some of you to death.
Lk 21:17 Καὶ ἔσεσθε μισούμενοι ὑπὸ πάντων διὰ τὸ ὄνομά μου.
17And indeed you will be hated by everyone because of my name.
Lk 21:18 Καὶ θρὶξ ἐκ τῆς κεφαλῆς ὑμῶν οὐ μὴ ἀπόληται.
18Yet not a hair of your head will perish:
Lk 21:19 Ἐν τῇ ὑπομονῇ ὑμῶν κτήσασθε τὰς ψυχὰς ὑμῶν.
19by your enduring, you shall gain your lives.[324]
Lk 21:20 Ὅταν δὲ ἴδητε κυκλουμένην ὑπὸ στρατοπέδων Ἱερουσαλήμ, τότε γνῶτε ὅτι ἤγγικεν ἡ ἐρήμωσις αὐτῆς.
20But when you see Jerusalem surrounded by armies, then you will know[325] that her desolation is near.

---

[324] **21:19** κτήσασθε (ℵ L R W Δ 047 131 1071 κτήσασθαι) D E G H K M X Γ Λ Π Ψ 063 2 69 118 157 180 205 565 (579 κτίσασθαι) 597 700 788 828* 892 1006 1009 1010 1071 1079 1216 1230 1241 1242 1243 1292 1342 1344 1365 1424 1505 1546 1646 2148 2174 2882 𝔐 *Lect* it[d,i] Origen Apostolic Constitutions Gregory-Nyssa Macarius/Symeon Marcus-Eremita Cyril Hesychius TR RP TH NA28 {C} ‖ κτήσεσθε (A 13 828[c] κτήσεσθαι) B Θ Ω f^{13} 1 33 124 346 1195 (1253 κτίσησθε) it[a,c,e,f,ff2,l,q,r1,s] vg syr[c,s,p,h,(pal)] cop[sa,bopt] arm eth geo slav Jerome Augustine WH Weiss Trg NA25 ‖ σώσετε (ἑαυτούς *for* τὰς ψυχὰς ὑμῶν) Marcion[acc to Tertullian] ‖ lac 𝔓45 𝔓75 C F N P Q T 28. The UBS editorial committee says it is slightly more probable that the reading of Codex Sinaiticus and many other early witnesses, is the correct one, which have the verb κτάομαι - ktáomai in the imperative mood. That would be a command to the disciples to preserve their lives. The committee says it would be more likely that copyists would have changed this verb to conform it to the future tense of the rest of the verbs in the context, more likely than the other way around. Note that the other gospels have the same idea in the future indicative. In some languages the difference between the two readings would not be translatable. I note that in the UBS4 apparatus, the reading of the Syriac is not given. (Is there a translatable difference between "you will gain your lives" and "you shall gain your lives"?) There is also discrepancy as to the reading of it[q]. And the apparatuses show f^1 in support of κτήσασθε, yet manuscript 1 itself, after which the whole family is named, supports κτήσεσθε.

[325] **21:20** The Greek word for "know" here, γινώσκω, is in the form of γνῶτε, which could be either imperative or subjunctive mood, since in this case the form would be identical. Imperative would be in English, "when you see Jerusalem surrounded by armies, then know - or then you should know,- that her desolation is near." Subjunctive would be in English, "when you see Jerusalem surrounded by armies, then you know - or would know - or will know, - or should know, that her desolation is near."

Lk 21:21 Τότε οἱ ἐν τῇ Ἰουδαίᾳ φευγέτωσαν εἰς τὰ ὄρη• καὶ οἱ ἐν μέσῳ αὐτῆς ἐκχωρείτωσαν• καὶ οἱ ἐν ταῖς χώραις μὴ εἰσερχέσθωσαν εἰς αὐτήν.

21Then, those in Judea should flee to the mountains, and those within Jerusalem should get without, and those in the fields should not go into her.

Lk 21:22 Ὅτι ἡμέραι ἐκδικήσεως αὗταί εἰσιν, τοῦ πλησθῆναι πάντα τὰ γεγραμμένα.

22For those are days[326] of vengeance, in fulfillment of all that is written.

Lk 21:23 Οὐαὶ ταῖς ἐν γαστρὶ ἐχούσαις καὶ ταῖς θηλαζούσαις ἐν ἐκείναις ταῖς ἡμέραις• ἔσται γὰρ ἀνάγκη μεγάλη ἐπὶ τῆς γῆς, καὶ ὀργὴ τῷ λαῷ τούτῳ.

23Alas for the ones who are pregnant, and the ones giving milk during those days! For it will be a great calamity upon the land, and wrath toward this people.[327]

Lk 21:24 Καὶ πεσοῦνται στόματι μαχαίρης, καὶ αἰχμαλωτισθήσονται εἰς τὰ ἔθνη πάντα• καὶ Ἱερουσαλὴμ ἔσται πατουμένη ὑπὸ ἐθνῶν, ἄχρι οὗ πληρωθῶσιν καιροὶ ἐθνῶν.

24And they will fall by the edge of the sword, and be taken captive to all the nations; and Jerusalem will be trampled over by Gentiles, until the times of the Gentiles are played out.

Lk 21:25 Καὶ ἔσονται σημεῖα ἐν ἡλίῳ καὶ σελήνῃ καὶ ἄστροις, καὶ ἐπὶ τῆς γῆς συνοχὴ ἐθνῶν ἐν ἀπορίᾳ, ἤχους θαλάσσης καὶ σάλου,

25And there will be signs in the sun, the moon and the stars, and on earth anxiety of the nations, in uncertainty over the roar and surge of the sea,

---

326 **21:22** In the Greek, the word for "day" is anarthrous here, that is, without the article. You will see some translations saying "the days" or "the time," and others saying "days," or "a time." This question regarding the Greek definite article is one of the translation issues most revealing of the translators' doctrinal preconceptions. Here, for example, it can reveal whether you believe that the prophecies will have a double fulfillment, or only one fulfillment. That is, are these prophecies partially fulfilled in the time and deeds of Titus in 70 A.D., and more fully fulfilled in the tribulation? Or are they solely fulfilled during the time of Titus? Or solely or primarily fulfilled in the tribulation? And prior to the time of Titus, some of God's people no doubt believed that these prophecies had been fulfilled during the time and deeds of Antiochus Epiphanes, either partially or primarily. I have 24 English translations on hand, and they split down the middle; half say "the days" and half say "days" or equivalent. We must interpret this passage by the rest of scripture, and do it in reliance on the anointing of the Holy Spirit, which leads us into all truth. We also must use common sense in light of the context here. This passage, in light of v. 24, seems to be including the destruction of the temple in 70 A.D. Therefore, we must say in v. 22 about the Great Tribulation, that those are "days" of tribulation, not the only ones.

327 **21:23a** txt τω λαω ℵ A B C D K L M N Π Ψ f^1 f^{13} 33 157 579 892 1241 2542 lat SBL TH NA28 {\} ‖ εν τω λαω E G H S U W Y Γ Δ Θ Λ Ω 2 124 346 565 700 1071 𝔐 syr^h TR RP ‖ επι τω λαω 1424 vg: *ira populo huic* (KJV) ‖ *lac* 𝔓^{45} 𝔓^{75} F P Q T 28. Sahidic & Bohairic: "for this people." Often too much is made of the Greek preposition εν, as it is often no more than a marker of the dative case. Modern Greek differs from New Testament Greek in many ways, and one of the biggest differences is that there are no longer any Dative Case inflections or suffixes on words like there were in Koine Greek. Instead, marker words or helper words came to be used.

Lk 21:26 ἀποψυχόντων ἀνθρώπων ἀπὸ φόβου καὶ προσδοκίας τῶν ἐπερχομένων τῇ οἰκουμένῃ• αἱ γὰρ δυνάμεις τῶν οὐρανῶν σαλευθήσονται.

26people holding their breath in fear and anticipation because of the things overtaking the world; for the forces of space will be shaken.

Lk 21:27 Καὶ τότε ὄψονται τὸν υἱὸν τοῦ ἀνθρώπου ἐρχόμενον ἐν νεφέλῃ μετὰ δυνάμεως καὶ δόξης πολλῆς.

27And then at that time they will see the Son of Man coming in a cloud, with power and great glory.

Lk 21:28 Ἀρχομένων δὲ τούτων γίνεσθαι, ἀνακύψατε καὶ ἐπάρατε τὰς κεφαλὰς ὑμῶν• διότι ἐγγίζει ἡ ἀπολύτρωσις ὑμῶν.

28So when these things are beginning to take place, stand yourselves tall and lift up your heads, because your redemption is drawing near."

Lk 21:29 Καὶ εἶπεν παραβολὴν αὐτοῖς, Ἴδετε τὴν συκῆν καὶ πάντα τὰ δένδρα•

29And he spoke a parable to them: "Consider the fig tree, indeed all the trees.

Lk 21:30 ὅταν προβάλωσιν ἤδη, βλέποντες ἀφ' ἑαυτῶν γινώσκετε ὅτι ἤδη ἐγγὺς τὸ θέρος ἐστίν.

30When they are now putting forth leaves, you see for yourselves *and* know that summer is now near.

Lk 21:31 Οὕτως καὶ ὑμεῖς, ὅταν ἴδητε ταῦτα γινόμενα, γινώσκετε ὅτι ἐγγύς ἐστιν ἡ βασιλεία τοῦ θεοῦ.

31So also you, when you see these things taking place, you know that the kingdom of God is near.

Lk 21:32 Ἀμὴν λέγω ὑμῖν ὅτι οὐ μὴ παρέλθῃ ἡ γενεὰ αὕτη, ἕως ἂν πάντα γένηται.

32Truly I tell you: this age will by no means pass away until this all has taken place.

Lk 21:33 Ὁ οὐρανὸς καὶ ἡ γῆ παρελεύσονται, οἱ δὲ λόγοι μου οὐ μὴ παρελεύσονται.

33Sky and earth will pass away, but my words will certainly not pass away.

Lk 21:34 Προσέχετε δὲ ἑαυτοῖς, μήποτε βαρηθῶσιν ὑμῶν αἱ καρδίαι ἐν κραιπάλῃ καὶ μέθῃ καὶ μερίμναις βιωτικαῖς, καὶ ἐπιστῇ ἐφ' ὑμᾶς αἰφνίδιος ἡ ἡμέρα ἐκείνη•

34But watch yourselves, that your hearts not be held back[328] by over-indulgence and drunkenness, and by ordinary concerns of this mortal life, and that day come upon you suddenly

Lk 21:35 ὡς παγὶς ἐπεισελεύσεται γὰρ ἐπὶ πάντας τοὺς καθημένους ἐπὶ πρόσωπον πάσης τῆς γῆς.

35like a trap. For it will come upon everyone who lives over the face of the whole earth.

---

328 **21:34** Or, "desensitized." The Greek word is βαρέω, which normally means "weighed down." But this is a metanymous meaning, as is also the word for heart. The heart is not literally weighed down. The spiritual strength, alertness, sensitivity, sharpness, and passion might be lessened by the things mentioned.

Lk 21:36 Ἀγρυπνεῖτε δὲ ἐν παντὶ καιρῷ δεόμενοι, ἵνα κατισχύσητε ἐκφυγεῖν ταῦτα πάντα τὰ μέλλοντα γίνεσθαι, καὶ σταθῆναι ἔμπροσθεν τοῦ υἱοῦ τοῦ ἀνθρώπου.

36So you must be watchful at all times, praying that you might manage[329] to avoid all these things about to come to pass, and stand before the Son of Man."

Lk 21:37 Ἦν δὲ τὰς ἡμέρας ἐν τῷ ἱερῷ διδάσκων• τὰς δὲ νύκτας ἐξερχόμενος ηὐλίζετο εἰς τὸ ὄρος τὸ καλούμενον Ἐλαιῶν.

37And he was spending the days teaching in the temple, and the nights he was going out and lodging on the hill called the Mount of Olives.

Lk 21:38 Καὶ πᾶς ὁ λαὸς ὤρθριζεν πρὸς αὐτὸν ἐν τῷ ἱερῷ ἀκούειν αὐτοῦ.

38And all the people would get up early to come to the temple and hear him.

Chapter 22

The Contract on Jesus

Lk 22:1 Ἤγγιζεν δὲ ἡ ἑορτὴ τῶν ἀζύμων, ἡ λεγομένη Πάσχα.

1And the Festival of Unleavened Bread, called Passover, was approaching,

Lk 22:2 Καὶ ἐζήτουν οἱ ἀρχιερεῖς καὶ οἱ γραμματεῖς τὸ πῶς ἀνέλωσιν αὐτόν• ἐφοβοῦντο γὰρ τὸν λαόν.

2and the chief priests and the Torah scholars were still yet looking for a way to put him to death, because they were still yet fearing the people.[330]

Lk 22:3 Εἰσῆλθεν δὲ Σατανᾶς εἰς Ἰούδαν τὸν καλούμενον Ἰσκαριώτην, ὄντα ἐκ τοῦ ἀριθμοῦ τῶν δώδεκα.

3Then Satan entered into Judas, the one called Ish Keriot, who was one of their number, of the Twelve.

Lk 22:4 Καὶ ἀπελθὼν συνελάλησεν τοῖς ἀρχιερεῦσιν καὶ στρατηγοῖς τὸ πῶς αὐτοῖς παραδῷ αὐτόν.

4And he went away, and discussed with the chief priests and the commanders of the temple guard how he might hand him over to them.

Lk 22:5 Καὶ ἐχάρησαν, καὶ συνέθεντο αὐτῷ ἀργύριον δοῦναι.

5And they were delighted, and contracted to give him silver.

---

[329] **21:36** txt κατισχυσητε ℵ B L T (W κατισχυσατε) Ψ 070 *f*[1] 33 157 892 1241 cop SBL TH NA28 {\} ‖ καταξιωθητε A C D E F G H K M N R S U Y Γ Δ Θ Λ Π Ω *f*[13] 2 124 565 700 1424 2542 𝔐 latt syr TR RP ‖ κατισχυσηται 0179 579 ‖ *lac* 𝔓[45] 𝔓[75] P Q 28.

[330] **22:2** This verse makes no sense unless you take into consideration the imperfect aspect of the Greek verbs for 'trying' and 'fearing.' Imperfect here means just that: incomplete and ongoing action. They had been trying to kill him already since Luke 19:47-48, and 20:19. The reason they still had not accomplished killing him, was because they were STILL YET fearing the people. So if someone tells you that the aspect (continuous vs. punctiliar) of N.T. Greek verbs is unimportant, don't believe them, no matter how big a name they are. Those big names are the ones who came up with the nonsensical mainstream rendering, as follows: "And the chief priests and the scribes were seeking how to kill him, for they feared the people." This makes it sound like the reason they wanted to kill Jesus was that they were afraid of the people. But that is not the case. The exact opposite is true: their fear of the people was what was still preventing them killing Jesus. See Endnote #4 on the linear aspect in Luke, which discusses this more fully.

Lk 22:6 Καὶ ἐξωμολόγησεν καὶ ἐζήτει εὐκαιρίαν τοῦ παραδοῦναι αὐτὸν ἄτερ ὄχλου αὐτοῖς.

6And he accepted, and was looking for the best time for handing him over to them, without the crowd.

The Passover Supper

Lk 22:7 Ἦλθεν δὲ ἡ ἡμέρα τῶν ἀζύμων, ᾗ ἔδει θύεσθαι τὸ Πάσχα.

7And the day of Unleavened Bread arrived in which it was customary to slaughter[331] the Passover.

Lk 22:8 Καὶ ἀπέστειλεν Πέτρον καὶ Ἰωάννην, εἰπών, Πορευθέντες ἑτοιμάσατε ἡμῖν τὸ Πάσχα, ἵνα φάγωμεν.

8And he sent Peter and John, saying, "Go, prepare the Passover for us so we can eat it."

Lk 22:9 Οἱ δὲ εἶπαν αὐτῷ, Ποῦ θέλεις ἑτοιμάσωμεν;

9And they said to him, "Where do you want us to prepare it?"

Lk 22:10 Ὁ δὲ εἶπεν αὐτοῖς, Ἰδού, εἰσελθόντων ὑμῶν εἰς τὴν πόλιν, συναντήσει ὑμῖν ἄνθρωπος κεράμιον ὕδατος βαστάζων• ἀκολουθήσατε αὐτῷ εἰς τὴν οἰκίαν εἰς ἣν εἰσπορεύεται.

10And he told them, "Behold, at the point of your arriving into the city a man carrying a water jar will encounter you. Follow him to whatever house he goes into.

Lk 22:11 Καὶ ἐρεῖτε τῷ οἰκοδεσπότῃ τῆς οἰκίας, Λέγει σοι ὁ διδάσκαλος, Ποῦ ἐστιν τὸ κατάλυμα, ὅπου τὸ Πάσχα μετὰ τῶν μαθητῶν μου φάγω;

11And say to the owner of the house, 'The teacher says to you, "Where is the guest room where I may eat the Passover with my disciples?" '

Lk 22:12 Κἀκεῖνος ὑμῖν δείξει ἀνάγαιον μέγα ἐστρωμένον• ἐκεῖ ἑτοιμάσατε.

12And that person will show you a large upstairs room all furnished. You shall prepare it there."

Lk 22:13 Ἀπελθόντες δὲ εὗρον καθὼς εἰρήκει αὐτοῖς, καὶ ἡτοίμασαν τὸ Πάσχα.

13So when they went, they found things just as he had told them; and they prepared the Passover.

Lk 22:14 Καὶ ὅτε ἐγένετο ἡ ὥρα, ἀνέπεσεν, καὶ οἱ δώδεκα ἀπόστολοι σὺν αὐτῷ.

14And when the hour had come, he reclined, and the disciples along with him.

Lk 22:15 Καὶ εἶπεν πρὸς αὐτούς, Ἐπιθυμίᾳ ἐπεθύμησα τοῦτο τὸ Πάσχα φαγεῖν μεθ' ὑμῶν πρὸ τοῦ με παθεῖν•

15And he said to them, "It is with great longing and anticipation I have wanted to eat this Passover with you before my suffering.

Lk 22:16 λέγω γὰρ ὑμῖν ὅτι οὐ μὴ φάγω αὐτό, ἕως ὅτου πληρωθῇ ἐν τῇ βασιλείᾳ τοῦ θεοῦ.

16For I tell you: I will certainly not eat it *again*[332] until such time it has been fulfilled in the kingdom of God."

---

331 **22:7** Greek: θύω. It could also be translated "to sacrifice," or, "to celebrate" the Passover. But the meaning "celebrate" only applied when the celebration included the slaughtering of something.

Lk 22:17 Καὶ δεξάμενος ποτήριον, εὐχαριστήσας εἶπεν, Λάβετε τοῦτο, καὶ διαμερίσατε εἰς ἑαυτοῖς·

17And after taking hold of the cup, he gave thanks, and said, "Take this, and share it among yourselves;

Lk 22:18 λέγω γὰρ ὑμῖν οὐ μὴ πίω ἀπὸ τοῦ νῦν ἀπὸ τοῦ γενήματος τῆς ἀμπέλου, ἕως οὗ ἡ βασιλεία τοῦ θεοῦ ἔλθῃ.

18for I tell you: By no means will I drink of the fruit of the vine from this point on until such time the kingdom of God has come."

Lk 22:19 Καὶ λαβὼν ἄρτον, εὐχαριστήσας ἔκλασεν καὶ ἔδωκεν αὐτοῖς, λέγων, Τοῦτό ἐστιν τὸ σῶμά μου τὸ ὑπὲρ ὑμῶν διδόμενον· τοῦτο ποιεῖτε εἰς τὴν ἐμὴν ἀνάμνησιν.

19And after taking the bread and giving thanks, he broke it and gave it to them, saying, "This is my body, being given for you. This you should do as a commemoration of me."[333]

Lk 22:20 Καὶ τὸ ποτήριον ὡσαύτως μετὰ τὸ δειπνῆσαι, λέγων, Τοῦτο τὸ ποτήριον ἡ καινὴ διαθήκη ἐν τῷ αἵματί μου, τὸ ὑπὲρ ὑμῶν ἐκχυννόμενον.

20And the cup after the meal[334] in the same way, saying: "This cup is the new covenant in my blood, being poured out for you.

Lk 22:21 Πλὴν ἰδού, ἡ χεὶρ τοῦ παραδιδόντος με μετ' ἐμοῦ ἐπὶ τῆς τραπέζης.

21But lo, the hand of the one betraying me is with mine on the table.

Lk 22:22 Ὅτι ὁ υἱὸς μὲν υἱὸς τοῦ ἀνθρώπου κατὰ τὸ ὡρισμένον πορεύεται· πλὴν οὐαὶ τῷ ἀνθρώπῳ ἐκείνῳ δι' οὗ παραδίδοται.

22Therefore indeed the Son of Man is going out exactly as is planned. Even so, woe to that man through whom he is betrayed!"

Lk 22:23 Καὶ αὐτοὶ ἤρξαντο συζητεῖν πρὸς ἑαυτοὺς τὸ τίς ἄρα εἴη ἐξ αὐτῶν ὁ τοῦτο μέλλων πράσσειν.

23And they began to debate with each other which of them therefore might be the one about to do this.

Lk 22:24 Ἐγένετο δὲ καὶ φιλονεικία ἐν αὐτοῖς τὸ τίς αὐτῶν δοκεῖ εἶναι μείζων.

24Then there also arose another dispute among them, as to which of them was considered to be greater.

---

332 **22:16** txt ὅτι οὐ μὴ φάγω 𝔓[75vid] א A B L 0211 it[a] cop[sa,bo] Apollinarus Cyr Tit-Bost Epiph TH NA28 {B} ‖ οὐκέτι μὴ φάγομαι D ‖ οὐκέτι οὐ μὴ φάγω C* N ‖ ὅτι οὐκέτι οὐ μὴ φάγω C[2] E P W 𝔐 it[aur,b,(d),e,f,ff2,i,(l),q,(r1)] vg arm eth (geo) Or[lat] TR RP ‖ *lac* 𝔓[45] Q T. The word "again" is not in the Greek, but implied. Thus, some copyists apparently felt obliged to add the Greek word οὐκέτι, to both clarify the meaning, and also to harmonize Luke with Mark 14:25, and perhaps also with Matthew 26:29, which says, "from now on."

333 **22:19** "This you should do" is referring to the Passover. From now on, they and we should do the Passover in commemoration of Jesus' death on our behalf. Both the unleavened bread and the Passover lamb or kid are His body figuratively. Note that Codex D has a much shorter reading of vss. 19-20, but it is alone in this, and is notoriously unreliable. So no serious consideration should be given it when it is all alone.

334 **22:20** Or possibly, "with" the meal.

Lk 22:25 Ὁ δὲ εἶπεν αὐτοῖς, Οἱ βασιλεῖς τῶν ἐθνῶν κυριεύουσιν αὐτῶν, καὶ οἱ ἐξουσιάζοντες αὐτῶν εὐεργέται καλοῦνται.

25And he said to them, "The kings of the nations lord it over them, and those exercising authority over them are called 'benefactors.'

Lk 22:26 Ὑμεῖς δὲ οὐχ οὕτως• ἀλλ' ὁ μείζων ἐν ὑμῖν γινέσθω ὡς ὁ νεώτερος• καὶ ὁ ἡγούμενος ὡς ὁ διακονῶν.

26But not so with you; rather, the greatest among you should be like the youngest,[335] and the leader as the one who serves.

Lk 22:27 Τίς γὰρ μείζων, ὁ ἀνακείμενος ἢ ὁ διακονῶν; Οὐχὶ ὁ ἀνακείμενος; Ἐγὼ δέ ἐν μέσῳ ὑμῶν εἰμι ὡς ὁ διακονῶν.

27For who is greater: the one reclining, or the one serving? Is it not the one reclining? Among you though, I am as the one serving.

Lk 22:28 Ὑμεῖς δέ ἐστε οἱ διαμεμενηκότες μετ' ἐμοῦ ἐν τοῖς πειρασμοῖς μου•

28But you are the ones who have stuck with me through my trials;

Lk 22:29 κἀγὼ διατίθεμαι ὑμῖν, καθὼς διέθετό μοι ὁ πατήρ μου, βασιλείαν,

29and I am assigning to you a kingdom, just as my Father did to me,

Lk 22:30 ἵνα ἔσθητε καὶ πίνητε ἐπὶ τῆς τραπέζης μου καὶ καθήσεσθε ἐπὶ θρόνων, τὰς δώδεκα φυλὰς κρίνοντες τοῦ Ἰσραήλ.

30such that you will eat and drink at my table in my kingdom,[336] and sit upon thrones, judging the twelve tribes of Israel.

Jesus Predicts the Disciples' Crisis of Faith

Lk 22:31 Σίμων, Σίμων, ἰδού, ὁ Σατανᾶς ἐξῃτήσατο ὑμᾶς, τοῦ σινιάσαι ὡς τὸν σῖτον•

31"Simon, Simon, behold, Satan has obtained permission to have you all, to sift you all like wheat.[337]

Lk 22:32 ἐγὼ δὲ ἐδεήθην περὶ σοῦ, ἵνα μὴ ἐκλίπῃ ἡ πίστις σου• καὶ σύ ποτε ἐπιστρέψας στήρισον τοὺς ἀδελφούς σου.

32But I have prayed for you, that your faith will not completely die. And you, when you have come back around, strengthen your brothers."

Lk 22:33 Ὁ δὲ εἶπεν αὐτῷ, Κύριε, μετὰ σοῦ ἕτοιμός εἰμι καὶ εἰς φυλακὴν καὶ εἰς θάνατον πορεύεσθαι.

33But he said to him, "Lord, I am prepared to go with you both to prison and to death."

---

335 **22:26** The youngest, as in Acts 5:6, customarily performed the menial tasks, and submitted to the elders.

336 **22:30** txt ἐν τῇ βασιλείᾳ μου 𝔓75 ℵ A B K L M N Q T U W Δ Θ Π Ψ 1 124 157 579 700 1071 1241 1582 latt syr cop TR HF SBL TH NA28 {\} ‖ ἐν τῇ βασιλείᾳ αὐτοῦ 69 ‖ ἐν τῇ βασιλείᾳ D itd,e,l vgmss syrc ‖ *omit* E F G H S V Y Γ Ω 047 2 22 174 230 565 1342 1424 1675 geo3 RP ‖ *lac* 𝔓45 C P 28 33 2882. MS 118?

337 **22:31** The Greek does not say "all," but we need to put in some indicator in English that the Greek pronoun "you" is in the plural. Jesus was not saying this about Peter only, but about all of the apostles.

Lk 22:34 Ὁ δὲ εἶπεν, Λέγω σοι, Πέτρε, οὐ φωνήσει σήμερον ἀλέκτωρ ἕως τρίς με ἀπαρνήσῃ εἰδέναι.

34But he said, "I tell you, Peter: the rooster will not crow this day, until you have denied three times that you know me."

Lk 22:35 Καὶ εἶπεν αὐτοῖς, Ὅτε ἀπέστειλα ὑμᾶς ἄτερ βαλλαντίου καὶ πήρας καὶ ὑποδημάτων, μή τινος ὑστερήσατε; Οἱ δὲ εἶπαν, Οὐθενός.

35And he said to them, "When I sent you without purse, knapsack and sandals, did you lack anything?" And they said, "Nothing."

Lk 22:36 Εἶπεν δὲ αὐτοῖς, Ἀλλὰ νῦν ὁ ἔχων βαλλάντιον ἀράτω, ὁμοίως καὶ πήραν• καὶ ὁ μὴ ἔχων, πωλησάτω τὸ ἱμάτιον αὐτοῦ, καὶ ἀγορασάτω μάχαιραν.

36Then he said, "But now, he who has a purse should bring it, or a knapsack likewise, and he who does not have a sword, should sell his cloak and buy one.

Lk 22:37 Λέγω γὰρ ὑμῖν ὅτι τοῦτο τὸ γεγραμμένον δεῖ τελεσθῆναι ἐν ἐμοί, τὸ Καὶ μετὰ ἀνόμων ἐλογίσθη• καὶ γὰρ τὸ περὶ ἐμοῦ τέλος ἔχει.

37For I tell you, this which is written has to be fulfilled in me: 'And he was considered one of the outlaws.'[338] Yes indeed, that about me is reaching fulfillment."

Lk 22:38 Οἱ δὲ εἶπαν, Κύριε, ἰδού, μάχαιραι ὧδε δύο. Ὁ δὲ εἶπεν αὐτοῖς, Ἱκανόν ἐστιν.

38So they said, "Lord, look. There are two swords here." And he said to them, "That is enough."

Gethsemane

Lk 22:39 Καὶ ἐξελθὼν ἐπορεύθη κατὰ τὸ ἔθος εἰς τὸ ὄρος τῶν Ἐλαιῶν• ἠκολούθησαν δὲ αὐτῷ καὶ οἱ μαθηταί.

39And after going out, he proceeded as was his custom to the Mount of Olives; and his disciples followed him also.

Lk 22:40 Γενόμενος δὲ ἐπὶ τοῦ τόπου, εἶπεν αὐτοῖς, Προσεύχεσθε μὴ εἰσελθεῖν εἰς πειρασμόν.

40And coming upon the place he said to them, "Pray not to come into temptation."

Lk 22:41 Καὶ αὐτὸς ἀπεσπάσθη ἀπ' αὐτῶν ὡσεὶ λίθου βολήν, καὶ θεὶς τὰ γόνατα προσηύχετο,

41And he withdrew from them, about a stone's throw away. And having dropped his knees, he was praying,

Lk 22:42 λέγων, Πάτερ, εἰ βούλει παρένεγκε τοῦτο τὸ ποτήριον ἀπ' ἐμοῦ• πλὴν μὴ τὸ θέλημά μου, ἀλλὰ τὸ σὸν γινέσθω.

42as follows: "Father, if you are willing, remove this cup from me. However, not my will, but yours be done."

Lk 22:43 Ὤφθη δὲ αὐτῷ ἄγγελος ἀπ' οὐρανοῦ ἐνισχύων αὐτόν.

43And an angel from heaven appeared to him, strengthening him.

---

338 **22:37** Isaiah 53:12

Lk 22:44 Καὶ γενόμενος ἐν ἀγωνίᾳ, ἐκτενέστερον προσηύχετο. Ἐγένετο δὲ ὁ ἱδρὼς αὐτοῦ ὡσεὶ θρόμβοι αἵματος καταβαίνοντες ἐπὶ τὴν γῆν.

44And being in agony, he was praying more earnestly; and his sweat became like drops of blood falling onto the ground.[339]

Lk 22:45 Καὶ ἀναστὰς ἀπὸ τῆς προσευχῆς, ἐλθὼν πρὸς τοὺς μαθητὰς εὗρεν κοιμωμένους αὐτοὺς ἀπὸ τῆς λύπης,

45And after rising from prayer and returning to the disciples, he found them sleeping, out of sorrow.

Lk 22:46 καὶ εἶπεν αὐτοῖς, Τί καθεύδετε; Ἀναστάντες προσεύχεσθε, ἵνα μὴ εἰσέλθητε εἰς πειρασμόν.

46And he said to them, "Why are you sleeping? Get up and pray, that you not go into temptation."

Jesus Arrested

Lk 22:47 Ἔτι αὐτοῦ λαλοῦντος, ἰδού, ὄχλος καὶ ὁ λεγόμενος Ἰούδας, εἷς τῶν δώδεκα, προήρχετο αὐτούς, καὶ ἤγγισεν τῷ Ἰησοῦ φιλῆσαι αὐτόν.

47While he was still speaking, behold, a crowd, and the one called Judas, one of the Twelve, was leading them. And he came up to Jesus, and kissed him.[340]

Lk 22:48 Ἰησοῦς δὲ εἶπεν αὐτῷ, Ἰούδα, φιλήματι τὸν υἱὸν τοῦ ἀνθρώπου παραδίδως;

48But Jesus said to him, "Judas, with a kiss you betray the Son of Man?"

Lk 22:49 Ἰδόντες δὲ οἱ περὶ αὐτὸν τὸ ἐσόμενον εἶπαν, Κύριε, εἰ πατάξομεν ἐν μαχαίρῃ;

49And seeing what was going to be happening, those around him said, "Lord, shall we strike with swords?"

Lk 22:50 Καὶ ἐπάταξεν εἷς τις ἐξ αὐτῶν τοῦ ἀρχιερέως τὸν δοῦλον, καὶ ἀφεῖλεν τὸ οὖς αὐτοῦ τὸ δεξιόν.

50And one of them struck the servant of the high priest, and cut off his right ear.

Lk 22:51 Ἀποκριθεὶς δὲ ὁ Ἰησοῦς εἶπεν, Ἐᾶτε ἕως τούτου. Καὶ ἁψάμενος τοῦ ὠτίου, ἰάσατο αὐτόν.

51But in response Jesus said, "Let that be enough of that." And he touched his ear and healed him.

Lk 22:52 Εἶπεν δὲ Ἰησοῦς πρὸς τοὺς παραγενομένους ἐπ' αὐτὸν ἀρχιερεῖς καὶ στρατηγοὺς τοῦ ἱεροῦ καὶ πρεσβυτέρους, Ὡς ἐπὶ λῃστὴν ἐξήλθατε μετὰ μαχαιρῶν καὶ ξύλων;

52Then, toward those coming against him, the chief priests, temple officers and elders, Jesus said, "As though after a bandit, you have come out with swords and clubs?

---

339 **22:43-44** Some consider the words in these verses to be an extra-canonical tradition which got added to the gospel of Luke. They are absent in very early and geographically widespread manuscripts and witnesses. See Endnote #3 at the end of this document wich discusses this.

340 **22:47** The Greek literally says, "And he came up to him, to kiss him." But this is probably a Semitism, called "the infinitive of result."

Lk 22:53 Καθ' ἡμέραν ὄντος μου μεθ' ὑμῶν ἐν τῷ ἱερῷ, οὐκ ἐξετείνατε τὰς χεῖρας ἐπ' ἐμέ. Ἀλλ' αὕτη ἐστὶν ὑμῶν ἡ ὥρα, καὶ ἡ ἐξουσία τοῦ σκότους.

53Every day with me being next to you in the temple you didn't lay your hands on me. But this is the hour for you, and the authority of darkness."

Peter's Denials

Lk 22:54 Συλλαβόντες δὲ αὐτὸν ἤγαγον, καὶ εἰσήγαγον εἰς τὴν οἰκίαν τοῦ ἀρχιερέως· ὁ δὲ Πέτρος ἠκολούθει μακρόθεν.

54And after seizing him, they took him and led him into the house of the high priest; and Peter was following at a distance.

Lk 22:55 Περιαψάντων δὲ πῦρ ἐν μέσῳ τῆς αὐλῆς, καὶ συγκαθισάντων, ἐκάθητο ὁ Πέτρος μέσος αὐτῶν.

55And since people had lit a fire in the middle of the courtyard and were all sitting together, Peter was sitting among them.

Lk 22:56 Ἰδοῦσα δὲ αὐτὸν παιδίσκη τις καθήμενον πρὸς τὸ φῶς, καὶ ἀτενίσασα αὐτῷ, εἶπεν, Καὶ οὗτος σὺν αὐτῷ ἦν.

56But a maidservant noticed him sitting toward the fire, and after studying him, she said, "This man also was with him."

Lk 22:57 Ὁ δὲ ἠρνήσατο, λέγων, Οὐκ οἶδα αὐτόν γύναι.

57But he denied it, saying, "I don't know him, woman."

Lk 22:58 Καὶ μετὰ βραχὺ ἕτερος ἰδὼν αὐτὸν ἔφη, Καὶ σὺ ἐξ αὐτῶν εἶ. Ὁ δὲ Πέτρος ἔφη, Ἄνθρωπε, οὐκ εἰμί.

58And shortly thereafter, another person who saw him was saying, "You are also one of them." And Peter was saying, "Man, I am not."

Lk 22:59 Καὶ διαστάσης ὡσεὶ ὥρας μιᾶς, ἄλλος τις διϊσχυρίζετο, λέγων, Ἐπ' ἀληθείας καὶ οὗτος μετ' αὐτοῦ ἦν· καὶ γὰρ Γαλιλαῖός ἐστιν.

59And after about an hour had passed, someone else was affirming, saying, "Definitely, this man **was** also with him; he is also Galilean."

Lk 22:60 Εἶπεν δὲ ὁ Πέτρος, Ἄνθρωπε, οὐκ οἶδα ὃ λέγεις. Καὶ παραχρῆμα, ἔτι λαλοῦντος αὐτοῦ, ἐφώνησεν ἀλέκτωρ.

60But Peter said, "Man, I do not know what you are talking about." And immediately as he was still speaking, a rooster crowed.

Lk 22:61 Καὶ στραφεὶς ὁ κύριος ἐνέβλεψεν τῷ Πέτρῳ. Καὶ ὑπεμνήσθη ὁ Πέτρος τοῦ ῥήματος τοῦ κυρίου, ὡς εἶπεν αὐτῷ ὅτι Πρὶν ἀλέκτορα φωνῆσαι σήμερον ἀπαρνήσῃ με τρίς.

61And the Lord turned and looked at Peter, and he remembered the statement of the Lord, how he had said to him, "Before the rooster crows today, you will deny me three times."

Lk 22:62 Καὶ ἐξελθὼν ἔξω ἔκλαυσεν πικρῶς.

62And he went off outside, and bitterly wept.

Before the Sanhedrin

Lk 22:63 Καὶ οἱ ἄνδρες οἱ συνέχοντες τὸν Ἰησοῦν ἐνέπαιζον αὐτῷ, δέροντες.

63And the men guarding Jesus were making fun of him as they beat him up.

Lk 22:64 Καὶ περικαλύψαντες αὐτόν, ἐπηρώτων λέγοντες, Προφήτευσον. Τίς ἐστιν ὁ παίσας σε;

64After blindfolding him, they were asking him, "Prophesy, who is it that hit you?"

Lk 22:65 Καὶ ἕτερα πολλὰ βλασφημοῦντες ἔλεγον εἰς αὐτόν.

65And they were saying many other insulting things against him.

Lk 22:66 Καὶ ὡς ἐγένετο ἡμέρα, συνήχθη τὸ πρεσβυτέριον τοῦ λαοῦ, ἀρχιερεῖς καὶ ἀρχιερεῖς τε γραμματεῖς, καὶ ἀπήγαγον αὐτὸν εἰς τὸ συνέδριον αὐτῶν,

66And as the day broke, the elders of the people and the high priests and the Torah scholars were assembled, and they brought him over into their Sanhedrin,

Lk 22:67 λέγοντες, Εἰ σὺ εἶ ὁ χριστός, εἰπὸν ἡμῖν. Εἶπεν δὲ αὐτοῖς, Ἐὰν ὑμῖν εἴπω, οὐ μὴ πιστεύσητε•

67saying, "Tell us whether you are the Christ." And he said to them, "If I told you, you would certainly not believe,

Lk 22:68 ἐὰν δὲ ἐρωτήσω, οὐ μὴ ἀποκριθῆτε.

68and if I asked questions, you would certainly not answer.[341]

Lk 22:69 Ἀπὸ τοῦ νῦν δὲ ἔσται ὁ υἱὸς τοῦ ἀνθρώπου καθήμενος ἐκ δεξιῶν τῆς δυνάμεως τοῦ θεοῦ.

69Nevertheless,[342] from now on, the Son of Man will be sitting at the right hand of the power of God."

Lk 22:70 Εἶπαν δὲ πάντες, Σὺ οὖν εἶ ὁ υἱὸς τοῦ θεοῦ; Ὁ δὲ πρὸς αὐτοὺς ἔφη, Ὑμεῖς λέγετε ὅτι ἐγώ εἰμι.

70So they all said, "You are the Son of God then?" And he was saying to them, "You are saying that I am."[343]

---

341 **22:68** txt αποκριθητε 𝔓^{75} ℵ B L T 1241 1278* cop^{bo} Apoll Cyr SBL TH NA28 {B} ‖ αποκριθητε μοι Θ *f*^{1} 22 157 205 579 1612 *pc*^{14} vg^{ms} cop^{sa} Ambrose ‖ αποκριθητε η απολυσητε 892 1505 *pc*^{38} ‖ αποκριθητε μοι η απολυσητε A D E G H K N S U W X Y Γ Δ Π Ψ Ω 0211 0233 *f*^{13} 2 28 180 565 597 700 1006 1010 1071 1243 1292 1342 1278^{c} 2786 𝔐 *Lect* it$^{aur,b,c,d,f,ff^2,(i),(l),q,r^1}$ vg syr^{c,s,p,h} arm geo slav Aug TR RP ‖ αποκριθητε μοι ουδε απολυσητε 1424 ‖ αποκριθητε μοι η απολυσητε με/μοι it^{a} *pc*^{5} ‖ απολυσητε 2542 ‖ *omit verse* 901 2729 it^{e} vg^{ms} ‖ *lac* 𝔓^{45} C F P Q 33

342 **22:69** txt δε 𝔓^{75} ℵ A B D L T SBL TH NA28 {\} ‖ *omit* E N W 𝔐 vg syr^{p} cop^{sa,bo} arm eth TR RP ‖ *lac* 𝔓^{45} C P Q

343 **22:70** "You are saying that I am" is literally what the Greek says, and this expression comes from the Semitic word " 'amarta." It is neither a yes nor a no. This was a Jewish idiom, and you can find some Rabbinic examples where it was understood as a Yes, and some where it would obviously NOT be understood as a yes. Therefore, we have to conclude that it is not a yes of any kind. At the same time, it is not a denial. Which sometimes some people might take as a yes. But as for translation, it should be translated literally, and left at that. No helper words should be added that might imply an affirmative answer. See the endnote on this topic at the end of my translation of Mark's gospel. The Sanhedrin would not be satisfied with anything less than a vehement denial from Jesus. Thus the Sanhedrin's reaction, of needing no more witnesses or evidence. But even what Jesus had already said here earlier, in 22:69, that Jesus would be seated at the right hand of God, that would be offense enough. What is different about Luke here, is that he uses ἔφη, the imperfect form of φημίhere, which I translated "kept saying." Luke does not use the continuous aspect indiscriminately or insignificantly.

Lk 22:71 Οἱ δὲ εἶπαν, Τί ἔτι ἔχομεν μαρτυρίας χρείαν; Αὐτοὶ γὰρ ἠκούσαμεν ἀπὸ τοῦ στόματος αὐτοῦ.

71And they said, "What more need do we have for witnesses? For we ourselves have heard from his own mouth."

Chapter 23

Jesus Before Pilate and Herod

Lk 23:1 Καὶ ἀναστὰν ἅπαν τὸ πλῆθος αὐτῶν, ἤγαγον αὐτὸν ἐπὶ τὸν Πιλάτον.

1And the whole assembly of them got up, and they took him before Pilate.

Lk 23:2 Ἤρξαντο δὲ κατηγορεῖν αὐτοῦ, λέγοντες, Τοῦτον εὕραμεν διαστρέφοντα τὸ ἔθνος ἡμῶν, καὶ κωλύοντα φόρους Καίσαρι διδόναι, καὶ λέγοντα ἑαυτὸν χριστὸν βασιλέα εἶναι.

2And they began to accuse him, as follows. "We found this man misleading our nation[344] and forbidding to give tribute to Caesar, and claiming to be a king himself, the Christ."

Lk 23:3 Ὁ δὲ Πιλάτος ἠρώτησεν αὐτόν, λέγων, Σὺ εἶ ὁ βασιλεὺς τῶν Ἰουδαίων; Ὁ δὲ ἀποκριθεὶς αὐτῷ ἔφη, Σὺ λέγεις.

3So Pilate examined him, saying, "Are you the king of the Jews?" And he in answer to him was saying, "You are the one saying that."[345]

Lk 23:4 Ὁ δὲ Πιλάτος εἶπεν πρὸς τοὺς ἀρχιερεῖς καὶ τοὺς ὄχλους, Οὐδὲν εὑρίσκω αἴτιον ἐν τῷ ἀνθρώπῳ τούτῳ.

4And Pilate said to the chief priests and the crowds, "I find no *causa capitalis* in this man."[346]

Lk 23:5 Οἱ δὲ ἐπίσχυον, λέγοντες ὅτι Ἀνασείει τὸν λαόν, διδάσκων καθ' ὅλης τῆς Ἰουδαίας, ἀρξάμενος ἀπὸ τῆς Γαλιλαίας ἕως ὧδε.

5But they were getting more insistent, saying, "He incites the people, teaching throughout the entire land of the Jews, starting from Galilee and all the way to here."

Lk 23:6 Πιλάτος δὲ ἀκούσας ἐπηρώτησεν εἰ ὁ ἄνθρωπος Γαλιλαῖός ἐστιν.

6And when Pilate heard this, he asked, "Is the man a Galilean?"[347]

---

344 **23:2** txt το εθνος ημων 𝔓[75] ℵ B D L N T lat syr SBL TH NA28 {\} ‖ το εθνος A E W 𝔐 it[a,r1] Marcion[E] TR RP ‖ *lac* 𝔓[45] C P Q. Both main text streams contain the definite article with ἔθνος, which article can serve as a weak possessive pronoun. Usually it is the Byzantine stream supplying the expressly possessive word, but here we have the roles reversed. The English translator could legitimately render both of these readings in English as "our nation." And that is what thetranslators of the Coptic may have done, as they read "our nation."

345 **23:3** The Greek says literally, "You are saying." See footnote on 22:70, and on Mark 15:3. It is not a "yes" answer.

346 **23:4** That is, basis for capital punishment. It was understood that the only reason the Jewish authorities would bring a criminal to Pilate, was for adjudication of the death penalty and execution. The Jewish authorities otherwise were allowed to execute judgment with their own courts and laws, short of execution; see John 18:31.

347 **23:6** The word εἰ here (usually "if") being an interrogative particle, introducing direct interrogative discourse, taking the place of ὅτι. See BAGD *in loc* V.; BDF § 440(3).

Lk 23:7 Καὶ ἐπιγνοὺς ὅτι ἐκ τῆς ἐξουσίας Ἡρῴδου ἐστίν, ἀνέπεμψεν αὐτὸν πρὸς Ἡρῴδην, ὄντα καὶ αὐτὸν ἐν Ἱεροσολύμοις ἐν ταύταις ταῖς ἡμέραις.

7And when he had confirmed that he was in fact from Herod's jurisdiction, he referred him to Herod, who was in Jerusalem too for those days.

Lk 23:8 Ὁ δὲ Ἡρῴδης ἰδὼν τὸν Ἰησοῦν ἐχάρη λίαν• ἦν γὰρ ἐξ ἱκανῶν χρόνων θέλων ἰδεῖν αὐτόν, διὰ τὸ ἀκούειν περὶ αὐτοῦ• καὶ ἤλπιζέν τι σημεῖον ἰδεῖν ὑπ' αὐτοῦ γινόμενον.

8Now Herod was very glad when he saw Jesus. He had been wanting for quite some time to meet him, because of hearing about him, and he hoped to see something miraculous happening through him.

Lk 23:9 Ἐπηρώτα δὲ αὐτὸν ἐν λόγοις ἱκανοῖς• αὐτὸς δὲ οὐδὲν ἀπεκρίνατο αὐτῷ.

9So he was plying him with a considerable amount of questions; but Jesus never gave any response at all.

Lk 23:10 Εἱστήκεισαν δὲ οἱ ἀρχιερεῖς καὶ οἱ γραμματεῖς, εὐτόνως κατηγοροῦντες αὐτοῦ.

10And the chief priests and the Torah scholars were standing there throughout, vehemently accusing him.

Lk 23:11 Ἐξουθενήσας δὲ αὐτὸν ὁ Ἡρῴδης σὺν τοῖς στρατεύμασιν αὐτοῦ, καὶ ἐμπαίξας, περιβαλὼν ἐσθῆτα λαμπράν, ἀνέπεμψεν αὐτὸν τῷ Πιλάτῳ.

11Then Herod, together with his soldiers, after treating him with contempt and mocking him by draping a splendid robe around him, sent him back to Pilate.

Lk 23:12 Ἐγένοντο δὲ φίλοι ὅ τε Ἡρῴδης καὶ ὁ Πιλᾶτος ἐν αὐτῇ τῇ ἡμέρᾳ μετ' ἀλλήλων• προϋπῆρχον γὰρ ἐν ἔχθρᾳ ὄντες πρὸς αὐτούς.

12Which caused Herod and Pilate to become friends with each other that same day (for they had previously always been hostile toward each other).

Lk 23:13 Πιλάτος δὲ συγκαλεσάμενος τοὺς ἀρχιερεῖς καὶ τοὺς ἄρχοντας καὶ τὸν λαόν,

13And Pilate summoned the high priest, together with the rulers and the people,

Lk 23:14 εἶπεν πρὸς αὐτούς, Προσηνέγκατέ μοι τὸν ἄνθρωπον τοῦτον, ὡς ἀποστρέφοντα τὸν λαόν• καὶ ἰδού, ἐγὼ ἐνώπιον ὑμῶν ἀνακρίνας οὐθὲν εὗρον ἐν τῷ ἀνθρώπῳ τούτῳ αἴτιον ὧν κατηγορεῖτε κατ' αὐτοῦ•

14and he said to them, "You have brought this man up to me as someone inciting the people to treason, and here now is my finding after trying him in your presence. I have found in this man no basis for the charges you are bringing against him.

Lk 23:15 ἀλλ' οὐδὲ Ἡρῴδης• ἀνέπεμψεν γὰρ αὐτὸν πρὸς ἡμᾶς, καὶ ἰδού, οὐδὲν ἄξιον θανάτου ἐστὶν πεπραγμένον αὐτῷ.

15And neither has Herod, for he has sent him back to us. So you see, nothing being done by him is worthy of death.

Lk 23:16 Παιδεύσας οὖν αὐτὸν ἀπολύσω.

16Therefore, having scourged him, I will release him."

[[Lk 23:17 Ἀνάγκην δὲ εἶχεν ἀπολύειν αὐτοῖς κατὰ ἑορτὴν ἕνα.]]

[[17Now he was obligated by custom according to the festival to release one person to them.]][348]

Lk 23:18 Ἀνέκραγον δὲ παμπληθεί, λέγοντες, Αἶρε τοῦτον, ἀπόλυσον δὲ ἡμῖν τὸν Βαραββᾶν•

18But they all together shouted back, saying, "Away with this man! Release to us Barabbas!"

Lk 23:19 ὅστις ἦν διὰ στάσιν τινὰ γενομένην ἐν τῇ πόλει καὶ φόνον βληθεὶς ἐν τῇ φυλακῇ.

19(He was someone who had been thrown in prison because of a certain uprising and murder that took place in the city.)

Lk 23:20 Πάλιν δὲ ὁ Πιλάτος προσεφώνησεν αὐτοῖς θέλων ἀπολῦσαι τὸν Ἰησοῦν.

20But Pilate, wanting to release Jesus, called out to them again.

Lk 23:21 Οἱ δὲ ἐπεφώνουν, λέγοντες, Σταύρου σταύρου αὐτόν.

21But they cried out, saying, "Crucify him, crucify him!"

Lk 23:22 Ὁ δὲ τρίτον εἶπεν πρὸς αὐτούς, Τί γὰρ κακὸν ἐποίησεν οὗτος; Οὐδὲν αἴτιον θανάτου εὗρον ἐν αὐτῷ• παιδεύσας οὖν αὐτὸν ἀπολύσω.

22But a third time, he said to them, "Why? What crime has this man committed? Having scourged him therefore, I will release him."

Lk 23:23 Οἱ δὲ ἐπέκειντο φωναῖς μεγάλαις, αἰτούμενοι αὐτὸν σταυρωθῆναι• καὶ κατίσχυον αἱ φωναὶ αὐτῶν.

23But with loud shouts the crowd kept urgently demanding that he be crucified. And their shouts prevailed.

Lk 23:24 Καὶ Πιλάτος ἐπέκρινεν γενέσθαι τὸ αἴτημα αὐτῶν.

24and Pilate decided to grant their request.

Lk 23:25 Ἀπέλυσεν δὲ τὸν διὰ στάσιν καὶ φόνον βεβλημένον εἰς φυλακήν, ὃν ᾐτοῦντο• τὸν δὲ Ἰησοῦν παρέδωκεν τῷ θελήματι αὐτῶν.

25And he released the man who had been thrown into prison for insurrection and murder, the one whom they had asked for, and Jesus he handed over to their will.

[348] **23:17** These words now called verse 17 are not found in 𝔓^{75} A B K L T Π 070 0211 892* 1241 it^{a} vg^{ms} cop$^{sa, bo^{pt.}}$ and included, with minor variants, as harmonized to Matthew 27:15 and Mark 15:6, in the following: ℵ E F G H (N συνήθειαν for ἀνάγκην) W Δ Θ Ψ*f*^{1} *f*^{13} 28 157 (180 579 εἶχον - imperfect) 205 565 597 700 892^{c} 1006 1010 1071 (1243 ἕνα δέσμιον one prisoner) 1292 1342 1424 1505 2882 *Byz Lect* it$^{aur, b, c, e, f, ff^2, l, q, r1}$ vg syr$^{p, h}$ (cop$^{bo^{ms}}$) arm eth geo slav Eusebian Canons; Augustine. And the following include these words in a different place- after verse 19: D it^{d} syr$^{c, s}$. There is over all a great variation in the additions, not detailed here, which is a sign of inauthenticity. The UBS editorial committee gives the omission an A rating of certainty.

The Crucifixion

Lk 23:26 Καὶ ὡς ἀπήγαγον αὐτόν, ἐπιλαβόμενοι Σίμωνά τινα Κυρηναῖον
ἐρχόμενον ἐρχομένου ἀπ' ἀγροῦ, ἐπέθηκαν αὐτῷ τὸν σταυρόν, φέρειν ὄπισθεν
τοῦ Ἰησοῦ.
26And as they led him away, they seized a Cyrenian, Simon, who was
returning from the country, and they placed the cross on him, to carry it behind
Jesus.
Lk 23:27 Ἠκολούθει δὲ αὐτῷ πολὺ πλῆθος τοῦ λαοῦ, καὶ γυναικῶν αἳ ἐκόπτοντο
καὶ ἐθρήνουν αὐτόν.
27And a great multitude of the people were following him, and women who
were mourning and lamenting him.
Lk 23:28 Στραφεὶς δὲ πρὸς αὐτὰς ὁ Ἰησοῦς εἶπεν, Θυγατέρες Ἱερουσαλήμ, μὴ
κλαίετε ἐπ' ἐμέ, πλὴν ἐφ' ἑαυτὰς κλαίετε καὶ ἐπὶ τὰ τέκνα ὑμῶν.
28But Jesus turned to them, and he said, "Daughters of Jerusalem, do not weep
for me, but weep for yourselves, and for your children.
Lk 23:29 Ὅτι ἰδού, ἔρχονται ἡμέραι ἐν αἷς ἐροῦσιν, Μακάριαι αἱ στεῖραι, καὶ αἱ
κοιλίαι αἳ οὐκ ἐγέννησαν, καὶ μαστοὶ οἳ οὐκ ἔθρεψαν.
29For behold, days are coming in which they will say, 'Blessed are the barren,
and the wombs that never bore, and the breasts that never nursed.'
Lk 23:30 Τότε ἄρξονται λέγειν τοῖς ὄρεσιν, Πέσετε ἐφ' ἡμᾶς• καὶ τοῖς βουνοῖς,
Καλύψατε ἡμᾶς.
30At that time they will begin to say to the mountains, 'Fall on us,' and to the
hills, 'Cover us.'[349]
Lk 23:31 Ὅτι εἰ ἐν τῷ ὑγρῷ ξύλῳ ταῦτα ποιοῦσιν, ἐν τῷ ξηρῷ τί γένηται;
31For if they do these things when the tree is green, what will happen when it
is dry?
Lk 23:32 Ἤγοντο δὲ καὶ ἕτεροι κακοῦργοι δύο σὺν αὐτῷ ἀναιρεθῆναι.
32Now two others, criminals, were also being taken with him to be
executed.[350]
Lk 23:33 Καὶ ὅτε ἦλθον ἐπὶ τὸν τόπον τὸν καλούμενον Κρανίον, ἐκεῖ
ἐσταύρωσαν αὐτόν, καὶ τοὺς κακούργους, ὃν μὲν ἐκ δεξιῶν, ὃν δὲ ἐξ ἀριστερῶν.
33And when they came to the place called The Skull [גָּלְגָּלְתָּא], there they
crucified him, along with the criminals, one on his right and one on his left.
Lk 23:34 Ὁ δὲ Ἰησοῦς ἔλεγεν, Πάτερ, ἄφες αὐτοῖς• οὐ γὰρ οἴδασιν τί ποιοῦσιν.
Διαμεριζόμενοι δὲ τὰ ἱμάτια αὐτοῦ, ἔβαλον κλήρους.
34And Jesus said, "Father, forgive them, for they do not know what they are
doing."[351] And they cast lots, for dividing out his clothing.[352]

---

349 **23:30** Hosea 10:8

350 **23:32** The Greek syntax here may be more properly translated, "Now two other criminals were also being taken with him to be executed." Later Greek manuscripts were possibly modified to take away this possibility. But Jesus had predicted in Luke 22:37 that he would be considered one of the outlaws.

351 **23:34a** txt Ὁ δὲ Ἰησοῦς ἔλεγεν, Πάτερ, ἄφες αὐτοῖς• οὐ γὰρ οἴδασιν τί ποιοῦσιν *with minor variants:* ℵ*,3 (A *omit* "Father") C D1 (E with *) F G H K L M N Q U Γ Δ Λ Π Ψ 0250 *f*1 (*f*13) 2 28 33 131 157 180 205 565 597C 700 828 892 1006 1010 1071 1243 1292 1342 1424 1505 2882 𝔐 *Lect*

Lk 23:35 Καὶ εἱστήκει ὁ λαὸς θεωρῶν. Ἐξεμυκτήριζον δὲ καὶ οἱ ἄρχοντες, λέγοντες, Ἄλλους ἔσωσεν, σωσάτω ἑαυτόν, εἰ οὗτός ἐστιν ὁ χριστός τοῦ θεοῦ ὁ ἐκλεκτός.

35And the people stood there, watching. Now the rulers were also there, sneering at him, saying, "He saved others; he should save himself, if this is the one chosen the Christ of God."

Lk 23:36 Ἐνέπαιξαν δὲ αὐτῷ καὶ οἱ στρατιῶται προσερχόμενοι, ὄξος προσφέροντες αὐτῷ,

36And the soldiers, when they were approaching bringing him vinegar, also made fun of him.

Lk 23:37 καὶ λέγοντες, Εἰ σὺ εἶ ὁ βασιλεὺς τῶν Ἰουδαίων, σῶσον σεαυτόν.

37They also were saying, "If you are the king of the Jews, save yourself."

Lk 23:38 Ἦν δὲ καὶ ἐπιγραφὴ ἐπ' αὐτῷ, Ὁ βασιλεὺς τῶν Ἰουδαίων οὗτος.

38Now there was also a notice inscribed above him:[353] "THIS IS THE KING OF THE JEWS."

Lk 23:39 Εἷς δὲ τῶν κρεμασθέντων κακούργων ἐβλασφήμει αὐτόν, λέγων, Οὐχὶ σὺ εἶ ὁ χριστός; Σῶσον σεαυτὸν καὶ ἡμᾶς.

39And one of the criminals hung there was deriding him, saying, "You are the Christ, aren't you? Save yourself and us."

Lk 23:40 Ἀποκριθεὶς δὲ ὁ ἕτερος ἐπιτιμῶν αὐτῷ ἔφη, Οὐδὲ φοβῇ σὺ τὸν θεόν, ὅτι ἐν τῷ αὐτῷ κρίματι εἶ;

40But in response the other one was rebuking him, saying, "Don't you fear God at all, considering that you yourself are in this same judgement?[354]

Lk 23:41 Καὶ ἡμεῖς μὲν δικαίως, ἄξια γὰρ ὧν ἐπράξαμεν ἀπολαμβάνομεν• οὗτος δὲ οὐδὲν ἄτοπον ἔπραξεν.

41And we indeed justly; for we have gotten back what was fitting to how we have lived. But this man, he has done nothing wrong."

Lk 23:42 Καὶ ἔλεγεν, Ἰησοῦ, μνήσθητί μου ὅταν ἔλθῃς εἰς τὴν βασιλείαν σου.

42And then he was saying, "Jesus, remember me when you come into your kingdom."

Lk 23:43 Καὶ εἶπεν αὐτῷ, Ἀμὴν σοι λέγω, σήμερον μετ' ἐμοῦ ἔσῃ ἐν τῷ παραδείσῳ.

43And Jesus said to him, "I tell you the truth, today you will be with me in Paradise."

---

it^{aur,b,c,e,ff2,l,r1} vg syr^{c,p,h,pal} cop^{bopt} arm eth geo slav Diatess Iren^{lat} Clement Or Euseb Chryst Cyr TR RP TH ‖ *omit* 𝔓^{75} א B D* W Θ 070 31* 38 435 579 597* 1241 1808* 2622L 2633 it^{a,b,d} syr^{s} cop^{sa,bomss} NA28 {A} ‖ *lac* 𝔓^{45} P T Y. See the Endnote about this verse at the end of this document.

352 **23:34b** יְחַלְּקוּ בְגָדַי לָהֶם; וְעַל-לְבוּשִׁי, יַפִּילוּ גוֹרָל. https://mechon-mamre.org/p/pt/pt2622.htm

353 **23:38** txt *omit* 𝔓^{75} א^{2a} C* B L 070 cop^{sa,bopt} SBL TH NA28 {\} ‖ γραμμασιν ελληνικοις ρωμαικοις εβραικοις א^{*,2a} D ‖ γραμμασιν ελληνικοις και ρωμαικοις και εβραικοις ουτος εστιν A N Q R W 0250 𝔐 lat syr cop^{bopt} TR RP ‖ *lac* 𝔓^{45} P T.

354 **23:40** Or, perhaps an Aramaism as follows, "since you are in this same fate?"

Jesus' Death

Lk 23:44 Καὶ ἦν ἤδη ὡσεὶ ὥρα ἕκτη, καὶ σκότος ἐγένετο ἐφ' ὅλην τὴν γῆν ἕως ὥρας ἐνάτης

44 And it was now about noon,[355] and darkness came across the whole land until 3:00 p.m.,

Lk 23:45 τοῦ ἡλίου ἐκλιπόντος, ἐσχίσθη δὲ τὸ καταπέτασμα τοῦ ναοῦ μέσον.

45 for the sun was darkened.[356] And the curtain of the temple was torn in two.

Lk 23:46 Καὶ φωνήσας φωνῇ μεγάλῃ ὁ Ἰησοῦς εἶπεν, Πάτερ, εἰς χεῖράς σου παρατίθεμαι τὸ πνεῦμά μου• τοῦτο δὲ εἰπὼν ἐξέπνευσεν.

46 And crying out with a loud voice, Jesus said, "Father, into your hands I commit my spirit."[357] And after he had said this, he expired.

Lk 23:47 Ἰδὼν δὲ ὁ ἑκατοντάρχης τὸ γενόμενον, ἐδόξαζεν τὸν θεόν, λέγων, Ὄντως ὁ ἄνθρωπος οὗτος δίκαιος ἦν.

47 Now the centurion when he saw what had happened, was giving glory to God, by saying, "This really must have been a righteous man."

---

[355] **23:44** Greek, "the sixth hour," that is, the sixth hour from 6 a.m. when the daytime starts, which makes this 12:00 noon. So also the remaining references to time in Luke: the darkness lasted until 3:00 p.m. (Grk-the ninth hour), when Jesus cried out to the Father. See the endnote in my Diatessaron regarding the differing clock systems and divisions of the day used by the synoptic evangelists in contrast to John.

[356] **23:45** txt τοῦ ἡλίου ἐκλιπόντος 𝔓^{75*} א C^{*vid} L 070 579 597 968 1012 1451 1626 2528 (2542 ἐκλάμποντος) 2705 0124? ℓ384$^{1/3}$ syr^{hmg} (syr^{h} σκοτισθέντος) slav Origen^{gr,lat} mss$^{acc. to Orig}$ SBL TH NA28 {B} ‖ τοῦ ἡλίου ἐκλείποντος 𝔓^{75C} B 597 ℓ68$^{1/2}$ ℓ76$^{1/2}$ ℓ211$^{1/2}$ ℓ387$^{1/2}$ ℓ770$^{1/2}$ ℓ773$^{1/2}$ ℓ813$^{1/2}$ ℓ950$^{1/3}$ ℓ1223$^{1/2}$ ℓ1780$^{1/2}$ cop^{bo} Origen ‖ ἐσκοτίσθη ὁ ἥλιος it^{a,b,c,e} arm geo Diatessaron ‖ καὶ ἐσκοτίσθη ὁ ἥλιος (A ἐσκορτίσθη) C^{3} (D it^{d} ἐσκοτίσθη δὲ) E G H K M Q R (S -ό) U W Γ Δ Θ Λ Π Ψ 0117? *f*^{1} *f*^{13} 1 2 28 118 157 180 205 565 700 892 1006 1009 1010 1071 1079 1195^{mg} 1216 1230 1241 1242 1243 1253 1292 1342 1344 1424? 1505 1546 1582^{*,c} 1646 2148 2174 2882 *Lect* it^{aur,f,ff2,l,q} vg syr^{c,s,p,pal} eth Marcion$^{acc. To Epiphanius vid}$ Origen^{lat} mss$^{acc. to Orig}$ TR HF RP ‖ τοῦ ἡλίου ἐκλιπόντος καὶ ἐσκοτίσθη ὁ ἥλιος C^{2vid} (UBS5) 22 *pc* (18) ‖ *omit* C^{2} (NA28) 33 159 443* 1137 1195* 1373* 1424? ‖ *lac* 𝔓^{45} F N P T. The phrase with ἐκλείπω could be translated, "from an eclipse of the sun." The Classical Greek writers Thucidides, Herodotus and Aristophanes used this word, when referring to the sun or moon, as meaning "suffer eclipse." But the event in this passage, Jesus' crucifixion, took place during Passover, which was always during a full moon, so an eclipse of the sun by the moon was not possible. Neither are there any astronomical records of the moon eclipsing the sun during that time. So the only rendering that is truly incorrect, would be "eclipse." To most people, an eclipse of the sun would mean that the sun was eclipsed by the moon. I imagine it is theoretically possible for some other kind of heavenly body to have eclipsed the sun, but I know of no astronomical records of such. Regardless, the rendering "eclipse" is just too misleading, since that word almost always means eclipse by the moon. The Majority text reads "καὶ ἐσκοτίσθη ὁ ἥλιος, "and the sun was darkened." But this textual variance need not make any difference, since the lexical authorites say that, in the passive voice, in which both ἐκλείπω and σκοτίζω are, either one of them can mean "was obscured."

[357] **23:46** This is as Jewish as King David who said it first, see Psalm 31:5 (6) in the Hebrew https://mechon-mamre.org/p/pt/pt2631.htm תהלים ל לא :

בְּיָדְךָ, אַפְקִיד רוּחִי

Lk 23:48 Καὶ πάντες οἱ συμπαραγενόμενοι ὄχλοι ἐπὶ τὴν θεωρίαν ταύτην, θεωρήσαντες τὰ γενόμενα, τύπτοντες τὰ στήθη ὑπέστρεφον.

48And all the crowds who had gathered around for this spectacle, when they observed what took place, they were turning away, beating their breasts.

Lk 23:49 Εἱστήκεισαν δὲ πάντες οἱ γνωστοὶ αὐτῷ ἀπὸ μακρόθεν καὶ γυναῖκες αἱ συνακολουθοῦσαι αὐτῷ ἀπὸ τῆς Γαλιλαίας, ὁρῶσαι ταῦτα.

49But all those who knew him, including the women[358] who had followed with him from Galilee, stood off at a distance throughout, watching these things.

Jesus' Burial

Lk 23:50 Καὶ ἰδού, ἀνὴρ ὀνόματι Ἰωσήφ, βουλευτὴς ὑπάρχων, ἀνὴρ ἀγαθὸς καὶ δίκαιος

50And behold, there was a council member named Joseph, who was a good and righteous man

Lk 23:51– οὗτος οὐκ ἦν συγκατατεθειμένος τῇ βουλῇ καὶ τῇ πράξει αὐτῶν– ἀπὸ Ἀριμαθαίας πόλεως τῶν Ἰουδαίων, ὃς προσεδέχετο τὴν βασιλείαν τοῦ θεοῦ•

51(he was not going along with their decision and actions), from Arimathea, a city in Judea, who was looking forward to the kingdom of God.

Lk 23:52 οὗτος προσελθὼν τῷ Πιλάτῳ ᾐτήσατο τὸ σῶμα τοῦ Ἰησοῦ.

52This man went to Pilate and asked for the body of Jesus.

Lk 23:53 Καὶ καθελὼν ἐνετύλιξεν αὐτὸ σινδόνι, καὶ ἔθηκεν αὐτὸν ἐν μνήματι λαξευτῷ, οὗ οὐκ ἦν οὐδεὶς οὔπω κείμενος.

53And when he had taken it down he wrapped it in linen, and laid it in a hewn-out tomb, which no one was lying in yet.

Lk 23:54 Καὶ ἡμέρα ἦν Παρασκευῆς καὶ σάββατον ἐπέφωσκεν.

54And it was the day of Preparation, and the Sabbath was coming on.

Lk 23:55 Κατακολουθήσασαι δὲ γυναῖκες, αἵτινες ἦσαν συνεληλυθυῖαι ἐκ τῆς Γαλιλαίας αὐτῷ, ἐθεάσαντο τὸ μνημεῖον, καὶ ὡς ἐτέθη τὸ σῶμα αὐτοῦ.

55Now some women had followed close behind, which were the ones who had come with him from Galilee. They observed the tomb, and how his body was interred.

Lk 23:56 Ὑποστρέψασαι δὲ ἡτοίμασαν ἀρώματα καὶ μύρα. Καὶ τὸ μὲν σάββατον ἡσύχασαν κατὰ τὴν ἐντολήν,

56Then when they returned home, they prepared spices and perfumes. And for the Sabbath though, they did rest, in keeping with the commandment;

---

[358] **23:49** Tatian's Diatessaron: "the wives of those who had followed with him." In Syriac the difference between "women" and "wives" was the letter *dalath*. With it meant "wives."

Chapter 24

The Resurrection

Lk 24:1 τῇ δὲ μιᾷ τῶν σαββάτων ὄρθρου βαθέως ἐπὶ τὸ μνῆμα ἦλθον φέρουσαι ἃ ἡτοίμασαν ἀρώματα.

1but at the crack of dawn on the first day of the week, they went to the tomb, carrying the spices they had prepared.[359]

Lk 24:2 Εὗρον δὲ τὸν λίθον ἀποκεκυλισμένον ἀπὸ τοῦ μνημείου.

2But they found the stone had been rolled away from the tomb.

Jesus Appears to the Women

Lk 24:3 Εἰσελθοῦσαι δὲ οὐχ εὗρον τὸ σῶμα τοῦ κυρίου Ἰησοῦ.

3And when they went inside, they did not find the body of the Lord Jesus.

Lk 24:4 Καὶ ἐγένετο ἐν τῷἀπορεῖσθαι αὐτὰς περὶ τούτου, καὶ ἰδού, ἄνδρες δύο ἐπέστησαν αὐταῖς ἐν ἐσθῆτι ἀστραπτούσῃ•

4And it happened that as they stood hesitating about this, behold, two men appeared to them, in gleaming robes.

Lk 24:5 ἐμφόβων δὲ γενομένων αὐτῶν, καὶ κλινουσῶν τὰ πρόσωπα εἰς τὴν γῆν, εἶπαν πρὸς αὐτάς, Τί ζητεῖτε τὸν ζῶντα μετὰ τῶν νεκρῶν;

5And when terror came over them, such that they had bowed their faces down to the ground, the *men* said to them, "Why are you looking for the living among the dead?

Lk 24:6 Οὐκ ἔστιν ὧδε, ἀλλὰ ἠγέρθη• μνήσθητε ὡς ἐλάλησεν ὑμῖν, ἔτι ὢν ἐν τῇ Γαλιλαίᾳ,

6He is not here, but is risen! Recall how he spoke to you while still in Galilee,

Lk 24:7 λέγων τὸν υἱὸν τοῦ ἀνθρώπου ὅτι δεῖ παραδοθῆναι εἰς χεῖρας ἀνθρώπων ἁμαρτωλῶν, καὶ σταυρωθῆναι, καὶ τῇ τρίτῃ ἡμέρᾳ ἀναστῆναι.

7saying that the Son of Man must be transferred into the hands of sinful mortals, and be crucified, and on the third day rise again."

Lk 24:8 Καὶ ἐμνήσθησαν τῶν ῥημάτων αὐτοῦ,

8And they did recall his statements.

Lk 24:9 καὶ ὑποστρέψασαι ἀπὸ τοῦ μνημείου, ἀπήγγειλαν ταῦτα πάντα τοῖς ἕνδεκα καὶ πᾶσιν τοῖς λοιποῖς.

9And when they returned from the tomb, they related all these things to the Eleven and to all the rest.

Lk 24:10 Ἦσαν δὲ ἡ Μαγδαληνὴ Μαρία καὶ Ἰωάννα καὶ Μαρία ἡ Ἰακώβου, καὶ αἱ λοιπαὶ σὺν αὐταῖς, ἔλεγον πρὸς τοὺς ἀποστόλους ταῦτα.

10Now it was the Magdalene Mary, and Joanna, and Mary *the mother* of James, and the others with them who were telling these things to the apostles;

---

359 **24:1** txt αρωματα 𝔓75 א B C* L lat copbopt syrpalms SBL TH NA28 ‖ αρωματα και τινες συν αυταις. *p*) ελογινζοντο δε εν εαυταις· τις αρα αποκυλισει ημιν τον λιθον 070 ‖ και τινες συν αυταις. *p*) ελογινζοντο δε εν εαυταις· τις αρα αποκυλισει τον λιθον D copsa ‖ αρωματα και τινες συν αυταις A E W 𝔐 itf,q,r1 (syr copbopt Eus) TR RP ‖ *lac* 𝔓45 N P Q T.

Lk 24:11 Καὶ ἐφάνησαν ἐνώπιον αὐτῶν ὡσεὶ λῆρος τὰ ῥήματα ταῦτα, καὶ ἠπίστουν αὐταῖς.

11and these statements appeared to them as nonsense, and they did not believe them.

Lk 24:12 Ὁ δὲ Πέτρος ἀναστὰς ἔδραμεν ἐπὶ τὸ μνημεῖον, καὶ παρακύψας βλέπει τὰ ὀθόνια μόνα• καὶ ἀπῆλθεν πρὸς ἑαυτὸν θαυμάζων τὸ γεγονός.

12But Peter got up and ran to the tomb, and after stooping down, he sees only the linen bandages. And he went away, wondering to himself what had happened.

On the Road to Emmaus

Lk 24:13 Καὶ ἰδού, δύο ἐξ αὐτῶν ἐν αὐτῇ τῇ ἡμέρᾳ ἦσαν πορευόμενοι εἰς κώμην ἀπέχουσαν σταδίους ἑξήκοντα ἀπὸ Ἱερουσαλήμ, ᾗ ὄνομα Ἐμμαούς.

13And behold, that same day, two of them were on their way to a village named Emmaus, which was seven miles[360] from Jerusalem.

Lk 24:14 Καὶ αὐτοὶ ὡμίλουν πρὸς ἀλλήλους περὶ πάντων τῶν συμβεβηκότων τούτων.

14And these two were conversing with each other about the outcome of all these things.

Lk 24:15 Καὶ ἐγένετο ἐν τῷ ὁμιλεῖν αὐτοὺς καὶ συζητεῖν, καὶ αὐτὸς Ἰησοῦς ἐγγίσας συνεπορεύετο αὐτοῖς.

15And it came about, that they are in conversation, and Jesus himself has come up, walking along with them.

Lk 24:16 Οἱ δὲ ὀφθαλμοὶ αὐτῶν ἐκρατοῦντο τοῦ μὴ ἐπιγνῶναι αὐτόν.

16Their eyes, however, were being restrained, so as not to recognize him.

Lk 24:17 Εἶπεν δὲ πρὸς αὐτούς, Τίνες οἱ λόγοι οὗτοι οὓς ἀντιβάλλετε πρὸς ἀλλήλους περιπατοῦντες; καὶ ἐστάθησαν σκυθρωποί;

17And he said to them, "What is this discussion you are having with each other as you walk along?" And they came to a stop,[361] looking dismal.

Lk 24:18 Ἀποκριθεὶς δὲ εἷς ὀνόματι Κλεοπᾶς, εἶπεν πρὸς αὐτόν, Σὺ μόνος παροικεῖς Ἱερουσαλήμ, καὶ οὐκ ἔγνως τὰ γενόμενα ἐν αὐτῇ ἐν ταῖς ἡμέραις ταύταις;

18And in response, the one named Cleopas said to him, "Are you just visiting Jerusalem,[362] and unaware of the things happening in it during these days?"

---

360 **24:13** Greek: sixty stadia, or about 11 kilometers.

361 **24:17** txt και εσταθησαν 𝔓^{75} ℵ A* B (L εστησαν) 070 079 it^{e} syr^{pal} cop^{sa,bo} SBL TH NA28 {B} ‖ και εστε A^{c} E N P W 𝔐 vg it$^{a,aur,b,f,ff^2,l,r^1}$ syr$^{(s,c),p,h}$ TR RP ‖ *omit* D it^{d} eth Cyr ‖ *lac* 𝔓^{45} C Q T. The Robinson-Pierpont also punctuates this differently. Whereas the NA28 text has a question mark after περιπατοῦντες, the RP has a comma. Thus the NA text reads " 'What is this discussion you are having with each other as you walk along?' And they came to a stop, looking dismal." The RP text reads, "What is this discussion you are having with each other as you are walking along and looking dismal?"

362 **24:18** Or possibly, "Are you the only one living near Jerusalem who is unaware of the things happening..." But this is less likely, because in the Greek, the word for "living," παροικέω, is in the present indicative, not a participle, neither a noun. It seems to be a transitive verb, expecting an object, such as "visitng Jerusalem," or, "living IN Jerusalem."

Lk 24:19 Καὶ εἶπεν αὐτοῖς, Ποῖα; Οἱ δὲ εἶπαν αὐτῷ, Τὰ περὶ Ἰησοῦ τοῦ Ναζαρηνοῦ, ὃς ἐγένετο ἀνὴρ προφήτης δυνατὸς ἐν ἔργῳ καὶ λόγῳ ἐναντίον τοῦ θεοῦ καὶ παντὸς τοῦ λαοῦ•

19And he said to them, "What things?" And they said to him, "The things concerning Jesus the Nazarene, who was a prophet powerful in deed and in word, in the eyes of both God and all the people;

Lk 24:20 ὅπως τε παρέδωκαν αὐτὸν οἱ ἀρχιερεῖς καὶ οἱ ἄρχοντες ἡμῶν εἰς κρίμα θανάτου, καὶ ἐσταύρωσαν αὐτόν.

20how the chief priests and our rulers handed him over for the sentence of death, and how they crucified him.

Lk 24:21 Ἡμεῖς δὲ ἠλπίζομεν ὅτι αὐτός ἐστιν ὁ μέλλων λυτροῦσθαι τὸν Ἰσραήλ. Ἀλλά γε καὶ σὺν πᾶσιν τούτοις τρίτην ταύτην ἡμέραν ἄγει ἀφ' οὗ ταῦτα ἐγένετο.

21And here we had been hoping he was the one who was going to redeem Israel. And what is more, he is already spending his third day *in the grave* since when these things took place.[363]

Lk 24:22 Ἀλλὰ καὶ γυναῖκές τινες ἐξ ἡμῶν ἐξέστησαν ἡμᾶς, γενόμεναι ὀρθριναὶ ἐπὶ τὸ μνημεῖον•

22And not only that, now some of our women have confounded us. They were at the tomb early this morning,

Lk 24:23 καὶ μὴ εὑροῦσαι τὸ σῶμα αὐτοῦ, ἦλθον λέγουσαι καὶ ὀπτασίαν ἀγγέλων ἑωρακέναι, οἳ λέγουσιν αὐτὸν ζῆν.

23and not finding his body, they came back, claiming also to have seen a vision of angels, which were maintaining that he was alive.

Lk 24:24 Καὶ ἀπῆλθόν τινες τῶν σὺν ἡμῖν ἐπὶ τὸ μνημεῖον, καὶ εὗρον οὕτως καθὼς καὶ αἱ γυναῖκες εἶπον• αὐτὸν δὲ οὐκ εἶδον.

24So some of our number went to the tomb, and found it just as the women had said; but him they did not see."

Lk 24:25 Καὶ αὐτὸς εἶπεν πρὸς αὐτούς, Ὦ ἀνόητοι καὶ βραδεῖς τῇ καρδίᾳ τοῦ πιστεύειν ἐπὶ πᾶσιν οἷς ἐλάλησαν οἱ προφῆται•

25And he said to them, "O you thick headed, and slow of heart to believe on all the things the prophets have spoken!

Lk 24:26 οὐχὶ ταῦτα ἔδει παθεῖν τὸν χριστόν, καὶ εἰσελθεῖν εἰς τὴν δόξαν αὐτοῦ;

26Were not these things required for the Christ to suffer in order to go on into his glory?"

And the phrase "who is not aware" would be a stretch. Moreover, the Greek does not say "in Jerusalem," but rather just "Jerusalem." The word παροικέω generally meant "living as a stranger, a pilgrim, living as a visitor," and only rarely meant just "live or inhabit next to" without the connotation of being an alien or stranger.

363 **24:21** DeBrunner says in §129 that rather than the impersonal "it is the third day," that this phrase τρίτην ταύτην ἡμέραν ἄγει ἀφ' οὗ ταῦτα ἐγένετο means "he is already spending the third day" [in the tomb]. Bauer agrees with this as well. The Greek does not supply a subject here, but some third person singular subject is implied, and the verb ἄγω in phrases about time, means "spend."

Lk 24:27 Καὶ ἀρξάμενος ἀπὸ Μωϋσέως καὶ ἀπὸ πάντων τῶν προφητῶν,
διερμήνευσεν αὐτοῖς ἐν πάσαις ταῖς γραφαῖς τὰ περὶ ἑαυτοῦ.
27And beginning with Moses, and through all the prophets, he interpreted for
them the things in all the writings that were about himself.
Lk 24:28 Καὶ ἤγγισαν εἰς τὴν κώμην οὗ ἐπορεύοντο• καὶ αὐτὸς προσεποιήσατο
πορρώτερον πορεύεσθαι.
28And they came near to the village to which they were going, and he
pretended to go on farther.
Lk 24:29 Καὶ παρεβιάσαντο αὐτόν, λέγοντες, Μεῖνον μεθ' ἡμῶν, ὅτι πρὸς
ἑσπέραν ἐστίν, καὶ κέκλικεν ἤδη ἡ ἡμέρα. Καὶ εἰσῆλθεν τοῦ μεῖναι σὺν αὐτοῖς.
29And they urged him insistently, saying, "Lodge with us, because it is near
evening, and the daylight is almost gone." And he went inside, to lodge with
them.
Lk 24:30 Καὶ ἐγένετο ἐν τῷ κατακλιθῆναι αὐτὸν μετ' αὐτῶν, λαβὼν τὸν ἄρτον
εὐλόγησεν, καὶ κλάσας ἐπεδίδου αὐτοῖς.
30And it came about that as he reclined with them, he took bread, gave thanks
and broke it, and was distributing it to them.
Lk 24:31 Αὐτῶν δὲ διηνοίχθησαν οἱ ὀφθαλμοί, καὶ ἐπέγνωσαν αὐτόν• καὶ αὐτὸς
ἄφαντος ἐγένετο ἀπ' αὐτῶν.
31Then their eyes were opened, and they recognized him. And he disappeared
from them.
Lk 24:32 Καὶ εἶπαν πρὸς ἀλλήλους, Οὐχὶ ἡ καρδία ἡμῶν καιομένη ἦν ἐν ἡμῖν, ὡς
ἐλάλει ἡμῖν ἐν τῇ ὁδῷ, ὡς διήνοιγεν ἡμῖν τὰς γραφάς;
32And they said to each other, "Were not our hearts burning within us as he
talked to us on the road, as he explained the scriptures to us?"
Lk 24:33 Καὶ ἀναστάντες αὐτῇ τῇ ὥρᾳ ὑπέστρεψαν εἰς Ἰερουσαλήμ, καὶ εὗρον
ἠθροισμένους τοὺς ἕνδεκα καὶ τοὺς σὺν αὐτοῖς,
33And after rising up that very hour, they returned to Jerusalem, and found
the Eleven and those with them all gathered together,
Lk 24:34 λέγοντας ὅτι Ὄντως ἠγέρθη ὁ κύριος, καὶ ὤφθη Σίμωνι.
34who were saying that the Lord really was risen, and had appeared to Simon.
Lk 24:35 Καὶ αὐτοὶ ἐξηγοῦντο τὰ ἐν τῇ ὁδῷ, καὶ ὡς ἐγνώσθη αὐτοῖς ἐν τῇ κλάσει
τοῦ ἄρτου.
35And then the former were recounting the events on the road, and how he
was made known to them in the breaking of the bread.

Jesus Appears to the Apostles

Lk 24:36 Ταῦτα δὲ αὐτῶν λαλούντων, αὐτὸς ἔστη ἐν μέσῳ αὐτῶν, καὶ λέγει
αὐτοῖς, Εἰρήνη ὑμῖν.
36And while they were speaking these things, he stood in the midst of them,
and he is saying to them, "Peace be with you."
Lk 24:37 Πτοηθέντες δὲ καὶ ἔμφοβοι γενόμενοι ἐδόκουν πνεῦμα θεωρεῖν.
37But alarmed they were, and terrified, thinking they were seeing a ghost.

Lk 24:38 Καὶ εἶπεν αὐτοῖς, Τί τεταραγμένοι ἐστέ, καὶ διὰ τί διαλογισμοὶ ἀναβαίνουσιν ἐν τῇ καρδίᾳ ὑμῶν;

38And he said to them, "Why are you troubled? And for what reason are doubts arising in your hearts?

Lk 24:39 Ἴδετε τὰς χεῖράς μου καὶ τοὺς πόδας μου, ὅτι ἐγώ εἰμι αὐτός• ψηλαφήσατέ με καὶ ἴδετε, ὅτι πνεῦμα σάρκα καὶ ὀστέα οὐκ ἔχει, καθὼς ἐμὲ θεωρεῖτε ἔχοντα.

39Behold my hands and my feet, that I am me. Touch me, and know, because a ghost does not have flesh and bones as you see me having."

Lk 24:40 Καὶ τοῦτο εἰπὼν ἔδειξεν αὐτοῖς τὰς χεῖρας καὶ τοὺς πόδας.

40And when he had said this, he showed them his hands and his feet.

Lk 24:41 Ἔτι δὲ ἀπιστούντων αὐτῶν ἀπὸ τῆς χαρᾶς καὶ θαυμαζόντων, εἶπεν αὐτοῖς, Ἔχετέ τι βρώσιμον ἐνθάδε;

41But, since they were still not believing, out of joy and astonishment, he said to them, "What do you have to eat in this place?"

Lk 24:42 Οἱ δὲ ἐπέδωκαν αὐτῷ ἰχθύος ὀπτοῦ μέρος.

42So they handed him a piece of broiled fish.[364]

Lk 24:43 Καὶ λαβὼν ἐνώπιον αὐτῶν ἔφαγεν.

43And he took it, and ate it in front of them.

The Ascension

Lk 24:44 Εἶπεν δὲ πρὸς αὐτούς, Οὗτοι οἱ λόγοι οὓς ἐλάλησα πρὸς ὑμᾶς ἔτι ὢν σὺν ὑμῖν, ὅτι δεῖ πληρωθῆναι πάντα τὰ γεγραμμένα ἐν τῷ νόμῳ Μωϋσέως καὶ τοῖς προφήταις καὶ ψαλμοῖς περὶ ἐμοῦ.

44And he said to them, "These are the words which I spoke to you while I was still with you, how all the things written about me in the law of Moses and the prophets and the psalms must be fulfilled."

Lk 24:45 Τότε διήνοιξεν αὐτῶν τὸν νοῦν, τοῦ συνιέναι τὰς γραφάς•

45Then at that time he opened their minds to understand the scriptures.

Lk 24:46 καὶ εἶπεν αὐτοῖς ὅτι Οὕτως γέγραπται παθεῖν τὸν χριστόν, καὶ ἀναστῆναι ἐκ νεκρῶν τῇ τρίτῃ ἡμέρᾳ,

46And he said to them, "This is what is written: the Christ was to suffer, and to rise from the dead the third day,

Lk 24:47 καὶ κηρυχθῆναι ἐπὶ τῷ ὀνόματι αὐτοῦ μετάνοιαν καὶ ἄφεσιν ἁμαρτιῶν εἰς πάντα τὰ ἔθνη, ἀρξάμενοι ἀπὸ Ἱερουσαλήμ.

47and that repentance and forgiveness of sins is to be preached in his name to all the nations, beginning from Jerusalem.

Lk 24:48 Ὑμεῖς μάρτυρες τούτων.

48You are witnesses of these things.

---

364 **24:42** txt μερος $\mathfrak{P}^{75}$ ℵ A B D L W it^{d,e} syr^{s} cop^{sa,bopt} Clem Or^{vid} Cyr½ Ps-Ath Aug¼ Diatess-Arab½ SBL TH NA28 {B} ‖ μερος και κηριον it^{a} Jerome Diatess-Arab½ ‖ μερος και απο μελισσιου κηριου E^{C} N 𝔐 it^{b,q} syr$^{c,p,pal,h\ with*}$ cop^{bopt} Justin^{dub} Amphil Tert Cyr½ Epiph Jer TR RP ‖ μερος και απο μελισσιου κηριον E* it$^{aur,t,ff^2,l,r^1}$ vg arm geo Cyril-Jerusalem Proclus; Aug¾ Varimadum ‖ *lac* $\mathfrak{P}^{45}$ C P Q T

Lk 24:49 Καγὼ ἀποστέλλω τὴν ἐπαγγελίαν τοῦ πατρός μου ἐφ' ὑμᾶς• ὑμεῖς δὲ καθίσατε ἐν τῇ πόλει ἕως οὗ ἐνδύσησθε ἐξ ὕψους δύναμιν.

49And I am sending what my Father promised down upon you. So you are to stay put in the city until such time you are endued with power from on high."

Lk 24:50 Ἐξήγαγεν δὲ αὐτοὺς ἔξω ἕως πρὸς Βηθανίαν• καὶ ἐπάρας τὰς χεῖρας αὐτοῦ εὐλόγησεν αὐτούς.

50Then he led them outside, as far as Bethany. And after lifting up his hands, he blessed them.

Lk 24:51 Καὶ ἐγένετο ἐν τῷ εὐλογεῖν αὐτὸν αὐτούς, διέστη ἀπ' αὐτῶν, καὶ ἀνεφέρετο εἰς τὸν οὐρανόν.

51And it came about that as he was blessing them, he parted from them, and was taken up into heaven.

Lk 24:52 Καὶ αὐτοὶ προσκυνήσαντες αὐτόν, ὑπέστρεψαν εἰς Ἱερουσαλὴμ μετὰ χαρᾶς μεγάλης•

52And they, after worshiping him, returned back to Jerusalem with great rejoicing.

Lk 24:53 καὶ ἦσαν διὰ παντὸς ἐν τῷ ἱερῷ εὐλογοῦντες τὸν θεόν.

53And throughout those days they were continually at the temple, praising God.

Endnote #1 – Matthew's vs. Luke's Genealogy

MATTHEW'S AND LUKE'S GENEALOGIES APPEAR TO GIVE CONFLICTING GENEALOGIES OF JOSEPH THE HUSBAND OF MARY.

Matthew 1:1-17; Luke 3:28-38

MATTHEW	LUKE
Abraham	Abraham
Isaac	Isaac
Jacob	Jacob
Judah	Judah
Perez	Perez
Hezron	Hezron
Aram	Aram
Amminadab	Amminadab
Nahshon	Nahshon
Salmon	Salmon
Boaz	Boaz
Obed	Obed
Jesse	Jesse
David	David
Solomon	Nathan
Rehoboam	Mattatha
Abijah	Menna
Asa	Melea
Jehoshaphat	Eliakim
Joram	Jonam
Uzziah	Joseph
Jotham	Judah
Ahaz	Simeon
Hezekiah	Levi
Manasseh	Matthat
Amos/Amon	Jorim
Josiah	Eliezer
Jeconiah	Joshua
Shealtiel	Er
Zerubbabel	Elmadam
Abiud	Cosam
Eliakim	Addi
Azor	Melki
Zadok	Neri

Achim	Shealtiel
Eliud	Zerubbabel
Eleazar	Rhesa
Matthan	Joanan
Jacob	Joda
Joseph	Josech
Jesus	Semein
	Mattathias
	Joseph
	Jannai
	Melki
	Levi
	Matthat
	Heli
	Joseph
	Jesus

It should be noted that though Matthew states in 1:17 that there are three sets of 14 generations, there are only 13 generations in his 3rd set. He also left out two generations from the second set which would have made that set 16 generations. After Josiah came Jehoiakim and Jehoiachin, according to 2 Kings 23:34 – 24:6. Thus it seems Matthew made these sets for some purpose such as to be a memorization aid or teaching aid.

Following is taken from an article on the Internet, formerly on carm.org:

Both Matthew 1 and Luke 3 contain genealogies of Jesus. But there is one problem. They are different. Luke's Genealogy starts at Adam and goes to David. Matthew's Genealogy starts at Abraham and goes to David. When the genealogies arrive at David, they split with David's sons: Nathan (Mary's side) and Solomon (Joseph's side).

There is no discrepancy because one genealogy is for Mary and the other is for Joseph. It was customary to mention the genealogy through the father even though it was clearly known that it was through Mary.

F**irst**, realize that the Bible should be interpreted in the context of its literary style, culture, and history. Breaking up genealogies into male and female representations was acceptable in the ancient Near East culture since it was often impolite to speak of women without proper conditions being met: male presence, etc. One genealogy is of Mary and the other of Joseph, even though both mention Joseph. In other words, the Mary was counted "in" Joseph and under his headship.

Second, do any critics actually think that those who collected the books of the New Testament, and who believed it was inerrant, were unaware of this blatant differentiation in genealogies? Does anyone actually think that the Christians were so dense that they were unaware of the differences in the genealogy lists, closed their eyes and put the gospels into the canon anyway hoping no one would notice? Not at all. They knew the cultural context and had no problem with it knowing that one was of Joseph and the other of Mary.

Third, notice that Luke starts with Mary and goes backwards to Adam. Matthew starts with Abraham and goes forward to Joseph. The intents of the genealogies were different which is seen in their styles. Luke was not written to the Jews, Matthew was. Therefore, Matthew would carry the legal line (from Abraham through David) and Luke the biological one (from Adam through David). Also, notice that Luke's first three chapters mention Mary eleven times; hence, the genealogy from her. Fourth, notice Luke 3:23, "And when He began His ministry, Jesus Himself was about thirty years of age, being supposedly the son of Joseph, the son of Eli," This designation "supposedly" seems to signify the Marian genealogy since it seems to indicate that Jesus is not the biological son of Joseph.

Finally, in the Joseph genealogy there is a man named Jeconiah. God cursed Jeconiah (also called Coniah), stating that no descendant of his would ever sit on the throne of David, "For no man of his descendants will prosper sitting on the throne of David or ruling again in Judah," (Jer. 22:30). But Jesus, of course, will sit on the throne in the heavenly kingdom. The point is that Jesus is not a biological descendant of Jeconiah, but through the other lineage -- that of Mary. Hence, the prophetic curse upon Jeconiah stands inviolate. But, the legal adoption of Jesus by Joseph reckoned the legal rights of Joseph to Jesus as a son, not the biological curse. This is why we need two genealogies: one of Mary (the actually biological line according to prophecy), and the legal line through Joseph.

Again, the early church knew this and had no problem with it. It is only the critics of today who narrow their vision and require this to be a "contradiction" when in reality we have an explanation that is more than sufficient.

Endnote #2

Did Jesus send out seventy, or seventy-two? (ἑβδομήκοντα or ἑβδομήκοντα δύο?)

Luke 10:1, 17; Diatessaron 18:10, 15

There are witnesses both ample and ancient ($\mathfrak{P}^{45}$ now is known to support 70 in 10:17) to both readings, though somewhat favoring "seventy-two." Both the Nestle-Aland 28th Edition and the UBS 5th Edition of the Greek text put the δυο, the "two," in square brackets, and the UBS editorial committee gives it a [C] rating of certainty. This means that they decided on "72," but had difficulty in deciding to do so, and therefore placed the δυο in brackets to indicate the great degree of doubt that it has a right to be there.

Since the manuscript consideration is almost a stand-off, interpreters then discuss what stronger or more likely numerological symbolism there is for one reading over the other. Discussion invariably leads to Genesis chapter 11, where God broke up the single world language into many nations. There, one can count seventy nations in the Hebrew text. Yet, in the Septuagint, the Greek translation of the Hebrew scriptures made by Jewish translators in Egypt before the time of Christ, one can count seventy-two nations. If it were only Alexandrian witnesses which read "72" in 10:1, an argument might be made that they were overly influenced by the Septuagint, which was also produced in Alexandria. But this is not the case, since the chief representatives of both the Alexandrian, as well as the Western groups of Greek manuscripts, read "72," along with most of the Old Latin and the Sinaitic Syriac. And on the other hand, Codex Sinaiticus, one of the primary Alexandrian manuscripts, reads "70."

The implication some interpreters make, is that by appointing 70, Jesus drew on the Jewish tradition of there being 70 nations in the world, to show that his message was intended for everyone in the whole world. And that that was intended to be in contrast to when he sent the Twelve out earlier, and forbade them to go into any Samaritan village; whereas here in the case of the 70 / 72, there is no such prohibition. Paul says, "the gospel is to the Jew first, and also to the Gentile." (Romans 1:16) The Lord himself said in John 10:16, "Other sheep I also have, which are not of this fold; those also I am to bring, and my voice they will hear, and the result will be one flock, one shepherd."

Regarding the above-mentioned decision by the Editorial Committee of the United Bible Societies' Greek New Testament to include the "-two" in square brackets, one of the members of the committee disagreed with that decision, for he regarded "72" as undoubtedly the original reading. That member was the late Kurt Aland. His written dissent, as published in the book, *A Textual Commentary on the Greek New Testament*, Metzger, Bruce M., on behalf of and in cooperation with the Editorial Committee of the United Bible Societies' Greek New Testament: Kurt Aland, Matthew Black, Carlo M. Martini, Bruce M. Metzger, and Allen Wikgren (Stuttgart, United Bible Societies, Corrected Edition, 1975), is worthy of being printed below, as follows.

> The concept of "70" is an established entity in the Septuagint and in Christian tradition. The number of examples of "70" in the Old Testament is overwhelming: there are always 70 souls in the house of Jacob, 70 elders, sons, priests, and 70 years that are mentioned in chronological references to important events. The number 72 appears only once, where, amid many other numbers, 72 cattle are set aside for a sacrificial offering (Num 31:38). If 72 occurs in the Letter of Aristeas (as the number of translators of the Septuagint) as well as in III Enoch, these sporadic instances are not to be compared in significance with the tradition involving 70.
>
> Consequently it is astonishing that the reading ἑβδομήκοντα δύο appears at all in [Luke] 10:1 and 17, and that it has such strong support. A reading that in the Gospels has in its support 𝔓[75] B D, the Old Syriac, the Old Latin, etc., etc., is ordinarily regarded at once as the original reading. If in addition the

> opposing reading lies under the suspicion of ecclesiastical "normalizing," the testimony becomes irrefutable. The opposing witnesses represent entirely an ecclesiastical normalizing. That they are in the majority is altogether understandable; if they are ancient, this only proves how early the normalizing process began to operate. For these reasons ἑβδομήκοντα δύο should be printed without square brackets. K.A.

In other words, why would some copyists change the number away from the symbolically significant "seventy" to a symbolically insignificant "seventy-two"? It is more likely that the copyists who did the changing of the originals were the ones who changed it to "seventy" in order to make it line up with the strong tradition of 70 in the Bible and Jewish tradition. (This latter is part of what Kurt Aland calls "normalizing." There are many instances in the Greek New Testament where the original reading is very obscure, or is poor grammar, or is a very unpopular teaching. Later copyists tended to smooth over these passages, or "normalize" them.)

There may be no symbolism at all involved in the number "seventy-two." Unless there is significance that it is divisible by twelve. Six times.

Well then, since the messengers were sent out two by two, let's examine how each number is divisible by two. If Jesus sent out seventy, that means there were 35 pairs of them. If Jesus sent out seventy-two, that means there were 36 pairs of them.

There may be no symbolism at all in what number of emissaries Jesus sent out. Yes, it is possible that he did intend some symbolism. But we should beware lest we change original holy writ just because we want a symbolism in it. It is possible Jesus did not intend any symbolism.

Here is a breakdown of some English translations I have checked. Those reading "**70**" are: Tyndale, KJV, NKJV, ASV, RSV, NRSV, NASB, AMP, CBW, CJB, ISV, HCSB, WEB, GW, EMTV, Phillips, Recovery, Darby, Weymouth. Those reading "**72**" are: CSB, DRP, DRB, GNB, JB, NIV, TNIV, REB, NLT, NCV, CEV, NET, ESV, MOUNCE, EHV; and the NAB reads "seventy[-two], and says "seventy-two" in the section heading. Note that the HCSB which read 70 has changed to 72 in the CSB.

Endnote #3

Luke 22:43-44

43And an angel from heaven appeared to him, strengthening him. 44And being in agony, he was praying more earnestly; and his sweat became like drops of blood falling down onto the ground.

Omit vv 43,44: 𝔓^{69,} 𝔓^{75} א^{2a} A B N R T W 0211 124 158 179 579 713 788 1071* *Lect*^{½} it^{f} syr^{s} cop^{sa,bomss} arm geo some Greek mss$^{acc. to Anastasius-Sinaita}$; Greek and Latin mss$^{acc to Hilary}$ Ambrose Jerome (Recent research by Thomas Wayment* has made the omission in 𝔓^{69} certain.)

Transpose Lk 22:43-44 after Mt. 26:39 f^{13}

Transpose Lk 22:43-45a (*add* καὶ ἀναστὰς ἀπὸ τῆς προσευχῆς) *after Mt. 26:39 Lect*^{½}

Include with minor variants: א^{*,2b} D E F G H K L M Q X Γ Δ* Θ Λ Π* Ψ 0171 0223 *f*^{1} 13^{c} 28 157 180 205 346 565 597 700 828½ 892* 1006 1009 1010 1071^{c} 1230 1241 1242 1243 1253 1292 1342 1344 1365 1424 1505 1546 1646 2148 2174 𝔐 ℓ184½ it^{a,aur,b,c,d,e,ff2,i,l,q,r1} vg syr^{c,p,h,pal} cop^{bopt} eth slav Diatessaron^{arm} Justin Irenaeus^{gr} Hippolytus$^{acc. to Theodoret}$ Origen^{dub} Ps-Dionysius Arius$^{acc. to Epiphanius}$ Eusebian Canons Didymus^{dub} Epiphanius Chrysostom Theodore Nestorius Theodoret all versions and most Greek mss$^{acc. to Anastasius-Sinaita}$ John-Damascus; Hil,ary Greek and Latin mss$^{acc. to Jerome}$ Augustine Quodvultdeus. The uncial 0171 is defective here, but indicates probable presence of the words.

Include with asterisks or obeli: Δ* Π^{c} 892$^{c mg}$ 1079 1195 1216 cop^{bomss}

Here is what the Editorial Committee of the United Bible Societies' Greek New Testament says about the passage in "A Textual Commentary on the Greek New Testament, corrected edition, 1975

> "The absence of these verses in such ancient and widely diversified witnesses as 𝔓$^{(69),75}$ א A B T W syr^{s} cop^{sa,bo} arm^{mss} geo Marcion Clement Origen *al*, as well as their being marked with asterisks or obeli (signifying spuriousness) in other witnesses (Δ* Π^{c} 892$^{c mg}$ 1079 1195 1216 cop^{bomss}) and their transferral to Matthew's gospel (after 26:39) by family 13 and several lectionaries (the latter also transfer ver. 45a), strongly suggests that they are no part of the original text of Luke. Their presence in many manuscripts, some ancient, as well as their citation by Justin, Irenaeus, Hippolytus, Eusebius and many other

> Fathers, is proof of the antiquity of the account. On grounds of transcriptional probability it is less likely that the verses were deleted in several different areas of the church by those who felt that the account of Jesus overwhelmed with human weakness was incompatible with his sharing the divine omnipotence of the Father, than that they were added from an early source, oral or written, of extra-canonical traditions concerning the life and passion of Jesus. Nevertheless, while acknowledging that the passage is a later addition to the text, in view of its evident antiquity and its importance in the textual tradition, a majority of the Committee decided to retain the words in the text but to enclose them within double square brackets.

In the 5th edition of their Greek New Testament, the committee gives the absence of these verses in the original text an A rating of certainty.

*Thomas A. Wayment, "A New transcription of P.Oxy 2383 (𝔓^{69}); NovT 50 (2008) 351-57

Endnote #4

Is the saying, "Father, forgive them, for they do not know what they are doing," original scripture?

Luke 23:34

The saying attributed to Jesus while on the cross, "Father, forgive them, for they do not know what they are doing" is not found in most of the earliest (pre-5th century) Greek manuscripts. Neither is it found in the earliest translations of Luke's gospel into other languages.

Omit: 𝔓$^{66, 75}$ א^{2a} B D* W Θ 070 0241 31* 38 435 579 597* 1241 1808* 2622L 2633 it$^{a,b^c,d}$ syr^{s} cop$^{sa,bo^{mss}}$

Include with minor variants: א^{*,2b} (A *omit* “Father”) C D^{3} (E with *) F G H (K ειπεν for ἔλεγεν) L M N Q U X Γ Δ Λ Π Ψ 063 0211 0250= ℓ1561 *f*^{1} (*f*^{13}) 2 28 33 131 157 158 180 205 565 597^{c} 700 713 828 892 1006 (1009 ποιῶσιν) 1010 1071 1079 (1195 ἅ for τί) 1216 (1230 1253 Ιησοῦς ἐσταυρωμένος ἔλεγεν) 1242 1243 1292 1342 1344 1365 1424 1505 1546 1646 2148 2174 𝔐 *Lect* it^{aur,b,c,e,ff2,l,r1} vg syr^{c,p,h,pal} cop$^{bo^{pt}}$ arm eth geo slav Diatess Irenaeus^{lat} Clement Origen Eusebius Chrystostom Cyr

Here is what the Editorial Committee of the United Bible Societies' Greek New Testament says about the passage in "A Textual Commentary on the Greek New Testament, corrected edition, 1975:

> "The absence of these words from such early and diverse witnesses as 𝔓[75] B D* W Θ it[a,d] syr[s] cop[sa,bo mss] is most impressive and can scarcely be explained as a deliberate excision by copyists who, considering the fall of Jerusalem to be proof that God had not forgiven the Jews, could not allow it to appear that the prayer of Jesus had remained unanswered. At the same time, the logion, though probably not a part of the original Gospel of Luke, bears self-evident tokens of its dominical origin, and was retained, within double square brackets, in its traditional place where it had been incorporated by unknown copyists relatively early in the transmission of the Third Gospel."

When I pondered what reasons could have possibly prompted copyists to add this passage to the gospel, it occurred to me that elements in the early church might not have wanted the Lord himself to be outshined by Stephen. For Stephen in Acts 7:60 said something similar. Yet Jesus himself predicted in John 14:12, "The person who believes in me, truly, truly I say to you, the works that I do, that one also shall do, and even greater than these *shall do*, because I am going to the Father." (DRP) On the other hand, Stephen may have done what he did because he was following Christ's known example.

Endnote #5

The Linear Aspect in the Gospel of Luke

The primary semantic content of a New Testament Greek verb, other than its lexical definition, was its "aspect" or "kind of action." Of these, there were three primary categories: the punctiliar aspect, the linear aspect, and the combined aspect. See Sections 318 through 356, in the book entitled, "A Greek Grammar of the New Testament and Other Early Christian Literature," by Blass and DeBrunner, and translated and edited by Funk, the University of Chicago Press, Chicago and London (1961).

Luke used the linear aspect much more discriminatingly than did Mark for example. Because of this, we should pay that much more attention to the linear aspect in Luke, and in fact, this makes all the difference for a proper understanding of several passages, some of which are shown and discussed below.

Luke 1:34 εἶπεν δὲ Μαριὰμ πρὸς τὸν ἄγγελον· Πῶς ἔσται τοῦτο, ἐπεὶ ἄνδρα οὐ γινώσκω;
34 And Mary said to the angel, "How will this happen, since I am not knowing a man?"

Mary asks how she could have a baby nine months from then, since she was not having sex with a man at the time, nor in the near future.

Luke 5:33
Οἱ δὲ εἶπαν πρὸς αὐτόν· Οἱ μαθηταὶ Ἰωάννου νηστεύουσιν πυκνὰ καὶ δεήσεις ποιοῦνται, ὁμοίως καὶ οἱ τῶν Φαρισαίων, οἱ δὲ σοὶ ἐσθίουσιν καὶ πίνουσιν.
33They then said to him, "The disciples of John are often fasting and making prayers, and likewise those of the Pharisees, but yours go on eating and drinking."

Luke 6:46 Τί δέ με καλεῖτε· Κύριε κύριε, καὶ οὐ ποιεῖτε ἃ λέγω;
46"And why do you keep calling me 'Lord, Lord,' and yet not do the things which I say?

Luke 11:9
Κἀγὼ ὑμῖν λέγω, αἰτεῖτε, καὶ δοθήσεται ὑμῖν· ζητεῖτε, καὶ εὑρήσετε· κρούετε, καὶ ἀνοιγήσεται ὑμῖν·
9So I say to you: ask, and it will be given to you; seek, and you will find; knock, and it will be opened to you.
Luke 11:10 πᾶς γὰρ ὁ αἰτῶν λαμβάνει, καὶ ὁ ζητῶν εὑρίσκει, καὶ τῷ κρούοντι ἀνοιγήσεται.
10For everyone who keeps asking, receives; and the person who keeps seeking, finds; and to the one who keeps on knocking, it will be opened.

The moral of that story is the virtue of brash persistence.

Luke 16:21
καὶ ἐπιθυμῶν χορτασθῆναι ἀπὸ τῶν πιπτόντων ἀπὸ τῆς τραπέζης τοῦ πλουσίου· ἀλλὰ καὶ οἱ κύνες ἐρχόμενοι ἐπέλειχον τὰ ἕλκη αὐτοῦ.
21and he kept longing in vain to eat the scraps dropping from the table of that rich man. In contrast, even the dogs at least would come and lick his sores.

In this passage, the contrast Jesus is making between the rich man and the dogs, would be lost unless our translations show the linear aspect. The point is that the beggar kept on longing to eat what was falling from the rich man's table, but never did. His longing never ceased, or ended. In contrast, the dogs would at least come and lick his sores.

Luke 18:3
χήρα δὲ ἦν ἐν τῇ πόλει ἐκείνῃ καὶ ἤρχετο πρὸς αὐτὸν λέγουσα· Ἐκδίκησόν με ἀπὸ τοῦ ἀντιδίκου μου.
3But there was a widow in that city, and she kept on coming to him, saying, 'Give me redress from my adversary.'

The linear aspect, the continuousness of the widow's coming, is the whole moral of the story. There are not separate Greek words in the Greek text specifically correspondng to "kept on" coming. That "kept on" aspect is indicated by the markers affixed to the verb stem, that is, the inflection.

Luke 18:7
ὁ δὲ θεὸς οὐ μὴ ποιήσῃ τὴν ἐκδίκησιν τῶν ἐκλεκτῶν αὐτοῦ τῶν βοώντων αὐτῷ ἡμέρας καὶ νυκτός, καὶ μακροθυμεῖ ἐπ' αὐτοῖς;
7So God, would he not bring about the avenging of his elect, who keep crying out to him day and night? And is he slow to respond to them?

Again, as in the previous example, the moral of the parable of the persistent widow, is to come "continually" and "persistently" and "habitually" with the same request, until you get it.

Luke 22:2
καὶ ἐζήτουν οἱ ἀρχιερεῖς καὶ οἱ γραμματεῖς τὸ πῶς ἀνέλωσιν αὐτόν, ἐφοβοῦντο γὰρ τὸν λαόν.
2and the chief priests and the Torah scholars were still yet looking for a way to put him to death, because they were still yet fearing the people.

This is the passage most dependent on the linear aspect. The passage does not make much sense without it. First, observe how various translations have rendered it. I have put them in groups according to how they rendered the Greek causal coordinating conjunction γαρ.

KJV And the chief priests and scribes sought how they might kill him; **for** they feared the people.
ASV And the chief priests and the scribes sought how they might put him to death; **for** they feared the people.
Darby and the chief priests and the scribes sought how they might kill him; **for** they feared the people.
YLT and the chief priests and the scribes were seeking how they may take him up, **for** they were afraid of the people.
WEB The chief priests and the scribes sought how they might put him to death, **for** they feared the people.
CBW So the high priests and the scribes continued to seek how they might put Him to death, **for** they were afraid of the people.
Phillips Now as the feast of unleavened bread, called the Passover, was approaching, fear of the people **made** the chief priests and scribes try desperately to find a way of getting rid of Jesus..
NASB and the chief priests and the teachers of the law were looking for some way to get rid of Jesus, **for** they were afraid of the people.
JB and the chief priests and the scribes were looking for some way of doing away with him, **because** they mistrusted the people.
RSV And the chief priests and the scribes were seeking how to put him to death; **for** they feared the people.

NKJV And the chief priests and the scribes sought how they might kill Him, **for** they feared the people.
NIV and the chief priests and the teachers of the law were looking for some way to get rid of Jesus, **for** they were afraid of the people.
TNIV and the chief priests and the teachers of the law were looking for some way to get rid of Jesus, **for** they were afraid of the people.
Recov. And the chief priests and the scribes were seeking a way to do away with Him, **for** they feared the people.
NAB and the chief priests and the scribes were seeking a way to put him to death, **for** they were afraid of the people.
REB and the chief priests and the scribes were trying to devise some means of doing away with him; **for** they were afraid of the people.
NRSV The chief priests and the scribes were looking for a way to put Jesus to death, **for** they were afraid of the people.
JNT and the head cohanim and the Torah-teachers began trying to find some way to get rid of Yeshua, **because** they were afraid of the people.
NCV The leading priests and teachers of the law were trying to find a way to kill Jesus, **because** they were afraid of the people.
CEV The chief priests and the teachers of the law of Moses were looking for a way to get rid of Jesus, **because** they were afraid of what the people might do.
ISV So the high priests and the scribes were looking for a way to put him to death, **for** they were afraid of the crowd.
NET The chief priests and the experts in the law were trying to find some way to put Jesus to death; **for** they were afraid of the people.
ESV And the chief priests and the scribes were seeking how to put him to death; **for** they feared the people.
HCSB The chief priests and the scribes were looking for a way to put Him to death, **because** they were afraid of the people.

Tyndl and the high Priests and Scribes sought how to kill him, **but** they feared the people.
Wey and the High Priests and the Scribes were contriving how to destroy Him. **But** they feared the people.
Mess The high priests and religion scholars were looking for a way to do away with Jesus **but**, fearful of the people, they were also looking for a way to cover their tracks.
BBE And the chief priests and the scribes were looking for a chance to put him to death, **but** they went in fear of the people.
NLT The leading priests and teachers of religious law were actively plotting Jesus' murder. **But** they wanted to kill him without starting a riot, a possibility they greatly feared.
GW The chief priests and the scribes were looking for some way to kill Jesus. **However**, they were afraid of the people.

I have found no grammatical or lexical authority for a purely adversative meaning for γαρ. The closest thing to an adversative use is said to be in one passage in Matthew where γαρ is used in combination with other conjunctions; but here in this passage it is used by itself. The Matthew passage:

Matt 15:27
ἡ δὲ εἶπεν, Ναί, κύριε, καὶ γὰρ τὰ κυνάρια ἐσθίει ἀπὸ τῶν ψιχίων τῶν πιπτόντων ἀπὸ τῆς τραπέζης τῶν κυρίων αὐτῶν.
27But she said, "True, Lord; yet the dogs certainly eat of the crumbs falling from their master's table."

If there is any adversative meaning here at all, it would be contained in the conjunction και, not in γαρ.

Perhaps The Message and the New Living Translation see an ellipsis implied in the passage. Perhaps that is why they supply so many English words that are not indicated in the Greek. I don't see an ellipsis.

I note that none of the above translations except the BBE conveys the imperfect aspect of the Greek verb for "fearing," that is, the leaders were still fearing the people; their fear was "imperfect," that is, ongoing.

Bible Translations Abbreviation Keys and Copyright Information

Tynd. = William Tyndale, 1527, public domain
Douay = The Douay-Rheims, by Martin, Allen and Bristow, New Testament published in 1582; Roman Catholic, public domain
KJV = King James Version, 1611, as revised by Blayney, 1769, or the Scrivener 1873 revision; Anglican, public domain
YLT = Young's Literal Translation, Robert Young, 1862, public domain
Darby = John Nelson Darby's translation, 1871, Brethren denomination, public domain
ASV = American Standard Version, 1901, public domain
Wey = Richard Francis Weymouth, published 1903, revised by James A. Robertson, 1924? public domain?
CBW = Charles B. Williams' translation, 1937, Copyright© 1986, Homan Bible Publishers, All rights reserved.
RSV = Revised Standard Version, 1946, 1971 Edition, Copyright © 1971, Division of Christian Education of the National Council of the Churches of Christ in the United States of America
ESV - English Standard Version, Copyright © 2001 by Crossway Bibles, a division of Good News Publishers, Wheaton, Illinois. All rights reserved.
HCSB = Holman Christian Standard Bible, © 2001, Broadman & Holman Publishers, Lifeway Christian Resources, 127 Ninth Avenue North, Nashville, TN 37234.
http://www.broadmanholman.com/hcsb/default.asp
BBE = The Bible in Basic English, 1949, 1964, Published by Cambridge Press. Now Public Domain in the USA, as far as I know.
Ampl. = Amplified Bible, 1954, Copyright © 1987 by the Lockman Foundation, a corporation not for profit, La Habra, California; All Rights Reserved
Phil = J.B. Phillips, 1958, Revised 1972, Copyright Mrs. Vera Phillips and the J.B. Phillips Estate?, published by Harper Collins
NASB = New American Standard Bible, 1963, 1995 updated edition, Copyright © 1995 by the Lockman Foundation, a corporation not for profit, La Habra, California; All Rights Reserved
JB = Jerusalem Bible, 1966, Copyright © 1968 by Darton, Longman & Todd, Ltd. and Doubleday & Company, Inc. (Roman Catholic)
NAB = New American Bible, 1970, New Testament revised 1986, Copyright © 1986 by Confraternity of Christian Doctrine (Roman Catholic), Washington D.C. All rights reserved.
NIV = New International Version, 1973, Copyright © 1984 by International Bible Society, Colorado Springs, Colorado, and Zondervan Publishing House, Grand Rapids, Michigan, and Hodder Headline, Plc., Sevenoaks, Kent, England. All rights reserved.
TNIV = Today's New International Version, Copyright © by the International Bible Society, Colorado Springs, Colorado. http://www.tniv.info/
NKJV = New King James Version, 1979, Copyright © 1982 by Thomas Nelson, Inc., Nashville, Tennessee

Recov. = Recovery Version, 1985, Revised 1991, Copyright © 1991 by Living Stream Ministry, Anaheim, California (the "Local Church"; notes by Witness Lee.)
NCV = New Century Version, 1987, Copyright © 1991 by Word Publishing, Nashville, Tennessee
NRSV = New Revised Standard Version, 1989, Copyright © 1989 by Division of Christian Education of the National Council of the Churches of Christ in the United States of America
JNT = Jewish New Testament, Copyright © 1989 by David H. Stern, All rights reserved. Published by Jewish New Testament Publications, Jerusalem, Israel
Mess = The Message, Copyright © 1993 by Eugene H. Peterson. All rights Reserved.
CEV = Contemporary English Version, 1995, Copyright © 1995 by the American Bible Society, New York, New York
GW = God's Word, 1995, GOD'S WORD is a copyrighted work of God's Word to the Nations. Quotations are used by permission. Copyright © 1995 by God's Word to the Nations. All rights reserved.
NLT = New Living Translation, 1996, Copyright © 1996 by Tyndale Charitable Trust, Wheaton, Illinois. All rights reserved.
WEB = World English Bible, "World English Bible" is a trademark of Rainbow Missions, Inc. Permission is granted to use the name "World English Bible" and its logo only to identify faithful copies of the Public Domain translation of the Holy Bible of that name published by Rainbow Missions, Inc. The World English Bible is not copyrighted. The domain names eBible.org and mpj.cx are trademarks of Michael Paul Johnson.
NET = New English Translation, Copyright © 1997, 1998, 1999 by Biblical Studies Press, L.L.C. and the authors. All rights reserved. For free usage information, please read the BSF web site copyright statement for fair use statements.
ISV = International Standard Version, 2000, Copyright © 2000 The ISV Foundation, Santa Ana, California, The Davidson Press, ALL RIGHTS RESERVED INTERNATIONALLY.
Wilt = Clyde Wilton, pastor of Emmanuel Baptist Church, Bryan, Texas, copyright unknown
Alex = Victor Alexander's translation of an Aramaic source text
DRP = David Robert Palmer, translations from the Greek. Download, copy, print, and quote them at will. Do not change them.

Table of Witnesses

Symbl	Alt	Date	Contents
$\mathfrak{P}^{3}$		VI/VII	7:36-45, 10:38-42
$\mathfrak{P}^{4}$		III	1:58-59,62-80,2:1,6,7, 3:8-38, 4:1,2,29-32,34,35, 5:3-8,30-39, 6:1-16
$\mathfrak{P}^{7}$		III-IV?	4:1-3
$\mathfrak{P}^{42}$		VII/VIII	1:54,55; 2:29-32
$\mathfrak{P}^{45}$		III	6:31-41,45-49, **7**:1-7; **9**:26-41, 45-62, **10**:1, 6-22, 26-42, **11**:1, 6-25, 28-46, 50-54, **12**:1-12, 18-37, 42-59, **13**:1, 6-24, 29-35, **14**:1-10, 17-33
$\mathfrak{P}^{69}$		III	22:41, 45-48, 58-61
$\mathfrak{P}^{75}$		early III	3:18-22,33-38; 4:1-2,34-44; 5:1-10,37-39; 6:1-4,10-49; 7:1-32,35-39,41-43,46-50; 8:1-56; 9:1-2,4-62; 10:1-42; 11:1-54; 12:1-59; 13:1-35; 14:1-35; 15:1-32; 16:1-31; 17:1-15,19-37; 18:1-18;22:4-71; 23:1-56; 24:1-53
$\mathfrak{P}^{82}$	P. Gr. 2677	IV/V	7:32-34, 37, 38
$\mathfrak{P}^{97}$		VI/VII	14:7-14
$\mathfrak{P}^{111}$		III	17:11-13, 22-23
$\mathfrak{P}^{141}$	P. Oxy 5478	III	2:32-34, 40-42; 24:22-28, 30-38
ℵ*	01	IV	Codex Sinaiticus, all of Luke
$\aleph^{1}$	1st corr.	IV-VI	$\aleph^{1a}$/$\aleph^{1b}$ for differences within the group
$\aleph^{2}$	2nd corr.	VII	$\aleph^{2a}$/$\aleph^{2b}$ for differences within the group
A	02	V	Codex Alexandrinus; all
B	03	IV	Codex Vaticanus; all
B^{1}		IV	all
B^{2}		VI-VII	all
C	04	V	Codex Ephraemi Syri Rescriptus; lacks 1:1-2; 2:5-42; 3:21- 4:25; 6:4-36; 7:17-8:28; 12:4- 19:42; 20:28- 21:20; 22:19- 23:25; 24:7-45
C^{1}		V	
C^{2}		VI	
C^{3}		IX	
D	05	V	Codex Bezae; all
E	07	VI	Codex Basilensis; all
L	019	VIII	Codex Regius; all
N	022	VI	Codex Petropolitanus Purpureus; lacks 1:1- 2:23; 4:3-19,26-35; 4:42- 5:12; 5:33- 9:7,21-28,36-58; 10:4-12; 10:35- 11:14; 11:23- 12:12,21-29; 18:32- 19:17; 20:30-21:22; 22:49-57; 23:41- 24:13,21-39,49-end
P	024	VI	Codex Guelferbytanus A; 1:1-13; 2:9-20; 6:21-42; 7:32- 8:2; 8:31-50; 9:26-36; 10:36- 11:4; 12:34-45; 14:14-25; 15:13-16:22; 18:13-39; 20:21- 21:3; 22:3-16; 23:20-33; 23:45- 24:1; 24:14-37
Q	026	V	Codex Guelferbytanus B; 4:34- 5:4; 6:10-26; 12:6-43; 15:14-31; 17:34- 18:15; 18:34-19:11; 19:47-20:17; 20:34- 21:8; 22:27-46; 23:30-49
R	027	VII	Codex Nitriensis; all, but lacunose
T	029, w/0113, 0125, 0139	V	Codex Borgianus; 6:18-26; 18:2-9,10-16; 18:32-19:8; 21:33- 22:3; 22:20- 23:20; 24:25-27,29-31
W	032	IV/V	Codex Washingtonianus; all
Ξ	040	VI	Codex Zacynthius; 1:1-9,19-23,27-28,30-32,36-66; 1:77-2:19,21,22,33-39; 3:5-8,11-20; 4:1,2,6-20,32-43; 5:17-

			36; 6:21- 7:6,11-37,39-47; 8:4-21,25-35,43-50; 9:1-28,32,33,35; 9:41- 10:18,21-40; 11:1-4,24-33
047		VIII	all
070	w/0110, 0124, 0178, 0179, 0180, 0190, 0191, 0193, 0202	VI	3:19-30; 8:13-19; 8:56- 9:9,12,13-16; 10:21-39,41-11:6,24-42; 12:5- 13:32; 16:4-12; 21:30- 22:2,54-65; 23:4- 24:26
079		VI	7:39-49; 24:10-19
0102		VII	3:23- 4:8,10-16,18,19,21-43;21:4-18
0108		VII	11:37-45
0116		VIII	3:1- 4:20
0147		VI	6:23-35
0171		300	22:44-56, 61-64
0181		IV/V	9:59-10:14
0182		V	19:18-20,22-24
0212	Diatessaron	III	23:49-51,54
0233		VIII	all
0239		VII	2:27-30,34
0250	ℓ1561	VIII	all
0253		VI	10:19-22
0265		VI	7:20,21,33-35
0266		VI	20:19-25,30-39
0267		V	8:25-27
0291		VII/VIII	8:45- 9:2
	LATIN		
it^{e}	2	V	Palatinus; lacks 8:30-48; 11:4-24
it^{a}	3	IV	Vercellensis; lacks 11:12-26; 12:37-59
it^{b}	4	V	Veronensis; lacks 19:26- 21:29
it^{d}	5	V	Bezae Cantabrigiensis; all of Luke
it^{ff_2}	8	V	Corbeiensis II; lacks 9:48- 10:20; 11:45- 12:6
it^{f}	10	VI	Brixianus; all of Luke
it^{l}	11	VIII	Rhedigeranus; lacks 11:28-37
it^{q}	13	VI/VII	Monacensis; lacks 23:23-35; 24:11-39
it^{r_1}	14	VII	Usserianus I; all of Luke
it^{aur}	15	VIII	Aureus; lacks 21:8-30
it^{a_2}	16	V	Curiensis; Luke 11:11-29; 13:16-34
it^{i}	17	V	Vindobonensis; 10:6- 14:2214:29- 16:4; 16:11-23:10
it^{π}	18	VII	Stuttgartensis; 14:8-13
it^{s}	21	VI/VII	Ambrosianus; 17:3-29; 18:39- 19:47; 20:46- 21:22
it^{β}	26	VII	Carinthianum; 1:64- 2:51
	SYRIAC		
syr^{c}	Curetonian	III/IV	
syr^{s}	Sinaitic	III/IV	Luke 2:48- 3:16, 7:33- 15:21, 17:24- 24:44
syr^{p}	Peshitta	V	
syr^{pal}	Palestinian	VI/VII	
syr^{h}	Harklean	VII	
	COPTIC		

cop^{sa}	Sahidic	IV	
cop^{fay}	Fayyumic	IV	
cop^{bo}	Bohairic	IX	
	ARMENIAN		
arm		V	
	GEORGIAN		
geo		V	
	ETHIOPIC		
eth		VI	

https://www.amazon.com/author/davidrobertpalmer

Printed in Great Britain
by Amazon

37141620R00099